BOOKS BY H. STUART HUGHES

Consciousness and Society:
The Reorientation of European Social Thought
1890–1930

(1958)

The United States and Italy

(1953)

Oswald Spengler: A Critical Estimate

(1952)

An Essay for Our Times

(1950)

MR. HUGHES HAS EDITED

Teachers of History:
Essays in Honor of Laurence Bradford Packard

(1954)

CONSCIOUSNESS
AND
SOCIETY

H. Stuart Hughes

CONSCIOUSNESS
AND
SOCIETY

THE REORIENTATION OF
EUROPEAN SOCIAL THOUGHT
1890-1930

LONDON

MACGIBBON & KEE

1967

FIRST PUBLISHED
IN THE U.S.A. BY ALFRED A. KNOPF, INC.
© H. STUART HUGHES 1958

PUBLISHED BY MACGIBBON AND KEE 1959
REPRINTED IN THIS EDITION 1967

PRINTED IN GREAT BRITAIN
BY COMPTON PRINTING WORKS LTD

To the memory of my father

Acknowledgments

IN COMPLETING this volume, I find my intellectual debts more than usually explicit and ramifying.

To my former teachers and present colleagues Crane Brinton and Charles H. Taylor I owe my original introduction to the theory and practice of intellectual history.

To the following I am deeply grateful for having sponsored this project at the time of its inception: Sir Isaiah Berlin, Felix Gilbert, Hajo Holborn, Clyde Kluckhohn, Donald C. McKay, David Riesman, Sir Llewellyn Woodward.

To my senior seminar students at Stanford University and my colleagues at the Center for Advanced Study in the Behavioral Sciences, I offer my thanks for having followed me patiently through lines of reasoning that were still in tentative form, and for having suggested new formulations and unsuspected lines of investigation.

I am indebted to the Guggenheim Foundation for a

traveling fellowship that enabled me to begin work on this study during the second half of 1955, and to the Center for Advanced Study in the Behavioral Sciences for the leisure and ideal working conditions that made possible the greater part of the actual writing during the first eight months of 1957.

My student and friend Allan Mitchell gave me valuable assistance in the research for Chapter 6. Mrs. Jeanne Gentry approached with unfailing intelligence and enthusiasm the taxing assignment of converting my nearly illegible handwriting into neatly typewritten prose. Franklin L. Baumer, Karl W. Deutsch, and Hans Meyerhoff generously gave a careful and judicious reading to the entire manuscript, and my wife added a number of discerning editorial suggestions.

I wish to thank Basic Books, Inc., for permission to quote from Ernest Jones: *The Life and Work of Sigmund Freud,* and The Free Press for permission to quote from Talcott Parsons: *The Structure of Social Action.*

Finally I should note that portions of the following chapters were originally delivered in lecture form: Chapter 2, at the Congress of the Historical Sciences in Rome in September 1955; Chapter 4, at Mills College in March 1957; Chapter 5, at Smith College in December 1955; Chapter 7, at the American Historical Association meeting in St. Louis in December 1956. In closing a word of warning: readers who are not particularly interested in the technical problems of intellectual history might do well to skip Chapters 1 and 3.

Contents

Contents

CONSCIOUSNESS
AND
SOCIETY

Some Preliminary Observations

THE PRESENT study is an essay in intellectual history. But to declare that one is writing intellectual history is really to say nothing until one has defined the term. History of this sort obviously deals with the thoughts and emotions of men—with reasoned argument and with passionate outburst alike. The whole range of human expression—as revealed in writing, speech, practice, and tradition—falls within its orbit. Indeed every declaration of mankind more explicit than a bestial cry may in some sense be considered the subject matter of intellectual history.

It might well be argued that this subject matter is not the deepest stuff of history. Below it (to use the workable but deceptively concrete metaphor of the "high" and "low" when dealing with the human psyche) lies the realm of unorganized sentiments and routine economic processes. Marx called this realm the "substratum." For Marx the important thing to know about it was the character of the regime of production that inexorably conditioned human life: for the great social

thinkers of the next generation the crucial concern was
the irrational, virtually unchanging nature of human
sentiments—what Freud usually referred to as "drives"
and what Pareto rather awkwardly termed "residues."
However radically these thinkers differed from Marx,
they at least agreed with him that what was "deepest"
in human conduct for the most part fell into a pattern
of mere repetition.

Or, to put the matter in moral terms, they agreed
that the basic characteristic of human experience was
the limited nature of its freedom. Men were masters
of their fate, they argued, only for limited periods and
in strictly limited segments of their activity. The eight-
eenth- or early nineteenth-century image of man as a
self-consciously rational being freely selecting among
properly weighed alternatives they dismissed as an antiquated illusion.

Some such conviction of the inevitable limitations on
human freedom—whether by physical circumstance or
through emotional conditioning—has become the unstated major premise of contemporary social science.
Sociologists and anthropologists, economists and psychologists are at one in confining within narrow limits
the realm of conscious choice. And historians—who are
customarily more squeamish about these matters—have
been profoundly shaken by a line of argument that
seemed to cut their very subject matter out from under
them. This subject matter had always been *res gestæ*—
the deeds of men. What was there to write of if these
deeds were to be dismissed as simply the product of
material and psychological conditioning? Were historians reduced to the necessity of becoming no more and
no less than social scientists?

The dilemma is at least as old as the 1860's and will
appear again in this study when we come to treat of
the late nineteenth-century vogue of positivism. But the
current strength and self-confidence of social science in
the United States has presented it in a particularly
acute form. Today an American historian may well suf-

fer from an uneasy conscience when he chooses to write of the "higher" things—of ethical aspiration and the freely speculating mind.

Viewed from a slightly different angle, however, this state of affairs looks a good deal less unpromising. Historians have always written of the "higher" things—but without exactly knowing why. They have felt temperamentally drawn to the realms of the great deed and the lofty thought. And this bent has not been seriously altered by their new awareness of social science. However much historians may have learned from Marx and Freud to consider the more conscious aspects of human experience mere "rationalizations," or from Pareto to call them "derivations," they have stubbornly continued to write about them. An obscure sense of the fitness of things has kept them to the familiar definition of their calling.

A moment's reflection will suggest that the current insistence on the "basic" in human conduct, far from robbing the historian of his traditional function, has for the first time given him an adequate explanation of why he felt drawn toward a certain type of subject matter. This subject matter, we now realize, cannot possibly be the merely repetitive. For the essence of history is *change*—and change must be at least partially the result of conscious mental activity. Somewhere at some time someone must have decided to do something. "Vast impersonal forces" are simply abstractions—the sum of an infinite number of small but strictly personal decisions. In a statistical sense, the outcome of a large number of choices may be predictable, but in a metaphysical and ethical sense most of us are convinced that each individual choice is free. Our vocabulary and categories of thought imply this conviction.[1] Hence Croce was right—although not quite in the way he imagined—when he insisted that history was necessarily the "story of freedom."

[1] Isaiah Berlin: *Historical Inevitability* (London, 1954), pp. 32–4.

The repetitive, the irrational, the quasi-instinctual may be the substratum of history—but it cannot be the subject matter of history itself. This can only be what is capable of coherent explanation in logically delimited time sequences. And in such an explanation deed and thought are inextricably entangled. Intellectual history means a way of treating this common material from the standpoint of the thought rather than of the deed.

The subject matter of intellectual history, then, is "rationalizations" of various levels of complexity. As such, it offers the trickiest sort of material with which historians are called on to deal. The pitfalls it presents are so numerous and so appalling as to prompt one to a veritable despair of reaching any adequate understanding or arriving at a comprehensible form of presentation.

Here, even more than elsewhere in historical scholarship, the student finds himself overwhelmed by the heterogeneity of his data. His materials are only in slight part measurable, nor, except to a very limited extent, are they comparable among each other. They are of all types and of all levels of intellectual sophistication: they extend all the way from the shoddiest journalism to the most abstruse scientific and philosophical investigations. Under these circumstances, the first and major temptation to be avoided is the urge to be encyclopedic. The perhaps laudable desire of the historian to "cover" his material adequately—to write some sort of "definitive" study—when applied to the field of ideas reveals itself as a dangerous illusion.

Whatever the situation may be in other branches of historical study, in intellectual history a work that purports to be definitive is an obvious absurdity: an encyclopedic investigation of the development of ideas—even in a limited area—would be an impossible assignment. A book of this sort would be obliged to shuttle constantly back and forth among incompatible levels of interpretation. Its author could not possibly have an expert knowledge of all the fields with which he was dealing: even the best-endowed historian possesses a satisfactory understanding of only a small number of subjects besides his own. The result of such an effort could scarcely fail to be unevenness and lack of focus— superficiality alternating with an overtechnical presentation of material. For the commonest error of the intellectual historian is to write about things that he does not really understand—things that he has not "internalized" and thought through again for himself. Yet without such a process, the historian can write no more than what Croce would call "chronicle"—material simply delimited, described, or catalogued—not true history as its best practitioners have always understood the term.

It is my hope that the present study avoids this first major pitfall. It is written in the conviction that only through rigorous selectivity and a sharp definition of the central problems to be investigated can the writing of intellectual history achieve artistic and logical integration.

A second set of dangers clusters around the question of the rationality of history. On the one hand there is the familiar temptation to see a clear design, to impose one's own neat pattern on the recalcitrant data. Of this danger most historians are well aware—perhaps even over-aware. They are so afraid of doing violence to the integrity of their materials that they shun any systematic presentation. Hence the invertebrate character of so much that passes for intellectual history. Yet surely to escape one trap does not mean that one must run blindly into another. An awareness of the fallacy of descrying an immanent reason in history does not imply that one must succumb to the converse fallacy of declaring its essential irrationality. If history obviously has no agreed-on rational pattern, the opposite is not necessarily true: even if one despairs of finding any manifest logic in history, one need not throw up one's hands and lament that all is chaos.

In any ultimate terms, the problem is insoluble. But

on the pragmatic level, it can be solved rather easily. Whatever may be the nature of history "as it actually happened," *statements about history* can only be logical—otherwise they would be incomprehensible. Whatever may be the ultimate "reality" (and I defy anyone to tell me), one can communicate one's findings about history only in rational terms, i.e., in terms that are coherent and reproducible, although not necessarily rigorous. Again, to make rational statements implies setting up some sort of structure or laying out some design. Even if this be advanced as only the most tentative sort of hypothesis, it is still a coherent product of the human brain: it did not emerge by some spontaneous process of generation from the womb of history itself. The present study, then, rests on the assumption that in order to say something worthwhile about the history of ideas one must not be afraid to advance hypotheses and to proceed in a logically ordered fashion: I shall not shy away from doing what the social scientists would call "structuring" my material.

Finally, there is the old but still relevant matter of the "spirit of the times." Most of us think that such a spirit exists. Few go along with Goethe's skeptical characterization of the *Geist der Zeiten* as the historians' "own spirit in which the times are reflected." [2] But who is bold enough to say exactly what this spirit is? Who is confident that he knows how to locate it or to define it? The paradoxical truth is that the discovery of the spirit of the times is at once a technical near-impossibility and the intellectual historian's highest achievement.

By its very delimitation in time and subject matter, the present study implies the existence of some such spirit. The effort will be to locate—at least among a selected number of thinkers—the common attitudes that

---

[2] "*Was ihr den Geist der Zeiten heisst,*
Das ist im Grund der Herren eigner Geist,
In dem die Zeiten sich bespiegeln."
                              Faust, Part I, "Night."

together constitute the emerging critical consciousness of the early twentieth century.

And so we come to the delimitation of the study itself. First, I should like to state what sort of intellectual history I am writing; second, I want to explain why I selected a certain place, a certain time, certain ideas, and certain people for treatment; finally, I should like to say a few words about the form of the book and the personal viewpoints I have brought to it.

As customarily written, intellectual history deals with either a "higher" or a "lower" level of thought. The first refers to intellectually clear and significant statements—the second to popular effusions in the nature of slogans. The second is characteristically supposed to represent what has "seeped down" from the first level after a generation or two of "cultural lag": in this new setting ideas nearly invariably figure in vulgarized or distorted form. The present study falls in the "higher" category. A few further distinctions will suggest why this is the case.

In casting my mind over the literature of intellectual history, I have been struck by the fact that there seem to be three manageable ways in which this sort of study can be approached. (I am not considering works that treat the history of a particular aesthetic field or learned discipline—art, literature, philosophy, economics, and the like—since these address themselves to a rather different set of problems and do not pose the central question of an integrating "spirit of the times.") The first is to deal with popular ideas and practices—with the whole vast realm of folklore and community sentiments. Historians interested in this sort of material proceed in much the same fashion in which anthropologists approach the study of "primitive" culture. Hence the efforts of such historians have quite properly been labeled "retrospective cultural anthropology." Second, there is the kind of history that Croce called ethico-political—the study of the activities and aspirations of ruling minorities and of the rival minorities striving to supplant them.[3] Finally there is the history of the enunciation and development of the ideas that eventually will inspire such governing élites. Proceeding on the assumption that only a small number of individuals are actually responsible for the establishment and maintenance of civilized values, history of this last type tries to determine the fund of ideas available at any particular time to men who have received a superior general education. Sometimes it is concerned with ideas that have *already* won acceptance—but in this case it shades off into the first category I have suggested. More commonly it deals with ideas that have still to win their way.

By now it is probably apparent that my own study falls into the final category. This, I am convinced, is the *via regia* of intellectual history. Not that the other types are not worth writing—far from it. But more closely examined they turn out to be something that is not quite the history of ideas. This consideration brings us back to the distinction between the "higher" and the "lower" levels. On the level of popular acceptance, ideas can scarcely be handled in intrinsic terms: they are not sufficiently explicit for that. Efforts on the part of historians to deal with them have all too frequently degenerated into a mechanical and boring catalogue of curious notions. Where they have been successfully (that is, meaningfully) handled, they have been integrated in a general structure of explanation covering all the interlocking practices of a given society. In short, they have become a constituent part of general social history. Perhaps that is what I really meant when I referred earlier to "retrospective cultural anthropology." This and *conceptualized*—not merely descriptive—social history amount very nearly to the same thing. Hence the first type of intellectual history that I identified may not have been intellectual history at all. As the only prac-

[3] This concept will be extensively discussed in Chapter 6.

ticable way of writing the history of ideas on the "lower" level, it may simply be one possible approach to the historical study of society—an enormously important pursuit but not the one that concerns us at present.

The same may be said with slight modifications about the "ethico-political" type of intellectual history. It is not entirely clear whether this sort of study is on the "higher" or on the "lower" level. Certainly the notions entertained by the members of governing minorities frequently differ only slightly if at all from the beliefs and practices of their countrymen in less exalted stations. At other times the governing élite—or at least certain influential members of it—may be far "in advance" of the ideas of the majority. In any case, except in periods of unusual ideological integration, the stock of convictions held by individuals within the ruling minority varies markedly from one person to another. It is extremely difficult to assess with any accuracy what the dominant ideas at any given time actually are. The most reliable indicator is not what people say but what they do—and thus we are led directly back to the history of action rather than of thought.

This is an initial reason for doubting whether ethico-political history is exactly what we are after—its tendency to revert to the historian's traditional concentration on political activity. Furthermore, even where it has tried to remain on the level of ideas (in the sense of ethical aspirations), it has succeeded in doing so only at the price of a radical simplification. One or two "great" ideas have necessarily been singled out as organizing concepts. And these leading ideas more often than not on closer inspection have proved to be the historian's own. Croce himself, the godfather of ethico-political history, was, as we shall subsequently observe, by no means exempt from the charge of reading his own ideas back into the past.

We are left with the third type of intellectual history—the study of major ideas in their pristine form on the higher levels. I shall say something shortly about what *kinds* of ideas I think deserve this sort of treatment; for obviously only a small portion even of the more influential ones can be dealt with in a study of this length—if again we are to avoid the danger of cataloguing. Meantime a final word on the character of the present volume. In brief, it is an attempt to fill a recognized gap: it is an effort to respond to what one recent writer on intellectual history has characterized as the chief need in this field—"detailed studies of the interrelationship of thought in relatively brief periods of time." And it addresses itself to the sort of questions that the same writer proposes as guides to future investigation:

> Do ideas readily cross over (although perhaps in disguised form) from one field of thought to another . . . ? What, if any, are the basic assumptions and presuppositions upon which all or most of the intellectuals ultimately agree? How much tension exists with respect to these assumptions? What are the most significant variations within the common intellectual framework? [4]

So much for the definition of the *type* of history this book exemplifies. It is now time to speak of its content—and even before that of its delimitation in space and time. The "unit of historical study"—to use Toynbee's phrase—is neither world-wide nor national. Nor is it that undefined entity, whose boundaries are never clear but in whose spiritual reality most of us believe, which we call Western civilization. Nor, finally, is it simply Europe. The geographical area of study is Europe in the narrower sense—the original "heartland" of Western society: France, Germany (including Austria), and Italy.

Why precisely this area? Initially it may be argued that from the Empire of Charlemagne to the present

[4] Franklin L. Baumer: "Intellectual History and Its Problems," *Journal of Modern History*, XXI (September 1949), 193-4.

six-nation community of "little Europe," an area approximating the one with which I am dealing has had a more intense European consciousness, a more identifiable sense of a common culture and common interests, than characterized the countries on the West European periphery. Scandinavia, the Iberian Peninsula, the British Isles—these have always seemed less self-consciously European than the states of the Continental core. And as for Eastern Europe, its participation in the family heritage has appeared even more doubtful. One has only to recall that speculative philosophers of history as divergent in other respects as Danilevsky, Spengler, and Toynbee have been at one in excluding Russia and most of the Slavic world from the main body of European culture.

Aside from these historical and perhaps excessively abstract reasons—whose further elaboration would take us too far afield—in the case of the present study there are more practical considerations dictating a limitation to the narrower community of the Western and Central European Continent. Its subject matter is general social thought in the period roughly from 1890 to 1930. And more particularly it deals with major innovators. In the course of the study I hope to establish that it was Germans and Austrians and French and Italians—rather than Englishmen or Americans or Russians—who in general provided the fund of ideas that has come to seem most characteristic of our own time. Moreover, they often arrived at strikingly similar theories within just a few years of each other. Sometimes this can be explained by personal friendship and intellectual exchange. More frequently it looks purely fortuitous: the two thinkers were in fact totally ignorant of each other's work. Yet there is more than accident to such a concatenation. To a far greater extent than was the case on the European periphery, the countries of the Western and Central European Continent shared institutions and an intellectual heritage—in philosophy, in law, and in the structure of higher education—that presented their leading social thinkers with a similar set of problems. And in the generation just preceding the First World War these thinkers similarly shared a wider experience of psychological *malaise*: the sense of impending doom, of old practices and institutions no longer conforming to social realities, which obsessed so many Continentals, reached the periphery only in attenuated form.

This sense of the demise of an old society, coupled with an agonizing uncertainty as to what the forms of the new society might prove to be, suggests how I came to fix the time-span of the study as I did. It extends through forty years from the *fin de siècle* to the beginning of the great depression of the 1930's. It straddles the First World War—although the period before the war figures more decisively than the one following it. The reasons for ascribing some sort of intellectual unity to this era will, I trust, emerge more fully as the study proceeds. Meantime it will perhaps suffice to suggest that what we are after is the initial definition and elaboration of the styles of thought that have come to characterize our century. We shall find the peculiar pathos of the period in its combination of intellectual creativity with a conviction of what the Germans call *Epigonentum*: the very individuals whose work established the guiding patterns of thought for the next fifty years were haunted by a sense of living in an age of merely derivative philosophy and scholarship.[5] Particularly those who died early had no notion of the enormous future influence of what they had written in a state of mortal pessimism and self-doubt.

From another standpoint also, the period under consideration may be regarded as manifesting in the same process the end of one type of intellectual activity and the beginning of another. A number of the major figures of this era—Freud, Croce, Pareto, to cite three very different ones—were builders of great inclusive systems.

[5] See, for example, Marianne Weber: *Max Weber: Ein Lebensbild*, new edition (Heidelberg, 1950), p. 151.

Yet at the same time they narrowed the range through which such general theorizing might operate and cast doubt on the future usefulness of intellectual operations of this type. Thus on the one hand they figured as the last in the long succession of system-builders descending from Aristotle. At the same time, by leaving their systems open and by passing on to their successors fewer solid answers than unproved hypotheses to be tested, they introduced an era of specialization in social theory and of concentration on discrete, finite problems. Personally they were humanists: they combined a philosophical with a scientific education, and they drew no clear line of demarcation between literature and social science. But by enunciating far more rigorously than their predecessors the criteria of social research, they almost necessarily precluded the formation of successors in their own image: these speculative, widely ranging minds have educated two generations of microscopic investigators.

In the shifting, transitional world of ideas in which they dwelt, the problem of consciousness early established itself as crucial. Another way of defining their intellectual epoch would be to suggest that it was the period in which the subjective attitude of the observer of society first thrust itself forward in peremptory fashion—hence the title of this study. Earlier it had commonly been assumed that this attitude presented no serious problem: rationalists and empiricists alike agreed on an identity of view between actor and observer in the social process, and on assuming this common attitude to be that postulated by scientific investigation or utilitarian ethics. All other standpoints, it had been argued, could be dismissed or discounted as intrusions of irrelevant emotion.[6] Now rather suddenly a number of thinkers independently began to wonder whether these emotional involvements, far from being merely extraneous, might not be the central element in the story. By

[6] In this connection see Talcott Parsons: *The Structure of Social Action*, second edition (Glencoe, Ill., 1949), p. 61.

slow stages of reorientation—and often against their
original intention—they were led to discover the importance of subjective "values" in human behavior. Man
as an actor in society, they came to see, was seldom decisively influenced by logical considerations: supra- or
infra-rational values of one sort or another usually
guided his conduct. And indeed the scientific observer—
however much his attitude might diverge from that of
the actor—was himself in no radically different situation: for him also a value-system, however little articulated, dictated the selection of the problems worthy of
investigation and thereby prejudiced the nature of their
solution.

Thus the various thinkers with whom we shall be
dealing were all in their different ways striving to com-
prehend the newly recognized disparity between external reality and the internal appreciation of that reality. The study of society they gradually came to see as a
vastly more complicated matter than one of merely fitting observed data into a structure of human thought
that was presumed to be universal. Such a "fit," they
recognized, was far from automatic: they saw themselves as removed by one further stage from the direct
confrontation of their materials which earlier thinkers
had taken for granted. In short, they found themselves
inserting between the external data and the final intellectual product an intermediate stage of reflection on
their own awareness of these data. The result was an
enormous heightening of intellectual self-consciousness
—a wholesale re-examination of the presuppositions
of social thought itself. "Seeing through"—probing in
depth—these are the hallmarks of early twentieth-century thinking.

Regarded in this fashion, the intellectual labors of
the forty years from 1890 to 1930 group themselves as a
series of attempts to solve the specific questions that
the new awareness of the problematical character of
social observation had thrust to the fore. Such attempts,
as we have just observed, notably raised the general

level of intellectual self-consciousness among social investigators. But this increase in sophistication also had its dangers. In nearly every case, it was to a greater or lesser extent self-defeating. The new self-consciousness could readily slip into a radical skepticism: from an awareness of the subjective character of social thought it was an easy step to denying the validity of all such thought—or, alternatively, to a desperate resolve to "think with the blood." In evaluating the permanent significance of the generation of the 1890's, we need constantly to bear in mind the central paradox of their achievement: more often than not, their work encouraged an anti-intellectualism to which the vast majority of them were intensely hostile.

Some of these thinkers never quite realized the implications of their own theories: they clung tenaciously to a set of philosophical presuppositions that their thought had long ago outgrown. A second group welcomed the advent of the irrational and sought to ground in "intuition" the social philosophy of the future. Finally there were a few thinkers—and I believe these were the greatest—who while fighting every step of the way to salvage as much as possible of the rationalist heritage decisively shifted the axis of that tradition to make room for the new definition of man as something more (or less) than a logically calculating animal.

Together these writers constitute what has been called a "cluster" of genius.[7] Why such a clustering should occur in history, why some periods seem to be richer in creative minds than others—this is a problem for which the historian can offer no satisfactory answer. Perhaps the whole thing is simply an illusion of perspective: those who look like geniuses to one era may a half-century later appear no more than talented jugglers of ideas. In any case, *from our present vantage-point*, the generation of social thinkers who came to maturity

[7] A. L. Kroeber: *Configurations of Culture Growth* (Berkeley and Los Angeles, 1944), pp. 10–16, 839.

in the 1890's bears the mark of major creativity: we are willing to acknowledge as our masters the men who established the styles of thought that are still our own.

"The notion of one generation" in history "is very elastic." But "it corresponds to realities which we feel to be very concrete. . . . There are . . . some generations which are long and some which are short. Only observation enables us to perceive the points at which the curve changes its direction." [8] Obviously all generations are overlapping: all are somewhat arbitrarily defined. But at the same time they tend to shape their own definitions through common experiences. Around such experiences a "clustering" again occurs. Thus individuals who have participated in psychologically decisive events in company with people fifteen years their seniors may feel closer to these latter than they do to individuals only slightly younger than themselves who just missed this great experience: the generations of the two world wars are cases in point. In the next chapter I shall try to suggest the common experience—both social and intellectual—that served to define the "generation of the 1890's."

In this case we are dealing with a long generation. Its period of creativity covers roughly forty years. And its youngest member is twenty-one years younger than its oldest. If we make an exception of Sorel and Pareto— born respectively in 1847 and 1848—who began their writing late and tended to associate intellectually with men much younger than themselves, the birth-dates of the thinkers with whom we are concerned fall between the years 1856 and 1877.[9] They cluster most heavily in

    [8] Marc Bloch: *Apologie pour l'histoire ou métier d'historien* (Paris, 1952), translated by Peter Putnam as *The Historian's Craft* (New York, 1953), pp. 186–7.
    [9] 1856, Freud; 1858, Durkheim, Mosca; 1859, Bergson; 1862, Meinecke; 1864, Weber; 1865, Troeltsch; 1866, Croce; 1867, Benda, Pirandello; 1868, Alain; 1869, Gide; 1871, Proust; 1873, Péguy; 1875, Jung, Mann; 1876, Michels; 1877, Hesse. Only two (Hesse and Jung) are still living.

the late 1860's. When the new century opened, the average age was somewhat over thirty.

Let us pass in review our *dramatis personæ*. Obviously the towering figure of the era is Sigmund Freud. Just behind him in importance comes Max Weber—legal scholar, economist, historian, sociologist, philosopher—a man of enormous intellectual power and versatility, who barely held together by force of an iron resolve the desperate contradictions that threatened his sanity. Perhaps next we should mention Benedetto Croce—a thinker of lesser originality, but whose influence in his own country, over which for a half-century he exercised a kind of literary and philosophical dictatorship, was without parallel in our time. To him we historians owe the most powerful contemporary critique of our methods and philosophical presuppositions. On the importance of these three there is little serious dispute.

Along with them some might rank Emile Durkheim. As the other "founding father"—besides Weber—of contemporary sociology, he obviously deserves our respectful attention. Yet I hope to establish that the precepts Durkheim left to posterity were necessarily less sharp and original than those of Freud or Weber or Croce. His is the classic case of a theorist confined within an intellectual structure from which his data were constantly escaping. And the same applies to a third major sociologist, Vilfredo Pareto. With Pareto we reach the level of thinkers about whom opinions have always been divided and controversy continues to rage. Three others in a similar case are the philosopher Henri Bergson, the absolutely unclassifiable Georges Sorel, and Freud's errant disciple Carl G. Jung.

For all of the foregoing, claims to world-shaking significance have at one time or another been seriously advanced, and their names continue to figure prominently in contemporary discussion. The same is not true of men like the political sociologists Gaetano Mosca and Robert Michels, the historian Friedrich Meinecke, the theologian Ernst Troeltsch, and the poet and "moral ist" Charles Péguy. Yet their indispensability to our account will, I hope, become apparent as the analysis unfolds. In addition to these, certain relatively minor writers will figure in a peripheral fashion by way of comparison and reference—notably the French essayists Julien Benda and Alain. And a few thinkers of greater importance older or younger than the generation of the 1890's will appear in the role of precursors or successors —among the former the philosopher Wilhelm Dilthey, among the latter the Marxist theoretician Antonio Gramsci, the speculative historian Oswald Spengler, the philosopher Ludwig Wittgenstein, and the sociologist Karl Mannheim.

Finally six imaginative writers will appear in illustrative and exemplary guise: Alain-Fournier, Gide, Proust, Mann, Hesse, and Pirandello. Their inclusion may occasion some surprise. In order to explain it I should enlarge a little further on what I mean by "general social thought."

Initially and most emphatically I should explain that I am not dealing with the technical development of social science. Hence I shall not consider thinkers whose importance lies chiefly within their own disciplines. I am interested only in ideas that transcend the scope of a technical intellectual pursuit and have relevance for other fields of knowledge: I shall restrict the study to those writings that have contributed to a common store of social and moral ideas available to men of a general humanistic education. Under this definition, I am excluding a large number of individuals coming from such diverse fields as economics, anthropology, logic, and metaphysics.

At the other extreme, I do not propose to deal with writers intimately and vociferously connected with political movements, whether of the Right or of the Left. I am interested only in thinkers who aimed at intellectually elevated and classic formulations, who strove for objectivity, and whose work was free from self-interested or propagandist intention. Some of the figures I have selected for consideration—we may think of Weber and Mosca—were actively involved in the politics of their day. But they at least strove—sometimes without success—to keep their scientific and their polemical writings separate. In any event, I shall deal with them primarily in their abstract capacity. And in the case of writers like Gramsci or Alain, who were frankly spokesmen for political parties, I shall refer only to those broader aspects of their writings which shed light on the abiding concerns of man in society. Obviously, then, the precursors of fascism have no place in this study: the reader will find nothing about French and Italian nationalism or German racism, however large these movements may have loomed in the years just preceding and just following the First World War. And Marxism will figure rather as a point of departure than as a line of thought to be given intrinsic consideration in its own right.

The case for including a limited number of imaginative writers may appear more questionable. Here again I propose to give no intrinsic treatment in an artistic sense. I am not writing literary history. But in our century I think it is apparent that imaginative literature—and more particularly the novel—has come to play a rather more serious and self-conscious role in the enunciation of values than was the case in the two preceding centuries. On the major novel or play has devolved the task of making concrete and thereby more readily approachable the abstract insights of the philosophers and social scientists. Imaginative literature in our time has of course done a great deal more than this: it has surrounded its depiction of society with a penumbra of symbol and suggestion that has resisted explicit categorization. And it has not only borrowed from social science: it has fed its own discoveries back into social theory in a dense interplay of mutual influence.[1] When we come in the

[1] In this connection see Thomas Mann: *Freud und die Zukunft* (Vienna, 1936), translated by H. T. Lowe-Porter as

next to last chapter to discuss the seeping down of ideas from the men who originally defined them to broader strata of the educated public, the relevance of novel and drama will, I think, become more apparent.

The meaning of "general social thought" may still not be entirely clear. In terms of a social-science discipline, sociology comes closest to what I am talking about. "Whereas in an age of liberal ideals philosophy best reflected the social and intellectual situation, today . . . [it] . . . is reflected most clearly in the diverse forms of sociology." [2] But by sociology I do not mean the highly specialized and fragmented discipline with which we are currently familiar in the United States. I mean a more universal social theorizing in the tradition of Montesquieu or Marx. This was the notion of sociology held by Weber or Durkheim or Pareto. However finite the problems to which they might address themselves, what they were really after was the over-all structure of society. And it is significant that they were all men of broad general education who came to sociology only after having received their original training in other fields. Indeed, in their day formal instruction in sociology was virtually non-existent, and what instruction there was could have helped them scarcely at all.

Within this broadly defined field—which includes besides sociology certain aspects of philosophy, psychology, history, and political theory—we are concerned not so much with the formal enunciation of concepts as with what we may call styles of thought. We are interested in establishing as many interrelationships as possible among our roster of early twentieth-century thinkers. We shall try to penetrate to the essential similarity of ideas in cases where their formulation or technical

---

"Freud and the Future," *Essays of Three Decades* (New York, 1947), pp. 412–15.
  [2] Karl Mannheim: *Ideology and Utopia*, expansion and translation of *Ideologie und Utopie* [Bonn, 1929], (London and New York, 1936), p. 226.

definition—for example, in terms of psychology or in terms of ethics—may be quite different. Eventually there may emerge a number of common assumptions that may be presumed to constitute the intellectual "style" of the era.

In this focus, the implications of ideas will frequently bulk larger than those ideas themselves. The underlying, only half-conscious attitudes of the individual thinkers will figure more prominently than their explicit formulations. In some cases, where the original terminology now sounds awkward and dated—Pareto's vocabulary is a case in point—I shall attempt a broader redefinition. In other cases, where problems that loomed large at the time now appear relatively trivial, I shall suggest a corresponding shift of emphasis. In such reinterpretations, I shall be guided by Croce's dictum that the historian's definition of his problem is necessarily and quite properly a reflection of the concerns of his own time.

Why, the reader may ask, have I chosen to concentrate on individual thinkers rather than to organize the study around ideas in themselves? The question is entirely legitimate and raises one of the most vexing problems in the writing of intellectual history. First, I should like to explain that the study is by no means simply a series of intellectual biographies: a glance at the table of contents will show where the analysis of the work of individual thinkers fits into a more general conceptual structure. Beyond that, however, I think it can be argued that charting the vicissitudes of an idea through time is a dangerous pastime: at any moment the temptation to arrange things in a tight pattern without gaps or uncertainties may become overpowering. To ward off such dangers, one must constantly refer to specific cases. Only in this fashion can the historical imagination be anchored in something approaching reality. The individual is, after all, the ultimate unit of historical study. Ideas themselves—like "trends," "movements," or "currents" of thought—are merely human constructions. An idea does not beget out of its own fullness the thought of an individual (although a number of great philosophers have imagined so): an idea has no actuality until a concrete individual somewhere in time and space has produced it from his own mind.

All of the foregoing may sound lamentably elementary. But it is important to be absolutely clear on these matters before proceeding any farther. The idealist tradition dies hard. And it is particularly important to put myself on record so early because *one form* of idealism will figure in a prominent and sympathetic role in the present volume. A study of individuals, then, it will be. And it will be a study not of ordinary individuals, but of highly superior ones. A moment back, I threw out in somewhat cavalier fashion certain ratings of greatness. I hope that the study itself will adequately explain the reasons for such a ranking. For one of its by-products will be a tentative assessment of what constitutes intellectual greatness in our time.

Throughout the study two central problems will occupy our attention. In the foreground, as the ostensible and more readily comprehensible subject of investigation, we shall find the theories of man's purpose—the definition of human nature—advanced by the leading social thinkers of the early twentieth century. Behind it, sometimes only implicit and never satisfactorily "solved," we shall glimpse the more perplexing question of how the human mind can arrive at knowledge of society at all—the age-old epistemological riddle that has never before been faced with so much courage and rigor as in our own era.

Such, I think, are necessarily the two major concerns of general social thought—the mainsprings of human activity in its broadest sense and the criteria for the human understanding of that activity. "Logico-experimental" as against irrational behavior, the character of individual and group dominance, the sources of social cohesion, the nature and function of religious sentiment —these and the parallel question of how one goes about

explaining them have constituted the familiar obses-
sions of major speculative minds. Philosophers in particular have traditionally regarded them as their special
preserve. In our own time, however, these questions
have tended to pass on the one hand into the field of
social science, on the other hand into that of imaginative literature—when they have not been neglected altogether. In the case of the immediate precursors of our
era—the generation of the 1890's—the major attempts
at explanation were grounded in epistemology and
metaphysics and terminated in psychology or sociology.
Indeed, one useful way of characterizing this group of
thinkers is as transition figures between philosophy and
social science. The questions they raised were universal
and highly speculative: the answers they gave represented only that small portion of the total problem area
that had proved amenable to quasi-scientific treatment.
Or—on the other horn of the dilemma—such answers
remained couched in frankly literary and metaphorical
language. The alternative to social science was literature: the two aspects of speculative thought that philosophy had once held together were now condemned
to part.

It must by now be evident that a number of the protagonists of the present study have influenced the presuppositions of the study itself. This duality of function
is quite intentional. I should not have chosen to write
about these men at all had I not believed that they
could help us to a more intelligent consideration of
man in society. The influence of Croce and Freud and
Weber will be apparent on nearly every page. The implicit notion of what constitutes history is basically
Crocean. Yet it is a Crocean attitude profoundly modified by psychoanalytic and sociological theory—things
to which Croce himself was temperamentally hostile.
Here lies an initial contradiction: the danger of falling
into a flabby eclecticism is all too obvious. Yet I trust
that I shall successfully surmount it.

This consideration leads me to the final duty that the conscientious historian of ideas owes to his readers. If he is not to palm off his own prejudices in surreptitious form under the guise of "objectivity," he must explain to them the educational influences and ethical values that lie behind his writing. Obviously he does not know them all: even the psychoanalyzed are not at home in every corner of their own minds. But he should do his best to explain what he *does* know.

In my own case, I might proffer the information that while I am American by nationality, my intellectual formation has been largely European. Originally it was Anglo-French: Cartesian logic, the common sense of Locke, the skepticism of Hume were already in the background of my education long before I had read a line of these philosophers. And I still fall most naturally into a "rationalistic" way of thought. But an exposure to Germany and to the German idealist tradition came early enough in my life to effect a radical change in orientation. More recently I have been primarily concerned with Italy, and the tranquil persuasiveness of Croce has been ever with me. Out of these contradictory influences there has come, I hope, some sort of intellectual balance. A now familiar tension has established itself between a temperamental leaning toward the reasonableness and humane ethic of England and France and a recognition of both the heady deceptions and the unparalleled critical contribution of German philosophy: against my will I have been drawn by historical study and reflection on method toward a quasi-idealist position. Perhaps this precarious balance will assure a certain measure of fairness to all parties. Let me say in addition that I shall endeavor to keep invidious national comparisons completely out of the present study: in intellectual history even more than in other branches of historical investigation, the play of group passions has no proper place. The only fitting attitude is that of the cosmopolitan, detached intellectual.

In this *obiter dictum* I have already anticipated another self-characterization. Throughout the study the point of reference, the base line from which the analysis will proceed, is the Enlightenment of the eighteenth century. My own position is quite consciously "eighteenth century." I believe that we are all to a greater or lesser extent children of the Enlightenment, and that it is from this standpoint that civilized members of Western society—the heirs to a humane tradition more than two centuries old—almost necessarily judge the political and social movements of their own time.

"More than ever before, it seems to me, the time is . . . ripe for applying . . . self-criticism to the present age, for holding up to it that bright clear mirror fashioned by the Enlightenment. . . . The age which venerated reason and science as man's highest faculty cannot and must not be lost . . . for us. We must find a way not only to see that age in its own shape but to release again those original forces which brought forth and molded" it. This profession of faith by the greatest contemporary historian of eighteenth-century philosophy I should like to make my own. And in so doing I associate myself with his view of the Enlightenment— a view that stresses the open, undogmatic quality of most eighteenth-century thought, its flexible use of the concept of reason, and its sympathetic understanding for "sensibility" and "the passions." Thus re-established in its original outlines the philosophy of the Enlightenment appears far less intellectualistic than as usually characterized, and its presumed fondness for mechanistic and materialistic explanations and naïve faith in human progress stand revealed as largely the product of subsequent critical distortion.[3]

Yet it would be foolish to imply that the critical la-

[3] Ernst Cassirer: *Die Philosophie der Aufklärung* (Tübingen, 1932), translated by Fritz C. A. Koelln and James P. Pettegrove as *The Philosophy of the Enlightenment* (Princeton, N.J., 1951), pp. xi–xii, 13, 55, 73, 90–2, 104–8, 169; see also Peter Gay: "The Enlightenment in the History of Political Theory," *Political Science Quarterly*, LXIX (September 1954), 374–89.

bors of the past two centuries have been in vain—that we need do nothing further than to take our stand with the Enlightenment. What I mean to suggest, rather, is that certain ethical postulates characteristic of the eighteenth century—chief among them the insistence, *where possible,* on rational solutions and humane behavior—represent an abiding legacy of overriding importance: as a guide for intellectuals no subsequently enunciated principles have been anywhere near as effective. Obviously it is our privilege—and duty—to accept as our own the nineteenth- and twentieth-century criticisms that have corrected the epistemology and psychology of the Enlightenment to the extent that they actually *were* shallow and mechanistic. And after the horrors of the past four decades it would be difficult to retain the full eighteenth-century confidence in man's potentialities for good. Yet as guides to conduct and intellectual investigation we can reject the principles of the Enlightenment only at our peril.

Here again the presuppositions of the present study reflect the concerns of the study itself. A critique of the Enlightenment was one of the central tasks that the major social thinkers of the early twentieth century set themselves. Sometimes they did this only implicitly— at other times by a highly self-conscious process of negation. Yet most of these thinkers were not so hostile to the eighteenth century as they have conventionally been depicted. The greatest of them applied "enlightened" criteria in their judgment of political and social phenomena. But they did this with evident embarrassment. Intellectual fastidiousness and a dislike of high-sounding phrases held them back from proclaiming their allegiance and made them sound "tougher" than they actually were. Only occasionally do they permit us to catch a glimpse of the intense moral feeling behind the wall of scientific objectivity with which they sought to protect their personal sentiments from the gaze of the profane.

Once more our task will be to discover the half-conscious attitude underlying the explicit theoretical formulation. And it will be our further responsibility to distinguish between different types of criticism of the Enlightenment. If the greatest minds of the early twentieth century, such as Freud and Weber and Croce, were actually "loyal" critics, some of those of second rank may properly be described as "disloyal": Sorel is the obvious example. Hence it is important to distinguish between those who in scoffing at the Enlightenment were consciously attacking the humane values of the West, and those who, by probing more deeply the problem of human motivation and the structure of society, sought to restate that tradition in terms that would carry conviction to a skeptical generation.

Actually much of the presumed anti-Enlightenment feeling of the generation of the 1890's had a different target. The hostility of these thinkers was directed not so much against the eighteenth-century tradition in its original guise as against its late nineteenth-century reincarnation—in travestied form—as the cult of positivism. The revolt against positivism will occupy us in the next chapter. Meantime it will suffice to say that the charge of mechanistic and materialistic thinking so often laid to the Enlightenment more properly regards the positivist philosophy in its various manifestations. For my own part, I admit frankly to a distaste for positivism: in this I share the viewpoint of most of the protagonists of my study. Yet here again a corrective is in order: a root-and-branch opposition to positivism would be ridiculous. The scientific rigor toward which the thinkers of this school aimed, their dedication to what they fancied to be objective investigation, may still command our respect. Indeed in their very failings we may discern one of the mainsprings of their achievements. "It was precisely . . . its faith in progress and its naïve realism . . . which enabled positivism to make so many significant contributions." [4]

[4] Mannheim: *Ideology and Utopia*, p. 79.

As a counterbalance to the positivist faith in exact science, a number of the young thinkers of the 1890's proposed to rely on "intuition." What they meant by this term varied notably from one to another, as did the amount of trust they vested in such a debatable type of cognition. The various uses of intuition will figure as one of the leading themes of the present study: the definition of the term—if a proper definition can ever be found—will gradually emerge from the discussion itself. For it must be apparent that simply to oppose "intuition" to "reason" as two contradictory (or complementary) paths to knowledge offers no real solution to the difficulty. It may be that the two are no more than different aspects of the same sort of psychological functioning—that what we call intuition is simply a combination of rational and affective processes too minute to be identified. While reasoning is almost wholly conscious, intuition is only partially so. Yet intuition is not an "unconscious" process in the Freudian sense: it goes on in the area that Freud called the "preconscious" and William James termed the "fringe of consciousness." It is characterized by a "fusion of intermediate steps" that resists precise identification. Of its importance "for all normal symbolic creative thinking, whether artistic or scientific," there can be little doubt. It alone "makes possible those . . . leaps in art and science by means of which the creative process sometimes dons seven-league boots." [5]

Even the most science-minded could scarcely object to such a characterization. For myself, I confess to more than a little tolerance for the intuitive approach—and with it, to a conviction of the decisive role of spiritual motivations. In this I align myself with most of the thinkers about whom I shall be writing: their insistence on the radical insufficiency of merely "naturalistic" explanations of human conduct was the crux of their po-

[5] Lawrence S. Kubie: "Problems and Techniques of Psychoanalytic Validation and Progress," *Psychoanalysis as Science*, edited by E. Pumpian-Mindlin (Stanford, Calif., 1952), pp. 50–1.

lemic with the generation of their fathers. Yet this insistence only rarely had anything to do with organized religion: if Weber and Pareto and Durkheim were fascinated by religion, it was not as a manifestation of their own faith but rather as a social phenomenon of vast importance that their immediate predecessors had omitted from their calculations. Hence the new attitude toward the spirit was usually expressed in the negative: few of the major social thinkers of the early twentieth century personally advocated specific spiritual values— they simply condemned as shallow the postulates of scientific and ethical naturalism. In this regard, the generation of the 1890's were far more cautious than their latter-day interpreters.

The same is true in my own case. This negative and skeptical attitude may perhaps best be suggested by citing one of the most forceful statements of naturalist faith to emerge from the imaginative literature of the years just preceding the outbreak of the First World War:

> I do not believe that mind and matter are mutually exclusive entities. The "soul" is a complex of psychic phenomena, and the body is a complex of organic phenomena. . . . I know that my personality is but an agglomeration of particles of matter, whose disintegration will end it absolutely.
>
> I believe in universal determinism; that we are conditioned by circumstances in all respects. . . .
>
> Good and Evil are mere arbitrary distinctions. . . .
>
> I believe that though all the phenomena of life have not yet been analysed, they will be analysed one day. . . .[6]

The author of these lines was himself profoundly divided. His novel, as we shall see in the next to last chapter, is a key document in the spiritual struggle of the

[6] Roger Martin du Gard: *Jean Barois* (Paris, 1913), translation by Stuart Gilbert (New York, 1949), pp. 255–6.

generation of Europeans who were reaching manhood on the eve of the First World War—the generation of the sons of those who had come to maturity in the 1890's. By 1913, such a profession of naturalism sounded old-fashioned: a quarter-century earlier it had been the dominant popular philosophy. But the generation of the 1890's had done no more than to deny the tenets of naturalism: they had not affirmed the contrary. They were content to dwell in a twilight zone of suspended judgment—open to metaphysical possibilities, yet wary of dogmatic assertion. I trust that I am not alone among the generation of their grandchildren in believing this to be the most valid philosophical position for the student of human society.

CHAPTER
2

The Decade of the 1890's:
The Revolt against Positivism

THERE are certain periods in history in which a number of advanced thinkers, usually working independently one of another, have proposed views on human
conduct so different from those commonly accepted at
the time—and yet so manifestly interrelated—that together they seem to constitute an intellectual revolution. The decade of the 1890's was one of such periods.
In this decade and the one immediately succeeding it,
the basic assumptions of eighteenth- and nineteenth-
century social thought underwent a critical review from
which there emerged the new assumptions characteristic of our own time. "A revolution of such magnitude
in the prevailing empirical interpretations of human society is hardly to be found occurring within the short
space of a generation, unless one goes back to about the
sixteenth century. What is to account for it?" [1]

[1] Talcott Parsons: *The Structure of Social Action*, second
edition (Glencoe, Ill., 1949), p. 5.

Nearly all students of the last years of the nineteenth century have sensed in some form or other a profound psychological change. Yet they have differed markedly in the way in which they have expressed their understanding of it. In the older, more æsthetically oriented interpretations (we may think of Henry Adams), the 1890's figured as the *fin de siècle:* it was a period of over-ripeness, of perverse and mannered decadence—the end of an era. We need not stop to ask ourselves how much of this was simply an artistic and literary pose. For our present purposes, it is irrelevant: the *fin de siècle* is a backdrop, nothing more.

Somewhere between an æsthetic and a more intellectual interpretation, we might be tempted to characterize the new attitude as neo-romanticism or neo-mysticism. This formulation has considerable plausibility. Unquestionably the turn toward the subjective that we find in so much of the imaginative and speculative writing of the quarter-century between 1890 and the First World War recalls the aspirations of the original Romanticists. It is not difficult to think of writers who in the 1890's or early 1900's felt that they were reaching back over a half-century gap to restore to honor those values of the imagination that their immediate predecessors had scorned and neglected. It was writers such as these who established the cult of Dostoyevsky and Nietzsche as the literary heralds of the new era. There is a pathetic paradox in the fact that the year of Nietzsche's madness—1889—coincides with the time at which his work, after two decades of public neglect, first began to find wide acceptance. Again and again in the course of the present study we shall find one or another social thinker elaborating more rigorously and systematically the suggestions with regard to unconscious strivings and heroic minorities which Nietzsche had thrown out in fragmentary form.

Yet to call Nietzsche a neo-romantic is surely misleading. Any such characterization does less than justice to the critical and Socratic elements in his thought.

And when it is applied to the social thinkers of the early twentieth century, it fits only a very few—and these are minor figures like Péguy and Jung. The truly great either were hostile to what they took to be neoromantic tendencies or, like Freud and Weber, sought to curb the romanticism they discovered within themselves. Durkheim was perhaps the most categorical of his contemporaries in protesting against what he called a "renascent mysticism," but he was not an isolated case.[2] It was rather the "mystic" Bergson (whom Durkheim may have been aiming at) who was less typical. Indeed, of the major new doctrines of the period, the Bergsonian metaphysics was unique in having frankly mystical aspects—and even this doctrine was couched so far as possible in acceptable philosophic terminology. It was on the "lower" levels of thought, rather—on the level of semipopular agitation—that the neo-romantic tendencies were to have their greatest effect. And it was here that their application to politics eventually produced that "betrayal of the intellectuals" which Julien Benda assailed with such telling effect three decades later.

If not "romanticism," will "irrationalism" serve as a general description? It is neat, it is frequently used, and it at least begins to suggest the real concerns of early twentieth-century social thought. Unquestionably the major intellectual innovators of the 1890's were profoundly interested in the problem of irrational motivation in human conduct. They were obsessed, almost intoxicated, with a rediscovery of the nonlogical, the uncivilized, the inexplicable. But to call them "irrationalists" is to fall into a dangerous ambiguity. It suggests a tolerance or even a preference for the realms of the unconscious. The reverse was actually the case. The social thinkers of the 1890's were concerned with the ir-

[2] Preface to the first edition of Emile Durkheim: *Les Règles de la méthode sociologique* (Paris, 1895), translated from the eighth French edition by Sarah A. Solovay and John H. Mueller as *The Rules of Sociological Method* (Chicago, 1938), p. xl.

rational only to exorcise it. By probing into it, they
sought ways to tame it, to canalize it for constructive
human purposes. Even Sorel, who has often been held
up as the supreme irrationalist, had as his life's goal the
enunciation of a political formula that would fit the
new world of industrial logic and the machine.

Sorel, Pareto, Durkheim, Freud—all thought of themselves as engineers or technicians, men of science or
medicine. It is obviously absurd to call them irrationalists in any but the most restricted sense. As a substitute,
the formula "anti-intellectualist" has sometimes been
employed.[3] This characterization is both flexible and
comprehensive. It suggests the revulsion from ideology
and the *a priori*, from the abstract thought of the century and a half preceding, which served to unite writers
otherwise so far apart as Durkheim and Sorel. It recalls
the influence and prestige of William James—an influence at the same time comparable, opposed, and complementary to that of Nietzsche. "Anti-intellectualism,"
then, is virtually equivalent to Jamesian pragmatism. It
offers a satisfactory common denominator for grouping
a large proportion of the intellectual innovations of the
1890's.

Yet it is at the same time too broad and too narrow.
It fails to take account of the unrepentant abstraction
and intellectualism in the thought of Benedetto Croce
—or, to take quite a different example, the later elaboration by Max Weber of social theory in terms of "ideal
types." It suggests, moreover, that the turn from the
principles of the Enlightenment was more complete
and decisive than was actually the case. The main attack against the intellectual heritage of the past was in
fact on a narrower front. It was directed primarily
against what the writers of the 1890's chose to call "positivism." By this they did not mean simply the rather
quaint doctrines associated with the name of Auguste

[3] For example, by Richard Humphrey in his *Georges Sorel:
Prophet without Honor: A Study in anti-Intellectualism* (Cambridge, Mass., 1951).

Comte, who had originally coined the term. Nor did they mean the social philosophy of Herbert Spencer, which was the guise in which positivist thinking was most apparent in their own time. They used the word in a looser sense to characterize the whole tendency to discuss human behavior in terms of analogies drawn from natural science. In reacting against it, the innovators of the 1890's felt that they were rejecting the most pervasive intellectual tenet of their time. They believed that they were casting off a spiritual yoke that the preceding quarter-century had laid upon them.

As a preliminary characterization, to speak of the innovations of the 1890's as a revolt against positivism comes closest to what the writers in question actually thought that they were about. Yet even this last formula has its pitfalls. We must be on guard against the tendency of someone like Croce to use positivism as a philosophic catch-all, to embrace under this epithet every doctrine for which he had a dislike. We must not forget the number of influential thinkers of the period —men like Durkheim and Mosca—who remained essentially in the positivist tradition. And, finally, we must take proper account of the others, like Freud, who continued to use mechanistic language drawn from the natural sciences long after their discoveries had burst the framework of their inherited vocabulary.

How, then, did positivism appear to the young rebels of the 1890's? To understand a new tendency in thought, we must necessarily look first at what the revolt is directed against.

I have already suggested that the late nineteenth-century critics of positivism did not write of it in any very precise terms. Apparently they regarded it as so familiar to their readers as not to require identification: they thought of it more as a diffused intellectual tendency than as a specific set of principles. Hence they used the word "positivism" almost interchangeably with a number of other philosophical doctrines that they regarded with equal disfavor—"materialism," "mechanism," and "naturalism." To describe the dominant tendency in late nineteenth-century thought as materialism was obviously a crude simplification. Few serious thinkers of any period have been true materialists. Indeed, the individual usually pointed to as the nineteenth-century prototype of this attitude—Ludwig Feuerbach—was far from being an unqualified materialist.[4] "Mechanism," on the other hand, was a rather more accurate characterization: it suggested the prestige of explanations drawn from the Newtonian physical universe and in particular from the recently developed field of electricity. Similarly the term "naturalism" evoked the biological explanations that had come increasingly into vogue as the nineteenth century advanced. This had been notably the case since the triumph of Darwinism in the 1860's.

With Darwinism in its applied or "social" form, we come to the central point of intellectual conflict. Some of Darwin's earliest supporters had beeen followers of Auguste Comte, and the second of the high priests of positivism, Herbert Spencer, had early rallied to Darwinism, sensing its possibilities as support for his own position.[5] With its Darwinian alliance, the positivist way of thinking underwent some curious changes. In its original eighteenth-century or Utilitarian form it had been an intellectualist philosophy, basing itself on the conviction that the problems of man in society were readily capable of a rational solution. Under the influence of Social Darwinism, however, the positivist creed began to shed its rationalist features: "heredity" and "environment" replaced conscious, logical choice as the main determinants of human action. A Hobbesian state of nature (now called "struggle for existence") was substituted for decorous social order as the characteristic

[4] Franco Lombardi: *Ludovico Feuerbach* (Florence, 1935), pp. 227–45.
[5] Jacques Barzun: *Darwin, Marx, Wagner: Critique of a Heritage* (Boston, 1941), pp. 37–42.

view of the relations between man and man. The result was a kind of scientific fatalism—the antithesis of the buoyantly optimistic attitude that had characterized the philosophers of the eighteenth century or the English Utilitarians of the first part of the century following. The ultimate irony of positivism was that what had started as an ultra-intellectualist doctrine became in effect a philosophy of radical anti-intellectualism.[6]

Hence in the perspective of a cultural scene dominated by Social Darwinism, the young thinkers of the 1890's can be regarded as aiming at precisely the opposite of what they have usually been accused of doing. Far from being "irrationalists," they were striving to vindicate the rights of rational inquiry. Alarmed by the threat of an iron determinism, they were seeking to restore the freely speculating mind to the dignity it had enjoyed a century earlier.

From our present-day vantage point, it is difficult to reconstruct in our minds the dominant intellectual temper of the 1890's. It is hard for us to conceive how men who are almost forgotten today could have wielded so much influence in their own time. In Italy, where the anti-clericalism of the governing classes reinforced the teachings of positivism to cast them in their crudest mold, the guardian of the cult was the defrocked priest Ardigò. In Germany, where positivism never took so firm a hold, the physiologist DuBois-Reymond pontificated at the University of Berlin. It was France, perhaps, that had produced the most distinguished positivist minds: the names of Taine and Renan may still command our respect as the exponents of a dedicated search for precise chains of causation and an ethic of dignified, urbane resignation. To the generation that had grown up under their direct influence, however, these teachings appeared rather more sinister. Taine's celebrated precepts—"virtue and vice are products like sugar and vitriol" or "genius . . . is a resultant of race, milieu, and the [proper] moment" or yet again "nature

[6] Parsons: *Structure of Social Action*, pp. 64, 67, 111–14.

and history are only the unrolling of universal necessity"—these dicta, which today strike us as merely excessive, then seemed crushing burdens under which the
youthful imagination felt stifled. Similarly Renan's
ultra-civilized relativism acted as an icy bath in which
ideal values simply dissolved. The novelist Romain Rolland has recalled how as a young lecturer on art and
music at the Ecole Normale Supérieure—the summit of
the French educational system—he and his friends had
striven for liberation from the prevailing attitude of
pessimistic skepticism:

> There we were, huddled together in anguish,
> scarcely breathing. . . . Ah! we spent difficult
> years together. Our masters do not suspect the anx-
> ieties with which our youth struggled under their
> shadow! [7]

It was not only in respect to the life of the mind that
young men began to feel stifled as the 1880's drew to a
close. In sober truth it had been a stuffy decade. It was
almost literally in order to breathe more freely that Nietzsche had withdrawn to his Alpine heights—away from
the smugness, the "philistinism," of upper middle-class
society. In the very character of its decorative arts the
epoch exuded a sense of heaviness, of material excess, of
confinement:

> Men of the seventies and eighties . . . were
> filled with a devouring hunger for reality, but they
> had the misfortune to confuse this with matter—
> which is but the hollow and deceptive wrapping
> of it. Thus they lived perpetually in a wretched,
> padded, puffed-out world of cotton-wool, card-
> board, and tissue-paper. In all their creations it is
> with the arts of adornment that imagination is con-

---

[7] Quoted in the first edition of Daniel Halévy: *Charles Péguy
et les Cahiers de la Quinzaine* (Paris, 1918), p. 30. The quotation has been omitted from the revised version, which has been
translated into English.

cerned: with the art of the upholsterer, the confec-
tioner, the stucco decorator. . . .[8]

The quotation is from one of the most imaginative and
least systematic of cultural historians. But it has deftly
caught the material background of bourgeois life in the
1880's.

With the new decade, particularly with its closing
years, the circumstances, social and political, that had
earlier inspired a sense of sober confidence began to
change. Both on the "lower" and on the "higher" levels of intellectual activity, doubts arose as to the reigning philosophy of the upper middle class—the self-satis-
fied cult of material progress which, in a vulgarized
sense, could also be termed "positivism." After two
decades of precarious equilibrium, the institutional ar-
rangements of the major Western European states were
again brought into question. The artificial, contrived
character of the regimes with which unification had
endowed Germany and Italy were revealed by their
malfunctioning—in the one case by the erratic changes
in policy that followed the resignation of Bismarck in
1890, in the other by the social disorders and authoritarian government with which the century came to a
close. In France the shock of the Dreyfus case acted as
a stimulus to the re-examination of the traditional ideologies on which both the defenders and the enemies of
the accused captain had rested their case.

Social disorder, economic crisis, and institutional malfunctioning had contributed to the growth of Socialist
parties and to the spread of Marxist doctrines. The decade of the 1890's was to be the great period of expansion in the history of European Socialism. At first sight
it might seem that Marxism—a critical as opposed to a
positive philosophy of society—could have offered to
the intellectual innovators of the 1890's a suitable
weapon with which to combat the dominant ideology

[8] Egon Friedell: *Kulturgeschichte der Neuzeit* (Munich,
1931), translated by Charles Francis Atkinson as *A Cultural History of the Modern Age* (New York, 1932), III, 299.

of the European middle class. Such was, indeed, briefly the case in Italy, under the revivifying influence of the lectures of Antonio Labriola at the University of Rome. But even here Labriola's student Croce was eventually impelled to arrive at his own critique of Marxist doctrine. Basically Marxism was to figure in the intellectual renovation of the 1890's as an aberrant, and peculiarly insidious, form of the reigning cult of positivism. It loomed on the cultural horizon as the last and most ambitious of the abstract and pseudoscientific ideologies that had bewitched European intellectuals since the early eighteenth century.

To come to terms with Marxism, then, was the first and most obvious task confronting the intellectual innovators of the 1890's. Some, like Freud, dealt with Marx only by implication—by extending social thought to new areas undreamed of in the socialist ideologies. Others, like Pareto, offered highly skeptical refutations of the central arguments of dialectical materialism. Still others, like Croce and Sorel, while maintaining the Marxist terminology, were to transmute it into something so different from the original intention as to leave little standing but a hollow framework—within which the earlier categories of thought had ceased to be actualities and had become mere symbols and methodological conveniences. Finally, a decade later than the rest, Max Weber was to propose a view of society that brought Marx's economic motivations into a tense and polar relationship to the deepest spiritual values of mankind.

This whole task of cultural re-evaluation, while concerned with common problems, had a different tone and character in each of the major national communities of Western and Central Europe. Of these Germany should probably occupy us first. Despite the fact that its finest days of intellectual leadership were over— the great century of creation from about 1760 to 1860 had now begun to slip into idealizing memory—Germany still held an almost unquestioned position of pre-eminence. France might be the nation *par excellence* of artists and novelists, but Germany was the land of thinkers and professors. It might be living on its intellectual capital, but it was still the goal of students from all countries in search of solid scientific and historical training. Hence in a brief survey of the character of intellectual communities and intellectual activity in the 1890's, Germany quite naturally takes precedence.

"In all Germany," wrote one of the great survivors of the period, in recalling the intellectual atmosphere of his young manhood after a gap of fifty years, "one can detect something new around 1890 not only politically but also spiritually and intellectually. . . . Politically things were going down; intellectually they were going up again." And this revival of spiritual interest expressed itself in a "new and deeper longing for what was genuine and true" and in a "new sense for the fragmentary and problematic character of modern life. . . . Stated in banal terms, the period after 1890 can at least boast of better taste . . . than what on the average had prevailed" during the two preceding decades.[9]

An initial sign of the changed times was the appearance in 1890 of an anonymous work entitled *Rembrandt als Erzieher*—Rembrandt as educator. The book created an unprecedented public furor. More than a quarter of a century was to pass before another such work would arouse so much general interest—Spengler's *Decline of the West*, which it resembled in its disorderly display of miscellaneous learning and in its "symptomatic meaning." [1]

The author—later identified as a certain Julius Langbehn—was a classic example of the "half-educated" man who declares himself with dogmatic confidence on

[9] Friedrich Meinecke: *Erlebtes 1862–1901* (Leipzig, 1941), pp. 167–8.
[1] Ernst Troeltsch, quoted in Liselotte Voss: *Rembrandt als Erzieher und seine Bedeutung* (Dissertation: n.p., n.d.), p. 71.

all subjects. He possessed little more than an artistic imagination, a rhetorical flair, and a wide but unsystematic education. It was characteristic of him that shortly after the onset of Nietzsche's madness he had appeared at the philosopher's home with the claim that he could effect a cure if the patient were left completely in his hands.[2]

Langbehn's book offered a grab-bag collection of ideas, with no one of them pursued to enough depth to weary the inattentive reader. It ranged over ethics, politics, science, art. Its conceptual apparatus was never clear. Hence it had advanced no farther at its end than on its first page (which was also its best). It had simply presented an enormous variety of examples from all phases of cultural life—some vastly illuminating, some questionable, and some merely comic—to illustrate its central thesis that Rembrandt deserved to be established as the guide and culture-symbol for the Germany of the future.

This contention Langbehn supported with a thoroughly specious vindication of his own, the northwestern or *niederdeutsch*, element in German life. Such special pleading need not detain us. Yet what rescued the book from mere fatuousness and gave it at least a symptomatic importance was its diagnosis of the German cultural situation. Langbehn attacked his own era as an age of decline—an age of Alexandrians. It was dominated, he said, by professors and specialists. "Goethe, who is honored by the Germans of today more in theory than in practice, could not stand people with glasses; now, however, Germany is full of people who wear glasses either actually or in the spirit." [3] More particularly Langbehn hit out at the cult of natural science and its "false objectivity." He saw—rather earlier than most—that the revival of cultural creativity in Germany

[2] Walter A. Kaufmann: *Nietzsche: Philosopher, Psychologist, Antichrist* (Princeton, N.J., 1950), p. 48.
[3] *Rembrandt als Erzieher: Von einem Deutschen* (Leipzig, 1890), p. 1.

was appearing on the periphery rather than at the center. And he pleaded for a more philosophical, a more synthesizing treatment of knowledge. Most concisely he demanded—and in the same breath predicted—a turn from an objective to a subjective emphasis in intellectual and artistic pursuits.

Langbehn was substantially right when he claimed that German intellectual life was dominated by the professors. This was perhaps what distinguished most sharply the German intellectual community from that of France or Italy. In the German-speaking lands, literary amateurs did not enjoy the same respect as in the Latin countries: the professors had the field very largely to themselves.

In the 1890's German professors, besides occupying a high social position, were still in the comparatively easy financial circumstances that were to last until the First World War. Those at the bottom of the academic hierarchy might be threatened with starvation (unless they came from affluent families, which was usually the case), but the holders of university chairs were free of financial worries. Their existences were alike hard-working and jovial. Beer and wine-drinking, Alpine vacations and pilgrimages to Italy, found their proper place in lives that were to seem in retrospect both cheerful and productive.

This academic intellectual community was far more dispersed than was the case in France. Small university towns such as Heidelberg or Göttingen or Bonn figured prominently in it. Yet the greatest intellectual center was undoubtedly Berlin, both as the national capital and as the seat of the university which, although less than a century old, was usually conceded to rank first in scholarly eminence. Berlin, however, had a somewhat ambiguous cultural ring: it suggested not only the freedom of speculation on which the Hohenzollern princes —with certain notable lapses—had prided themselves since the days of Frederick the Great, but also the expectations of a loyal and disciplined intellectual per-

formance that had earned for its university faculty the
nickname of "First Guards Regiment of Learning." [4]
And in the late 1890's and early 1900's it seemed in partial eclipse, at least in the realm of historical studies,
for which it had won its greatest fame: the philosopher
of history Wilhelm Dilthey was still teaching, but the
great modern historians Ranke and Droysen had died
in the mid-1880's, followed by Sybel and Treitschke a
decade later.

In implicit opposition to Berlin, the southern capital
of Munich seemed raffish and Bohemian. It was known
as a city of painters and creative writers, of French influence, and of a teasing *esprit frondeur*. In the prevailing humorlessness of Wilhelminian Germany, the Munich review *Simplizissimus* was almost the only voice of
irony and satire. Aggressively individualistic in tone, it
not only mocked established institutions but also acted
as the "organ of Impressionist culture" and the "Impressionist style of life." It was no accident that the
young Thomas Mann—like many another refugee from
the unsympathetic north—just after the turn of the century should have settled in Munich and associated himself with *Simplizissimus*.[5]

Yet in the sense of intellectual, as opposed to artistic
leadership, Munich possessed fewer major figures than
some of the smaller cities of the southwest. We may
mention the university towns of Heidelberg and Freiburg—and along with them the Alsatian city of Strassburg (then in German hands) and Basel, just over the
border in Switzerland, over whose patrician cultural life
the aged Jacob Burckhardt presided until his death in
1897. These together formed a kind of "cultural province of the upper Rhine." With Berlin living on its reputation, the universities of the southwest began to bulk
larger on the German intellectual horizon. Here there

---

[4] Friedrich Meinecke: *Strassburg/Freiburg/Berlin 1901–1919:
Erinnerungen* (Stuttgart, 1949), p. 145.
[5] Arnold Bauer: *Thomas Mann und die Krise der bürgerlichen Kultur* (Berlin, 1946), pp. 17, 20–1.

settled a number of young scholars with fresh ideas—
philosophers, historians, and sociologists who were trying "to bring art and science into inner alliance." Indeed, people spoke of a "southwest German philosophy," of a markedly anti-positivist character, when
they coupled the names of Wilhelm Windelband and
his student Heinrich Rickert: Windelband's rectoral
address at the University of Strassburg in 1894 sounded
to his contemporaries like a "declaration of war against
positivism." With these philosophers, the young scholar
who was to rank as the most influential historian of
twentieth-century Germany, Friedrich Meinecke, found
himself in spiritual communion. And he also felt that
he was pulling "in the same harness" with Max Weber
—like himself a Berliner transplanted to the upper
Rhine. From Weber paths of association led to Ernst
Troeltsch, who was to share with him a house in Heidelberg in the years just before the First World War.[6]

Not all of these scholars remained permanently in
the southwest. Weber, indeed, spent his whole mature
intellectual life there, chiefly in Heidelberg, but also
for brief periods at the beginning and end of his academic career, in Freiburg and Munich. Meinecke would
have been content to do the same; he felt in his element in the southwest, first in Strassburg and later in
Freiburg. But the call to a chair in Berlin was something that practically no German scholar could resist—
least of all one like Meinecke whose entire youth had
been passed in the capital. Just as the war was breaking
out he moved back to the north, followed a year later
by Troeltsch, whose close friend he was to become during the war years.

The southwest, however, had left its mark upon
them. Even a loyal Prussian and Berliner could never
be quite the same again after he had dwelt for a while
in the cultural province of the upper Rhine. For in this
region of Germany which was closest, both geographi-

[6] Meinecke: *Strassburg/Freiburg/Berlin*, pp. 48–51, 102.

cally and culturally, to France, they had breathed an
atmosphere of gentle and tolerant liberalism. Heidelberg and Freiburg were both within the jurisdiction of
the Grand Duchy of Baden—and Baden, which was
governed in almost British fashion as a parliamentary
democracy, ranked as the most "enlightened" of the
German states, the alternative model to Prussia. The
Baden ruling house took pride in its two great universities: the state government supervised their faculties
in a sympathetic and understanding fashion.[7] It is
worth recalling that when at the very end of the war
Germany undertook its brief experiment in parliamentary monarchy, a prince of the house of Baden was
named chancellor.

There was another influence in the southwest that
was to change the mental orientation of transplanted
Prussians. In the gray political landscape of the Wilhelminian era, in which leaders of any personal stature
seemed almost totally lacking, one figure alone caught
the imagination of the younger scholars. Pastor Friedrich Naumann was both a Württemberg liberal and a
German patriot. As a politician he was calamitously unsuccessful: he failed in his effort to build a new party
that would unite Germans of good will by cutting
across the old political and class cleavages. But as a
personal force, a man of rectitude and social vision, he
drew into his orbit men like Weber and Meinecke who
were seeking a way out of the political impasse into
which Germany had blundered.

To us today Naumann's program may seem hopelessly contradictory: he wanted to reconcile nationalism
and socialism, and these in turn with political democracy. But in these very contradictions we may discern
the central dilemmas with which liberal-minded German intellectuals were struggling in the pre-war years.

[7] As, for example, in the case of Max Weber's severe depression and withdrawal from active teaching. See Marianne Weber:
Max Weber: Ein Lebensbild, new edition (Heidelberg, 1950),
pp. 277, 299.

Nearly all of them were unquestioning patriots. The advancement of Germany's national strength they accepted as dogma. Their fathers' generation had acquiesced without protest or even with enthusiasm in the solution that Bismarck had given to the problem of German unity, with its implied sacrifice of liberal to national values. This was the atmosphere in which men like Weber and Meinecke had grown up: both of them during their younger days had been sufficiently conformist to join student dueling fraternities. It was only with the greatest reluctance that they could pass into even qualified opposition to the dominant values of their society.

Yet this was what was eventually to happen under the pressure of external events—and of residence in the southwest. All three of the chief German protagonists of this study—Weber the earliest and most decisively, Meinecke only hesitantly, Troeltsch not until the war years—were to cross the invisible barricade that separated the opponents from the supporters of the regime. And they did it with the deepest sorrow, driven against their will by the irresponsible behavior of the young Emperor, the calamitous mistakes in foreign policy, the unyielding resistance to democratization of the constitutions of Prussia and of the Reich. These things added up in their minds to evidence of an incurable idiocy on the part of Germany's ruling classes. With each year of postponed reform, they felt the chances growing dimmer of saving their country from a major catastrophe.

Already well before the outbreak of the world conflict, then, the ground was prepared for that concerted political attack on the part of liberal German intellectuals which was to culminate after the war in the foundation of the Democratic party. This effort will appear in its proper place toward the close of the study. For the present it is sufficient to note that the German intellectual of the Wilhelminian era was in a peculiarly ambiguous relationship to his own political and social milieu. The polarity between the attractions of Berlin

and those of the southwest was paralleled by a tension
between political acceptance and opposition. Nearly all
the more distinguished intellectuals found something
repellent about the social atmosphere of Wilhelminian
Germany—its bragging, its parvenu vulgarity, and the
obsequiousness that they termed "Byzantinism." Yet at
the same time they were tied by countless threads to
the ruling powers within that society. As professors,
they were firmly anchored in the upper middle class and
were frequently state functionaries of a government—
like that of Prussia—of whose constitution they thoroughly disapproved.

Thus despite the seriousness of their scholarship and
the dignity of their personal situation, the German professors were the prisoners of their own exalted station.
The public treated them with a respect and followed
their abstract debates with a passionate interest that
may strike us as little short of miraculous, but, like
most of the state government that employed them, it
expected of its professors a thoroughly conformist attitude toward the national community. And the professors were not too loath to conform: some of them might
criticize with violence the *internal* character of the regime, but in the realm of foreign policy virtually all
remained within the nationalist frame. Most of them
were only dimly aware of these inconsistencies. Weber
alone, perhaps, possessed the intellectual ruthlessness
to expose the situation with stark clarity. Moreover,
since for the greater part of his academic career he held
only an honorary professorship and did no teaching, he
enjoyed an unusual measure of personal independence.
In his own national emphasis, Weber never wavered.
Yet he was sufficiently honest to recognize the pious
shams of German university life—that it was idle to talk
of true academic freedom in a situation where Georg
Simmel as a Jew and Robert Michels as a Socialist were
systematically excluded from university chairs.[8]

---

[8] Ibid., pp. 360, 395-6.

Both spiritually and in practical terms, the creative writers were less dependent on the support of society. With them we encounter most forcibly that situation on the periphery of national life, that "unseasonableness," on which Nietzsche had insisted. Thomas Mann came from the Baltic seaport of Lübeck, the only one of the three remaining free cities which had failed to adjust to the world of industrialism. He had grown up among the patrician archaisms of *Buddenbrooks*, his first novel. From the archaic his path led to the *avantgarde*—from Lübeck to Munich. Yet he at least remained within the national community. With Hermann Hesse, the artist's sense of alienation from his society was still more radical. Even before the outbreak of the war, disgusted and frightened by the prevailing militarism, he had left his own country for lifelong exile in Switzerland. Two decades before most intellectuals awoke to their peril, he had sensed the radical evil in German life that in the 1930's was to drive thousands of them into headlong flight.

From 1890 to 1914, then, we can detect in Germany two complementary and contradictory processes—a cultural revival and the beginnings of a "secession of the intellectuals." The tension between the two was to give a character of painful self-searching to German intellectual life in its most critical quarter-century.

In the case of the Vienna of Sigmund Freud, the temptation is almost irresistible to link up the work of the founder of psychoanalysis with some of the more obvious and celebrated features of the Austrian capital. Indeed, Freud's concern with the sexual and psychopathic has not infrequently been ascribed to the character of life in the Vienna of his day. This character was presumably embodied in the combination of charm and erotic "decadence" that we find in the theater of Arthur Schnitzler.

The Viennese of the 1890's and early 1900's certainly enjoyed Schnitzler's plays—as they appreciated the poetry of Hugo von Hofmannsthal and the music of Gustav Mahler. But the city of Schnitzler or Hofmannsthal or Mahler was not precisely Freud's Vienna. It is true that he came into personal contact with two of these figures: from 1906 on, he occasionally corresponded with Schnitzler, whom he greatly admired and in whom he found an "uncanny" reflection of his own interests; and in 1910, just one year before Mahler's death, Freud gave the composer a sensationally brief (and successful) treatment for a temporary obsessional neurosis.[9] These, however, were isolated events in a busy professional life. Freud was thoroughly unmusical, and in his youth, at least, his taste ran more to the classics than to the literature of his own day. Moreover, the type of life he led kept him out of the main current of self-consciously "advanced" culture. Rather than being an intellectual in the conventional sense, Freud was a medical man and an inordinately hard-working one. It was only in the latter part of his life that he formed friendships with such leading novelists as Hermann Hesse, Thomas Mann, Romain Rolland, and Arnold Zweig. Earlier his personal associations had been almost exclusively with physicians like himself—most of them Jewish—or with members of the Jewish lodge to which he belonged. His patients, furthermore, were not altogether typical of Viennese society: a large number of them were foreigners from Eastern Europe.

The disabilities under which Freud labored as a Jew, more particularly the official prejudice that delayed for years his appointment to a professorship at the University, further suggest one of the least attractive features of the Vienna of his day. The antagonism among nationalities and classes characteristic of the last decades of the Austrian empire reached its sharpest form in the popular anti-Semitism of the Vienna streets: the city of Freud's maturity was also the Vienna of Hitler's youth.

[9] Ernest Jones: *The Life and Work of Sigmund Freud*, II: *Years of Maturity 1901–1919* (New York, 1955), pp. 79–80; III: *The Last Phase 1919–1939* (New York, 1957), pp. 84, 443–4.

Hence we can understand the former's dislike of his home city and his constant longing to escape to the more liberal atmosphere of England—a wish that was to be granted under tragic circumstances one year before his death.

It would be wrong, however, to leave the impression that the intellectual resources of the Austrian Empire in its last phase were confined to the circle around Sigmund Freud or to the literary and musical world of Vienna. Austria might have little cultural cohesion—its leading citizens tended to be hostile to the more unconventional varieties of social speculation—but the very antagonisms within its society gave a special variety and excitement to its intellectual products. At its best, the Austrian Empire served as a link between the Germanic and the Slavic worlds. In the years just prior to the First World War, the bilingual city of Prague sheltered both the Slavic cultural studies of the future Czechoslovak president Thomas Masaryk and the tormented imaginings of that young master of German prose, Franz Kafka. Somewhat earlier it had been the home of the physicist Ernst Mach—the most influential contemporary philosopher of science. When in the mid-1890's Mach moved to Vienna, his scientific career was nearly over. But his influence was subsequently to manifest itself in a renewal of philosophical inquiry that had Vienna as its center. Mach was the last and most sophisticated product of nineteenth-century positivism. It was fitting that the city in which he spent his old age should have given its name to the post-war movement in philosophy that once again made the word "positivist" a term of honor rather than reproach.

When we look at French intellectual life in contrast to that of Germany, we can scarcely fail to be struck by two notable differences—the centralization of cultural activities, and the comparatively favorable attitude of the more critically minded intellectuals toward their own national government.

Perhaps these two things have something to do with the fact that while there are more Frenchmen than Germans in our *dramatis personæ*, we find among them no giants on the model of Weber or Freud. The external circumstances of French life in the 1890's and early 1900's were favorable to the life of the mind—perhaps more favorable than those of any other European country. But in a sense they were too satisfactory. In a situation in which official pressure and provincial isolation did not, as in Germany, act as serious hindrances to thought, the intellectual was thrown less on his own devices. He felt supported and encouraged both by the liberal attitude of the state and by the companionship of his peers. Hence the lonely genius was a less characteristic cultural product in France than in Germany. By the same token, the two French "moralists" of the early twentieth century who came closest to that image, Sorel and Péguy, were both self-consciously provincial. And even these two did not work in true isolation: they lived in Paris, they were members of regularly constituted intellectual circles, and for more than a decade they enjoyed each other's friendship.

The unique, the overpowering position of Paris in French cultural life is a fact that has often been deplored by the French themselves. Already in the 1890's conservatives and admirers of local tradition were arguing that the concentration of talent in the capital, far from maximizing France's cultural assets, actually reduced them: cut off from the childhood associates among whom they might otherwise have risen to a position of natural leadership, the young intellectuals who congregated in Paris simply got in each others' way and wasted their substance in the sterile debates of literary coteries. Maurice Barrès's novel *Les Déracinés*—the uprooted—published in 1897, gave persuasive voice to this argument from the standpoint of a provincial nationalist. And, a decade later, from the other end of the political spectrum, the essays of Alain were to convey an equally passionate protest from the countless small

cities of France against the overweening pretensions of
the capital.

Yet this concentration of talent had its obvious ad-
vantages. In a situation in which every writer who
counted was presumed, more or less, to know everyone
else, intellectual life attained to a pace, an excitement,
a vitality that were lacking in Germany or Italy. Public
and semi-public discussion of ideas in the columns of
reviews or across the tables of cafés ranked as a genuine
source of enlightenment. And it was no mere convention that the leading intellectuals knew each other. We
have seen that Sorel and Péguy were good friends. They
in turn regarded themselves, somewhat at a distance it
is true, as disciples of Bergson. And through the good
offices of Daniel Halévy—one of those *littérateurs* of
lesser rank who perform the indispensable functions of
clarifiers and go-betweens—they were linked to the literary world of Gide and the *Nouvelle Revue Française*.

Some of these intellectual friendships dated back to
school days in one or another of the famous Parisian
lycées. But only about half of the writers we are considering were Parisians by birth. Actually the most usual
place in which lifetime associations were formed was
that unique French institution of higher learning, the
Ecole Normale Supérieure. Placed above and outside
the University of Paris, this extraordinary school was
intended to train the best minds of the nation for humanistic teaching in the higher educational system. Its
students were selected by rigorous competitive examinations. And, in contrast to the usual situation in Continental universities, they lived and ate together in an
ideal setting for intense intellectual exchange.

The method of recruitment of this future educational
élite was intentionally democratic. In France, no less
than in Germany, *in practice* very few individuals who
were not of middle-class origin succeeded in breaking
into the cultural stratosphere. But in France the theory at least was democratic, which in Germany it was
not. This difference says a good deal about the attitude

of the French state toward intellectual life, and helps
suggest why the intellectuals themselves were less dissatisfied with their government than was the case in
Germany after 1890.

Every one of the French protagonists of this study
was in some sense or other a republican. Only Durkheim, perhaps, was enthusiastic about the institutions
under which he lived, but all the others endorsed with
greater or less qualification the Republic and political
democracy. (Sorel's apostasy came only after the turn
of the century.) When in the late 1890's, in the tumults
of the Dreyfus case, the very existence of the Republic
seemed threatened, they all rallied to its defense. It may
be objected in this connection that at the turn of the
century royalism and other forms of anti-republican
activity were fashionable in French literary circles: in
the Dreyfus case the intellectuals were almost evenly
divided. But the anti-Dreyfusard writers were in general
those of lesser rank—novelists like Barrès and Bourget
whose reputations have not stood the passage of time,
and the more conventional sort of university professors.
The great and sensitive minds in the field of social
thought were without exception Dreyfusards.

It is also relevant to recall that what gave the *affaire*
its particular vehemence was the fact that Captain
Dreyfus was a Jew. It is difficult, indeed impossible, to
imagine a Dreyfus case in the Germany of the same
period. In the first place, no German Jew had the re-
motest chance of becoming, like Dreyfus in France, a
member of the Army General Staff. Beyond this, the
attitude toward the Jews of liberal-minded German intellectuals was more ambiguous than that of their
French counterparts: men like Weber and Meinecke
opposed the conventional anti-Semitism of the German
upper classes, but they qualified their opposition in a
fashion that in France would have been quite unacceptable. In the country of Voltaire, an attitude of doctrinaire "enlightenment" was the rule rather than the exception. At Normale, a former student recalled: "We

had always lived with our Jewish comrades in the same
intimacy as with those who were Christians; it did not
enter our heads that they could be different from us;
and the idea that a man should have to suffer for his
religion and his race seemed intolerable to us." [1]

Of the French protagonists of this study, three—
Bergson, Benda, and Durkheim—were of Jewish origin,
and Proust had one Jewish parent. This high proportion
suggests the extent of the assimilation and participation
of the Jews in French intellectual life. But it would be
wrong to imply that there was anything approaching a
Jewish cohesiveness in cultural circles—as the anti-
Semites were wont to assert. A certain number of Jews,
it is true, after the turn of the century congregated
about Péguy and his curious periodical, the *Cahiers de
la Quinzaine*. But it was more usual to find Jewish intellectuals scattered in different coteries and sometimes
in strong opposition: Bergson's most persistent opponent was his co-religionist Julien Benda, who conducted
against him a personal vendetta extending over more
than forty years. [2]

In this connection it is instructive to observe the
parallel careers of Bergson and Durkheim, both of
whom eventually attained the highest academic honors
in the award of the French state. As Jews, they came
from quite different backgrounds. Bergson was thoroughly assimilated: the son of a prosperous Parisian
couple of Polish origin, he had attended one of the
most respectable of the city's *lycées*. Durkheim, on the
contrary, was the son of a rabbi from Alsace—where
more Germanic conditions prevailed. Born one year
apart, they met at the Ecole Normale Supérieure: Berg-

[1] Jérôme and Jean Tharaud: *Notre Cher Péguy* (Paris, 1926),
I, 134.

[2] Besides writing two books directed specifically against Bergson (*Le Bergsonisme, ou une philosophie de la mobilité* [Paris,
1912] and *Sur le Succès du bergsonisme* [Paris, 1914]), Benda
dealt extensively with the Bergsonian philosophy in at least four
of his other works. See Robert J. Niess: *Julien Benda* (Ann Arbor,
Mich., 1956), pp. 95–143.

son (although he was the younger) arrived in 1878,
and Durkheim a year later. Yet they never seem to have
become very well acquainted. Both enjoyed the reputation of being coldly intellectualist. We have a glimpse
of the disputatious Durkheim shouting logical riddles
from the head of the stairs, and of Bergson taking advantage of his position as an assistant librarian to with-
draw from the noisy disputes and gaiety of his fellow-
students. Once when a pile of books was lying on the
floor, one of Bergson's teachers turned to him with the
reproach: "Your librarian's soul must suffer"—to which
his fellow-students answered in chorus: "He has no
soul"—a strange commentary on the youth of the man
who was to do more than any other twentieth-century
figure to restore to philosophy the notion of spiritual
values! [3]

Both Bergson and Durkheim received major teaching
chairs in Paris. One was to rank as *the* philosopher, the
other as *the* sociologist, of early twentieth-century
France. Yet they were at the two extreme poles of intuitionism and residual positivism in the intellectual
critique of the 1890's. Their careers suggest the extent
of divergence within one or two commonly held assumptions that characterized not only the French Jews
but French intellectual life as a whole in the first decade
and a half of our century.

The Republic, then, was not only acceptable. On occasion it even seemed worth defending with some vehemence. And this was particularly true of the Jews, to
whom the word "equality" in the national motto meant
more than an empty symbol. [4] For them republican patriotism was a natural product of profound gratitude:
the accusers of Captain Dreyfus committed a catastrophic error in imagining that he could possibly betray
his country. Indeed, among French intellectuals as a

[3] Jacques Chevalier: *Bergson*, revised edition (Paris, 1948),
pp. 42–5.
[4] Julien Benda: *La Jeunesse d'un clerc* (Paris, 1936), pp.
36–42.

whole patriotism was a natural, almost instinctive emotion, less talked about than in Germany because it was
taken more for granted. There was a certain innocence
about the unquestioning national loyalty of the French:
it had little of that aggressive, hyper-tense quality of
the "demonic" that the more sensitive Germans feared
even as they detected it in their own souls. The patriotism of a Péguy—the most "nationalist" of our sample—was that of a peasant tenaciously defending his
soil.

By the same token, the French intellectuals were not
even remotely tempted to renounce their national allegiance. The self-exile of Romain Rolland during the
First World War remained a unique phenomenon.
The French writer or scholar simply assumed that his
country was the center of the civilized world, as its language was the most perfect vehicle for intellectual communication. He could not imagine how it was possible
to live anywhere else—just as he could not conceive of
permanent residence away from Paris. André Gide complained all his life of the climate and distractions of the
capital—but he never succeeded in breaking away from
it. Similarly someone like Benda who untiringly de-
nounced the corrupting influence of Parisian coteries
had been himself deeply involved in salon life. To the
French intellectual the stimulation of his fellows was a
necessity of life. Take him away from Paris, and he
would perish.

What were the new interests that were agitating
these writers as the decade of the 1890's wore on? The
great influence of Nietzsche still lay in the future: only
at the end of the century would a significant number
of young Frenchmen became professed Nietzscheans.[5]
Yet already in France, as in Germany, there was a growing awareness of the things of the spirit: the teaching of
the philosopher Emile Boutroux, and later of Bergson
himself, at the Ecole Normale Supérieure worked in

[5] Geneviève Bianquis: *Nietzsche en France* (Paris, 1929), pp.
13–15.

this direction. Among the *normaliens*, however, the strongest influence did not come from the faculty at all, but from Lucien Herr, the librarian of the school during the critical decades after 1886.

Lucien Herr is one of the most curious figures in the intellectual history of France. Although he never wrote a line that counted, he deserves to figure in an important capacity in any survey of ideas at the turn of the century. An Alsatian, like Durkheim, and apparently marked out for a brilliant intellectual career, he had surprised his contemporaries by fixing on the modest position of librarian.

> It was the job he wanted and he settled down to it. . . . There, invariably seated at his imposing desk, he watched the groups of young men go by. . . . He supplied them with reading matter and laid his own immense scholarship at their service. . . . He won respect by his spiritual as well as his physical stature, equally exalted and excellent. . . . Lucien Herr was born to serve a church and to propagate a faith. . . . A good Catholic . . . by origin . . . , he had given it all up . . . and . . . put his name down for the Socialist Party. This throws some light on his choice of a career.[6]

As a young man of thirty, Lucien Herr, stubborn Alsatian that he was, had seen that the library of the Ecole Normale Supérieure offered the most strategic spot in France from which to make distinguished converts to Socialism. And in this self-chosen mission he proved spectacularly successful. The greatest of the conversions to Socialism, however, just preceded Herr's arrival—that of the future "tribune" Jean Jaurès. Noisy, affable, self-confident, and intellectual facile, Jaurès

[6] Daniel Halévy: *Péguy and* Les Cahiers de la Quinzaine (translation by Ruth Bethell of the revised version, published in France in 1940, of Halévy's *Charles Péguy et les Cahiers de la Quinzaine*) (London, 1946), p. 31.

was the acknowledged chief of the "promotion" of
1878, which was also Bergson's class.[7] In the competitive examination for the *agrégation* in philosophy three
years later, Jaurès felt himself "dishonored" to rank
third—after Bergson, who placed second, and the now
unknown figure that came in first. Jaurès was a southerner who had matured early and early marked out his
course in life: to his more timid classmates, it seemed
natural to follow where he had given the lead.

Subsequently, when he was already an influential
young politician and professor, Jaurès would return to
his student haunts and, in afternoon gatherings around
Herr's desk, reinforce the precepts of the librarian. The
combined pressure of two such different temperaments
must have been overwhelming. We should bear it in
mind when we recall the near unanimity with which
the *normaliens* aligned themselves behind Captain
Dreyfus at the end of the decade.[8]

The sequel, however, was to be less attractive. The
triumph of the Dreyfusards was their undoing. With
the exploitation of the victory of the republican Left,
a growing disillusionment gripped the consciences of
the intellectuals—now entering middle age—who had
fought the good fight for what they took to be abstract
justice. Defense of the Republic, party Socialism—these
things to which they had given the best energies of
their youth now seemed tarnished. Many of them
turned away from Socialism—some even, like Sorel, to
a denial of democracy itself. And at the same time the
conservatives who had lost the ideological battle began
to find new and more attractive grounds from which
to make their appeal to traditional values. At the turn
of the century these things still lay in the future.
We shall consider them more fully when toward the
end of the study we encounter the new "generation of
1905."

[7] "Promotions" at Normale were dated by the year of arrival
rather than of graduation.

[8] Tharaud: *Péguy*, I, 91, 97–8.

In Italy it is not possible to detect the same sort of large, influential intellectual community as existed in France and Germany. For much of Italy was still too provincial, and its educated stratum was not sufficiently broad, to support universities and reviews of a caliber similar to the German or the French. Nor was Rome, far from being a Paris, even on a par with Berlin. Italy, like Germany, still reflected in the scattering of its intellectual life the disunity of its past. And, as opposed to Germany, the center of administration was by no means the intellectual capital. Rome in 1890 was still a city of priests, tourists, and civil servants. Turin, Milan, Florence—above all, Naples—the great regional capitals still thought of themselves as culturally superior to Rome. And it was true that the most lively intellectual activity frequently manifested itself in local groupings of individuals with like interests, such as the Florentine Academy of the Georgofili to which Pareto belonged from the mid-seventies to the mid-nineties and the circle of Neapolitan scholars to which the young Croce read his first essays on the philosophy of history.

This is not to say that the Italian contribution to the intellectual renovation of the 1890's was unimportant or undistinguished—far from it. A limited number of Italian writers and scholars already ranked among the greatest in Europe: we have only to think of the literary historian and critic Francesco de Sanctis, who taught at the University of Naples from 1871 to his death in 1883. But there were too few of them and they did not receive sufficient moral support from the society in which they lived. Moreover in Italy, still more than in Germany, the period from the mid-century to the 1890's seemed lamentably lacking in major figures. It was as though in both countries creative talent had been diverted and burned out in the fatigues of unification. In the parliamentary state whose leading exponent for the entire decade from the mid-seventies to the mid-eighties was the pallid, deftly corrupting Agostino Depretis, men of large views were either lacking or unappreciated. It was symptomatic that after years of vainly seeking a university chair in his own country, Pareto was eventually obliged to accept the offer of a professorship in French Switzerland. And it is further noteworthy that the date of Pareto's departure—1893— marked the beginning of seven years of civic tumults that in retrospect were to appear the necessary prologue to a renewal of political and cultural life.

In Italy, at least as much as in Germany, the period from the 1890's to the First World War was to rank as a literary and philosophical renaissance. And this was to an extraordinary extent the work of a single man— as Benedetto Croce admitted without modesty when he came to write the history of his own time.[9] Croce worked all his life as a private scholar: he never held a university chair. But perhaps for that very reason his voice carried farther. Radiating out from his beloved Naples, Croce's influence gradually became all-pervasive. And the task that he set himself was precisely what Italy most required. As a "cosmopolitan intellectual," a "man of the Renaissance," like Erasmus, Croce undertook to "de-provincialize [Italian] culture and manners . . . , to raise the tone of intellectual life through contact and exchange of ideas" with the outside world.[1]

So much for the cultural setting. Against this background we may outline in preliminary and schematic form the major ideas that were initially stated in the 1890's, preparatory to their fuller elaboration in the first decade of the twentieth century.

1. Most basic, perhaps, and the key to all the others was the new interest in the problem of consciousness and the role of the unconscious. It was the problem

---

[9] *Storia d'Italia dal 1871 al 1915* (Bari, 1928), translated by Cecilia M. Ady as *A History of Italy 1871–1915* (Oxford, 1929), pp. 242–6.

[1] Antonio Gramsci: *Il materialismo storico e la filosofia di Benedetto Croce* (*Opere*, vol. 2) (Turin, 1952), pp. 246–8.

implicit in the title of Bergson's first book, the *Essay on the Immediate Data of Consciousness*. In it he had tried to distinguish between a "superficial psychic life" to which the scientific logic of space and number could properly be applied, and a life in the "depths of consciousness" in which "the deep-seated self" followed a logic of its own: he had come to the conclusion that the world of dreams might offer a clue to this secret and unexplored realm. "In order to recover this fundamental self," he had added, "a vigorous effort of analysis is necessary." [2] A decade later, and proceeding from a philosophic and professional preparation almost totally in contrast to that of Bergson, Freud began to carry out the program that the former had outlined. Freud's first major work, *The Interpretation of Dreams*, built on his own "vigorous effort" of self-analysis a theory of unconscious motivation to which the life of dreams offered the key.

2. Closely related to the problem of consciousness was the question of the meaning of time and duration in psychology, philosophy, literature, and history. It was the problem to which Bergson was to return again and again in an effort to define the nature of subjective existence as opposed to the schematic order that the natural sciences had imposed on the external world. It represented one aspect of the task that Croce had set himself in trying to establish the qualitative and methodological differences between the realm of history and the realm of science. In somewhat different form it was the problem with which the natural scientists were themselves contending in postulating a universe that no longer strictly conformed to the laws of Newtonian physics. Finally it was the dilemma that obsessed the novelists of the first two decades of the new century—Alain-Fournier, Proust, Thomas Mann—the tor-

[2] *Essai sur les données immédiates de la conscience* (Paris, 1889), authorized translation by F. L. Pogson as *Time and Free Will: An Essay on the Immediate Data of Consciousness* (London and New York, 1910), pp. 125–7, 129.

menting question of how to recapture the immediacy of past experience in language that in ordinary usage could reproduce no more than the fragmentized reality of an existence that the logical memory had already stored away in neat compartments.

3. Beyond and embracing the questions of consciousness and time, there loomed the further problem of the nature of knowledge in what Wilhelm Dilthey had called the "sciences of the mind." In the early 1880's Dilthey had attempted to establish rules that would separate the areas in which the human mind strove for some kind of internal comprehension from the realm of external and purely conventional symbols devised by natural science. A decade later Croce had resumed the task, with his first important essay, "*La storia ridotta sotto il concetto generale dell'arte.*" Croce soon abandoned the simple solution of including history among the arts. But his conviction of the radical subjectivity of historical knowledge remained. By 1900 it was apparent to the more imaginative of Croce's contemporaries that the nineteenth-century program of building an edifice of historical and sociological knowledge by patient accumulation and painstaking verification no longer sufficed. By such means it would prove forever impossible to penetrate beneath the surface of human experience. One had, rather, a choice between the exercise of the sympathetic intuition postulated in Croce's neo-idealistic theory of history, and the creation of useful fictions, as Max Weber was later to elaborate them, as models for critical understanding.

4. If the knowledge of human affairs, then, rested on such tentative foundations, the whole basis of political discussion had been radically altered. No longer could one remain content with the easy assurances of the rationalistic ideologies inherited from the century and a half preceding—liberal, democratic, or socialist as the case might be. The task was rather to penetrate behind the fictions of political action, behind what Sorel called the "myths," Pareto the "derivations," and Mosca the

"political formulas" of the time. Behind these convenient façades, one could postulate the existence of the actual wielders of power, the creative minorities, the political élites. The discussion of politics, then, had been pushed back from the front of the stage to the wings—from the rhetoric of public discussion to the manipulation of half-conscious sentiments.

Such, indeed, is the most general characterization we may give to the new intellectual concerns of the 1890's. They had displaced the axis of social thought from the apparent and objectively verifiable to the only partially conscious area of unexplained motivation. In this sense the new doctrines were manifestly subjective. Psychological process had replaced external reality as the most pressing topic for investigation. It was no longer what actually existed that seemed most important: it was what men thought existed. And what they felt on the unconscious level had become rather more interesting than what they had consciously rationalized. Or—to formulate the change in still more radical terms—since it had apparently been proved impossible to arrive at any sure knowledge of human behavior—if one must rely on flashes of subjective intuition or on the creation of convenient fictions—then the mind had indeed been freed from the bonds of positivist method: it was at liberty to speculate, to imagine, to create. At one stroke, the realm of human understanding had been drastically reduced and immensely broadened. The possibilities of social thought stretched out to infinity. It was perhaps this that Freud had in mind when in 1896 he spoke of "metapsychology"—the definition of the origin and nature of humanity—as his "ideal and problem child," his most challenging task for the future.[3]

---

[3] Jones: *Freud, I: The Formative Years and the Great Discoveries 1856–1900* (New York, 1953), p. 294.

3

The Critique of Marxism

T HE INTELLECTUAL legacy that Karl Marx had left to
future social thinkers was both untidy and ambiguous. By the 1890's it was no longer possible to dismiss
him as just another proletarian agitator: the size of the
political parties that recognized him as their prophet
and the seriousness of the economic investigations that
he had initiated had made him a massive force that demanded to be related in some way or other to the major
traditions of European thought. As the decade wore
on, a number of "bourgeois" economists and social
thinkers of the most varying intellectual orientations
found themselves compelled to come to grips with his
doctrines. Yet it was not entirely clear with what part
of the Marxian heritage they should grapple. Were they
to treat Marx in the abstract as a "scientific" social
thinker, or more pragmatically as the initiator of an extraordinarily successful political movement?

Marx himself, of course, had thought he was both,
and had argued that the two aspects of his activity were
necessarily inseparable. Theory, he maintained, grew

out of action and action out of theory in an inextricable
dialectical relationship, and the pretended objectivity
of "bourgeois" social science was patently a fraud. Yet
a careful examination of Marx's own statements revealed that the entanglement of scientific investigation
and practical precept was not so tight as he had imagined. In the vast, overlapping, disparate corpus of
Marxian writings—which, if we add the works of Engels
written after Marx's death, extended through the half-
century from the mid-forties to the mid-nineties—there
were certain sequences of doctrine that could be separated from those with which they had originally been
aligned, and were hence capable of independent application.

It was not necessarily true, for example, that Marx's
theory of history pointed inexorably to socialism, or
that the inevitable triumph of socialism which he had
postulated implied that one felt any moral compulsion
to hasten that victory. The Marxian interpretation of
history—commonly referred to as historical materialism
—had no necessary connection with socialism: in
slightly modified form, it was capable of being applied
to conservative ends, as the first decades of the twentieth century were to prove. And a conviction of the inevitability of a socialist society did not invariably lead
to the parallel conviction that such a change was desir-
able; indeed it might lead to the very opposite conclusion—witness the writings of the "defeatist" conservatives of our time, of whom Joseph Schumpeter was the
most distinguished example.[1]

As the writings of Marx began to be subjected to the
sort of close textual scrutiny which they were least capable of bearing, it soon became apparent that they
contained a number of peripheral—or even accidental—
features which had loomed very large in the original
thinking of their author, but which, as the decades
passed, began to reveal themselves as unessential en-

[1] See his *Capitalism, Socialism, and Democracy*, third edition
(New York, 1950).

cumbrances. Their Hegelian structure could plausibly be dismissed as the time-bound product of Marx's philosophical instruction in Berlin in the 1830's. It accounted for a good deal that was cumbersome about his theories: even the dialectical method—ostensibly the priceless jewel in the Hegelian inheritance—proved to be far less impressive when applied to concrete social situations than when merely talked about. Similarly, the economics of Marx rested on two or three central pillars that with the passage of years began to seem perilously shaky—the complementary "laws" of the falling rate of profit and the increasing misery of the working class, and the labor theory of value, with its still more questionable corollary of exploitative "surplus" value. It was no wonder that most critics came to find Marxism more impressive as a canon of historical interpretation—or as speculative sociology—than as technical economics.

Indeed—as countless students of Marxism can bear witness—what gradually emerged from a careful reading of the texts was that the powerful personality of their author and his unshakable conviction of the rightness of his cause had fused together in a fiery synthesis the most disparate philosophical and social elements. On the plane of abstract social theory, Marx had coupled Hegel to Ricardo and Ricardo in turn to the great Utopians. On the plane of revolutionary action, it was still more apparent that the author of the *Manifesto* and *Capital* had aligned in apparently logical sequence a number of assertions for whose necessary connection he offered little proof beyond his own profound moral conviction. Could one be sure that the triumph of socialism would assure the primacy of the working class? The subsequent experience of the Soviet Union would appear to disprove it. Would this primacy in turn eventually disappear in an apocalyptic end of all classes? Again the Soviet example would suggest the contrary. Still more, was not the very notion of an apocalypse a radically unhistorical idea that ran counter to the whole

development of historical thinking in the nineteenth
century?

These were some of the questions that Marx's critics
of the 1890's—sympathetic and unsympathetic alike—
began to put to themselves as they pored over his writings. And in coming to rest on the apocalyptic pronouncements that were at the very center of the Marxian doctrine, they discovered the familiar contrast
between Marx the social thinker and Marx the political
agitator—a contrast that today can be more starkly recast as an image of Marx the nineteenth-century scientist at war with Marx the Old Testament prophet. In
the 1890's it was not yet possible to discern the unconscious revelations of ancestral thought-patterns that lay
scattered through the Marxian writings: it would take
the work of Freud and his successors to assess at its full
value the religious imagery in the vocabulary of a man
who believed himself a convinced materialist. Yet even
before 1900 a scholar like Durkheim could assert that
it was moral passion rather than systematic research
which had inspired and given their force to Marx's doctrines.

This contrast between Marxism as social science and
Marxism as moral preachment brings us to a final question—a question that the critics of the 1890's rather
posed by implication than consciously formulated. As
a social scientist Marx was clearly in the rational tradition of the Enlightenment. In his more scholarly guise,
he could be both generous and fair-minded, and he rendered full justice even to the works of his enemies—the
capitalists and the industrial bourgeoisie. As prophet,
however, Marx was a man of wrath, vicious in polemic
and showering scorn on his adversaries. In this latter
guise, his works were to serve as manuals for the gravediggers of the Enlightenment, from the Right and the
Left alike. If a reassessment of Europe's eighteenth-century heritage was to be one of the central tasks of
the new social thinkers of the 1890's, then it was essen-

tial for them to determine—if only by implication—to what extent Marx could be considered a child of the Enlightenment.

The antithesis between the Marx of wrath and the Marx of sweet reason had, of course, always existed. But it was not until more than a decade after his death that the controversy over his heritage really began— when, with the decease of his collaborator Friedrich Engels in 1895, the last link with the canonical past had snapped, and there was no one left with full authority to reconcile the contradictions inherent in the original doctrine. The way was now open for younger men to choose one or the other horn of the dilemma that Marx had bequeathed to them, and to push his contrasting tendencies to their logical conclusions.

On the political plane, the antithesis expressed itself as a conflict within the European Socialist parties between "revisionists" or "reformists" on the one hand and revolutionaries on the other. By the turn of the century there had already delineated themselves the factions that two decades later were to split the movement into the mutually antagonistic camps of democratic Socialism and Communism. In a systematic sense, it was the revisionists who inaugurated the debate. Their spokesman, the German Social Democrat Eduard Bernstein, had tarried too long in England to preserve his Marxist purity and had become severely contaminated by Fabianism. In a series of magazine articles published between 1896 and 1898, and, more coherently, in his book *Evolutionary Socialism* which came out a year later, Bernstein advanced a number of propositions that were unquestionably Fabian in inspiration. A great deal of Marx's economics, he argued, and most of Marx's predictions for the future had been disproved by the developments of the last decades. "Peasants do not sink"—he noted in a scribbled summary of his theory— "middle class does not disappear; crises do not grow ever larger; misery and serfdom do not increase." [2] Under these changed circumstances, Bernstein argued, the only logical tactic for European Socialists was to exploit to the full the potentialities of gradual reform through parliamentary action.

Initially the response to Bernstein came in shocked outbursts from Karl Kautsky and the other self-constituted guardians of party orthodoxy. Most of these simply obscured the logic of the revisionist position by making a dogged effort to reconcile revolutionary theory with the legalistic practice of the Social Democratic parties. The real rejoinder to Bernstein—in the sense of radical intellectual rigor—came from quite a different quarter. It was not one of the pontiffs of Marxism but the comparative neophyte Lenin who in his pamphlet of 1901 entitled *What Is To Be Done?* first met head-on the issues that Bernstein had raised. Lenin refused to be daunted by the patent ambiguities of the Marxian tests. Boldly drawing the opposite conclusions from the evidences of *embourgeoisement* that Bernstein had assembled, he argued for the necessity of a tight, conspiratorial party, tirelessly pursuing its aim of revolutionary subversion.

Both Bernstein and Lenin were primarily party polemicists. Either one could have become a first-rank social thinker if he had chosen to cast his writings in more abstract form. But Bernstein was obliged to spend virtually his whole professional life in defending the position that he had marked out in the late 1890's, and Lenin, after one foray into the field of abstract reasoning, returned to the more familiar ground of party tactics. And it is significant that this one venture, the book *Materialism and Empirio-Criticism* which he published in 1909, while ostensibly a defense of materialist metaphysics against the neo-Kantian epistemology that was

---

[2] Bernstein Archives: cited by Peter Gay in *The Dilemma of Democratic Socialism* (New York, 1952), p. 244. The original title of Bernstein's book is *Die Voraussetzungen des Sozialismus und die Aufgaben der Sozialdemokratie.*

gaining converts even among Marxists, was actually written to settle an obscure factional dispute within the Russian Social Democratic party.[3]

We shall see subsequently how the doctrinal crisis within organized Socialism overlapped with and was intensified by the investigations of more disinterested social thinkers. These latter obviously constitute our real subject, and the factional fights within European Social Democracy are important to us only as suggesting one of the reasons why a number of extremely able intellectuals not previously interested in Marxism began to turn their attention to it in the 1890's. Marx, they had come to realize, was too important to be left to the propagandists and party hacks.

All of them were looking to him for intellectual renewal. The standpoints, however, from which they approached him and the things they found in him were as diverse as their philosophical origins. Emile Durkheim—positivist in orientation, but dissatisfied with the positivist tradition as handed down by Comte and Spencer—found in the systematic study of Marxian socialism an intellectual introduction to a new sociology based on empirical data rather than on abstract speculation. Vilfredo Pareto—also a positivist, but more hostile to Marx and judging him primarily from the standpoint of technical economics—discovered through the demolition of socialist myths the initial outlines of a more general theory of social conflict. For Georges Sorel, Marxian socialism was a grab-bag of novelties that required a painstaking sorting-out; half nineteenth-century scientist half twentieth-century prophet, Sorel was to return again and again to Marx, now for intellectual clarification, now for moral uplift. Benedetto Croce, coming from the most unlikely preparation in historical erudition and aesthetics, stumbled on Marx almost by accident and abode with him only long enough to say four or five supremely intelligent things

[3] See the chapter "Lenin as Philosopher" in Bertram Wolfe's *Three Who Made a Revolution* (New York, 1948), pp. 496–517.

and then pass on to more permanent concerns; for him Marxism offered both a stick with which to beat the positivists and a corrective to his own idealist view of history based on literary and artistic models.

Positivism and anti-positivism, admiration and hostility to Marx—these overlap bewilderingly in the critique of the 1890's. Durkheim, in fact, presented his course of lectures on socialism largely to justify his own ambivalence. Pareto the Marx-slayer, Sorel the most subtle of Marx's modernizers, and Croce the cool dissector of historical materialism were all united by a mutual esteem verging on friendship. Yet their association was based on something more solid than an agreement to differ. They were all absorbed by the crucial question of Marx's claim to "scientific" validity. And in asking themselves whether Marxism could properly be considered a science, they were inevitably led to pose the further question of what one meant by a science of society and the extent to which such a body of scientific knowledge was attainable at all.

The study of Marxism, then, offered them a kind of proving-ground—an initial test both of the general canons of social science and of the more personal theories that began to emerge out of the confrontation with the Marxian texts. In his own lifetime Marx had been fond of obstetrical metaphors and had characterized force as the "midwife" of social change. In similar vein, the Marx who less than fifteen years after his death had been transformed into an ideological institution could properly be called the midwife of twentieth-century social thought. For in the process of discarding what they had found invalid in Marxism and explaining what aspects of it had proved helpful and suggestive, the innovators of the 1890's took their first steps toward constructing a more general theory of social reality.

1. *Durkheim and Marxism as Moral Passion*

Emile Durkheim conventionally ranks as the founder of contemporary sociology, and it is in this guise that we shall encounter him later in the present volume.[4] As early as 1880, he had been initiated into the intricacies of Marxian socialism as a student at the Ecole Normale Supérieure, where he had made a lasting friendship with his fellow *normalien* the future Socialist tribune Jean Jaurès. Yet it was not until fifteen years later that he expressed himself systematically on the subject, and it was to be three decades more before his lectures on socialism—still in unfinished form—were posthumously published. The explanation for these delays seems to lie in the fact that for Durkheim Marxism offered no more than one of the several possible avenues to an investigation of society, and he was constantly being diverted from a full analysis of it by the pressure of more empirical studies.

Durkheim, his closest collaborator tells us, had originally intended to write a book on socialism and the individual. But the project gradually extended itself into a study of the individual and society in general, and this in turn into an effort to re-establish on a more solid base the new discipline of sociology, which the heirs of Auguste Comte had left in a state of disrepute. Hence he was led to interrupt his study of socialism and to deal in his university lectures with the concrete problems of suicide and of the division of labor, which were to become the subjects of his early major works.

In the academic year 1895–6, Durkheim, now thirty-seven years old and professor at the University of Bordeaux, at last turned his attention to the problem of socialism. His purpose was at least as much moral as scientific—just as he was to emphasize the moral element in his analysis of Marxism. He was trying to jus-

[4] See Chapter 8.

tify to himself, to the outside world, and to his students
—some of the best of whom were socialists—his own
ambiguous relationship to organized Socialism. "All his
life he shrank from adhering to Socialism in the narrower sense only on account of . . . its violent character, its class character . . . , and also its political
character. . . . Even the social and moral crisis of the
Dreyfus case, in which he played a great part, did not
change his opinion. . . . He 'sympathized' . . . with
the Socialists, with Jaurès, with Socialism. He never
gave himself to them." [5]

The course of lectures, we understand, was a great
success, but it was never completed by the two succeeding courses that would have brought the subject up
through Marx. Hence we are left with a volume that
deals primarily with socialism in general and with
Saint-Simon—and only in brief and tantalizingly suggestive passages with the problem of Marxism itself. In
sum, the view that Durkheim advanced was that most
of the current criticisms of socialist doctrine hit wide of
the essentials since they took at face value its claim to
scientific validity. The economists like Böhm-Bawerk
and the members of the "Austrian" school, who were
so painstakingly refuting Marxism dogma by dogma,
were engaged in a "Penelope's labor, constantly need-
ing to be renewed." By these methods, socialism could
never be touched more than externally: its inner force
would always escape the weapons of analysis.[6]

For socialism, Durkheim argued, could not properly
be attacked in the abstract. It was "entirely directed toward the future" rather than toward an "actually existing object" and hence did not possess a "truly scientific character." Socialism was in fact "an ideal":

No doubt, even in its most utopian forms, it has
never scorned the support of facts, and it is even

[5] Introduction by M. Mauss to Emile Durkheim: *Le Socialisme: sa définition, ses débuts, la doctrine saint-simonienne*
(Paris, 1928), pp. v–ix.
[6] Ibid., p. 10.

true that in more recent times it has more and more assumed a certain scientific cast. It is incontestable that in so doing it has perhaps helped social science more than it has been helped by it. For it has awakened reflection; it has stimulated scientific activity . . . to such an extent that in more than one respect its history blends with that of sociology. Nevertheless, how can one fail to be struck by the enormous disproportion that exists between the rare and thin data that it borrows from the sciences and the extent of the practical conclusions which it draws from them and yet which are the very heart of the system? [7]

Even the work of socialist thinking that was "most powerful, most systematic, richest in ideas . . . Marx's *Capital*" could not be considered an exception.

What a lot of statistical data, of historical comparisons, of studies would be indispensable to settle a single one of the innumerable questions it treats! . . . The truth is that the facts and observations gathered in it . . . figure there as little more than arguments. The research . . . was undertaken to establish the doctrine . . . , far from the doctrine resulting from research. . . . It was passion that inspired all these systems; what gave birth to them and constitutes their strength is the thirst for a more perfect justice. . . . Socialism is not a science, a sociology in miniature: it is a cry of pain. . . .

Its perennial appeal, then, could be explained only by searching behind the scientific pretenses of its doctrine, for the concrete social circumstances out of which it arose. And in so doing, the sole attitude that a conscientious social scientist could adopt—and one to which an equally conscientious socialist could never

[7] Ibid., pp. 3–4.

consent—was an attitude of "reserve and circumspection." [8]

II. *Pareto and the Theory of the Elite*

Vilfredo Pareto's *Les Systèmes socialistes*, originally published in 1902, early established itself as the classic refutation of Marxian economics and sociology. Legend has it that it caused Lenin graver worry than any other anti-Marxist writing, and that he took more than one sleepless night to work out his own counter-refutation. Certainly it is a biting, spirited, witty book—a magnificent polemic. Yet as one begins to recover from the initial effect of bedazzlement it produces, one detects its gaps, its slips in reasoning—and its literal-mindedness. Although coming later in time than Croce's and Sorel's initial writings on Marxism, and building on these writings, *Les Systèmes socialistes* in a number of respects stopped short of the conclusions that its author's predecessors and intellectual companions had reached. Its polemical construction proved inadequate to embrace a full critique of the Marxian doctrine.

Pareto's work on socialism marks the transition in his thought from problems of technical, and more particularly mathematical, economics to a system of general sociology. Like Durkheim, Pareto came to sociology by way of socialism. By training an engineer and public servant, the Marchese Pareto displayed a curious combination of an aristocrat's distaste for the multitude and a technician's respect for facts. In 1893, disgusted with what he regarded as his own country's squalid parliamentary regime, he had retired to a comfortable exile on the Lake of Geneva as professor of economics at the University of Lausanne. The study and teaching of economics had led logically to an interest in Marxism, and in the same year, 1893, we find him writing an introduction to a French translation of extracts from

[8] Ibid., pp. 5–6.

Marx's *Capital* selected by the latter's son-in-law Paul Lafargue. Eight more years of study resulted in *Les Systèmes socialistes*, the second volume of which was devoted primarily to Marx.

A positivist, like Durkheim, Pareto followed the French sociologist's lead in denying scientific validity to nearly all of Marx's work. And he similarly agreed with Durkheim in drawing a sharp distinction between the logical value of socialist doctrines—which he found virtually nil—and the social reality they reflected. But while Durkheim had simply thrown out this suggestion as a precept for future investigation, Pareto was to exploit it in methodical fashion as the starting-point of a system of sociology that would work from substantially Marxian premises to diametrically opposed conclusions. As Marx himself had once claimed to have turned Hegelianism right side up, so Pareto would now subject Marx to the same treatment.

Obviously Pareto approached his socialist studies with a temperamental hostility that was far removed from Durkheim's attitude of qualified sympathy. All class prejudices aside, his position as a classical economist and his dogmatic free-trade convictions made all types of socialism profoundly distasteful to him. And this temperamental dislike was reinforced by the economist's fastidious annoyance at the "sophistries" in which the socialist writers had indulged. Hence Pareto could not resist the sort of intellectual fencing with his adversaries which Durkheim had rejected as pure waste motion.

These spirited skirmishes took up the greater part of Pareto's two thick volumes. Yet in the retrospect of a half-century they provide little more than entertainment value. What is of immediate concern to us now is Pareto's central contention—the core of validity that he discovered in the Marxian doctrine. "There is in Marx," he affirmed, "a sociological part, which is superior to the other parts and is often in accord with reality. Marx has one very clear idea—that of class conflict; it is this idea that inspires all his practical action, and he subordinates to it all his theoretical researches." [9]

The task of the social scientist, then, was to accept in their broad outlines the Marxian theories of class struggle and subsequently to disentangle in them what was true from what was false. This task was complicated by the fact that *Capital*, "the holy book of socialism," possessed "to a high degree the characteristics that one encounters in all holy books, that is to say vagueness and obscurity." And these complications were compounded by the fact that the works of Marx and Engels presented "a happy mixture of passion and reason, calculated to satisfy the exegesis both of the vulgar and of the learned." The former were impressed with Marx's literary vigor and the colorful fashion in which he depicted capitalist oppression; the latter were entranced by his subtleties and by the flattering "idea that while the true meaning escapes the run of mankind, we alone have succeeded in discovering it." It was this second or learned exegesis—however tortuous it might be—that Pareto found of interest to the social scientist. "The learned interpretation of the materialist conception of history," he affirmed, "leads us toward reality and has all the characteristics of a scientific theory." [1]

Yet, considered in this guise, historical materialism was "at bottom, no more favorable to socialism than to any other doctrine"; it could "even be said to be absolutely opposed to sentimental and ethical socialism." For—as a passing bow to Darwin suggested—the class struggle had nothing whatever to do with the humanitarian sentiments with which the vulgar socialists chose to adorn it. These sentiments existed—to deny their existence would be "to fall headlong into the error of the people who imagine that man can get along

    [9] *Les Systèmes socialistes*, second edition (Paris, 1926), I, 16; II, 338.
    [1] Ibid., II, 333, 393, 402.

entirely without religion"—but they were not of the essence of class conflict.[2]

As this conflict had ramified into ever greater complexities, it had become apparent that the student of society was confronted with more than a simple struggle between "bourgeois" and "proletarians." Not only had it developed that these two classes in turn were falling into warring divisions. It was also evident that the proletarians were only ostensibly fighting in their own cause. Surface appearances were deceptive—in actuality, the social struggle had never been one of aristocrats against the "people." Throughout history, the so-called popular leaders had simply been disgruntled individuals of superior ability who had felt themselves barred from effective power. The great revolutions had been no more than the struggle of a new élite to displace an old one—with the "people" serving as its humble soldiers. These latter doubtless believed that they were fighting "for what they call justice, liberty, humanity," and many of their leaders imagined "in good faith" that they were doing the same. What was really at stake, however, was the class or personal advantage of the new élite.

Hence it would be an illusion, Pareto concluded, to think that the end of the struggle between "capital" and "labor" would bring an end to class conflict in the wider sense. Even in a collectivist society, conflicts would arise "between the different kinds of workers in the socialist state, between 'intellectuals' and 'nonintellectuals,' between different kinds of politicians, between politicians and those administered by them, between innovators and conservatives."[3] The socialist apocalypse could be dismissed as a mirage.

Such was the fashion in which Pareto turned Marx on his head. The class conflict, he was quite willing to grant, had a real existence, but its determinants were

[2] Ibid., II, 405, 413.
[3] Ibid., I, 35–7; II, 430, 467.

far more complex than simply the laws of economics.[4] Sentiments, "ideals"—non-logical motivations of all sorts that were essentially religious in nature—played the dominant role, and it was these that the great popular leaders of history had known so well how to manipulate. If it was true, as Pareto asserted, that the mass of the population could never be more than a passive instrument in revolutions and civil wars, then the "scientific" part of Marx need not point inevitably toward socialism. Historical materialism could be turned in a conservative direction to give the threatened élites a new toughness and self-confidence. With the completion of *Les Systèmes socialistes*, Pareto had already formulated in rough outline the theories of social organization that fourteen years later were to make him justly celebrated as the great rationalizer of authoritarian conservatism in our time.[5]

iii. *Croce and Historical Materialism as a Canon of Interpretation*

In his discussion of the "learned exegesis" of Marxism, Pareto had cited as "two Marxists of great talent" his intellectual companions Benedetto Croce and Georges Sorel, and in the subsequent chapter he had added that a knowledge of the writings of the former—and of those of his master in things Marxist, Antonio Labriola—was "indispensable for appreciating the present state of the question of *historical materialism*." [6]

As applied to Sorel the epithet "Marxist" might perhaps serve as a rough approximation, but in Croce's case it was woefully inappropriate. Croce's five-year brush with Marxism bore little relation to what had come before it in his intellectual life and to what were

---

[4] See Erwin Schuler: *Pareto's Marx-Kritik* (Tübingen, 1935), pp. 15–21.
[5] See Chapter 7.
[6] *Les Systèmes socialistes*, II, 333, 402.

to be his major concerns in the future. He happened upon it rather casually, he extracted from it what he needed in order to enrich his canons of historical interpretation, and then—when he found that there was no further profit to be derived from it—he dropped it as suddenly as he had taken it up. While his interest lasted, however, he pursued his Marxist studies with feverish enthusiasm, and he even succeeded in mastering the technical discipline of economics that was so alien to his aesthetic and literary bent.

Hence it was not surprising that Pareto, who was able to follow Croce's thought only from a distance, should have taken him for a Marxist. In fact, in collecting for publication his scattered essays on historical materialism, Croce voiced the complaint that he had been more than once described as a "rigid orthodox Marxist" who had gradually changed into a critic and opponent. It was true, he granted, that the subjective coloring of his thought had varied during the period of his Marxist studies—one could find in his essays both "enthusiasm" for a "work of genius" and "disgust" with the "pedantries, sophistries, and emptiness" of its later commentators—but the thought itself had remained constant. This, he claimed, represented "the same tendency that has been developing almost simultaneously in France through the work of Sorel and that has succeeded in freeing the healthy and realistic kernel of Marx's thought from the metaphysical and literary flourishes of the author himself, and from the imprudent exegesis and deductions of his school." [7]

In late April of 1895, the twenty-nine-year-old Croce —who was growing slightly bored with his life as a private scholar immersed in the antiquities of his native city of Naples—received from his former teacher Labriola a letter that galvanized him into new and unfamiliar activity. In it the older scholar announced the appearance in Paris of a Marxist journal entitled *Deve-*

[7] Preface of 1899 to *Materialismo storico ed economia marxistica*, ninth edition revised (Bari, 1951), pp. viii–ix.

nir social. Labriola was the only serious theoretical Marxist in Italy, and the newly founded review at last gave him the literary outlet he needed. What he asked of Croce was, first, to subscribe to *Devenir social,* and, second, to advise him on an article he had prepared for publication in it.

In this somewhat accidental fashion there began the curious collaboration of Labriola and Croce in Marxist studies. The younger man had been Labriola's student at the University of Rome in the 1880's, and he knew that the latter had subsequently begun to give lectures on historical materialism, but his residence in Naples had prevented him from attending them. Hence he awaited Labriola's article with intense anticipation. And on reading and rereading it he found his "inflamed" mind filling with strange new "concepts" and "visions" that literally constituted a "revelation." He wrote back offering to serve as editor for this first essay and for the others which it was Labriola's "duty to compose." [8]

From the start there was an ambiguity in the relationship between the two men which—however diplomatically Croce might try to conceal it—was bound eventually to come to the surface. Labriola might be a philosopher and scholar, but he was also, in political terms, a convinced socialist. For him Marxism represented a lifetime commitment. For Croce, however, who stood outside partisan politics, Marxism was simply an exciting intellectual novelty. Hence in the warm exchange of correspondence between them and in the long conversations that marked their meetings, there was always a lurking danger that this basic misunderstanding would break forth. All went well so long as Croce was simply the student—commenting only rarely on Labriola's flood of elaborations and interpretations—but when he began himself to write on Marx-

[8] "*Come nacque e come morì il marxismo teorico in Italia* (1895–1900)," printed as appendix to sixth (1941) and later editions of *Materialismo storico,* pp. 272, 274.

ist subjects, his doubts and criticisms soon became apparent.

Already in his first essay on historical materialism—a critique of the theories of Professor Loria, Italy's leading Marxist vulgarizer who also ranked as Labriola's *bête noire*—he had not completely satisfied his master. For the latter had discovered that Croce could not possibly fulfill the "greater hopes that he had . . . vested" in him as "his colleague and successor in the guardianship and defense of the true Marxist tradition." Croce, Labriola complained, was too much of an "intellectual," a "*littérateur*," a "contemplative epicurean." And when, after almost a year of reflection, Croce came to present his own ideas on historical materialism, they were in fact, if not in appearance a critique of Labriola's views. Croce's essay—which he read in May 1896 before an academic circle in Naples—constituted a punctiliously respectful commentary on Labriola's collected Marxist writings that had just appeared in book form. The younger man took pains, as he himself relates, to present what he had to say "as though it were not a question of my own thought, but of something that was already in Labriola and in Marx himself." Hence, for the moment at least, Labriola did not detect "what Dante called 'the poison in the argument.' " [9]

Obviously such an ambiguous situation could not go on indefinitely. As the next two years passed and Croce continued to write with ever greater independence on Marxist topics, Labriola's expressions of annoyance became more open and pointed. In 1898 the long-delayed explosion occurred. This was the year of the "crisis of Marxism"—the year of Bernstein's heresy. Quite unwittingly, Croce had stumbled into the center of the doctrinal furor within European Social Democracy. For by this time Bernstein had become interested in Croce's work as potential support for his own position and, in all good faith, had written Labriola to inquire about it.

[9] Ibid., pp. 293–6.

The latter was, of course, appalled: he tormented himself with the thought that his own pupil "had helped to overturn and put in mortal peril the doctrine to which he [Labriola] . . . had introduced" him. And in his urgent letters to Croce, Labriola in effect requested of him that he explain to one and all that he was a "mere literary fellow," a "mere intellectual and *raisonneur*," who marveled at the fact that his "demonstrations" and "authority" could be used "to promote a thing of such gravity as the crisis of Marxism!" [1]

Croce, of course, never made any such statement. He simply withdrew gracefully from the whole dispute. For by this time he had said nearly all he had to say on Marxian topics. By 1899 he was ready to close the "Marxist parenthesis" of his life. And at roughly the same time Labriola also dropped his socialist studies. For his part, Croce was "glad to have passed through" the doctrine of historical materialism; had he not done so, he would have felt "a sense of void" in his "mentality as a modern man." [2]

There was, then, in Croce's writings on Marxism, an implicit confusion arising from the overlayering of Labriola on Marx, and of Croce in turn on Labriola. Despite the limpidness of Croce's own literary style, he was treading his polemical way so carefully that the reader was obliged to remain always on the alert for half-veiled meanings. This danger, however, did not worry Croce himself. He frankly admitted that he was not treating Marx historically, that he was not trying "to interpret his expressions literally." On the contrary, Croce felt free to give them a "more acceptable" meaning by selecting the interpretations which appeared "theoretically true and defensible." As Sorel was simultaneously doing, Croce was trying to search out the

---

[1] Ibid., pp. 305–8.
[2] "*Marxismo ed economia pura*," added to second (1906) and later editions of *Materialismo storica*, p. 175.

meaning that Marx's words bore—or, perhaps, should have borne?—"in the writer's inmost thoughts." [3]

Croce was primarily a philosopher of history. Hence his grapplings with Marx's theories gave him a welcome opportunity to clarify the notions of historical interpretation that were already arranging themselves in his own mind. And similarly it was natural that he should fasten on the Marxian doctrine of historical materialism. This he dealt with—in his customarily tidy and efficient fashion—by successively reducing it within ever narrower limits. First he denied that it was a philosophy of history at all. Indeed, he went on to exclude the possibility of there being any such thing as a philosophy of history in the sense of determining the laws of historical development. Second he insisted that the correct doctrine of historical materialism was not to be confused with the "metaphysical" materialism of Marx's vulgarizers. These latter, he found, had virtually deified "matter" in the same fashion in which the Hegelians had deified "the Idea." But when all this was eliminated, what was there left to historical materialism? There was left a new *method* of procedure, as both Engels and Labriola had clearly stated, or to put it more accurately, a new *content* for history—since the technical methods of historical investigation remained the same as in the past.

Historical materialism, in short, amounted to a "mass of new data" and of "new experiences." It was not an invariable rule of procedure but rather a "warning to keep its observations in mind as a new aid to the understanding of history." It was a "canon" of interpretation, a way to orient oneself in the maze of historical data. As Sorel so aptly expressed it, it "illuminated"

[3] "Concerning the Interpretation and Criticism of Some Concepts of Marxism," *Historical Materialism and the Economics of Karl Marx*, translated by C. M. Meredith (London, 1914), pp. 79, 81. This translation, evidently made from the second edition of Croce's *Materialismo storico*, does not include all of the essays that are in the original Italian version. I have taken the liberty of correcting the translation in several places.

matters rather than explained them in scientific fashion.[4]

To explain matters scientifically, Croce argued, meant to arrive at universal formulas of general application. This Marx had thought he was doing—but in fact his theory had arisen "out of the need to account for a definite social phenomenon": it was inextricably bound up with the passions of the "politicians and revolutionists" who had created it. Where Marx had gone wrong, Croce discovered, was in trying to extend his history-grounded knowledge too far beyond its point or origin. In so doing, he had arrived at "ideal and schematic" definitions that bore no exact relationship to any known society.[5]

Out of such "ideal and schematic" formulations, Max Weber was soon to construct a systematic theory of social-science types. But to these possibilities Croce's mind remained closed. He continued to insist on a sharp separation between quasi-scientific hypotheses and the specific data of history. Hence, while agreeing with Durkheim and Pareto in denying Marxism the character of a science, he went beyond them to extend his Marxian reflections to the definition of scientific method in the study of society as a whole. Durkheim and Pareto had contented themselves with the simple and essentially positivist formula of making "logical deductions from the facts." [6] With such a summary definition the more fastidious Croce could not possibly rest satisfied. "All scientific laws," he argued, were "abstract laws." But—and here came his decisive deviation from his contemporaries—

---

[4] "Concerning the Scientific Form of Historical Materialism," *Historical Materialism*, pp. 3–5, 8–9, 12, 20; "Concerning the Interpretation and Criticism of Some Concepts of Marxism," ibid., p. 77; "*Marxismo ed economia pura,*" *Materialismo storico*, p. 165.
[5] "Concerning the Scientific Form of Historical Materialism," *Historical Materialism*, pp. 16–17; "Concerning the Interpretation and Criticism of Some Concepts of Marxism," ibid., pp. 50, 56–8.
[6] *Les Systèmes socialistes*, I, 6.

there is no bridge over which to pass from the concrete to the abstract; just because the abstract is
not a reality, but a form of thought, one of our
. . . abbreviated ways of thinking. And, although
a knowledge of the laws may illuminate our perception of reality, it cannot become *this perception
itself*.[7]

Otherwise stated, the laws of social science could never
bear any sure relation to the concrete data of experience. Historical and social study would be obliged to
seek a different path if it was ever to reach psychological
certainty. With his critique of Marxism—and with the
further critique of all contemporary social science that
it implied—Croce had come close to formulating his
own neo-idealist canon for the study of human activity.

Thus Croce had reduced Marx's theories to a collection of more or less useful "general aphorisms" and
"particular applications." [8] In his procedure of discarding and selecting, he had arrived at a series of judgments that became very nearly standard for later social scientists. At a moment when he felt an intellectual
need for it, Marxism had come his way and he had
taken from it only what he strictly required. It had interested him in at least two ways: first, as a critical doctrine, with a direct appeal to the imagination and to
youth, which could "fill the void created . . . by the
devastating work of positivism and its accompanying
pessimism"; second, as a means of revivifying the study
of history, which, in Croce's own case, had threatened
to succumb to antiquarianism. But this was all. For
Croce, Marxism signified nothing further. When its
lessons had been "well digested," it would no longer
need to be spoken of.[9]

[7] "Concerning the Interpretation and Criticism of Some Concepts of Marxism," *Historical Materialism*, p. 104.

[8] "*Le teorie storiche del Prof. Loria*," *Materialismo storico*,
p. 27. See also Mario Corsi: *Le origini del pensiero di Benedetto
Croce* (Florence, 1951), p. 150.

[9] *Storia d'Italia dal 1871 al 1915* (Bari, 1928), translated by
Cecilia M. Ady as *A History of Italy 1871–1915* (Oxford, 1929),

IV. *Sorel and Marxism as "Social Poetry"*

Of all the critics of Marxism—French, Italian, and German—the most probing and persistent, the one who worried about it over the longest period of time and reinterpreted it in most original fashion, was the retired engineer of Boulogne-sur-Seine, Georges Sorel. We have seen how Croce regarded him as his own French counterpart. Sorel returned the compliment by describing his Italian friend as "a writer full of tact and finesse" and frequently citing his work with approval.[1] Indeed, the two maintained a warm correspondence through nearly a quarter of a century. Similarly in the case of Pareto, there was a relationship of mutual esteem which lasted until the deaths of the two scholars just a year apart: despite his own more favorable attitude toward Marx, Sorel cited Pareto's *Systèmes socialistes* with respect,[2] and the latter found Sorel at fault only in having corrected the "honeyed and sickly-sweet" aspect of socialism with too much "exaggeration." [3] Toward Durkheim, Sorel maintained an attitude of slightly ironical deference. In fact, he has been accused of cribbing from Durkheim without acknowledgment [4]—although he referred to the great sociologist at least three times in his Marxist writings,[5] and he could scarcely have been expected to cite Durkheim's lectures on socialism, which

---

p. 149; "*Marxismo ed economia pura*," *Materialismo storico*, p. 176. For a more extended discussion of Croce, see Chapter 6.

[1] *La Décomposition du marxisme*, second edition (Paris, 1910), p. 5.

[2] "*Avant-propos*" (1914), *Matériaux d'une théorie du prolétariat* (Paris, 1919), pp. 36, 48.

[3] *Les Systèmes socialistes*, II, 408.

[4] John Bowle: *Politics and Opinion in the Nineteenth Century* (Oxford, 1954), p. 452n.

[5] "*Avenir socialiste des syndicats*" (1898), *Matériaux*, pp. 83, 124–8; "*La necessità e il fatalismo nel marxismo*," *Saggi di critica del marxismo* (Milan, 1903), p. 80.

had not yet been published. So far as I know, Durkheim expressed no similar sentiments toward Sorel.

Sorel stood, then, after the turn of the century, at the focal point of the critique of Marxism. He summed up and went beyond the implicit antagonism in the attitudes of Pareto and Croce to develop the hints thrown out by both of them. For three decades—from 1893, when he first became interested in socialism, to his death in 1922—he maintained an interest in Marxist theory which wavered only briefly, and he produced an abundant stream of miscellaneous articles on the subject. The more important of them he collected into two volumes—the first of which was published in Italy, reflecting the fact that he was appreciated earlier there than in his own country.[6] These two books, plus a little work on the "decomposition" of the Marxist doctrine, rather better than his more famous *Reflections on Violence*, embody his reinterpretation of the major European socialist tradition.

There is, however, in Sorel's attitude toward Marx a steady evolution that lands him in apparently insoluble contradictions. In 1899 we find him taking his stand with Bernstein and the revisionists. Eight years later in his *Reflections* he is applying Marxist theory to the practice of revolutionary syndicalism. At the end of his life he makes a final appearance as an apologist for Lenin. These contrasting positions are part of the larger problem of Sorel's central ambivalence that will occupy us in a subsequent chapter.[7] For the present we may limit ourselves to trying to understand the rationale of his changes and the extent to which we can detect in them an underlying unity of view.

Initially, in terms of Sorel's own biography, it seems clear that his shift from revisionism to the advocacy of violence reflected an enormous disillusionment with

---

[6] The *Saggi* and *Matériaux* already cited.
[7] See Chapter 5.

the democratic process. Like so many other French intellectuals, he had been a militant Dreyfusard, and his revisionist position of the late 1890's logically paralleled the "optimistic" phase of unity between Socialists and middle-class democrats that the great *affaire* had inspired. Subsequently, however, he took his place among that die-hard minority who were disgusted by the exploitation of the Dreyfusard victory for sectarian and careerist ends; [8] the little book in which he vented his pent-up wrath contained some of the bitterest pages he ever wrote.[9] However much his subsequent political allegiance might vary, he never returned to a faith in parliamentary democracy.

In the second place, Sorel was not one to worry about inconsistency. He even believed that it could be a virtue—an aid in arriving at a more rounded notion of social reality. In writing an introduction to the second of his collections of Marxist essays, he explained that he had intentionally refrained from revising them to bring them into harmony with each other. This procedure he justified by citing his own peculiar social-science method—a method which he baptized *diremption* and which consisted in willfully wrenching out certain aspects of reality from the context that enveloped them and examining them independently one from another.[1] To juxtapose a number of mutually incompatible statements, Sorel argued, meant to illuminate aspects of reality that might otherwise have passed unobserved.

Hence as individual *diremptions*, a statement in praise of Bernstein and a statement endorsing revolutionary syndicalism could figure simultaneously as separate and complementary approaches to the understanding of Marx. And regarded in this fashion, Marx-

---

[8] Pierre Andreu: *Notre Maître, M. Sorel* (Paris, 1953), pp. 138, 143–4.
[9] *La Révolution dreyfusienne*, second edition (Paris, 1911).
[1] "Avant-propos," *Matériaux*, pp. 3–6. On *diremption*, see further in Chapter 5.

ism itself could be considered one grand *diremption*. Like Croce, Sorel believed that what Marx had offered had been a necessarily *partial* view of social reality, and that it would be wrong to expect in him a precision of thought that could not possibly be there.

> Marx's language frequently lacks precision because he tries to embrace in a single expression the totality of a historical movement, and *to think it in all its complexity*. The [human] intelligence does not have the means to express such a synthesis.

Yet at the same time "Marx was right . . . in not sticking to empirical descriptions of social complexity and in presenting the great conflict . . . in the form of struggles . . . between *antagonistic partners*." [2] The author of *Capital*, in short, had done well to oversimplify the issues.

Why was Marx "right"? Obviously for pragmatic reasons. Here we come to the crux of Sorel's reinterpretation—the point at which he diverged from both Pareto and Croce to find a new standing-ground on which to reconcile his contradictions. This new stance implied a thoroughgoing redefinition of Marxism—in terms of science, of moral teaching, and of symbolic meaning.

The socialists, Sorel argued, had a "false idea" of science. They thought of it as a "mill into which problems are poured and from which solutions come out." In actuality, science had an "infinitely more modest . . . function"; it simply tried "to understand and to perfect the trials and attempts of experimental workers." [3] Like Croce, Sorel defined science in essentially practical terms. But he differed from Croce in making no sharp separation between concrete reality and the abstractions of science. There was, he found, no break in continuity between the patient efforts of engineers

[2] "*La necessità e il fatalismo nel marxismo*," *Saggi*, p. 61; "*Préface pour Colajanni*," *Matériaux*, pp. 186–7.
[3] "*La necessità e il fatalismo nel marxismo*," *Saggi*, p. 92.

like himself to bend to their purposes the resistance of inert nature, and the speculations of the most abstract theorists; indeed, the latter had customarily arisen almost by accident out of problems posed by the practical exertions of the technicians.

Hence a scientific statement could never be more than an approximation or working hypothesis. And—in the field of social science—it was one of such approximations which Marx had offered. Obviously it was incomplete; obviously it was partial and freighted with emotion. But on that account did one need to deny it all scientific validity? Sorel himself was inclined to relegate Marxian theory to the realm of "common sense" rather than to assign it to that of science. But as he had rephrased the question, it had become largely a matter of words; the answer depended on the amount of precision one demanded in a scientific formula. Like Croce, Sorel was casting about for a new definition of what social science consisted of. Meantime, in the form in which he had restated it, the old problem as to whether or not Marxism could be considered "scientific" had simply fallen to the ground.

It was Marx's successors, Sorel maintained, rather than Marx himself, who had confused the issue by their crude abuse of the notions of "necessity" and "fatality." [4] Sorel agreed with Croce—and, by implication at least, differed from Pareto—in finding no place for determinism in social science. Yet once more he went beyond his Italian friends by turning his attention to the sentimental aspects of the Marxian appeal. Pareto had stressed the importance of the non-logical in assessing the social behavior of human beings, but he had approached the subject with an evident distaste. For Croce, the realm of the irrational was always repellent and he avoided it as much as possible. Of the major critics of Marxism, Sorel alone saw a positive value for human understanding in an entanglement of "objective" and emotional elements.

[4] Ibid., pp. 69, 93–4.

This is the moral or psychological aspect of his re-interpretation. Sorel, as we shall subsequently notice, was primarily a moralist: the ethical aspect of social and historical problems was always of critical concern to him, even when he did not express it in so many words. The same, of course, was true of Durkheim—and, to a lesser extent, of Croce also—but they chose to remain detached scholars, free from personal involvement in the socialist movement. For Sorel, such detachment was a psychological impossibility. Some sort of social commitment was a necessity of his being, and during the war years, when he had no political movement in which to vest his hopes, he was acutely unhappy. In a lesser man, such an attitude could easily have degenerated into propagandism. In Sorel it opened the way to sympathetic understanding of the aspects of social behavior that had heretofore eluded exact analysis.

Whether a revisionist or an apologist for violence, whether in or out of working-class movements, Sorel never wavered in his contention that Marxism as abstract statement could never present more than half the story. Both Durkheim and Pareto had seen that it was moral passion rather than scientific rigor that gave the doctrine its perennial appeal. But Sorel alone went on to suggest that a sympathetic involvement in the great moral movements themselves was essential to understanding their character. Anticipating a position of which Karl Mannheim was later to become the most persuasive advocate, he implied that in the political and social sphere one could understand only what one had actually or vicariously *experienced*. "To judge properly," it was essential "to put oneself into the movement and to acquire an intellectual sympathy for it; otherwise one could not get to the bottom of things." [5] Hence even incompatible political positions could prove mutually helpful in illuminating a constantly fluctuating reality. And hence also one could learn, from sym-

[5] Letter of 1910 to Agostino Lanzillo, cited by Andreu: *Sorel,* p. 77.

pathetic participation in one current of sentiment, to transfer one's understanding to another and ostensibly alien movement—witness Sorel's parallel interest in Marxism and religion, and the fashion in which he was able to apply to socialist themes experience derived from the history of Christianity.[6]

Thus for Sorel Marxism, like religion, eventually became a body of imprecise meanings couched in symbolic form. To the scandal of revisionists and orthodox revolutionaries alike, he found it "necessary to abandon every thought of transforming socialism into science" and to redefine it as "social poetry." Marx, he declared, had dealt in symbols without realizing it: he had uttered his thought in "summary and symbolic formulas" that almost always hit home.[7] It was idle to complain, as most Marxists did, that when it came to specific individual challenges these formulas proved lamentably vague. That was not the real question: the real question was to understand what actually moved men to become actors in the great events of history. In redefining Marxism in symbolic terms, Sorel had completed his own intellectual preparation for a wider restatement of social action as the visible expression of the psychological reality of myth.

Postscript: Gramsci and Marxist Humanism

Stated in the broadest possible terms, what the critics of the 1890's had done was to displace in radical fashion the central emphasis in the Marxian tradition. They had shifted it from economics to the moral and cultural aspects of life in society. In so doing, they had focused attention on what in Marx's teaching could be presumed to have some general validity beyond the tactical requirements of the political movement that

[6] "*Le Caractère religieux du socialisme*" (1906), *Máteriaux*, pp. 309–63; *Décomposition*, pp. 67–8.
[7] "*Introduzione*," *Saggi*, p. 13; *Décomposition*, pp. 50, 59n.

honored his name. And thus they had accomplished the essential task of separating out the general social theory from the mass of revolutionary precepts in the Marxian writings. Once "decontaminated" in this fashion, Marxism could be absorbed into the main stream of European social thought. From 1900 on, the Marxian doctrine led a double life: on the one hand it continued to inspire the party activities of Socialists and Communists; on the other hand, as the first comprehensive social theory to lay claim to scientific validity, it provided an initial test of the canons of empirical social science. It was not only that such of its central elements as the theories of class conflict and of the material conditioning of cultural activities won wide acceptance among the more imaginative of European social thinkers. Its combination of dogmatic method with flexibility of interpretation also challenged these thinkers into formulating more convincingly their own concepts of social reality.

Moreover, apart from all considerations of scientific method, the critics of the 1890's had agreed that Marx had exerted his influence primarily as an ethical leader, and hence, presumably, that he could be placed in the lineage of great secular reformers descending from the eighteenth century. But they had done no more than imply this: they had refrained from relating Marx more specifically to the Enlightenment or suggesting where their own writings in turn derived from a similar heritage. Why this manifest reluctance? Why do we find in the critique of the 1890's no more than a grudging recognition of the Enlightenment inheritance? The answer is not hard to find. In the context of the *fin de siècle*, the thought of the eighteenth century seldom figured in its pure or original form: it appeared overlaid with the late nineteenth-century accretions that had deformed it—materialism, positivism, and the more vulgar forms of humanitarianism. Even such acute theorists as Pareto and Croce and Sorel could seldom bring themselves to think of the Enlightenment in the ab-

stract: they customarily considered it only with reference to the doctrines they most disliked. Their verdict,
then, was almost necessarily negative. Durkheim alone
—the most "eighteenth century" of the four—failed to
make any specific condemnation of the Enlightenment
tradition.

Consequently, they left their critique of Marxism incomplete. They recognized only in part how much of
the Marxian theory they had left standing—more particularly the class interpretation of history that would
stimulate the renewal of sociological analysis a decade
later. Similarly they neglected to make explicit the common eighteenth-century presuppositions that lay behind their own work and the writings of Marx alike.
This recognition Sorel was never to effect: to the end
he remained unregenerate in his opposition to the Enlightenment. But in the case of Pareto and Croce—as
we shall subsequently observe—their later writings quite
clearly suggested a more positive evaluation of the doctrines they had originally assailed with scorn.[8]

To remind the critics of the 1890's of their debt to
Marxism and at the same time to restate that tradition
itself in a more self-consciously "enlightened" form are
tasks that recur constantly in the Marxist theoretical
writings of the second and third decades of the new
century. For it would be incorrect to leave the impression that Durkheim and Pareto, Croce and Sorel, by
absorbing what they required of the Marxian inheritance into their own thought, had thereby finished it
off as a living doctrine. In the years just preceding the
First World War, and in the decade that followed it,
the ideological body of Marxism remained paradoxically
alive and growing.

On the Social Democratic wing of the movement,
parliamentary leaders such as Léon Blum developed
the permissive and humanist features that had already
been implicit in the work of Bernstein. To the "left"

[8] See Chapters 6 and 7.

of them, precariously balanced between revolutionary theory and reformist actuality, the supreme pontiff of orthodox Marxism, Karl Kautsky, and the more supple Viennese theorists Bauer and Adler strove to keep organized Socialism on a course that would combine proletarian vitality with democratic procedure. On the Communist wing, Georg Lukács gave the traditional doctrine a firmer grounding in sociological and philosophical theory. And in imaginative literature also, novelists like Romain Rolland and Henri Barbusse found in Marxism the intellectual rationale for a humanitarian revulsion from the horrors of the First World War.

Of all these twentieth-century theorists and practitioners, the one who gave to Marxist thought its most subtle and original turn—the one who attempted the most difficult synthesis of its contradictory impulses toward freedom and toward compulsion—was the patron saint of the Italian Communist party Antonio Gramsci. A generation younger than his countryman Croce, Gramsci was born in 1891 of petty bourgeois parents on the island of Sardinia, the most remote and impoverished region of Italy. Throughout his life the Sardinian influence remained—in his intimate feeling for those who labor close to nature and his combination of revolutionary intransigence with the emphasis on humanist culture characteristic of a highly endowed young man growing up in an atmosphere alien to thought.[9] Gramsci's childhood had been inordinately hard: he had gone to work at the age of eleven, and many a night he had "wept in secret because his whole body hurt him." In long retrospect he was to reflect that he had "known almost always only the most brutal aspect of life." [1]

Yet through diligence and self-sacrifice he had man-

---

[9] Aldo Garosci: "*Totalitarismo e storicismo nel pensiero di Gramsci*," *Pensiero politico e storiografia moderna: saggi di storia contemporanea,* I (Pisa, 1954), p. 194.

[1] Antonio Gramsci: *Lettere dal carcere* (*Opere*, vol. 1) (Turin, 1947), p. 207.

aged to educate himself and to reach the University of Turin. A more dramatic contrast to Sardinia could scarcely be imagined: in the early twentieth century, as today, the Piedmontese capital took pride in its twin position of leadership in culture and in advanced industrial technique. Both of these aspects of life in Turin contributed decisively to the formation of Gramsci's thought: at the university he found an intellectual atmosphere of markedly positivist tone in which a reaction toward Marxism came naturally; in the factories he made the acquaintance of intelligent, highly trained, and class-conscious workers with whom an intellectual like himself—acquainted with poor people from childhood—could maintain a creative exchange of ideas. Out of this exchange there emerged just after the war the periodical *Ordine nuovo* with its imaginative concept of spontaneously organized factory councils as the peculiarly Italian form of the coming revolution.

Hence it was natural that when the Italian Communist party split off from the Socialists in 1921, Gramsci's circle of Torinese intellectuals and skilled workers should have been among the original organizers. And it was doubtless a wise choice on the part of the leaders of the Third International when, on a visit to Moscow the following year, Gramsci was chosen to head the Italian party. Yet this position of party leadership at Russian direction suggests the crucial difficulty in an assessment of Gramsci's career. On the one hand, he was an orthodox Communist who invariably referred to Lenin with admiration. On the other hand, even before Stalin had come into full control, Gramsci expressed his misgivings about the course of the intraparty struggle within the Soviet Union; it is significant that his works in that country have never been absorbed into the official Marxist canon.[2]

Gramsci's period of leadership was too short, moreover, to have given an unequivocal direction to the Ital-

[2] Garosci: *"Totalitarismo e storicismo,"* pp. 195–8, 200–2, 207–8.

ian Communist party. Arrested by Mussolini in 1926, he remained in prison until 1937, when he emerged shattered in health, just three days before his own death. It is one of the major ironies of interwar history that the one man capable of swinging at least part of international Communism in the direction of humane and tolerant values should have languished a prisoner during the decisive years of Stalinist orthodoxy and the Popular Front.

Thus it is only on the fragmentary writings dating from his years of imprisonment—more particularly the period 1929 to 1935—that we can judge him. These reveal Gramsci as a Marxist thinker of unparalleled range and depth of culture: alongside them, Lenin's theoretical works look crude indeed. And their qualities appear still more remarkable when we reflect on the desperately difficult circumstances of their composition: restricted in the use of books, subject to all sorts of petty inconveniences, plagued with multiple maladies, Gramsci was obliged to cast his writings in the form of letters and brief notes in which the key terms of Marxist theory were reduced to mere euphemisms or filtered through a transparent code.

In these writings the paradoxes within Gramsci's thought stand out in startling fashion. In their insistence on a necessary "hegemony" of the workers and ideologically advanced strata of society, they followed Lenin to the letter. This notion of "hegemony" was only verbally distinct from Leninist practice: it was not much more than another euphemism. As happened so often in Gramsci's writings, a totalitarian thought was clothed in liberal guise. By hegemony, Gramsci meant a situation in which the philosophy and practice of society would fuse—in which intellectual direction would be accepted as arising naturally out of a situation that had been freely recognized as one of revolutionary change. Hence there was something innocent about the totalitarian aspects of Gramsci's thought. Like Marx himself, he failed to draw the final implications of his

own thinking, and quite sincerely believed he was aiming at human liberation. Spiritually he dwelt in the
pre-1914 world: he never understood totalitarianism in
its twentieth-century incarnation.[3]

In tone and content, then, Gramsci's understanding
of proletarian dictatorship was quite different from Lenin's. He had almost nothing to say about the practical
problems of political leadership and revolution that had
riveted his Russian master's attention. What interested
him was the character of the new culture that would
develop *after* the proletarian assumption of power—
and more particularly the function of intellectuals like
himself in the socialist society.

Hence, almost alone among major Communist leaders, Gramsci took seriously the Marxian notion of a
"leap into freedom" as the decisive change from the old
society to the new. Like Lenin, he criticized the "economist," mechanistic, and determinist interpretations
that had deformed the original teachings of Marx and
Engels. He agreed with Lenin in returning to an emphasis on human will and the crucial importance of individual initiative. But he was not content to leave the
problem there: he searched for a definition of the cultural values that must inspire the leaders of the proletariat, and the relation of these values to the traditional
assumptions of the so-called cultivated classes. This was
the grand theme of his prison writings.

The new-type intellectual, Gramsci suggested, would
no longer be the bearer of a merely literary culture that
had little regard for popular needs and aspirations: he
would combine this traditional education with a specific technical competence. In thus insisting on the
necessity of cultural values growing naturally out of the
requirements of an industrial society, Gramsci resembled Sorel—an author to whom he returned again
and again. One was orthodox and one was heretical,
but they lay close to the same ideological dividing-line.
Like Sorel, Gramsci was primarily a moralist: he was

[3] Ibid., pp. 233, 239, 253–4.

3. *The Critique of Marxism* 103

searching for that ethical impetus—giving a new *quality* to life under socialism—that the former had "glimpsed . . . in a dispersed fashion." [4] And, like Sorel, he was fascinated by the phenomenon of popular Catholicism—by the cleavage that ever since the Renaissance had separated the ideal world of the common people from the intellectualist and liberal culture of the educated strata.

In his ethical search, Gramsci was inevitably led to assess the work of his most influential fellow countryman, Benedetto Croce. Even more than Sorel's, Croce's name recurs constantly in Gramsci's writings. And the relationship is a curious one of mixed respect and blame. Gramsci was fond of comparing Marxism to the Protestant Reformation or the Enlightenment of the eighteenth century. Like them, he argued, it had the function of creating a "new integrated culture" of a "mass character." Hence it "did not matter" that it was originally based on "mediocre philosophical works." The Marxist writings that would have the "classical characteristics of Greek and Renaissance culture" would come later. Meantime, Gramsci argued, in his role as a highly educated leader of European thought, Croce was wrong to turn his back on Marxism. He was behaving like Erasmus and the other Renaissance humanists who were repelled by Luther's crudities. Impatient for an immediate refinement of thought, Croce refused to recognize a new culture in embryo: he forgot that it had taken German Protestantism three centuries to produce a Hegel. [5]

Hence, Gramsci contended, by viewing Marxist philosophy as a mere "parenthesis" in his intellectual life, Croce had blinded himself to the potential importance of his own thought in the culture of the future. He had not only refused to recognize how much Marxism had left with him after his adventures of the 1890's—he

[4] Antonio Gramsci: *Il materialismo storico e la filosofia di Benedetto Croce* (*Opere*, vol. 2) (Turin, 1952), pp. 84–6, 243.

[5] Ibid., pp. 105, 199–200, 224–5.

had also denied himself a truly popular influence. For the wider strata of the population, Gramsci reasoned, the Crocean philosophy held the promise of raising the intellectual level of twentieth-century Marxism in the same fashion in which Hegelianism had given to the doctrine its original philosophical categories.

The argument was ingenious but totally ineffective. Enunciated in the isolation of a prison sentence, it could obviously have no direct influence in its own time. But now, a generation later, it may serve as a reminder—to use Gramsci's own words—of the " 'implicit,' unrecognized absorptions" of Marxism that have come about through its being a "diffused atmosphere which has modified the old ways of thinking through actions and reactions that are not immediately apparent." [6] And it may further suggest the paradoxical fashion in which Marxist thought eventually came full circle. In Gramsci's hands the doctrine returned to its idealist beginnings. It was in the consciousness of intellectuals alone, he recognized, that the great social ideas had their origin. They did not spring spontaneously from material conditions and economic relationships. They had an irreducible autonomy of their own. And their relationship to popular consciousness was neither necessary nor automatic: indeed, it offered the central problem in the interpretation of contemporary society. The final pathos of Gramsci's work lies in its combination of ideological certainty—a nineteenth-century inheritance—with a recognition of the problematical character of all intellectual endeavor that is entirely of our own time.

---

[6] Ibid., p. 83.

The Recovery of the Unconscious

1. The Philosophical and Scientific Setting

For the social thinkers whose central concern was the problem of unconscious motivation—for Bergson and Freud and Jung—the example of Nietzsche would logically seem to be paramount. Certainly, as I have already suggested, their words echo in quasi-scientific and explicit form what Nietzsche had discovered through poetic insight: the more systematic of his writings dating from the late 1880's—*Beyond Good and Evil* and *The Genealogy of Morals*—contain a theory of natural "drives," of rationalizations, of sexual masochism and sublimation, of guilt as a product of cultural thwarting, which readily translates itself into Freudian terms; and the Nietzschean notion of a "will to power" seems to be quite close to what Freud later called the "libido" and Bergson termed the "*élan vital.*" Yet the paradoxical fact is that the *direct* influence of Nietzsche on these great successors was almost nil. There is no evidence that Bergson ever profited by his example.[1] And Freud, although he admired Nietzsche, occasionally quoted him, and declared that "he had a more penetrating knowledge of himself than any other man who ever lived or was ever likely to live," firmly maintained that Nietzsche had not influenced his own ideas. Abstract philosophy was not to his taste: "he had tried to read" Nietzsche, "but found his thought so rich that he renounced the attempt."[2] It is only when we come to Jung that we find a specific Nietzschean inheritance.

The same is true for Schopenhauer. Indeed, what strikes one about both Bergson and Freud is the extent to which they worked without reference to the more obvious influences of their predecessors and contemporaries. Like so many original thinkers, they were not interested in finding the sort of respectable philosophical pedigree that has proved reassuring to lesser men: after a certain point in their work, they grew impatient of systematic research. Hence we find that their ideas parallel rather than directly reflect a philosophical and scientific current with which they had much in common—the thinking in terms of hypothesis and convenient fiction associated with such men as Ernst Mach, Henri Poincaré, and Hans Vaihinger. Of such methodological influence Bergson and Freud show almost no trace: it is with Pareto and Sorel, rather, that it first becomes manifest.

More particularly, the theories of Mach and Vaihinger offered a possible way out of the positivist and anti-positivist antithesis. Yet neither Bergson nor Freud —for quite different reasons—was especially interested in this sort of help. Both of them skirted rather than directly faced the central philosophical issue posed by "fictional" thinking. Bergson had early taken his stand

[1] Geneviève Bianquis: *Nietzsche en France* (Paris, 1929), p. 100.
[2] Ernest Jones: *The Life and Work of Sigmund Freud*, II: *Years of Maturity 1901–1919* (New York, 1955), p. 344.

against positivism and "scienticism": this radical opposition became his main intellectual stock-in-trade, and there would have been no point in his allowing it to be whittled away by a more conciliatory attitude. Moreover, the basis of Mach's and Vaihinger's doctrines was Kantian, and Bergson had declared in his first book that Kant's epistemology was fundamentally mistaken.[3] In Freud's case, as we shall shortly observe, the ultimate metaphysical and epistemological problems were never really confronted: Freud did not believe that his own theory of the mind required explicit philosophical buttressing.

Yet eventually these ultimate questions would press to the fore. The problems that Bergson and Freud merely side-stepped worried Sorel deeply, and forced even the anti-metaphysical Pareto into some careful programmatic pronouncements. Neither, however, succeeded in applying the "fictional" approach to the study of society in a fashion that would prove satisfactory to subsequent investigators. Too much of a traditional respect for scientific categories remained. Only with Max Weber do we reach a theory of fictions that has had enough internal consistency to maintain itself as a permanent contribution to social thought.

In this metaphysical and epistemological context, Kantianism offered the bridge across which the most diverse contradictions could be reconciled. Both the positivists and their opponents respected the same master. Throughout the nineteenth century virtually every educated German had cut his philosophical teeth on Kant. The same was true in France after the war of 1870, when German influence triumphed in the philosophy curriculum of the *lycées*. Mach himself has recalled how at the age of fifteen his first acquaintance

[3] *Essai sur les données immédiates de la conscience* (Paris, 1889), authorized translation by F. L. Pogson as *Time and Free Will: An Essay on the Immediate Data of Consciousness* (London and New York, 1910), Conclusion.

with Kant "made . . . a powerful and ineffaceable impression upon me, the like of which I never afterwards
experienced in any of my philosophical reading." [4]

From Kant, Mach went on to Schopenhauer and
Berkeley, from whom he learned that it was possible to
philosophize without postulating an essence or "thing
in itself." On this "sensationalist" basis, he proceeded
to formulate his own theory of knowledge. In his long
career as a professor of physics and the philosophy of
science, first in Prague (1867–95) and then in Vienna
(1895–1902), Mach refined the original naïve positivist
viewpoint almost beyond recognition. While adhering
to a "rigorously positive" attitude toward scientific theory, he discarded the mechanistic and quasi-material-
istic explanations that were so popular in his own day.
The whole concept of substance, he suggested, was unnecessary: human experience could be explained more
simply and efficiently in terms of sensations. And toward the end of his career he evolved more and more
toward a philosophical subjectivism. Mach was not always totally clear in what he meant by scientific laws.
At one moment they seemed to consist of "comprehensive descriptions" of "facts": at another time they were
simply "guides for our mental activity." It is in this latter guise, however, that Mach has chiefly impressed
subsequent scientific investigators.

> Before James, Mach proclaimed that the truth
> of our knowledge, even scientific knowledge, con-
> sists in its efficacy in giving a practical account of
> facts . . . , and ultimately in its utility for life.
> Before Poincaré, he showed that the principles
> on which our mathematical and natural sciences
> rest are only conventional hypotheses, which rec-
> ommend themselves by their convenience.

[4] *Die Analyse der Empfindungen und das Verhältnis des
Physischen zum Psychischen,* fifth edition (Jena, 1906), translated by C. M. Williams and Sydney Waterlow as *The Analysis
of Sensations and the Relation of the Physical to the Psychical*
(Chicago and London, 1914), p. 30n.

Before . . . Bergson, he pointed out that if reality is a constantly moving process of "becoming," the function of our intelligence is to immobilize it through words and concepts that seize only what is permanent and identical in the flow of phenomena.[5]

It seems almost incredible that Freud should have drawn so little on the work of Mach. The latter's *Analysis of Sensations* had first appeared in 1886, at the period when Freud, under Breuer's influence, was turning from neurology to clinical psychology. From the mid-nineties to the older man's death in 1916, the two were fellow townsmen in Vienna and, eventually, university colleagues. But by the time Mach reached Vienna, Freud's course was already set: he was no longer questioning his scientific postulates or reaching out for suggestions from philosophy.

It was not so much through Mach as through Poincaré that the notion of science as conventional hypothesis began to reach the attention of the more speculative social thinkers. Born just after the middle of the century—two years earlier than Freud, and five years before Bergson—Henri Poincaré before the age of thirty was already established in a chair at the University of Paris. During the three decades from the early 1880's to his death in 1912, he ranked as France's most influential natural scientist. Mathematician, astronomer, and physicist all in one, Poincaré possessed in addition a graceful literary style. He was admirably equipped to pass on to the wider reading public the results of the enormous work of self-criticism in physics and astronomy that had substituted for the earlier certainties of the Newtonian universe the notion of alternative and even contradictory explanations.

But this wider public pounced all too eagerly on what

[5] Robert Bouvier: *La Pensée d'Ernst Mach: Essai de biographie intellectuelle et de critique* (Paris, 1923), pp. ix, 111, 132, 306, 321, 325–6.

he had offered. The logicians and literary men pushed Poincaré's theories to the extreme of paradox.[6] It was perhaps for this reason that Bergson referred only rarely to his great contemporary, and Sorel rebuked him for having "expressed doubts on the reality of science." Pareto alone of the major social thinkers of the early twentieth century drew explicit profit from Poincaré's scientific precepts.[7]

Similarly, Pareto and Freud were the only ones to reflect, even by implication, Hans Vaihinger's celebrated definition of knowledge in terms of "as if." [8] Of all the philosophical formulas that we have been reviewing, Vaihinger's came the closest to providing social thought with the highly flexible criterion of investigation it required: his notion of a fiction in science was approximately the same as what Weber was to call an "ideal type." But Vaihinger's work remained almost unknown for the greater part of his academic life. This neglect was owing to the fact that his major work, *The Philosophy of 'As If'*, although its first version had been completed as early as 1877, was not published until 1911, when its author was nearly sixty years old.

Like Mach, Vaihinger had come to philosophy by way of Kant, Schopenhauer, and the English empiricists. Actually his views closely paralleled those of Mach, particularly in the latter's final and most subjective stage, but he persisted in referring to Mach as a positivist. His own position, on the other hand, he variously defined as "positivist idealism," "idealistic positivism," "critical positivism," or even "logical positivism"—the last of which anticipated a philosophical school that was to rise to major importance after the

     [6] Léon Husson, *L'Intellectualisme de Bergson: Genèse et développement de la notion bergsonienne d'intuition* (Paris, 1947), p. 89.

     [7] See Chapters 5 and 7.

     [8] G. H. Bousquet, *Vilfredo Pareto: sa vie et son œuvre* (Paris, 1928), pp. 32, 163; Sigmund Freud: *Die Zukunft einer Illusion* (Vienna, 1927), translated by W. D. Robson-Scott as *The Future of an Illusion*, Anchor edition (New York, 1957), p. 49.

First World War. Most of Vaihinger's book did no more than to spin out in longer and more explicit form a view of the fictional character of intellectual generalizations that had come to be common property in the first decade of the twentieth century. But Vaihinger went one step beyond this. He drew a sharp distinction between "fiction" and "hypothesis"—concepts that tended to blur in the work of Mach and Poincaré. "The real difference between the two," Vaihinger argued, "is that the fiction is a mere auxiliary construct, a circuitous approach, a scaffolding afterwards to be demolished, while the hypothesis looks forward to being definitely established. The former is artificial, the latter natural. What is untenable as an hypothesis can often render excellent service as a fiction." [9]

By this means Vaihinger accomplished the trick of keeping a foot in both camps. His insistence on the "natural" character of scientific hypotheses aligned him with the positivists. His emphasis on the artificiality of fictions opened the way to the bold imaginative constructions of their enemies. But for the most part Vaihinger's notion of an irremediable distinction between hypothesis and fiction failed to hold up: subsequent social thinkers were content to treat the two as roughly equivalent—just as they simplified the issue by classifying Mach as *the* positivist and Vaihinger as *the* pragmatist among their forebears. In so doing, they displayed a greater receptivity to William James's pragmatism than to what Vaihinger had called "fictionalism."

Here again Vaihinger had been careful to draw a distinction. He was willing to grant that pragmatism had "done something to prepare the ground" for the reception of his own views. "In practice," he recognized, "they may find much in common." But "in principle" they were "diametrically opposed": pragmatism equated usefulness with truth; "fictionalism," on the other hand,

[9] *Die Philosophie des Als ob* (Berlin, 1911), translated by C. K. Ogden as *The Philosophy of 'As If'* (London, 1924), pp. xxvii–xxx, xxxiv, xli, 64, 88, 163.

maintained that the two questions were separate—that an idea might be palpably false but nonetheless have "great practical importance." [1]

Once again Vaihinger was arguing in vain. After the turn of the century the influence of William James began its triumphant progress. I doubt whether ever before or since an American thinker has enjoyed such prestige on the European Continent. For with the advent of James—with the publication of his *Varieties of Religious Experience* in 1902, and more particularly with the *Pragmatism* of 1907—the intellectual horizon suddenly seemed to clear: everything became simple, direct, unequivocal. No longer was it necessary to break one's head over Kantian metaphysics and Teutonic hair-splitting. The sage from the New World had once for all displayed how the most vexing problems of traditional philosophy were simply not worth the trouble of worrying over them.

In the course of the present study we shall find the name of William James bobbing up again and again. We shall find Weber referring to him in connection with his own religious studies, Pareto objecting to his casual attitude toward science, Sorel hailing him as a philosophical savior. With Bergson, James shared a cult of mutual admiration. When the American philosopher greeted the appearance of Bergson's *Creative Evolution* as "divine" and a "marvel," the latter returned the compliment by describing *Pragmatism* as an "arresting and charming" work. For James, Bergson was the "Copernicus" who had effected a revolution in philosophy: for Bergson, James was a man whom it was a "joy" to know, who ardently loved truth and sought it with a "passion." [2] In the annals of philosophy it is difficult to find

---

[1] "Preface to the English Edition," ibid., p viii.

[2] Jacques Chevalier: *Bergson*, revised edition (Paris, 1948), p. 58; Henri Bergson: "Sur le Pragmatisme de William James. Vérité et réalité" (1911), *La Pensée et le mouvant: Essais et conférences* (Paris, 1934), pp. 239, 251. For the correspondence between Bergson and James, see Ralph Barton Perry: *The*

two men so different in intellectual origin and temperament who were bound together by such profound esteem.

Between James and Freud, the respect was more onesided. We have no evidence that the latter ever profited from reading James's psychological works: he was not given to the study of academic psychology. But on James's side the token of regard was unqualified and deeply touching. When in 1909 Freud gave the lectures at Clark University that for the first time were to spread his fame beyond the circle of the convinced adherents of psychoanalysis, James, although fatally ill himself, came to hear him. At the close of the lecture series, he told the visitor from Vienna: "The future of psychology belongs to your work." [3] There is no more dramatic moment in the intellectual history of our time.

II. *Bergson and the Uses of Intuition*

Does Bergson really belong in a study of social thought? Freud's place is obvious, but in Bergson's case it may be argued that he was, after all, primarily a metaphysician, and that his present-day influence is almost nil. All this is true—but at the same time the conscientious historian of ideas is obliged to give some account of Bergson's forays into moral speculation, and to try to explain why it was that he was so highly regarded in his own time. In the intellectual critique of the 1890's Bergson figured on the extreme "intuitionist" wing. And it was in this guise that those social thinkers who took him seriously—men like Sorel and Péguy—believed that his teachings could be applied to the discussion of human affairs. A consideration of Bergson, then, may be the best way to assess the potentialities of the

Thought and Character of William James (Boston, 1935), II, 605–34.
[3] Jones: *Freud*, II, 57. Contrast the account in Perry: *William James*, II, 122–3.

intuitive approach to the study of society in the quarter-century preceding the First World War.

Up until the severe illness that crippled his intellectual activity in the last twenty years of his life, Bergson's career had been a succession of triumphs. We have seen already how he had received the best secondary education that Paris provided and made a brilliant record at the Ecole Normale Supérieure. There followed the usual teaching assignments at a number of provincial *lycées*, a transfer to Paris, and three years as *maître de conférences* at Normale itself—the three critical years of the Dreyfus case, during which Péguy was his student. In 1900 Bergson was appointed to the chair of philosophy at the Collège de France—a position of even greater eminence than a professorship at the Sorbonne. He was subsequently elected to the French Academy and received the Nobel Prize for literature. There were apparently no further honors left to attain. The friend of Bergson's youth who gave the address of welcome to the Academy in 1918 recalled of him: "You were already famous. You have always been famous. You know how—with what intense curiosity—one looks, the first time one sees a famous man or even a famous child; the picture is forever engraved in the memory." [4]

And that was how the general public felt, particularly after the publication of *Creative Evolution* in 1907. Bergson's lectures became major events. Tourists and society ladies flocked to them, as to one of the sights of the capital. And Bergson did not disappoint his auditors: he lectured

> without a note, . . . his forehead enormous, his bright eyes . . . like two lights under his thick eyebrows, and his features of a delicacy that emphasizes the power of his forehead and the immaterial radiance of his thought. He speaks as slowly, nobly, and regularly as he writes, with an

[4] Quoted in Chevalier: *Bergson*, p. 37.

extraordinary sureness and a surprising precision, with caressing, musical intonations. . . . The form is . . . so perfect . . . that one scarcely detects its artfulness . . . : it is [the perfection] of a philosopher who thinks that "even in its most profound analyses and highest syntheses, philosophy should speak the language of every day." [5]

People left the auditorium with a sense of "liberation." They felt uplifted in the spirit as in the mind. Of all the intellectual innovators of the 1890's, Bergson was the one with the greatest *charisma*, the one whose direct personal influence was most compelling.

As an apologist for the values of sentiment and of the spirit, Bergson was in lineal descent from a tradition in French thought that since the seventeenth century had kept up a tranquil, insistent, sometimes almost stifled opposition to the dominant current of Cartesian rationalism. Through his own philosophical master Boutroux, through the latter's master Lachelier, through the early nineteenth-century metaphysician Maine de Biran, Bergson's antecedents traced back ultimately to Pascal. Like Pascal he was to oppose the *"esprit de finesse"* to the ruling *"esprit de géométrie,"* and to give to religion a frankly non-intellectual justification that might be on the edge of heresy, but that proved supremely attractive to the youth of the early 1900's.

Bergson's aggressive anti-positivism—like so many polemical positions—arose from a repudiation of an earlier allegiance. At the *lycée* his love had been mathematics, and at Normale, as we have seen, he was suspected of being a mechanist in his thinking, even, perhaps, a materialist. And it was true that he had fallen under the spell (if it is possible to speak of the spell of so pedestrian a thinker) of the ubiquitous Herbert Spencer.[6] But one day in his late twenties—he was then teaching

[5] Ibid., p. 55.
[6] *"Introduction," Pensée et mouvant*, p. 2.

at Clermont-Ferrand, the native city of Pascal—Bergson was taking his customary afternoon walk, having just explained to his pupils the teachings of Zeno and the Eleatic school, when the central intuition out of which his whole subsequent philosophy was to grow, quite suddenly came to him. For the following half-century Bergson was to follow through the infinitely ramifying implications of one simple flash of understanding.

The starting-point of his line of argument was Zeno's famous paradox of Achilles' race with the tortoise: by dividing into constantly smaller segments the course of both man and beast, the worthy pre-Socratic had proved the impossibility of Achilles' ever catching up. The obvious absurdity of all this from the standpoint of common sense suggested to Bergson that the reason why the paradox had never been satisfactorily refuted might be that it had always been approached in the wrong terms. And from here it was only a short step to questioning the whole basis of mechanistic and intellectualist thinking. What was wrong with this approach, Bergson reasoned, was that it confused motion with distance traversed, and time with space. Hence it could express the former only in terms of the latter. Time and space, Bergson argued, were radically incommensurable concepts. And, as usually practiced, natural science and logic succeeded in talking only of space—or of matter, its metaphysical double—never of time in the sense of experienced continuity.

This time-as-experience Bergson termed *duration*. In his first two books, the *Essay on the Immediate Data of Consciousness*, published in 1889, and *Matter and Memory*, of 1897, he analyzed the meaning of the term and its implications for the human consciousness. Duration, Bergson contended, could be sensed and understood only through introspection: only through a concentration on one's own consciousness could one arrive at a realization of human experience in its fullness and actuality—not as it was customarily chopped up into discrete portions. And this process of sympathetic comprehension was what was commonly called *intuition*. As Bergson expressed it in his essay "An Introduction to Metaphysics," published in 1903, which summarized in compact form his intellectual progress up to that date:

> There is one reality, at least, which we all seize from within, by intuition and not by simple analysis. It is our own personality in its flowing through time—our self which endures. We may sympathize intellectually with nothing else, but we certainly sympathize with our own selves. . . .
>
> Our intelligence . . . can place itself within . . . mobile reality, and adopt its ceaselessly changing direction; in short, can grasp it by means of that *intellectual sympathy* which we call intuition. This is extremely difficult. The mind has to do violence to itself, has to reverse the direction of the operation by which it habitually thinks. . . . But in this way it will attain to fluid concepts, capable of following reality in all its sinuosities and of adopting the very movement of the inward life of things.

Thus would it be possible to catch the flux of reality, as it were, on the wing—instead of freezing it, as was customarily done, into stable, ready-made categories. And, further, the philosopher would be able to accomplish what Kant and the others had ruled out as unattainable: to transcend the symbolical world of natural science—the mere understanding of a phenomenon in terms of something else—and to arrive at *absolute knowledge.*[7]

In Bergson's hands time became a positive concept. It ceased to be the mere source of "change and decay"

[7] *"Introduction à la métaphysique"* (*Pensée et mouvant,* pp. 177–227), authorized translation by T. E. Hulme as *An Introduction to Metaphysics,* new edition (New York, 1949), pp. 24, 50, 53.

that poets and thinkers had tried to hold back through the quest for immortality, and was established as the vehicle of spontaneous creation. To apply this new time-sense to the realm of values in life and society was the task that Bergson set himself in his last two major works, *Creative Evolution* and *Two Sources of Morality and Religion*.

The first of these, although it was the book that made its author famous, from the intellectual standpoint was less impressive than its predecessors. To put it uncharitably, it was a kind of majestic biological fantasy. Building out from the metaphysical positions established in Bergson's earlier work, it equated intuition with the instinct of the animal world and postulated an all-pervading vital impulse, an *élan vital* that came "gushing out unceasingly . . . from an immense reservoir of life." It further expressed the resolve that the "philosophy of intuition" would set "the life of the body . . . where it really is, on the road that leads to the life of the spirit." "All the living," Bergson proclaimed, "hold together, and all yield to the same tremendous push. . . . And the whole of humanity . . . is one immense army galloping beside and before and behind each of us in an overwhelming charge able to beat down every resistance and clear the most formidable obstacles, perhaps even death." [8]

Creative Evolution was a repetitious and elusive work. Its argument rested on a series of exceedingly shaky biological analogies, and Bergson's word magic only just succeeded in concealing its logical insufficiencies. Its underlying drift, however, was quite clear. Bergson had already set his course toward that suave advocacy of "higher" spiritual and moral values, that coquetting with the idea of personal immortality, which at the end of his life was to bring him into whole-

[8] *L'Evolution créatrice* (Paris, 1907), authorized translation by Arthur Mitchell as *Creative Evolution*, Modern Library edition (New York, 1944), pp. 270, 293, 295.

hearted sympathy if not actual communion with the Roman Catholic Church.

How far this evolution had gone was not made explicit until a quarter-century later with the publication of *Two Sources of Morality and Religion.*[9] But in the meantime the younger generation had taken the hint. The long-deferred appearance of Bergson's last major work proved that his more enthusiastic auditors had been quite correct in treating his message as a religious one and in rushing headlong from his lecture hall to throw themselves at the feet of a priest.[1] And it also showed that Péguy had been right in defending Bergson against his Catholic critics. It was futile, Péguy had argued, to try to prevent the students in the seminaries from reading him: indeed, the result would be self-defeating; were Bergson to be put on the Index, it would be Spencer rather than Saint Thomas who would be the gainer. As a convert to Catholicism, Péguy correctly saw that Bergson's line of reasoning, which professed to meet modern science on its own ground, offered the best possible avenue for winning back to religious belief a generation that had been suckled on positivism—that beneath all the surface divergences there was a profound "parallel between . . . the teaching of the Church . . . and the theories . . . of memory and habit that are one of the irreversible conquests of Bergsonian thought." [2]

On his death in 1941 Bergson gave the final confirmation. His last will revealed that it was only a sense of solidarity with the sufferings of his Jewish co-religionists under Nazi rule that held him back from formally ad-

[9] See Chapter 10.
[1] See Chapter 9.
[2] *Note conjointe* (Péguy's last work, comprising "Note sur M. Bergson et la philosophie bergsonienne" and "Note conjointe sur M. Descartes et la philosophie cartésienne," the former originally published in the *Cahiers de la Quinzaine*, April 26, 1914, the latter left unfinished at his death) (Paris, 1935), pp. 116, 300–1.

hering to Catholicism, and he asked that a priest read the prayers at his funeral.[3]

To a social scientist or to a student of social thought in a more discursive sense, Bergson presents a considerable puzzle. His work is a curious combination of poetic flights of fancy and a specifically French logic and clarity: it is the artistic fusion of the two that explains its persuasiveness and its almost magical appeal. Basically what Bergson did was to codify in quasi-scientific terminology certain central truths about human experience that the great religious mystics had always known.

Except for William James, the other leading philosophers of the day were almost unanimous in opposing him: both George Santayana and Bertrand Russell have attacked Bergson as a man who simply could not reason straight. For Julien Benda, Bergson was an intellectual trickster, a philosopher of sensualism and action, whose salon popularity betrayed the vice of his whole system. To demolish Bergson's philosophy from the standpoint of logic—Aristotelian or mathematical, as the case might be—was nothing very difficult to accomplish. "To criticize an intuitive philosophy is so easy"—Bergson wrote in his own defense—"that it will always tempt the beginner." [4]

Systematic logic is not the field of the present study. From our standpoint, it is more relevant to ask whether Bergson's intuitive approach can justify itself by its accomplishments *in practice*. Can a "fluid" philosophy, which aims to establish an actual communion between the human mind and the realm of external reality, add something to our knowledge that is lacking in the traditional metaphysics, with its categorical distinction between reality and idea? Here Benda's polemic hit the mark. Intuition, he claimed, could add nothing. If Bergsonism, like any mystical doctrine, were to remain "faithful to its principle," it could "logically do noth-

---

[3] Chevalier: *Bergson*, pp. xv–xvi.
[4] "Introduction," *Pensée et mouvant*, p. 33.

ing more than utter simple negations or mere cries of enthusiasm." [5] It could not *explain* anything: indeed, in trying to explain himself at all, Bergson had become as "intellectualist" as his enemies.

Before granting Benda's point, however, it is only fair to add that Bergson conscientiously believed that he had discovered something new, that he was not merely repeating in a more scientific terminology what the mystics had always said. He has told us that he hesitated a long time before adopting the term "intuition," whose use by the German Romantic philosophers in a sense of radical opposition to rational intelligence was quite different from what he himself intended. Far from being the negation of intelligence, Bergson explained, intuition, in the sense in which he employed the term, was its parallel and complement. Far from having proposed an anti-scientific philosophy in the Romantic tradition, he had raised science to an even loftier height than had positivism itself.[6] Bergson's expositors have echoed this self-defense: in their view, Bergson insisted so strongly on the virtues of intuition only because the preceding age had vested its whole trust in the intellect. Hence there was inevitably "a certain lack of balance . . . in his work." With the balance properly restored, however, Bergson's intuition can appear in its true guise as "not anti-intellectual but supra-intellectual: it does not exempt us from the work of the intellect; it completes this work, and in completing it, it presupposes it." [7]

This is the sense in which Sorel and Péguy understood the term. For Péguy, Bergson's supreme achievement had been to assault at its center the literal-mindedness of the intellectualist philosophies. In a "Napoleonic maneuver," Bergson had aimed "to wedge

[5] Robert J. Niess: *Julien Benda* (Ann Arbor, Mich., 1956), p. 117.

[6] "*Introduction*," *Pensée et mouvant*, pp. 25, 71.

[7] Chevalier: *Bergson*, pp. 303, 305; see also Husson: *L'Intellectualisme de Bergson*, pp. 12, 214, 224–5.

himself into the enemy's very heart, and then to defeat him in detail wherever he might appear." [8] Thus from the central Bergsonian intuition all sorts of applications would open up. Sorel was more explicit in his expectations. Taking his cue from a passage in *Creative Evolution* in which Bergson had argued that human logic grew out of the fact that men were "born artisans," Sorel pointed out the "remarkable . . . analogies" between Bergsonism and historical materialism—which were all the more noteworthy since the author of *Creative Evolution* was not yet familiar with the work of Marx. "One cannot be too grateful" to Bergson, Sorel commented, "for having tried to make our contemporaries understand the necessity of adapting their mode of thought to their revolutionary conditions of life." [9]

In short, Sorel found in Bergson support for his own contention that a new society would inevitably arise out of new techniques and new conditions of labor. But in the end—like all his other masters—Bergson disappointed him. [1] Shortly after the publication of *Creative Evolution*, Sorel expressed the hope that its author would stop trying to apply his philosophy to the realm of natural science and would turn instead toward "the great social movements." A few years later, however, he was obliged to admit that Bergson had not followed his advice: the latter had, rather, found his greatest success in the field of religion. [2] In the end, Sorel came to the unexpected conclusion that it was "musical influences, above all" that gave Bergsonism its particular character. "In pointing out the family relationship that exists between music and Bergson's philosophy, one creates grave doubts as to the latter's continuing life.

[8] *Note conjointe*, pp. 20, 93, 270.

[9] *Creative Evolution*, pp. 152–5; Georges Sorel: *"Critique de l' 'Evolution créatrice,'" De l'Utilité du pragmatisme* (Paris, 1921), pp. 393, 416.

[1] See Chapter 5.

[2] Pierre Andreu: *"Bergson et Sorel," Les Etudes bergsoniennes*, III (Paris, 1952), pp. 48, 50.

It is not likely that it will disappear as a mere fad, in the way that its detractors claim. But it might very well have significance only as a transition." [3]

Thus the most eminent of Bergson's disciples was finally driven to admit that his master's work had found no useful application in social theory: for Sorel, Bergsonism was a way-station to Jamesian pragmatism. He had correctly seen that Bergson's importance was little more than "transitional." With the passage of the years after the publication of *Creative Evolution,* the conviction had gradually been borne in upon him that nothing constructive would develop out of the Bergsonian philosophy. In 1914, Péguy died, leaving as his sole tribute to his philosophical master a collection of fragmentary notes and suggestions. Other Bergsonians, younger than Péguy and far younger than Sorel, began to apply the doctrine to the politics of reaction, of which Bergson himself, as a good democrat, thoroughly disapproved.[4] By the end of the First World War the professed Bergsonians had gone in all possible directions besides the one course of spiritual elevation *within* a free society which the author of the doctrine was to advocate in his last book.

Moreover, in taking his final stand with William James rather than with Bergson, Sorel was simply following the logic of the situation. To the extent that it actually could be applied to the study of society, Bergsonism—in its emphasis on the fluid character of reality—could be considered the equivalent of pragmatism. And in this realm James was the clearer thinker. Unlike Bergson, he did not push his case too far by laying a claim to "absolute" knowledge. Indeed, the whole idea would have struck James as very odd indeed. And the absolute was the last thing in which most social scientists were interested.

[3] *"Critique de l' 'Evolution créatrice,' " Pragmatisme,* pp. 449-451.
[4] See Chapter 9.

There were at least two other directions in which
Bergson's philosophy could serve as a transition. The
emphasis on duration—on the radical incompatibility
between the method of natural science and the method
of intuitive sympathy or inner understanding—led directly into the problem of historical knowledge. What
the Germans called *Verstehen*, what Croce called the
"lightning-flash" of historical comprehension—these
things were implicit in the Bergsonian metaphysics.[5]
But few practicing historians or students of society
chose to come to them via the Bergsonian route. An
even closer affiliation might logically be found to the
Freudian theory of psychoanalysis: what Bergson referred to as the deeper layers of consciousness, in which
the logic of space and number did not apply, Freud
more precisely termed the unconscious. And in so doing, Freud opened up a realm of knowledge into which
Bergson had merely peeped. The new understanding of
memory and habit that Péguy had hailed as one of
Bergson's "irreversible conquests" had in reality been
no more than a glimpse from afar: the actual conquest
was Freud's.

Although there are striking parallels between the theories of Bergson and those of Freud, the two bear no
organic relation to each other. If the former's second
book, *Matter and Memory*, said some of the same
things about the imperishability of recollection that
Freud was to develop more systematically two years
later in his *Interpretation of Dreams*, it was little more
than a dramatic coincidence and a sign that a certain
idea was "in the air." Freud owed nothing to Bergson,
and the latter apparently did not learn of Freud's work
until after the First World War. But in the meantime
they had covered much of the same ground. Both had
arrived at their theories of unconscious memory through
the scientific study of aphasia, or speech impairment.
Both had come by way of physiology to an essentially
immaterial concept of the human consciousness. As

5 See Chapters 6 and 8.

Bergson himself wrote toward the end of his life: "Our idea of a total conservation of the past . . . has more and more found its empirical verification in the vast mass of experiments undertaken by the disciples of Freud." [6]

In 1934, when these words were published, Freud's immortality was already established and Bergson was nearly forgotten: in the history of psychoanalytic theory he did not even rank as a great precursor.

III. *Sigmund Freud: Epistemology and Metaphysics*

"Is, then, Freud a metaphysician? Yes, but he does not know it." Thus quipped Egon Friedell, who for once knew what he was talking about.[7]

For Freud did indeed have a metaphysic and a theory of knowledge, as he had a coherent philosophy of society. But they were only implicit: both Freud's formal philosophy and his social theory remained on the level of *obiter dicta* or unstated assumption throughout the main body of his work; he hinted at them rather than fully explaining them—or he simply took them for granted and got on with his empirical labors. To dredge out these philosophical suggestions from the mass of Freud's writing, to establish them in logical sequence and relate them to the work of his contemporaries— this, rather than a discussion of the clinical methods of psychoanalysis, is the task of the present study. Let me insist once again: I am writing intellectual history, not a history of psychology. In what follows I shall reverse Freud's order of procedure: the revolutionary clinical innovations through which he established the primacy of the unconscious will remain in the background; the foreground will be occupied by the assumptions and

[6] *"Introduction," Pensée et mouvant*, p. 81.

[7] *Kulturgeschichte der Neuzeit* (Munich, 1931), translated by Charles Francis Atkinson as *A Cultural History of the Modern Age* (New York, 1932), III, 479.

corollaries that Freud never had time to develop to the full.

As a Jew born of a German-speaking family in the Czech province of Moravia, Sigmund Freud from the start lacked clear identification. When he was four years old his parents moved to Vienna, where he spent virtually his whole adult life in the study and practice of medicine. By nationality he remained an Austrian—but his spiritual home was England. Or, more precisely, "he lived the life of the free-floating intelligence. . . . Above nation, beyond class, outside time, such a man could know all, see all, tell all." [8]

However much Freud's thought strove to be universal in its range, it was obviously bound by its creator's own mental endowment and early experience: Freud himself invented the tools that have enabled his biographers to explain his insights and limitations. His childhood fixation on his mother was inordinately strong. The curious structure of his family, in which generations overlapped and roles were confused, helped open his eyes to the play of sexual attraction and aggression in parent-child relationships. When his self-analysis had taught him to look back to his childhood for an explanation of his adult interests, he came to the realization that it was the infant's thirst for sexual enlightenment which had been at the source of his later quest for scientific knowledge. This insight he later universalized. In the most attractive of his books—the one that Freud himself called "the only pretty thing" he had ever written—the study of Leonardo da Vinci published in 1910, he was bold enough to apply the fruits of his own introspection to a great historical figure: in this first psychoanalytic biography Freud worked from the slimmest sort of evidence toward an interpretation of the career

[8] Richard L. Schoenwald: *Freud: The Man and His Mind 1856–1956* (New York, 1956), p. 80.

of Leonardo in terms of latent homosexual tendencies sublimated into scientific inquiry and artistic creation.[9]

Leonardo is a good book with which to begin an analysis of Freud's only half-recognized assumptions. It clearly showed his self-identification in his middle years with the figure of Leonardo—as in his old age he was to see himself in the image of Moses. In his sympathetic understanding of the Florentine painter's bisexuality he reflected the androgynous tendencies he had discerned in himself—and that through his patients he was to find in mankind in general. Still more, his emphasis on Leonardo's conflicting aspirations mirrored his own dualistic view of the universe. This again was an inheritance from earliest childhood. Ten years before he had written: "My warm friendships as well as my enmities with contemporaries went back to my relations in childhood with a nephew who was a year my senior. . . . My emotional life has always insisted that I should have an intimate friend and a hated enemy. I have always been able to provide myself afresh with both." [1]

In childhood friend and enemy had been one. A duality, a polarization, in Freud's thought had arisen naturally out of early conflicts. To the end of his life he expressed himself in dualistic terms: it was a standing joke among his friends that "he had never learned to count beyond the number two." This polarization is central to an understanding of his creative drive. Like Leonardo, he was "torn by two impulses: the passion for scientific knowledge and the passion for creating works of art." Throughout his life Freud was both sci-

[9] Jones: *Freud,* II, 432–4; *Leonardo,* originally published as Heft 7 of the *Schriften zur angewandten Seelen Kunde,* has been translated by A. A. Brill as *Leonardo da Vinci: A Study in Psychosexuality,* Modern Library edition (New York, 1947).

[1] *Die Traumdeutung* (Leipzig and Vienna, 1899), translated from the eighth edition (1930) by James Strachey as *The Interpretation of Dreams* (*The Standard Edition of the Complete Psychological Works of Sigmund Freud,* IV and V) (London, 1953), V, 483.

entist and artist—but it was the latter tendency that
finally gained the upper hand. In his childhood, the two
had been combined: the thirst for understanding had
been universal in its range. In his early maturity, however, he forced himself to narrow his focus onto the
problems of exact science. "As a young man," Freud
explained, "I felt a strong attraction toward speculation
and ruthlessly checked it." It was only gradually that he
permitted himself to return to his first interest—the
world of cultural history and "the great problem of how
man came to be what he is"—until in his later years he
was able to think of his medical career as simply one
vast detour. "Freud was perhaps one of those whose
bent towards speculative abstractions is so powerful that
he is afraid of being mastered by it and feels it necessary
to counter it by studying concrete scientific data." [2]

From one standpoint Freud was right in believing
that he must at all costs curb his impulse toward flights
of fancy. For there was in him a "deep current of romanticism . . . —a sense of the role of impulse, of the
drama of life, of the power of symbolism, of ways of
knowing that were more poetic than rational in spirit,
of the poet's cultural alienation." His sense for the dramatic attracted him to Shakespeare and to the Greeks:
it was from Sophocles' *Œdipus* that he drew the parable
that became the focal point of his theory. "The sense
of the human tragedy, the inevitable working out of the
human plight—these are the hallmarks of Freud's case
histories." Indeed his psychoanalytic theory was itself
couched in terms of a dramatic conflict:

> The characters are from life: the blind, . . . pleas-
> ure-seeking id; the priggish and punitive super-ego;
> the ego, battling for its being by directing the en-
> ergy of others to its own use. The drama has an
> economy and a terseness. The ego develops canny

[2] Jones: *Freud*, I: *The Formative Years and the Great Discoveries 1856–1900* (New York, 1953), pp. 27–9; II, 320, 422,
432.

mechanisms for dealing with the threat of id impulses: denial, projection, and the rest. Balances are struck between the actors, and the balance is character and neurosis.[3]

Hence the streak of "gullibility" on which even the most sympathetic of Freud's interpreters have commented. "He was willing to believe in the improbable and the unexpected—the only way, as Heraclitus pointed out centuries ago, to discover new truths." It is easy to compile a long list of Freud's successive infatuations. In his early career as a medical researcher, there was his strenuous advocacy of the therapeutic virtues of cocaine—an error that very nearly wrecked his prospects at the start. Then came his friendship with Wilhelm Fliess: today it seems almost incredible that Freud should have given credence to this intellectual crank, whose fantasies ranged from the meaning of numbers to the inflammations of the nose, and should have allowed himself to become so dependent on Fliess's moral support. At the same period we find him taking literally his patients' fantasies of childhood seductions by close relatives. And even when he had corrected himself—even when he realized that these seductions corresponded only to "psychical reality"—his imagination still remained uncurbed.[4] There followed the explicit formulation of the Œdipus complex in his *Interpretation of Dreams.* This was unquestionably one of the most brilliant discoveries in the history of the human mind. But once Freud had found what he was seeking, he was not content to leave it in the form of a suggestion for further research. He had to establish it as the key to virtually all psychological riddles.

Hence the Œdipus complex became the ground on which sociologists, anthropologists, and academic psychologists chose to do battle with Freud's theories.

[3] Jerome S. Bruner: "Freud and the Image of Man," *Partisan Review*, XXIII (Summer 1956), 343, 346.
[4] Jones: *Freud*, I, 265–7, 287; II, 430.

[It] was first framed without any reference to the sociological or cultural setting. This was only natural, for psycho-analysis started as a technique of treatment based on clinical observation. It was subsequently expanded into a general account of neuroses; then into a theory of psychological processes in general; finally it became a system by which most phenomena in body and mind, in society and culture were to be explained.

It was not surprising, then, that even those social scientists who were well impressed with Freud's work should have found his claims "too ambitious" and should have urged that "some of its formulæ" be made "more elastic." [5] But this was just the sort of "watering down" that Freud was not interested in. He was stubborn as well as credulous. So instead of modifying his theory of the Œdipus complex to give it a more acceptable form, he made it "worse" by adding to it a vast anthropological fantasy—the story of the "primal horde" and the banding of the sons together to slay their father and eat of his flesh, first expounded in the *Totem and Taboo* of 1912 and 1913. On this excessively speculative foundation, Freud was to build out the whole ramifying structure of his subsequent social theory.

Were the primal horde and the primal crime mere figures of speech or were they historical actualities? The question brings us to the very center of Freud's implicit philosophy. Today most professed Freudians ascribe to the master's "anthropological speculation only . . . *symbolic* value." [6] But such a tepid allegiance would not have satisfied Freud himself. Down to his very last book he insisted that he had written of a historical event—many times repeated—for which the presumptive evidence was overwhelming. Nor did it worry him

[5] Bronislaw Malinowski: *Sex and Repression in Savage Society*, Meridian edition (New York, 1955), pp. 77, 123.
[6] See, for example, Herbert Marcuse: *Eros and Civilization: A Philosophical Inquiry into Freud* (Boston, 1955), p. 60.

that this claim involved postulating the inheritance of memory traces in a fashion that came dangerously close to Jung's notion of a "collective unconscious." [7] Freud had stated his theory, and he stuck by it. He had fought his way loose from his dependence on clinical and empirical data, and was not prepared to return to his earlier bondage. So much the worse if his wide-ranging speculations had put him in strange company—not only with Jung but with Spengler and the other architects of all-inclusive historical metaphors.[8]

For Freud's ultimate aim was to impose an order on the chaos of reality. Originally his goal had been relatively modest—to understand the human unconscious. In this narrower realm Freud's theories have won general acceptance today. It is at his more inclusive intellectual ambitions, rather, that subsequent investigators have boggled. For these ambitions paradoxically placed him in a line of descent from Plato and Hegel and the great system-builders. Despite his ostensible empiricism—despite his faith in the exact methods of natural science—at a deeper level Freud longed for a metaphysic and a cosmology that would bring into one coherent explanation the last riddles of human existence. As he grew older he insisted more and more strongly on his two vast interlocking metaphors of the Œdipus complex and the primal crime. In his last book he at length revealed the self-image that for three decades had been struggling for expression—the image of Moses the lawgiver.

In turning now from Freud's metaphysic to his theory of knowledge, we are obliged to retrace our steps

[7] *Moses and Monotheism*, first published in full in London in 1939 after the first two parts had appeared in German in *Imago*, XXIII [Heft 1 and 3, 1937], translated by Katherine Jones, Vintage edition (New York, 1955), pp. 71, 127; Ernest Jones: *The Life and Work of Sigmund Freud*, III: *The Last Phase 1919–1939* (New York, 1957), p. 313.

[8] See Chapter 9.

back to his original role as a modest, painstaking man of
science. This picture of himself Freud never entirely
abandoned. In their *explicit* form, his epistemological
assumptions remained those of a nineteenth-century scientific investigator.

Freud's theories arose in a fashion that would have
been highly gratifying to Georges Sorel: they developed
out of the practical demands of applied science. Freud
arrived at his theoretical discoveries as by-products of
his clinical work—the technique of free association that
gradually evolved between 1892 and 1895 and his own
self-analysis beginning in 1897 and culminating in the
publication of *The Interpretation of Dreams* two years
later. This book remained the bedrock of Freud's theoretical structure. Its central assertion—that *"the interpretation of dreams is the royal road to a knowledge
of the unconscious activities of the mind"*—constituted
his basic line of defense from which neither doubts nor
attacks could ever dislodge him. As Freud explained in
introducing the second edition of the book: "During
the long years in which I have been working at the problems of the neuroses I have often been in doubt and
sometimes been shaken in my convictions. At such
times it has always been the *Interpretation of Dreams*
that has given me back my certainty." And two decades
later he added: "Insight such as this falls to one's lot
but once in a lifetime." [9]

Was Freud a positivist? Certainly he never doubted
the reality of the external world, nor was he interested
in speculating on the nature of that reality. He "came
from his early training deeply imbued with . . . belief
in the universality of natural law. . . . He does not appear ever to have expressed any opinion on the general
theory of causality, but he presumably held the simple
nineteenth-century view of invariable antecedents. . . .
In all this Freud was the child of his time and we have
no reason to think that he ever indulged in individual

[9] *Interpretation of Dreams*, pp. xxvi, xxxii, 608.

speculations beyond those prevailing in his milieu." [1] Within the general framework of the present study, then, Freud in his original guise ranks as a positivist.

Was he a materialist? The answer is quite definitely in the negative. Although he denied the possibility of immortality—"no mind could exist apart from a brain" —he "held that . . . the essential nature of both mind and matter" was "quite unknown." Indeed, "they were so intrinsically different in kind as to make it a logical error to translate a description of processes in the one into terms of the other." Matter might be essential to the workings of the mind—but there was no "clue for elucidating the direct relationship of one to the other." [2]

Was he a determinist? Here the answer is somewhat harder to give. It is easy to cull specifically determinist passages from Freud's work. Already in his book on dreams we find him rebuking his predecessors for having "underestimated the extent to which psychical events are determined. There is nothing arbitrary about them." [3] But in insisting on the lawfulness of mental behavior, Freud was postulating a rather different sort of determinism from what had earlier been called by that name. He had pushed the determining forces back from the conscious to the unconscious level. And with the prime movers thus located beyond conscious recognition, he found it perfectly logical for human beings to behave *as though* their wills were free. Indeed, in his own conduct of life, Freud—like most philosophical determinists—acted in a highly self-confident and responsible manner. Furthermore, it was apparent to Freud that at the unconscious level the determination of choice was by no means a simple affair. It was customarily a question of plural causation; most psychic events were "over-determined." Hence it was usually impossible to ascribe to them a mechanical one-to-one rela-

---

[1] Jones: *Freud*, I, 365–7.
[2] Ibid., pp. 368–9.
[3] *Interpretation of Dreams*, p. 514.

tionship of cause to effect. There was plenty of room for alternative hypotheses.

"Paradoxically," however, "while Freud stressed the factor of over-determination rather than unitary determinants in regard to his clinical data, he searched for a unitary source of these data." [4] We have seen earlier how entranced he was with his sweeping metaphors of the Œdipus complex and the primal crime. Similarly in regard to the workings of the mind he sought to subsume his discoveries under a few large figures of speech. In what he called his "metapsychology" he gave an account of the mind in terms of metaphors derived from economics, topography, and dynamics. But only with the last of these did he succeed in outlining a theory that has carried conviction to the layman. This description of the mind in terms of metaphors drawn from physics leads us to the final and most significant aspect of Freud's residual positivism.

To the end of his life Freud used a mechanistic vocabulary. This he had learned from his teacher Ernst von Brücke, through whose efforts "the language of physics . . . had been grafted on to the data of physiology." [5] Sometimes Freud's metaphors were hydraulic—more often they were drawn from the field of electricity. There were flows and dams, charges and discharges, excitations and cathexes. Freud himself and his subsequent expositors have insisted that these figures of speech should not be taken too literally—that things did not "really" happen this way. But the defense is only partially convincing. If the mind did not really function in this fashion, how else might it be described as functioning? Was there an alternative set of metaphors that would fit? Freud never provided any. A thinker is, after all, partly judged on the basis of the

---

[4] E. Pumpian-Mindlin: "The Position of Psychoanalysis in Relation to the Biological and Social Sciences," *Psychoanalysis as Science*, edited by E. Pumpian-Mindlin (Stanford, Calif., 1952), p. 154.
[5] Jones: *Freud*, I, 369.

figures of speech he uses, and in Freud's case, the thought never got beyond a fairly simple vocabulary drawn from nineteenth-century physics.

Freud's theory, then, remained couched in positivist terms—and those were of a rather crude order. The longer he lived the more inappropriate this vocabulary became. What had begun in the 1890's as a convenient path to comprehension on the part of a public steeped in the cult of natural science had by the 1930's become at best a quaint anachronism. In Freud's later work of social speculation his fancy was constantly escaping from the pedestrian images to which it was attached. The creative imagination—the work of the unconscious itself—refused to be tied down by a vocabulary that had originally been devised for quite different purposes.

Toward the end of his life, as we have seen, Freud began to give free play to the imagination that he had earlier so "ruthlessly curbed." By the same process he began to grant greater scope to the qualities which formerly had figured only on the periphery of his achievement—the tolerance of uncertainty and doubt that led him to greet Poincaré's work with approval, the ease and grace of his own literary style—indeed, the whole taste for the literary and the mythical aspects of human life. As Thomas Mann said of him, Freud had come to his theories without benefit of the literary and philosophical predecessors who might have helped him along his way—Nietzsche, Schopenhauer, Novalis, Kierkegaard.[6] But with the world of literature he had always felt profound affinities. By the end of his life he had become at least as much a philosophical and literary figure as a man of science and of medicine. The positivist vocabulary remained—but the positivist mentality had been largely sloughed off.

Unlike Bergson, however, Freud was not content to express the recovery of the unconscious in terms of a

---

[6] *Freud und die Zukunft* (Vienna, 1936), translated by H. T. Lowe-Porter as "Freud and the Future," *Essays of Three Decades* (New York, 1947), p. 412.

merely literary sensation of time-as-experience. He felt
driven to make a coherent explanation of its workings.
Rather than simply affirming that the unconscious did
not follow the usual rules of logic, he attempted to define the strange rules by which such illogical logic
operated. In this mighty effort—despite all its limitations of vocabulary and conceptualization—our whole
contemporary view of the human mind has had its
origin.

IV. *Sigmund Freud: Social Philosophy*

It was not until the last decade and a half of his life
that Freud turned his attention explicitly to the problems of man in society. Why he did so cannot be explained in any simple terms. There are a number of
possible reasons—the emotional and moral shock of the
First World War, which had brought financial ruin and
the collapse of the political system under which he
lived; his own ill health, which made sustained clinical
work increasingly difficult; perhaps more than anything
else, the specter of death, which after 1923 was always
with him. Freud never spoke of his personal emotions
except when driven to it by the necessities of theoretical exposition: we are left to guess at the reasons for his
dramatic change in intellectual orientation.

Already in the first of the short, speculative works
characteristic of his late production—*The Future of an
Illusion*, published in 1927—Freud revealed in stark
terms the ambivalence of his view of society. On the
one hand we find a deeply pessimistic assessment of the
potentialities of civilization. "One gets the impression,"
Freud writes, "that culture is something which was imposed on a resisting majority by a minority that understood how to possess itself of the means of power and
coercion." Could this state of affairs be changed?
Would it be possible to arrive at a "reorganization of
human relations . . . which, by abandoning coercion

and the suppression of the instincts," would enable men to "devote themselves to the acquisition of natural resources and to the enjoyment of the same?" Freud thought not. "That would be the golden age, but it is questionable if such a state of affairs can ever be realized. It seems more probable that every culture must be built up on coercion and instinctual renunciation." The best that could be hoped for would be to diminish somewhat "the burden of the instinctual sacrifices imposed on men," and by finding some sort of compensation, to reconcile mankind to the sacrifices "that must necessarily remain." [7]

Freud called himself a conservative. And in his skepticism about the possibilities of a just society, we find a parallel to the attitude of Pareto and Mosca and the other conservative theorists of the early twentieth century. Indeed, we can even detect echoes of a Marxism that had been redefined as an intuitive sociology of mass protest. But Freud was not content, like Pareto, to dismiss this protest as simply mistaken. He sympathized with it and he sought for ways to grant it recognition. There was at least one avenue, he surmised, by which the lot of mankind might possibly be improved. Human beings, after all, were "equipped with the most varied instinctual predispositions." The "experiences of early childhood" ordinarily bent these instincts toward conformity to an ethic of coercion and renunciation. But perhaps it did not need to be this way. Perhaps it would eventually prove possible to train the instincts to non-repressive living. Thus mankind might succeed in producing a "throng of superior, dependable and disinterested leaders," who could "act as educators of the future generations." Freud did not think it very likely. But he concluded that "one cannot deny the grandeur of this project and its significance for the future of human culture." [8]

[7] *Future of an Illusion*, pp. 4–6.
[8] Ibid., p. 9.

Ordinarily Freud's interpreters have stressed the negative aspects of his writings on society. They have inferred from the fact of man's biological and instinctual limitations—from Freud's discovery that it was man's unconscious rather than his reason that was in ultimate control—that there was little hope for him to improve his lot. The human condition, they have argued, has been fixed for all eternity by the unconscious drives. More recently, however, a number of American commentators have picked up the threads of optimism that lie scattered through Freud's later writings and have tried to weave them into a coherent theory. Lionel Trilling has asked us "to consider whether this emphasis on biology . . . far from being a reactionary idea . . . is actually a liberating idea. It proposes to us that culture is not all-powerful. It suggests that there is a residue of human quality beyond the reach of cultural control, and that this residue . . . , elemental as it may be, serves to bring culture itself under criticism and keeps it from being absolute." [9] Similarly, Herbert Marcuse has traced the "subterranean" current in Freud's theory—the "elements that break through" the "rationalization" that a "non-repressive civilization is impossible." Freud's social speculation, Marcuse argues, "is an ever-renewed attempt to uncover, and to question, the terrible necessity of the inner connection between civilization and barbarism, progress and suffering, freedom and unhappiness." [1]

Are these writers correct in their reassessment? Are they justified in following Thomas Mann, who two decades earlier greeted Freud as the "path-finder towards a humanism of the future"? [2] This is our problem —and we may best approach it by first inquiring into Freud's personal ethic, and subsequently tracing the

---

[9] *Freud and the Crisis of Our Culture* (Boston, 1955), p. 48.
[1] *Eros and Civilization*, pp. 16–17.
[2] "Freud and the Future," p. 427.

stages through which his more explicit social philosophy unfolded.

I have said that Freud did not like to talk about his personal attitudes and values. These he held so deeply that it would have been both unnecessary and indelicate to probe into them. Kindness and integrity he regarded as simple absolutes. In Freud, "honesty . . . was more than a simple natural habit. It became an active love of truth and justice. . . . A moral attitude was so deeply implanted as to seem a part of his original nature. He never had any doubt about what was the right course of conduct," and he cited with approval the saying: "Morality is self-evident." Although—to quote his own words—he stood "for an incomparably freer sexual life," he "made very little use of such freedom." [3] Indeed, in terms of present-day morality he could almost be considered a prude. One of the most curious paradoxes about Freud is that in his personal conduct he never followed up the relativist implications of his own theories.

Freud's "penetrating, attentive eyes had not only the simplicity and innocent clear-sightedness of a child— one for whom nothing is too small, and nothing either common or unclean—there was also in them a mature patience and caution, and a detached inquiry." [4] For the Freud who looked out on the world with the eyes of a child was also Freud the scientist. We have noted already the intensity of his craving for knowledge, and the extent to which he held to a fairly simple nineteenth-century faith in the virtues of science. This faith was, in fact, the mainspring of the more optimistic features of his social philosophy. "No," he wrote toward the end of his life, "science is no illusion. But it would

[3] Jones: *Freud*, II, 416, 418, 426.
[4] Joan Riviere: "An Intimate Impression" (*The Lancet*, Sept. 20, 1939), quoted in Jones: *Freud*, II, 405.

be an illusion to suppose that we could get anywhere else what it cannot give us." [5]

"Anywhere else" meant, of course, the promises of religion. Toward these Freud was uncompromisingly hostile. His attitude was more militantly free-thinking than that of a Durkheim who regarded religious phenomena with a lively and even sympathetic curiosity, or of a Weber whose intellectual interest was reinforced by at least a remnant of personal faith. In *The Future of an Illusion*, the book in which Freud most explicitly subscribed to the principles of the Enlightenment, he put religion in the category of dreams, as just another example of "wish-fulfilment." Some religious doctrines, he added, "are so improbable, so very incompatible with everything we have laboriously discovered about the reality of the world" as to rank in the category of "delusions." "Where questions of religion are concerned people are guilty of every possible kind of insincerity and intellectual misdemeanour. . . . Think of the distressing contrast between the radiant intelligence of a healthy child and the feeble mentality of the average adult. Is it so utterly impossible that it is . . . religious upbringing which is largely to blame for this relative degeneration?" If religion, Freud continued, "had succeeded in making happy the greater part of mankind, in consoling them, in reconciling them to life, . . . then no one would dream of striving to alter existing conditions. But instead of this what do we see? . . . For many thousands of years," religion "has ruled human society; it has had time to show what it can achieve." [6] And indeed that had been very little.

Few thinkers of our time have been so outspoken. Yet Freud's hostility toward religion as an institution did not prevent him from maintaining good relations with a few individuals of deep religious faith. In the annals of psychoanalysis there is no more curious chapter than that of the intellectual and personal loyalty to

[5] *Future of an Illusion*, p. 102.
[6] Ibid., pp. 54, 56, 66, 84.

Freud of the Swiss pastor Oskar Pfister. An amateur in the field of psychiatry, Pfister had adhered to Freud's doctrines along with Jung and the Swiss contingent that represented the first large body of recruits to psychoanalysis from outside Freud's immediate circle of Viennese co-workers. When, shortly before the First World War, Jung and the other Swiss broke away *en masse,* Pfister was the only one to remain with Freud—thereby gravely imperiling his position as a minister of the gospel. Indeed, he was one of only four non-Jews—one of the others being Freud's subsequent biographer, Ernest Jones—to stick by the founder during the inner turmoil which shook the psychoanalytic movement in the immediate pre-war years.

In his correspondence with the Swiss pastor, Freud made no special allowances. He conceded, however, that "in itself psychoanalysis is neither religious nor the opposite, but an impartial instrument which can serve the clergy as well as the laity when it is used only to free suffering people." Yet on the central tenets of his doctrine Freud was uncompromising. One of these was his sexual theory, and he rebuked Pfister for contradicting it. He added the teasing query: "How comes it that none of the godly ever devised psychoanalysis and that one had to wait for a godless Jew?" [7]

Pfister replied with perfect logic that Freud was not a Jew. In a religious sense this was true: Freud obviously subscribed to no faith. But in a non-religious sense Freud was ready and proud to regard himself as Jewish. In his early professional career he had suffered on account of his origin, and in later life he was always ready to spring to the defense of other Jews who had been discriminated against or persecuted. He could never forget the shame of hearing how his father had submitted without protest to anti-Semitic insults. Before the period of his fame Freud had been an active mem-

[7] Letters of February 9, 1909, and October 9, 1918, included in the Appendix to Jones: *Freud,* II, 439–40, 457–8.

ber of the B'nai B'rith, and when he had become more
prominent, he served as a governor of the Hebrew University in Jerusalem. But it was with the great persecu-
tions of the 1930's that his Jewish allegiance became
most militant. Behind the uncommitted man of science
the angry figure of an Old Testament prophet began
to delineate itself. The personality of Moses had always
fascinated Freud: as early as 1913 he had written an
extraordinarily acute analysis of Michelangelo's statue
of the lawgiver. It was only in his last book, however,
that he gave free rein to this self-identification.

Moses and Monotheism is the strangest of Freud's
works. The very circumstances of its composition were
unusual. At first he ventured to publish only a fragment
of it, since he hesitated to offend the Catholic Church,
which seemed to be serving as the shield of a free Austria against the Nazi menace. But when this shield had
collapsed—once more organized religion had proved to
be "a broken reed"—and when, with the German occupation of his country, he had himself been obliged to
seek refuge in London, his hesitations vanished.[8] Only
a few months before his own death he gave to the world
his last word both on religion and on the historical role
of the Jewish people.

The book might well have offended Christian and
Jew alike. In its strictly naturalistic interpretation of
the origins of monotheism, it was a challenge to all revealed religion. And Jews in particular might object to
Freud's paradoxical assertion that Moses was actually
an Egyptian who had been slain by the children of
Israel after serving as their adopted prophet. Careful
readers, however, could detect in the work a streak of
triumphant pride in the way the Jews had borne their
tragic history. The tenacity, the indomitable stubbornness of the Jewish people appealed to the Freud who
was forever fighting for what he regarded as science and
truth.

[8] "Prefatory Notes" to Part III, *Moses and Monotheism*, pp.
66–71.

Freud died on September 23, 1939, three weeks after the outbreak of the Second World War. He was not granted time to comment on the conflict he had clearly seen approaching. On the First World War, however, he had spoken with an earnestness that revealed how deeply it had tried his soul. Prior to the war, Freud had taken no very active interest in public affairs. He had sympathized in a somewhat tepid fashion with the aims of the Austrian Socialist party, and he had of course opposed the anti-Semitic movement that was so powerful in Vienna politics. But it was only with the war that his attention became focused on the conduct of men in society.

The brutality of the conflict only confirmed what Freud in his more personal statements and in his formulations of psychoanalytic theory had been saying for many years. As the war was drawing to a close he wrote to Pastor Pfister: "I have not found much 'good' in the average human being. Most of them are in my experience riff-raff." Four years earlier he had written to a Dutch colleague in more specific terms:

Psychoanalysis has concluded from a study of the dreams and mental slips of normal people, as well as from the symptoms of neurotics, that the primitive, savage and evil impulses of mankind have not vanished in any individual, but continue their existence, although in a repressed state . . . and that they wait for opportunities to display their activity.

It has furthermore taught us that our intellect is a feeble and dependent thing, a plaything and tool of our impulses and emotions. . . .

And now just look at what is happening in this wartime, at the cruelties and injustices for which the most civilized nations are responsible, at the different way in which they judge of their own lies, their own wrong-doings, and those of their enemies, at the general loss of clear insight; then you must confess that psychoanalysis has been right with both its assertions.[9]

The war, Freud noted in his most extended discussion of the psychological effects of the conflict, had at least the merit of having destroyed a number of illusions. One could offer oneself a certain wry consolation through recognizing that: "In reality our fellow-citizens have not sunk so low as we feared, because they had never risen so high as we believed." Yet it would be foolhardy to resume one's earlier illusions once the war was over. The future would have to live on rather more modest hopes. "War," Freud concluded, "is not to be abolished; so long as the conditions of existence among the nations are so varied, and the repulsions between peoples so intense, there will be, must be, wars." [1]

From our consideration of Freud's personal attitudes we are led to a basically negative conclusion: Freud's own ethical standards were high, but he neither expected very much of his fellow men nor held out much hope to them.

What about his more explicit writings on social philosophy? Initially we should note that Freud had been from the start a rather special kind of social theorist. Although he began only late in life to apply to the world of human communities the insights that he had earlier derived from the study of individuals, in one sense he had all along been writing about society. For he had written of individuals *in families*: the relation of child to parent and of brother to sister had been at the basis of his theory of personality formation. From the family he branched out to the wider communities that were the products of civilization: the transition was perfectly natural.

[9] Letters of December 28, 1914, and October 9, 1918, included in Jones: *Freud*, II, 368–9, 457–8.
[1] "Thoughts for the Times on War and Death" (first published in *Imago*, V [1915]), authorized translation under the supervision of Joan Riviere, *Collected Papers*, IV (London, 1925), pp. 300, 316.

Hence it was logical that his first book of social theory—*Totem and Taboo*—should have been an inquiry into the primeval family. I have already called this work an anthropological fantasy: as an abstract parable of the foundation of society it was at least as remote from verifiable reality as Rousseau's *Social Contract*. Moreover, it betrayed the limitations of its author's social horizon. In an anthropological sense, it proved that Freud was "culture-bound." He looked out at the world through the eyes of a late nineteenth-century physician, for whom the main features of Western and Central European society were simply assumed. Hence he equipped his "primeval horde . . . with all the bias, maladjustments and ill-tempers of a middle-class European family . . . let loose in a prehistoric jungle to run riot in a most attractive but fantastic hypothesis." [2]

This hypothesis, however, as we have already seen, Freud refused to abandon or even to modify. The story of the slaying of the primeval father is repeated almost verbatim in his subsequent works of social speculation. For the death of the father was to Freud the supreme drama in the history of humanity. As he had discovered from his self-analysis, his own father's death had been "the most important event, the most poignant loss" of his whole life. [3] And this personal insight Freud enlarged—as he was so fond of doing—into a generalization about the rest of his fellow men.

How could the sons slay—or, in the case of civilized men, unconsciously long to slay—the father who had begotten them, and at the same time, once his death had actually occurred, be inconsolable in their grief? This paradox brings us to the center of Freud's social theory: it suggests why that theory is necessarily ambivalent. On the surface, of course, the explanation is simple: the sons had feared and hated their father because he monopolized the women of the horde; with

---

[2] Malinowski: *Sex and Repression*, p. 146.
[3] Preface to the second edition, *Interpretation of Dreams*, p. xxvi.

his death, however, came "remorse"—and the recognition of how much they had also loved him. At the same time the sons saw that they themselves would have to replace the father's vanished authority with a new moral imperative. Thus the foundation of social institutions was based on the realization that a desperate act of self-denial was required if humanity was not to perish utterly in a bloody strife of brother against brother.[4]

The result was the taboo on incest, which Freud established as the founding ordinance of civilized society. With primitive man, Freud surmised, as with the children that he had himself studied, the first act of the self-discipline on which civilization rested had been the curbing of incestuous fantasies. But this renunciation had never been complete. The forbidden desire for the mother and the sister had lingered on in repressed form. Mankind dimly understood the deeper reality, and hence from that time forth labored under an almost intolerable burden of guilt.

This is the more basic explanation for the ambivalence of Freud's social theory. The original prohibition of incest, Freud reasoned, had been followed by other moral imperatives, which in time had become equally binding. These ethical precepts had been indispensable—without them civilization could never have been built—but at the same time they had grievously thwarted man's deepest urges. It was for this reason that Freud insisted so strongly on the necessary connection between civilized society and a coercive social order.

In his works of social speculation published subsequent to the war—*The Future of an Illusion, Civilization and Its Discontents,* and *Moses and Monotheism* —Freud enlarged on his concept of the nature of guilt as the motive force of social solidarity. It was no acci-

---

[4] *Totem und Tabu* (Leipzig and Vienna, 1913), translated from the fifth edition (1934) by James Strachey as *Totem and Taboo* (*Standard Edition*, XIII, 1–162) (London, 1955), p. 143.

dent that the murder of a father figure—the ritualistic re-enactment of the primal crime—should have been at the origin of the Jewish religion and of monotheism as we know it in the Western world today. "In the course of the . . . development of religions," Freud had argued, "the two driving factors, the son's sense of guilt and the son's rebelliousness, never became extinct. Whatever . . . kind of reconciliation was effected between these two opposing mental forces, sooner or later broke down. . . . The son's efforts to put himself in the place of the father-god became ever more obvious." [5] Thus it was that Christianity, in the wake of a number of other Near Eastern cults, discovered the image of the god-as-son, whose sacrifice of his own life could alone atone for the original crime against the father. And in this fashion Freud was brought back to the question of anti-Semitism and the historical fate of the Jews:

> The poor Jewish people, who with its usual stiff-necked obduracy continued to deny the murder of their "father," has dearly expiated this in the course of centuries. Over and over again they heard the reproach: "You killed our God." And this reproach is true, if rightly interpreted. It says, in reference to the history of religion: "You won't *admit* that you murdered God" (the archetype of God, the primeval Father, and his reincarnations). Something should be added—namely: "It is true, we did the same thing, but we *admitted* it, and since then we have been purified." [6]

It was in *Civilization and Its Discontents,* published in 1930, that Freud most explicitly came to grips with this vast burden of guilt. "Since culture," he reasoned,

> obeys an inner . . . impulse which bids it bind mankind into a closely knit mass, it can achieve

[5] Ibid., p. 152.
[6] *Moses and Monotheism,* pp. 114–15.

this aim only by means of its vigilance in foment-
ing an ever-increasing sense of guilt. That which
began in relation to the father ends in relation to
the community. If civilization is an inevitable
course of development from the group of the family to the group of humanity as a whole, then an intensification of the sense of guilt . . . will be inextricably bound up with it, until perhaps the sense
of guilt may swell to a magnitude that individuals
can hardly support.[7]

Earlier Freud had postulated in the human psyche a
reality-principle and a pleasure-principle, whose contest
for control he roughly equated with the struggle between the ego and the id. One represented the consciously formed personality, the other the undifferentiated, amoral realm of primitive yearning. Obviously in
the work of building civilization the ego was obliged
to curb the id—the reality-principle to dominate over
the pleasure-principle. Moreover, in this two-way struggle the super-ego also figured, as the dwelling-place of
guilt and of the internalized values of the father.[8] From
one standpoint the super-ego seemed to be the main
motive-force in the construction of civilization: by constantly punishing the ego it drove the latter to ever
greater feats of self-deprivation. But the irony of the
matter was that a radically different power was also at
work: Eros—the thirst for affection characteristic of
the id. Love as well as self-punishment pushed man toward life in society. For Eros was not merely a blind
striving for instinctual gratification. It aimed "at binding together single . . . individuals, then families, then
tribes, races, nations, into one great unity, that of hu-

---

[7] *Das Unbehagen in der Kultur* (Vienna, 1930), translated
by Joan Riviere as *Civilization and Its Discontents* (London,
1930), pp. 121–2.
[8] *Das Ich und das Es* (Vienna, 1923), authorized translation
by Joan Riviere as *The Ego and the Id* (London, 1927), pp. 30,
44–5.

manity." [9] Love and self-punishment were combined in the vast paradox of civilization.

This, then, was the problem for modern man. How was he to maximize the potentialities of Eros—the aspect of civilization that grew from love and human solidarity—without threatening the aspects that had their origin in self-punishment and renunciation? Freud, as we have seen, was skeptical as to how much could be done. A certain measure of instinctual renunciation, he asserted again and again, was of the essence of civilization. If left to themselves, the id and the pleasure-principle would simply drift along in passive fashion, experiencing, as a baby does, one happy or uncomfortable sensation after another. Even if the more pressing requirements of the struggle for existence were eventually eliminated, a minimum of painful effort would always be required.

There was one realm, however, in which self-punishment had been carried to completely irrational extremes. By its code of sexual behavior Western society had so narrowed the range of erotic satisfaction that the sexual life itself had ended by being "seriously disabled." [1] In this area, Freud believed there was much that could be done. It was the only subject about which he was constantly militant, and the public, in its thirst for sensation, was not too far wrong in concentrating its attention on Freud's scientific investigations in the field of sex. Next to the discovery of the unconscious it was certainly the most significant aspect of his work. Indeed, the fact that Freud himself ranked his *Three Essays on the Theory of Sexuality*, published in 1905, alongside *The Interpretation of Dreams* as the second of his major books, suggests how much he thought of the revelation of infantile sexuality it contained. [2]

[9] *Civilization and Its Discontents*, p. 102.
[1] Ibid., p. 76.
[2] *Drei Abhandlungen zur Sexualtheorie* (Leipzig and Vienna, 1905), translated from the sixth edition (1925) by James Strachey as *Three Essays on the Theory of Sexuality* (*Standard Edition*, VII, 123–245) (London, 1953).

The simple facts about the sexual life of the very young—although they must have been common knowledge among nurses and everybody else who, unlike nineteenth-century men of science, knew children at first hand—had been systematically hushed up. And when the children themselves were slightly older, they had been kept in ignorance of their own sexual constitution. This, Freud believed, had reinforced the effects of early religious teaching to stultify still further the intellectual life of adults. Sexual enlightenment, he implied, could do only good. And similarly he recommended a more humane attitude toward homosexuals and others against whom social convention had unforgivingly set its face.

Among the latter was the vast mass of young people who were not yet in a position to marry. As a young man Freud had been engaged for a period of four years. He had suffered desperately from this long waiting—indeed, there is evidence that his subsequent emotional life was partially crippled by it—and he wrote with the liveliest sympathy of the trials of engaged couples. Echoes of his own experience were clearly discernible in his first significant publication on social theory, the paper entitled " 'Civilized' Sexual Morality and Modern Nervousness," which appeared three years after the *Three Essays* and four years before *Totem and Taboo*. It was an unsparing dissection of sexual ethics and of the realities of marriage as Freud knew them through the confessions of his patients. True emotional satisfaction, he concluded, was almost impossible in the marriage bond as Western society had devised it. And this was particularly the case with regard to women. As a reward for their submission to the dictates first of their parents and later of their husbands, mature married women had "only the choice between unappeased desire, infidelity, or neurosis." [3]

[3] " 'Civilized' Sexual Morality and Modern Nervousness" (first published in *Sexualprobleme*, IV [1908]), authorized translation

The picture of "civilized" sexual conventions that Freud drew in this first essay and in his subsequent contributions to social theory is, in a number of important respects, almost unrecognizable today. The fact that in the course of half a century so much has changed— that men and women have become at least to some extent freer and more joyous in their relations to each other—is obviously due in part to Freud's own teachings.[4] In this change we can find a direct answer to his doubts as to whether it was possible to make the lot of mankind more bearable. Far beyond his own anticipations, Freud's labors as ethical liberator and educator were to affect the character of the society whose dictates he had criticized, but which in most of his work he had treated as essentially unalterable.

What are we to conclude? How did the balance fall between skepticism and hope? Obviously Freud had few illusions. He had probed too deeply into his own unconscious and that of his patients to retain much conventional confidence in man's potentialities for good. He recognized without flinching that

> men are not gentle, friendly creatures . . . , who simply defend themselves if they are attacked . . . ; a powerful measure of desire for aggression has to be reckoned as part of their instinctual endowment. The result is that their neighbour is to them not only a possible helper or sexual object, but also a temptation to them to gratify their aggressiveness on him, to exploit his capacity for work without recompense, to use him sexually without his consent, to seize his possessions, to humiliate him, to cause him pain, to torture and to kill him.[5]

---

under the supervision of Joan Riviere, *Collected Papers*, II (London, 1924), p. 93.
[4] Jones: *Freud*, II, 293.
[5] *Civilization and Its Discontents*, p. 85.

These lines, written just four years before the advent of Hitler, showed that for Freud the future would hold few surprises.

Thus from one standpoint his discoveries seemed to throw into the discard the optimistic anticipations inherited from the Enlightenment. From another standpoint, they were a triumphant vindication of those same anticipations. The paradox of the matter is that "Freud, the man who above all others is supposed to have destroyed the justification of Enlightenment rationalism, was the greatest child of the Enlightenment which our century has known." For "his fundamental assumption" was "that the search for truth must never stop, that only knowledge allows reason to function, and that only reason can make us free." [6]

Freud's own career offered the best possible proof that his faith in human reason was no mere illusion. For by the use of his faculties of observation and analysis he added more to our knowledge about humanity than any other thinker of our time. Moreover this faith enabled him to face the future with serenity—and to put his own discoveries in proper perspective:

> We may insist as much as we like that the human intellect is weak in comparison with human instincts, and be right in doing so. But nevertheless there is something peculiar about this weakness. The voice of the intellect is a soft one, but it does not rest until it has gained a hearing. Ultimately, after endlessly repeated rebuffs, it succeeds. This is one of the few points in which one may be optimistic about the future of mankind, but in itself it signifies not a little. And one can make it a starting-point for yet other hopes. The primacy of the intellect certainly lies in the far, far, but still probably not infinite, distance.[7]

[6] Peter Gay: "The Enlightenment in the History of Political Theory," *Political Science Quarterly*, LXIX (September 1954), p. 379.
[7] *Future of an Illusion*, pp. 96–7.

Freud looked out on the world without illusion, yet with "warm humanitarian feeling." [8] "Man at his best and man at his worst," he saw, was "subject to a common set of explanations: . . . good and evil" grew "from a common process." Thus Freud "provided an image of man that . . . made him comprehensible without at the same time making him contemptible." [9] He confronted the facts of existence with a judicious combination of reason, realism, and humanity. He had the courage to deny himself the comfort of religion, and the still greater courage to attest frankly to his purely secular faith. In his latter years he was in constant pain, which he bore with fortitude. "If you would endure life," he had advised, "be prepared for death." [1]

v. *Jung and the "Collective Unconscious"*

Carl Gustav Jung is at the meeting-point between Bergson and Freud. In redefining Freud's notion of the *libido* as a generalized overflowing of life energy—in depriving it of the sexual connotations that Freud attached to it—Jung specifically equated it with Bergson's *élan vital*. This would be reason in itself for giving some consideration to Jung's theories. Beyond that, however, we have the authority of Freud's biographer for ranking Jung as the most important of the successive "heretics" who broke away from orthodox psychoanalysis. The other defector commonly mentioned in the same category, Alfred Adler, Freud simply did not take seriously. "What Adler had to offer was so superficial and indeed banal that it could seldom make any appeal to serious investigators." And indeed, Adler's real influence was to come only after the Second World War with the success of the "neo-Freudian" current represented by Erich Fromm, Karen Horney, and the like.

[8] Jones: *Freud*, II, 293.
[9] Bruner: "Freud and the Image of Man," pp. 342, 347.
[1] "Thoughts for the Times," p. 317.

"Jung, on the other hand, began with a far more extensive knowledge of psychoanalysis than Adler ever had . . . his intellectual ability and the width of his cultural background far transcended Adler's . . . , and what he offered the world was an alternative explanation of at least some" of Freud's discoveries.[2]

Moreover, there was an element of deep personal hurt in the rupture between the two. The adherence to psychoanalysis, beginning in 1904, of the Swiss group that included Jung had been the first great success of the doctrine beyond Freud's immediate circle. And of the Swiss, Jung was by far the most promising. Vigorous, intelligent, martial in bearing, with a youthful enthusiasm for psychoanalysis and all its works—Jung appealed strongly to a Freud who already felt himself aging. It was not long before the latter was treating Jung as his adopted son and successor-designate. The young Swiss was twenty years Freud's junior and seemed well fitted to carry on the doctrine after its founder had been carried off by early death (which was one of Freud's settled convictions). Nor was the fact that Jung was non-Jewish, and highly "respectable" from every other standpoint, of negligible importance in Freud's desire to push him forward. Conversely the suspicion of anti-Semitism lingered around Jung's activities both before and after the break.

At the International Psychoanalytic Congress of 1910 —the second major gathering of Freud's adherents—the founder of psychoanalysis saw to it that Jung was elected president of the association. The previous year, however, the strain between the two had already begun. Its origin seems to go back to Freud's trip to the United States, when Jung accompanied him and shared honors with him at the epoch-making lectures at Clark University. During the next three years misunderstandings and tensions mounted, until Jung's publication of the first version of his essay *On the Psychology of the Un-*

2 Jones: *Freud*, II, 137–8, 283.

conscious showed that an official rupture was not far away. By 1914, all communication between the two had ceased. How desperately Freud suffered from the loss was evidenced by the fact that he fainted on two different occasions of maximum strain.

What were the grounds of the separation? Initially and most obviously, there was the fact that Jung had gradually "watered down" the sexual basis of psychoanalytic theory until it had virtually disappeared. Freud and his loyal followers suspected that Jung's reasons for doing so were not exclusively scientific: they accused him of cowardice; the Swiss, they reasoned, as members of a patrician, conservative society, were peculiarly vulnerable to the opprobrium that the sexual aspects of psychoanalytic theory aroused. But this difference in the interpretation of neurotic symptoms was merely the most apparent manifestation of a deeper and more generalized psychological incompatibility. Freud and Jung had minds that worked quite differently: it was only on the grounds of fantastic anthropological speculation that the two—despite their mutual denials—remained on a parallel course. Otherwise—in intellectual training, in methodology, in implicit philosophy—they were poles apart. An analysis of these differences may be the best way to approach the central question that Jung presents—did he "deepen" Freud's theories, as his apologists claim, or, as the orthodox Freudians assert, was he little more than an intellectual charlatan who "perverted" the findings of psychoanalysis beyond recognition?

One of the most persuasive of Jung's interpreters has stated the difference between him and Freud as follows: "Freud . . . missed up on two main points: he did not understand history, and he did not understand religion." [3] About the latter statement, I think, there would be little serious dispute: even among the skeptics

---

[3] Ira Progoff: *Jung's Psychology and Its Social Meaning*, Evergreen edition (New York, 1955), p. 9.

of his generation, Freud lacked the sympathetic under-standing of religious sentiment that characterized the work of Weber or Sorel. The former assertion is more doubtful; yet it at least suggests a cleavage between Freud and Jung that existed from the start.

While Freud's training had been almost exclusively scientific and medical, Jung came to psychoanalysis steeped in philosophy, literature, and history. A citizen of Basel—the most proudly aristocratic and self-con-sciously cultured of Swiss cities—Jung had imbibed the tradition of Nietzsche, of Burckhardt, and of J. J. Bach-ofen, the speculative ethnologist and student of my-thology who ranked as the third of the intellectual lumi-naries associated with Basel. There had been both pastors and physicians in his family—as Jung himself was to be a bit of both. One suspects that he never had a truly scientific mind: his career in clinical psychiatry was—far more than in Freud's case—a detour from his real intellectual interests.

These were of a boldly imaginative order. Even more than Bergson, Jung turned increasingly toward mys-ticism in the course of his long life. And it is fair to say that this intellectual bent gave him a sense for the ambiguities of history which was closer to that of the true historian than Freud's. In Freud's ventures into historical and anthropological speculation, there was always a lingering trace of the mechanistic and the uni-lateral. In Jung's case, history led naturally into myth, and myth in turn to religion. By the time that his theory was fully developed—although it continues to this day to ramify and to alter—Jung had become a frank intuitionist and irrationalist. "We ought to be particularly grateful to Bergson," he wrote, "for having broken a lance in defence of the irrational." [4] Yet Jung himself went far beyond Bergson. As we have already

---

[4] "*La Structure de l'inconscient,*" *Archives de Psychologie,* XVI (1916), translated by R. F. C. Hull as "The Structure of the Unconscious," *The Collected Works of C. G. Jung* (Bol-lingen Series XX), VII (New York, 1953), p. 283.

noted, he and Péguy are the only members of the *dramatis personæ* of this study who can be called romanticists or irrationalists in any proper sense.

In his clinical treatment Jung veered farther and farther away from the orthodox methods of psychoanalysis. As a logical corollary to his denigration of sexuality, he diverted his attention from the problems of children and the young toward those of people in the latter half of life. For them, he argued, a mere sexual adjustment was insufficient: in the years of man's decline, spiritual force alone could provide the courage to go on living. Hence—although he professed no formal religion himself—Jung urged on his patients the virtues of religious practice. Those who had retained some connection with the faith of their fathers were advised to return to it. The others could follow Jung himself in his studies of the esoteric symbolism of Asian religions.

The great symbols of religion, the sense of mystic participation in a spiritual world-force—these became the most celebrated features of Jung's teaching. He and his patients set out in quest of the "archetypes"—the prime symbols of humanity that maintained themselves intact across the barriers of culture and of time. Through the archetypes, they hoped to enter into communion with the "collective unconscious"—the memory of the race in which the deepest wisdom lay stored. Beyond "the working of the intellect," Jung asserted,

> there is a thinking in primordial images—in symbols which are older than historical man; which have been ingrained in him from earliest times, and, eternally living, outlasting all generations, still make up the groundwork of the human psyche. It is only possible to live the fullest life when we are in harmony with these symbols; wisdom is a return to them.[5]

[5] *Modern Man in Search of a Soul* (including most of the essays published in *Seelenprobleme der Gegenwart* [Zürich, 1931]), translated by W. S. Dell and Cary F. Baynes (New York and London, 1947), pp. 129–30.

The collective unconscious, as the central feature of Jung's teaching, is a good point at which to shift over to the arguments of his critics. Before doing so, however, we should frankly recognize that Freud himself had placed the orthodox in a somewhat difficult position by himself postulating a psychological factor that came close to Jung's racial unconscious. *Totem and Taboo* had originally been intended as a rebuke and corrective to the mythological speculations on which Freud had earlier encouraged Jung to enter, but which had subsequently gone far afield: its date of publication coincided with the final break between the two. Yet *Totem and Taboo* itself, with its story of the slaying of the primeval father, was almost as fanciful as Jung's speculations; in assuming a universal sense of guilt, it implied the inheritance of collective memory traces. Indeed, Freud wrote quite specifically of a "collective mind." [6] In what respect, the uninitiated might wonder, was this different from Jung's "collective unconscious"?

The orthodox have been rather hard put to it to give a satisfactory answer—to demolish Jung without including Freud himself in the carnage. Personally I find the greater part of their arguments on this issue both strained and unconvincing. The most sensible thing they have done has been to discount the idea of the inheritance of memory traces as one of those lapses to which all great minds are subject, and as unessential to the main outlines of Freud's theory. [7] Once they have surmounted this hurdle, however, they have had comparatively easy going. It has not been difficult for them to deal unmercifully with Jung's collective unconscious. For they have quite thoroughly demonstrated that far from "deepening" Freud's theory, the notion of a collective layer below the "personal" unconscious has added nothing to it; on the contrary, it has actually

[6] *Totem and Taboo*, p. 157.
[7] See Edward Glover: *Freud or Jung?* Meridian edition (New York, 1956), pp. 39–43.

"flattened it out." Since the collective unconscious in practice proves to be a realm in which anything or nothing may occur—since it has no unequivocal meaning either for clinical purposes or in scientific understanding—the only tangible result of its construction has been to force the personal unconscious into an extremely narrow area. Caught between the realm of the primordial symbols and the realm of ordinary conscious processes, the Jungian personal unconscious leads a restricted and precarious existence.

This is the most telling feature of the orthodox criticism of Jung's work. Under such rigorous scrutiny his teaching turns out to be little more than another one of those academic, "conscious" psychologies whose insufficiencies Freud devoted his life to exposing. Basically it is a doctrine of moral and spiritual uplift, little else. It has added virtually nothing to what the mystics have always known—and which, as we earlier observed, is not really *communicable*. Indeed, it is far vaguer than most mystic teaching. For Jung has not been in the proper sense a religious leader, much as he has liked to surround himself with an atmosphere of devotion to his own person: he has propounded no defined religious doctrine. He has simply recommended religion— any religion—to his patients from "the standpoint of psychic hygiene." [8] Such an instrumental attitude toward religious faith could scarcely fail to prove offensive to a truly devout person.

Once the factitious character of Jung's mysticism has been exposed, it has been almost too easy to deal with the rest of his theories. His elaborate charting of psychological types, his creation of such psychic individualities as the *animus*, the *anima*, the *persona*, and the "shadow," suggest the aberrations of a basically intuitive mind that has felt a compulsion to arrange things in neat categories. His dabblings in the history of alchemy, his experiments with symbolic artifacts and the

---

[8] *Modern Man in Search of a Soul*, p. 129.

drawing of dreams, betray a restless imagination in search of new stimulation. Obviously only a man of enormous intelligence and versatility could have thought up all the odd devices that have entranced Jung and his disciples over the past half-century.

Hence it would be wrong to dismiss him as a charlatan. Jung has understood things about history, religion, and mythology that escaped Freud's more disciplined mind. It is perhaps for this reason that he has appealed almost as much as Freud—or, as in the case of James Joyce and Hermann Hesse, still more than Freud—to the creative writers of our century. But his wider understanding was of no profit to him: he was unable to express what he had learned in any unambiguous form. His mind was profoundly confused, and his writings are a trial to anyone who attempts to discover in them a logical sequence of ideas.

It would be impossible and unprofitable, then, to try to sort them out one by one. The best we can do is to conclude that Jung is a mystagogue who first erupted on the intellectual scene in the incongruous guise of a man of science and follower of Freud. In trying to deepen Freud's teaching, he did just the opposite. He retreated from all the advanced positions that psychoanalytic theory had staked out. He abandoned or completely watered down the concepts of "the unconscious, infantile sexuality, repression, conflict and transference" that were its minimum principles.[9] His critics are on firm ground in calling him a "reactionary."

5

Georges Sorel's Search for Reality

SOMETIME in the early 1930's, in parallel and almost simultaneous *démarches*, the Russian and Italian ambassadors to France proposed to erect a monument above the grave of Georges Sorel, which, they understood, had fallen into a state of disrepair during the decade that had elapsed since his death.[1] Thus had the official representatives of Fascism and Communism chosen to honor in similar fashion the thinker whom they both regarded—with some justice—as an ideological forebear.

The episode is characteristic of the ambiguity that has surrounded Sorel's memory. His mind was a windy crossroads by which there blew nearly every new social doctrine of the early twentieth century. We have already met him in his capacity as the most imaginative of the critics of Marxism. Yet Marxian socialism was only one of the successive political positions to which he adhered—and this he espoused in at least three dis-

[1] Preface by Daniel Halévy to Pierre Andreu: *Notre Maître, M. Sorel* (Paris, 1953), pp. 19–20. The story may be apocryphal.

tinct forms. At the beginning of his intellectual career, he raised his voice as a provincial conservative, in passionate reaction against the intellectualist cleverness of Paris. In the 1890's, with his discovery of Marx, he began the revisionist phase of his career that was to take him through the earlier and more "idealistic" of the vicissitudes of the Dreyfus case. In the succeeding decade, the central and most fruitful period of his life, he reached a third position, which at last brought him a substantial, if rather special measure of fame. From 1898, when he published the first of his essays on syndicalism, to 1908, when his two most influential works appeared, the *Reflections on Violence* and *The Illusions of Progress*, Sorel was occupied with elaborating the doctrine of spontaneous, non-rationalized activity on the part of the proletariat, with which his memory was chiefly to be associated. It was also in this period that he experienced the influence of the two contemporary philosophers who were most profoundly to mark his thought, Henri Bergson and William James.

Sorel might well have stopped at this point. He was more than sixty years old, and he had at least two lives behind him. Yet he went on to the final phases of his intellectual quest which have subsequently tormented his biographers—his elaborate flirtation with monarchist nationalism in the period 1910 to 1913, his despairing uncertainties of the war years, his triumphant salute to Lenin in 1919,[2] and his equivocal, half-admiring references to Mussolini, who was to come to power only two months after his own death. One has the impression that physical weakness and death alone could bring to an end this baffling accumulation of paradoxes and contradictions.

Nor did revolutionary theory and practice exhaust the range of his interests. Classical scholarship, the history of Christianity, epistemology, and the rationale of the natural sciences all provided continuing suste-

[2] "*Pour Lénine,*" published as an appendix to the fourth French edition of the *Reflections on Violence*.

nance for his restless curiosity. Technical economics
and the cultural sociology of the European bourgeoisie
caught his interest more sporadically. It would be impossible to fit Sorel into any neat academic category.
He was a philosopher and historian, a sociologist and
propagandist, all rolled into one. Above all, he was what
the French call a "moralist."

Regarded from one point of view, Sorel was more
centrally located—in an intellectual sense—than any of
his contemporaries. The roster of his literary friendships
was one of unparalleled distinction. We have noticed
already the relation of mutual esteem that bound him
to Croce and Pareto. With the former—despite the increasing divergence of their interests—he continued to
correspond until the eve of his death. The latter—who
detested sentimental effusions—wrote of his departed
friend with unprecedented warmth. Since they had first
become acquainted in 1897, Pareto declared in an
obituary article, "no cloud had troubled" their friendship: their temperaments had been radically opposed,
but partly because they *were* so opposed, they had been
able to understand each other. And in his search for the
truth, Pareto added, Sorel had always displayed an absolute rectitude.[3]

In the circle of young men which gathered around
Charles Péguy and the *Cahiers de la Quinzaine*, Sorel
played the role of an older mentor.[4] And he shared with
Péguy an enthusiasm for the metaphysics of Bergson
that made them both regular auditors of the latter's
celebrated lectures at the Collège de France. Bergson
himself quite correctly refused to regard Sorel as a
disciple. The author of the *Reflections on Violence*, he
sensibly remarked, was "too original and too independent a spirit to enroll himself under anyone's banner."
But he added that Sorel had accepted some of his views
and had understood him perfectly. Sorel himself re-

[3] Vilfredo Pareto, "*Georges Sorel*," *La Ronda*, IV (September
and October 1922), 541–2, 547–8.
[4] See Chapter 9.

ported in 1910 that Bergson had told him—doubtless
with polite exaggeration—that "no one up to now had
penerated as well as I had, what he had tried to do."
And Bergson's favorable reception of the essays on his
own philosophy that Sorel had included in his last book
was one of the few happy events relieving the gloom
of his final months.[5]

Yet despite the impressive support of those who respected his work and called him friend, Sorel remained
an isolated figure. He could maintain contact with
Croce and Pareto only from a distance; he eventually
fell out with Péguy; and with Bergson his relations
never advanced beyond a reserved respect. Moreover,
while the great and original minds among his contemporaries appreciated him at his full worth—with the significant exception of Lenin, who called him a "noto-
rious muddlehead"[6]—the general public found him
much too hard to follow. Sorel was well aware of this.
"The defects of my manner of writing," he admitted,
"prevent me getting access to a wide public." But he
refused to be troubled by it:

> I put before my readers the working of a mental
> effort which is continually endeavouring to break
> through the bonds of what has been previously
> constructed for common use, in order to discover
> that which is truly personal and individual. The
> only things I find it worth while entering in my
> notebooks are those which I have not met else-
> where; I readily skip the transitions between these
> things, because they nearly always come under the
> heading of commonplaces.[7]

[5] Letter of Bergson to Gilbert Maire, cited by Gaétan Pirou:
Georges Sorel (1847–1922) (Paris, 1927), pp. 56–7n.; Letter of
Sorel to Edouard Berth (November 1910), cited by Andreu:
Sorel, p. 241; Ibid., p. 262.

[6] *Materialism and Empirio-Criticism* (Collected Works, XIII)
(New York, 1927), p. 249.

[7] Introduction in the form of a letter to Daniel Halévy,
Réflexions sur la violence (Paris, 1908) (earlier published as a
series of articles in *Mouvement socialiste*, 1906), translated by

Sorel knew his own weaknesses. At the same time he knew that these very failings could eventually rank as his strengths. They reflected his eccentric working-methods: the whole voluminous, disorderly corpus of his writings—at least thirteen books and countless articles on an appalling variety of subjects—has been described as a collection of personal notes and polemics on his vast reading. Throughout his work, however, he systematically avoided the banal. Sorel can be exasperating, tiring, and terribly wrong-headed. But he is almost never obvious nor smug.

Hence in a study such as the present one it seems best to treat Sorel in a chapter by himself. To set him off in this fashion does not mean to rank him as the greatest of his contemporaries—he was far from that. But it means that he must be regarded as *sui generis*—a phenomenon defying exact classification.

To the English-speaking public, Sorel is known almost exclusively for his *Reflections on Violence*, the only one of his books that has been translated. And this is quite understandable in terms of the work's intrinsic merit. As the most impressive product of Sorel's central creative period, it gave the classic formulations to the ideas commonly associated with his name—the notion of violence as a purifying force "without hatred and without the spirit of revenge"; the characterization of historical "myths," and in particular the syndicalist myth of the general strike, as "pictures of battles" which were alone capable of arousing the inert mass of mankind to concerted action; and the more paradoxical assimilation of this thinking in terms of myth to the methodology of modern science.[8] These were the ideas that subsequent social thinkers were most frequently to adopt and exploit in tidier form. But they

---

T. E. Hulme and J. Roth as *Reflections on Violence*, new edition with an introduction by Edward A. Shils (Glencoe, Ill., 1950), pp. 33-4.

[8] Ibid., pp. 48-9, 132, 170.

represented only a small selection of the bewildering number of suggestions that Sorel had scattered abroad in such generous profusion.

The *Reflections on Violence*, then, does not give an adequate idea of Sorel's range or his power of self-contradiction. The most systematic of his books, it had benefited by the editorial labors of one of his younger friends, the gifted writer Daniel Halévy. To understand Sorel's work in its full complexity one must grapple with his other writings—or at least with those that treat of the methods and subject matter of the social sciences.

It so happens that in the year 1951 three different American scholars simultaneously published full-scale analyses of Sorel's ideas and influence. Their subtitles reveal the contrasting conclusions that their authors reached. For Richard Humphrey, Sorel is a "prophet without honor"—an inadequately recognized precursor of relativity in science and instrumentalism in social thought; [9] for Scott H. Lytle, he is an "apostle of fanaticism"—more destroyer than constructive thinker; [1] for James H. Meisel, the most subtle of Sorelian scholars, the path to understanding lies through a minute examination of Sorel's "formative period." [2] In comparing their meticulously documented studies, I have been struck once again with William James's contrast between "tough-" and "tender-mindedness." One interpreter chooses to stress the "open" and humane aspects of his subject's work; another is more impressed with its "closed" and intolerant quality. In the case of a writer as equivocal as Sorel, it is virtually impossible to write about him at all without putting a disproportion-

[9] *Georges Sorel: Prophet without Honor: A Study in anti-Intellectualism* (Cambridge, Mass., 1951).

[1] "Georges Sorel: Apostle of Fanaticism," *Modern France: Problems of the Third and Fourth Republics*, edited by Edward Mead Earle (Princeton, N.J., 1951), pp. 264–90.

[2] *The Genesis of Georges Sorel: An Account of His Formative Period Followed by a Study of His Influence* (Ann Arbor, Mich., 1951).

ate emphasis on one or the other aspect of his thought. Yet in this very difficulty lies the challenge that Sorel presents. What is "tough" and what is "tender" in his writing are inextricably entangled. The two aspects are inseparable: indeed, it is the tension between them that gives Sorel's work both its quality of illuminating reality and its fatal weakness. This concern with the definition of reality is the central problem that I should like to treat in Sorel. Relegating to the background the successive political positions that have usually occupied the attention of scholars, I shall concentrate on Sorel's contribution to the presuppositions and practices of contemporary social thought. By bringing together in coherent sequence the contrasting elements that went into his search for reality, we can perhaps discern a unity in his quest transcending his ideological shifts and contradictions. And I shall try to suggest that it was the very quality of fanaticism and extremism in his thought which enabled him to see things that had escaped the attention of earlier writers—just as it was this same quality that permitted him to go so far and no farther in the definition of social reality.

A number of initial clues to Sorel's highly eccentric position may be found in the salient points of his biography. As opposed to the vast majority of the leading French intellectuals of his day, Sorel was not a scion of the upper bourgeoisie, enjoying the freedom from financial worries and the secure social status that went with such an origin. Nor was he like Péguy that rare specimen among the French intelligentsia, a true son of the people. Sorel was a bourgeois, and he remained such all his life; but he was a bourgeois of a rather special sort. The son of a Norman couple of middling income and with intellectual ambitions for their children, he had doubtless been shaken by the financial reverses his father had suffered during his childhood: these calamities had necessitated an inordinately austere mode of living and had tended to isolate the Sorel family from their own social class.[3]

Moreover, in radical contrast to the customary path of fledgling French intellectuals, Sorel had pursued a technical rather than a literary and humanistic education. In 1865, when he was nearly eighteen, he was admitted to the Ecole Polytechnique—the scientific and military counterpart to that other summit of the French educational system, the Ecole Normale Supérieure, where so many of the intellectual luminaries of his day were to receive their training. In 1870 he began his professional career as an engineer for the government department of bridges and roads. The next two decades were to see him moving about from one provincial center to another, pursuing with quiet efficiency his honorable calling and in his spare time reading voraciously.

This self-education in the provinces doubtless had a good deal to do with Sorel's subsequent independence and originality. By throwing him on his own and keeping him clear of the coteries of Paris, it encouraged his tendencies toward intellectual self-reliance. Sorel himself said in later life that he had spent twenty years unlearning what he had retained from his formal education.[4] After a decade and a half of this sort of preparation, he was ready for the expression of his own ideas: his first two books appeared in 1889, while he was still in government employment. Three years later, having received the recognition he considered proper with the award of the Legion of Honor, Sorel resigned from the service and settled down in the Parisian suburb of Boulogne-sur-Seine to live on a modest inheritance. The next thirty years—the years of his second life—were to see practically no change in the outward circumstances of his quiet existence. But they were to be full of the tumults aroused by his irrepressible disputatiousness.

[3] Andreu: *Sorel*, pp. 25–6.
[4] Letter to Daniel Halévy, *Reflections*, p. 32.

One further circumstance separated Sorel from his intellectual peers. His common-law wife, whom respect for his family's wishes alone kept him from marrying, was a peasant girl almost without education. Sorel carefully nurtured her mind, and she in turn, by bringing him closer to the common people, inspired his socialist studies. Her simple religious convictions were also in part responsible for the unvarying respect with which Sorel treated the history of the Catholic Church. On her death in 1897, her husband vowed the rest of his life to the cultivation of her memory.

The two earliest and most constant of the intellectual elements which produced the curious amalgam that was Sorel's mind were already in implicit contrast. By training and profession he was an engineer; by temperament he was a moralist.

The imprint of Sorel's work as an engineer never vanished from his mind. Although he completely abandoned his professional career and spent the last thirty years of his life in literary pursuits, he retained the engineer's cast of thought. His respect went to the "*makers* and *doers*" of the world: "the way of perception he most trusted was through the hand; the kind of people he most trusted were those who used their hands to deal with the world—working people and artists." [5] And he had a similar respect for the machine. The world of nature, on the other hand, he feared and distrusted. Or, more precisely, he disliked what he called "natural nature," as contrasted with the "artificial nature" that scientists and technicians imposed on the chaos of reality. This distinction between the impenetrable mysteries of nature itself and the artificial constructions of science that alone enabled man to tame it—and thereby to understand it—was absolutely central to Sorel's thought. The positivists, he argued, had never had the wit to see the difference—hence the

[5] Humphrey: *Sorel*, p. 64.

scorn that Sorel professed for what he called their
"petite science." [6]

To create "an artificial world of order"—that was
Sorel's basic and unvarying aim.[7] Even the notion of
the political myth that was to make him famous did
not contrast so totally with the thought-structure of the
technician as might at first appear. For the myth also
was an artificial construction—a handle with which to
get a hold on social reality. Similarly, it is by this route
that we can begin to discover the relation between Sorel's engineering mentality and the other original element in his psychology—his unbending moralism.

As a moralist, Sorel was old-fashioned and even prud-
ish. His rigor in sexual matters was altogether extraordinary: one can think of no other of his contemporaries
who would have argued in all seriousness that "the
world will become more just only to the extent to which
it becomes more chaste." [8] Sorel himself recognized
how deeply he felt about moral questions. In thanking
Croce for the favorable review of his *Reflections on
Violence* which the Italian scholar had published, he
noted that Croce had well discerned what was "the
great preoccupation" of his "whole life: the historical
genesis of morality." [9] This ethical rigor gives the clue
to the conservative aspects of Sorel's thought that have
appeared to be in hopeless contradiction to his better-
known insistence on revolutionary violence. If, in his
first book, on Socrates' trial, he took the unusual position of siding with the Athenian state against the philosopher, it was because he felt that Socrates was in
sober truth a corrupter, an agent of dissolution in a
society that still respected the heroic ideals of a simpler
age. Similarly, Sorel's abiding hostility to eighteenth-

[6] *"L'Expérience dans la physique moderne," De l'Utilité du
pragmatisme* (Paris, 1921), pp. 336–7; *Reflections*, p. 162.

[7] Humphrey: *Sorel*, p. 13.

[8] *"Préface pour Colajanni"* (1899), *Matériaux d'une théorie
du prolétariat* (Paris, 1919), p. 199.

[9] Letter of May 6, 1907, *La Critica*, XXVI (1928), 100.

century thought has been ascribed to his sense of shock at the "loose morality" of that era.[1]

Thus in ethical questions also it was Sorel's aim to impose an order—this time not on inanimate nature, but on primitive, brute humanity. Sorel claimed to have few illusions about mankind. His own pessimism, he declared, was essentially a "philosophy of conduct."[2] "Movements toward greatness," he explained to Croce, were "always *an effort,* and movements toward decadence always *natural.*" "Our nature," he added, "is invincibly borne toward what the philosophers of history consider as bad, whether it be barbarism or whether it be decadence."[3] Hence his lifelong quest was for a *ricorso*—a renewal of human history through the restoration of archaic and heroic values. This concept of the *ricorso*—literally a "rerunning"—Sorel had derived from Giambattista Vico, whom he had discovered even before Croce, and to whom he had devoted one of his earliest essays.[4]

Like Vico, in his attitude of "moral pessimism," Sorel warned far more against decadence than against barbarism. He even found positive virtue in a certain kind of barbarism. In common with Nietzsche, he discovered a life-giving force in the "master" morality of heroic ages.

The influence of Nietzsche on Sorel has been the subject of considerable debate. On occasion their names have been linked with Freud's as "the great prophets of the modern age."[5] Unquestionably, many of Sorel's ideas echoed those of Nietzsche: they were both implacable opponents of bourgeois mediocrity and advocates of an unsentimental ethical integrity. Yet there appears to be no evidence of a direct influence. At the time of his earliest work, which proposed an interpretation of Greek civilization strikingly similar to Nie-

---

[1] Pirou: *Sorel,* p. 14.
[2] Letter to Daniel Halévy, *Reflections,* p. 38.
[3] Letter of January 25, 1911, *La Critica,* XXVI (1928), 343.
[4] See Chapter 6.
[5] Humphrey: *Sorel,* p. 218.

tzsche's, Sorel had not yet heard of the German philosopher. A full discussion of Nietzsche's ethical theories came only in his mature writings—notably in the *Reflections on Violence*. Here once again in the history of ideas we find two thinkers independently and almost contemporaneously hitting upon the same notions.[6]

Moreover, as opposed to Nietzsche, Sorel sought a practical political manifestation of his ethical aspirations. This search for a *ricorso* offers the key to his bewildering political changes: he was constantly seeking and constantly meeting disappointment. Yet despite the pessimistic philosophy to which he formally subscribed, Sorel was blessed with a marvelous resilience. Again and again it enabled him to triumph over discouragement and to discover a new movement in which to vest his hope.

Once more the mentality of the engineer and the ethical quest of the moralist seem to have diverged. Yet once more they can be brought together—this time through the mediating influence of Vico. Vico's central dictum—that man can understand the "civil world" because he *made* it—is similarly central for Sorel. Through Vico, he had learned to associate the act of doing and the act of knowing. Scientific construction, political engagement, understanding were for Sorel simply different aspects of the same search. In his mind the *practical* concept of understanding associated with the craftsman's or technician's calling was inseparable from the notion of moral commitment, if for no other reason because the craftsmen and technicians—the heroes of the machine age—offered the loftiest contemporary examples of morality. This association will emerge more clearly when we turn to examine the successive intellectual techniques by which Sorel sought to gain a firm grip on the elusive stuff of reality.

. . .

[6] Note the contrasting statements in Meisel: *Sorel*, p. 13, and in Geneviève Bianquis: *Nietzsche en France* (Paris, 1929), pp. 83–4. The former, I believe, is the more correct interpretation.

Initially he developed the concept of *diremption*. This technique we have already encountered in discussing Sorel's reworking of Marxism. We should now look at it in the broader context of general social theory.

Sorel's clearest definition ran as follows: *diremption* meant "to examine certain parts [of a situation, a series of events, or the like] without taking into account all of the ties which connect them to the whole, to determine in some manner the character of their activity by isolating them." It offered, Sorel subsequently explained, "a symbolic knowledge of what history creates by means incommensurate with our intelligence." [7] In brief, *diremptions* were arbitrary abstractions from reality—approximately what Max Weber was to call "ideal types" or what subsequent social scientists were to speak of as "models."

But the similarity was no more than approximate. Actually Sorel's notion of an abstraction in social science was far less precise than what Weber and his intellectual descendants proposed. For an engineer, Sorel was curiously distrustful of precision. Or perhaps for that very reason he was unimpressed by it. As opposed to the social theorists who knew little of natural science and hence overvalued it, Sorel was well acquainted through personal experience with the tentative character of most scientific propositions. He knew how often their apparent precision masked the doubts and hesitations of the original researchers.

And so he warned against taking his *diremptions* too literally. Like other kinds of symbols, they should not be applied too far from the context that originally produced them: otherwise "their sense" would become "vague, their usage arbitrary, and . . . their clarity deceptive." Similarly one should "beware of . . . too great rigor in language, because it would be in contradiction with the fluid character of reality." "One should

[7] Appendix 1: "Unity and Multiplicity," added to second (1910) edition of *Reflections*, p. 287; "*Avant-propos*" (1914), *Matériaux*, p. 7.

proceed," Sorel advised, "by feeling one's way; one should try out probable and partial hypotheses, and be satisfied with provisional approximations, so as always to leave the door open to progressive correction." Moreover, many of the vaunted abstractions of social theory would on closer consideration reveal themselves as originating in the "region of common sense. . . . In this region everything blends with everything else; formulas are true and false, real and symbolical, excellent in one sense and absurd in another; everything depends on the use one makes of them." [8]

Sorel's distrust of precision, then, sprang in part from his own practical knowledge of the limitations of theory. But it also reflected a more positive aim—a desire to embrace in his writing "the fluid character of reality" itself. This was an extraordinary, indeed, an almost unique ambition in a twentieth-century social theorist. Earlier writers had thought that they were doing just that—but their notions of what constituted the world of experience had been far more summary. In general, social theorists of our own time have argued the impossibility of following the exact configurations of observed experience: they have stressed the need for setting up clarifying abstractions. And this was the attitude that Sorel himself expressed toward the physical world when he differentiated "natural" from "artificial" nature. Why, we may ask, did he attempt something so much more difficult when he approached the universe of social relations?

Herewith we come to the second formulation of his social-science method—a formulation overlapping and subtly altering the simpler concept of a *diremption*. It was a direct manifestation of the influence upon him of Henri Bergson, which, as we have seen, was particularly strong during the central years 1906–8, when he wrote

<hr />

[8] Ibid., p. 15; "*Avenir socialiste des syndicats*" (1898), *Matériaux*, p. 58; "*La necessità e il fatalismo nel marxismo*," *Saggi di critica del marxismo* (Milan, 1903), pp. 68–9.

the *Reflections on Violence* and *The Illusions of Progress*.

In this second formulation—which he actually applied contemporaneously with the first—Sorel combined his old emphasis on the changing character of all social phenomena with a new and fuller recognition of non-logical motivation. Such a recognition had always been implicit in his interest in religion and sexual morality: it now became dominant in his thought. It emerged in explicit form in the concept of the "myth."

Superficially considered, the myth would seem to be simply a rather special kind of *diremption*. Each represented a symbolic way of thinking. As Sorel used the term, however, a myth appeared to be both more and less than a *diremption*. It was more because it was not just a methodological abstraction: it was a "complex of pictures" rather than a single element taken in isolation. Hence it reflected reality at more than one point. Moreover, a myth was a non-logical, irrational affair; for that very reason it approached closer to "the fluid character of reality" than did the logically ordered abstractions that social theorists usually devised. Finally, it was what human beings in fact *acted upon*—a merely logical abstraction left them cold: in this sense also it possessed a kind of reality.

On the other hand, the myth was less than a normal *diremption* in that it was less susceptible to empirical control. As Sorel had defined the use of abstractions in social theory, they were to be constantly subject to change and correction as circumstances and the knowledge of the observer also changed. These correctives, he quite explicitly stated, applied to *diremptions*. But they did not apply to myths. The latter were autonomous, perfect in themselves, and should not be tampered with. "One must not try to analyze such complexes of pictures," Sorel warned, "as one would break a thing down into its elements; . . . one must take them as a whole, as historical forces, and . . . must above all refrain from comparing actual accomplishments with the images of them that had been generally accepted before the action." [9]

The result was a kind of sociological mysticism. Now that Sorel had given full and explicit recognition to the realm of the irrational, he did not know what to do with it. He had discovered "what Heraclitus called the 'whirl,' what Bergson called the 'flux' of cosmic process," but he refused to follow the latter's procedure of "immersion" in the flux itself.[1] He remained too much the scientist for that. He was left high and dry on the shore—alone with his inexplicable symbols. Hence he could only conclude in a kind of desperation that history presented an "inextricable complexity" and that reality remained "protected by . . . obscurity." [2]

The paradoxical result of Sorel's effort to approach closer to reality through the concept of myth had been to carry him, in the sense of comprehensible explanation, farther from it. The *diremption* method had always implied some congruence with reality. The concept of the social myth dismissed the whole question as unimportant. From this methodological *impasse* Sorel was saved, provisionally at least, by the agency of William James.

The third and final formulation of Sorel's intellectual method was in terms of philosophic pragmatism. He had reached a position similar to that of James before he had heard of the American philosopher: his unvarying insistence on the origin in *practical action* of all valid social theory already implied a pragmatic approach. Like James, Sorel distrusted merely intellectualist formulations—hence his running skirmish with eighteenth-century theories of progress and with nineteenth-century positivism. But he also agreed with James in setting strict limits to his own anti-intellectualism. Indeed he protested against the use of the term

---

[9] Letter to Daniel Halévy, *Reflections*, p. 49. I have altered the translation somewhat.

[1] Humphrey: *Sorel*, p. 136.

[2] *Les Illusions du progrès* (Paris, 1908), p. 2.

at all as a characterization of what he and James were doing: far from being anti-intellectualists, they were trying "to dispel the confusions produced by *scientism*," and so "to create full confidence in the results of the legitimate work of the intellect." [3] Both James and Sorel had no quarrel with the classic, rational, humanist tradition of European letters; indeed it was in this tradition that they had trained their minds and from it they had drawn the richness of their imagery. It was only against its abuse, in the form of merely verbal philosophic solutions, that they protested.

Hence it was natural that in his last book of essays Sorel should have tried to promote James's ideas in France and to associate them in the public mind with his own. To this cozy fraternity he added Bergson— which again was natural in view of the French philosopher's enthusiasm for his American colleague. But just as he refused to follow Bergson all the way, so Sorel felt free to criticize James in detailed respects. More particularly he argued that James had been imprudent in enrolling as philosophic allies people like Henri Poincaré, who, under the guise of "explaining in an easy fashion the revolutions that the *artificial nature* of the physicists has undergone in our era, have . . . expressed doubts on the reality of science." [4]

"The reality of science"—here, as in sexual morality, lay one of Sorel's most sensitive nerve centers. And his sensitivity on the topic prevented him from enjoying to the full his new-found pragmatist allegiance. James's blithe agnosticism toward the categories both of science and of common sense made him extremely nervous. Although Sorel was now prepared to put his trust in common sense to a far greater extent than in the past, he was constitutionally unable to share James's robust confidence in rough-and-ready intellectual procedures. Too much fastidiousness had carried over from his engineering days.

[3] "*Avant-propos*" (1917), *Pragmatisme*, pp. 2–3n.
[4] "*De Kant à William James*," ibid., pp. 84–5.

Hence the final formulation of Sorel's thought remained problematical. Indeed, it was not really a final formulation at all. "I have never asked myself," he had written to Croce, "what would be the synthesis of my various writings. I write from day to day according to the needs of the moment." [5] In this sense Sorel's method had always been pragmatic. Through the agency of William James, he had come to recognize in explicit fashion his own philosophic pluralism. But he had refused to associate himself with the skeptical and relativist attitude that such a position usually implied. He insisted on clinging to the certainties of "artificial" nature. Hence his search for reality never reached its goal. He never discovered exactly what the term meant for him. Was the notion of reality merely a methodological convenience, as James had implied? Or was there some certainty of its congruence with the world of sense experience, as the natural scientists customarily assumed? To these questions Sorel could find no clear answer. And he failed to find it because the mental formation that had given him so penetrating an insight into the social and intellectual problems of his era, at the same time held him back from developing this insight into a coherent theory of social action.

It is unquestionable that from the standpoint of Western democratic values Sorel's basic attitude was, in the words of a leading American sociologist, "morally and politically pernicious." [6] To fail to recognize all that was irrational, quixotic, and hateful in Sorel's work would be to fall into the grossest errors of "tender-mindedness." It would be equally misleading to look at Sorel *sub specie æternitatis*—to view him simply as an abstract thinker and not as a highly passionate and "committed" mortal operating in a specific historical situation. With Sorel, as with Nietzsche, it is essential

[5] Letter of April 28, 1903, *La Critica*, XXV (1927), 372.
[6] Introduction by Edward A. Shils to *Reflections*, p. 29.

to remember that he regarded his own era as one of cultural and moral slackness, and that he believed it his duty to combat "bourgeois mediocrity" by enunciating a sterner and more strenuous ethic. Hence much that we today find repellent in Sorel—notably his hatred of parliamentary Socialism and of middle-class democracy—can be ascribed to the situation in which he wrote (or better, what he believed that situation to be). Once we have recognized it for the manifest prejudice that it is, we may pass on to more abstract topics.

It is also important to stress once more—in the wake of Humphrey and Meisel, who have set the record straight—that Sorel ranks as a precursor of Communism and Fascism only in the most indirect sense. His influence on Lenin was nil: we have seen that toward Sorel the founder of modern Communism expressed sentiments far removed from the respect that the Soviet ambassador manifested in inquiring about his grave. In the case of Mussolini the problem is more complicated. Certainly Sorel said complimentary things about the future Duce both during the latter's early career as a revolutionary Socialist and during his march to power as leader of the new Fascist movement. In fact, he was almost unique in having divined as early as 1912 the unconventional course that Mussolini was to follow. But it is questionable whether Mussolini ever learned anything specific from him. He was well acquainted with Sorel's work before the war—he successively praised it and damned it as Sorel's political position changed—but there is no truth in the legend that the two knew each other personally. Essentially Mussolini seems to have arrived at his notions of political action by himself. These notions paralleled Sorel's while omitting their subtleties. Mussolini did not need Sorel to teach him how to climb to power: he was a far better political tactician than his presumed master. But once he was safely installed there he found it convenient to cite Sorel's writings to rationalize and give intellectual re-

spectability to what he had done on his own—just as
he was to cite Nietzsche and William James and a number of others.[7]

When all this has been said, we can safely return to
Sorel as a social thinker in the broader sense. As I stated
at the beginning of the chapter, it is extremely difficult
to classify him or to rank him among his contemporaries. As one of the loosely associated group of French
writers who sought to correct the long-standing Gallic
tradition of "general ideas" and Cartesian categories,
he was a better thinker than Péguy but less influential
than Bergson. As a sociologist, he ranks far below Max
Weber or Durkheim or even Pareto: his method was
too discursive for the elaboration of systematic social
theory. As a philosopher of history, he could see many
of the same problems as Croce, but he saw them less
clearly. Why, then, do we bother so much about him?

Sorel, I believe, is one of those thinkers who are important for the problems they raise rather than for
those that they solve. He is in the tradition of the great
questioners, the great troublers of the ready-made and
the generally accepted, men such as Peter Abelard and
Nietzsche—and Socrates. The Socratic parallel may
seem odd in view of the unkind things that Sorel wrote
in his first book, but it is as apt as any other. Indeed,
we who have never known Sorel personally are in no
position to judge his influence fully: those who did
know him testify that he was at his best not in his writings but in the more Socratic relationship of personal
intellectual exchange.[8] The ruddy cheeks, the white
beard, the flashing blue eyes—these physical attributes,
to which Sorel's younger contemporaries have so often
alluded, underscored the *brio* of his conversation to
make an indelible personal impression.

Sorel was most effective, then, as a *critical* thinker.
His passionate personal engagements, his tackings, veer-

[7] Andreu: *Sorel*, pp. 106–9; Gaudens Megaro: *Mussolini in
the Making* (London, 1938), pp. 228–45.
[8] Andreu: *Sorel*, pp. 286–7.

ings, and inconsistencies—the whole complex of emotions that has been called his "fanaticism"—gave him a unique critical stance from which to demolish intellectual humbug. The very astigmatic quality of his vision made it all the more penetrating. At the same time, his intellectual eccentricity landed him in inextricable confusions. Two at least of these antinomies deserve some final consideration.

In the first place, Sorel never succeeded in achieving the minimum of separation between his abstract social theories and his political commitments which would have made the former viable in their own right. Indeed he believed that it would be fruitless to try to do so. Here Sorel was stating in an extreme and indefensible form what has become a truism of contemporary social theory. Obviously he was right in maintaining that no sociologist nor political writer could completely divorce himself from his own ethical presuppositions. But he failed to recognize the extent to which this was indeed possible, just as he failed to discern the complexity of the problem of "objectivity" in social science as Max Weber was to define it in classic form.[9] Hence I think that Pareto was only half correct when he wrote in his obituary article that one could accept the analytical part of Sorel's work while rejecting the latter's ethical aspirations for the future.[1] These aspirations were too tightly woven into the analysis itself to be readily separable from it.

In the second place, Sorel never found a proper vocabulary nor a suitable conceptual scheme into which he could fit what his critical intelligence had taught him. Like Freud, he had inherited from his early training a mechanistic vocabulary that only inadequately expressed his later discoveries. And when he tried to find a substitute for it, he hit on nothing more helpful than the colorful but imprecise metaphor of the social

---

[9] See Chapter 8.
[1] Pareto: "Sorel," p. 545.

myth. Sorel knew that the positivists were in error. But he discovered no new concept of scientific understanding that would carry a conviction of certainty equal to theirs. Sorel had embarked on his course of abstract inquiry too late in life: he found himself hovering in a twilight zone between nineteenth-century faith in naturalistic science and twentieth-century confidence in the construction of precise abstractions. He was sufficiently discriminating to make the all-important distinction between "natural" and "artificial" nature. His *"diremptions"* and "myths" offered the elements at least of a coherent theory. But he was unable to fit the pieces together. Men half a generation younger than he, Benedetto Croce and Max Weber, were to be the first to approach the resolution of the dilemmas that had left Sorel at a loss.

6

Neo-Idealism in History

1. The German Idealist Tradition

IN Germany positivism never gained as great a hold
as in France or Italy. To a German, an idealist philosophy was a kind of second nature. For it was in this
mold that German thought had been cast in the great
era from the mid-eighteenth century to the Revolution
of 1848. Kant, as we have seen, remained the dominant
formative influence on the German mind. And Kant's
contemporaries Goethe and Schiller—the classical writers on whom German schoolboys were nurtured—
taught what was usually taken to be a similar lesson. A
generation later, and in more dogmatic and eccentric
form, Hegel had reinforced the same precepts: like his
predecessors, he had built out his doctrine from the
idealist premise that the ultimate reality of the universe
lay in "spirit" or "idea" rather than in the data of sense
perception.

This conviction was what separated most decisively
the German philosophic tradition from the European

norm. In the dominant Anglo-French tradition the primacy of sense perception and the validity of empirical procedures were taken for granted as naturally as the supremacy of the "idea" was accepted in Germany. And from these assumptions there followed certain familiar consequences: utilitarianism and positivism, democracy and natural science, in Britain and France became logical sets of partners. In Germany it was quite otherwise. Hence there came about that parting of the ways, that separation of Germany from the main stream of Western European social thought, which was to torment the minds of Ernst Troeltsch and Friedrich Meinecke.[1] Why was it, they asked themselves, that from "shallow" philosophies of history and society the British and the French had been able to develop political practices that were both viable and humane, whereas the Germans, with their "deeper" understanding, not only had failed to achieve a social equilibrium, but as the twentieth century advanced, were ever more obviously succumbing to the "demon" of naked physical power?

This was the political form in which the question presented itself to the minds of sensitive Germans. In its political guise the problem of Germany's divergence from the main stream of Western European development is only peripheral to the present study. But it suggests the central paradox of the idealist tradition. In the period from about 1770 to 1840 the German philosophers and writers had been the schoolmasters of Europe: from them the French and British and Italians had learned to be dissatisfied with merely intellectualist explanations and to seek out the living and growing stuff of history and society themselves. From the influence of the German school of historical idealism the canons of social study emerged immeasurably enriched. Yet in the sense of *applied* wisdom this teaching came

[1] Hajo Holborn: "*Der deutsche Idealismus in sozialgeschichtlicher Beleuchtung,*" *Historische Zeitschrift,* CLXXIV (October 1952), 359–60.

to next to nothing. The great political innovations of the nineteenth century were based on presuppositions derived from the century preceding and, in a philosophical sense, already out of date.

Once again in the period from the 1880's to the First World War, the revivifying breath was to come from Germany: figures as diverse, as independent one of another, and as mutually contradictory as Nietzsche and Dilthey were to serve as the heralds of the intellectual renewal of the 1890's. Yet once again these new teachings came to nothing—or, perhaps, in view of the experience of the 1930's and 1940's, to what we may consider worse than nothing. The paradox remained—indeed, was intensified: intellectual creativity and destruction flowed from a common source. This consideration, I reiterate, figures only in the background of the present study. But it suggests why any pragmatic judgment on the German idealist tradition must necessarily be ambivalent.

In the study of history and society, the reign of Hegel had been dramatic but brief. After the middle of the century, he remained little but a memory. Only through his Marxist heirs did he survive as a living force. The more permanent influence was that of a man twenty-five years Hegel's junior—and who had the good fortune to outlive him by more than half a century—the historian Leopold von Ranke. In his incredibly long career as a practicing historian, which embraced the six decades from the mid-1820's to his death in 1886, Ranke attained to a position of unexampled pre-eminence. The leading professors of Germany had been his students—foreigners eager to learn the new method of German historical scholarship came to work in his seminar—even the study of economics in Germany was reinforced in its characteristically historical cast through the labors of Ranke's pupil Wilhelm Roscher.

Ranke was closer than Hegel to the spiritual world of Romanticism. For all his emphasis on meticulous research methods, Ranke's categories of thought resem-

bled those of the Romantics. Like them, he dealt in
spiritual entities that were "intuited" and "contem-
plated" in semi-mystical fashion, rather than in firm
concepts, empirically tested or logically analyzed. And
in these procedures, Ranke's method was typical of
German idealism. In history and in economics, in sociology and in law, social thought in Germany was
based on a few fairly simple principles, which, across all
differences of method and field, remained surprisingly
uniform.

The basic tenets of idealist social thought can be
briefly summarized.[2] Between the phenomenal and the
spiritual world, between the world of natural science
and the world of human activity, a radical cleavage was
presumed to exist. Hence the Germans came to draw
a sharp distinction between *Naturwissenschaft*, or natural science, and the *Geisteswissenschaften*, the "cultural sciences" or "sciences of the mind"—including
both what we would call the humanities and what we
would call history or social science. The cultural sciences, then, could not possibly take their cue from natural science, as the positivists advocated. Indeed, they
could not search for general "laws" at all. "Hence the
tendency for the idealistic interest in human action to
issue in two main directions—detailed, concrete history
on the one hand, the philosophy of history on the
other."[3] The painstaking investigators of minute detail were obviously at home in the German tradition.
At the other end of the scale, the builders of vast, metaphysically based historical systems, like Hegel, or the
architects of ambitious critiques of historical thinking
itself, like Dilthey or Rickert, were equally, or even
more, in their element. The middle level of social study,
however, the level of careful synthesis and the modest
testing of hypothesis, tended to drop out entirely. This

[2] I am following the schema presented by Talcott Parsons in
his *The Structure of Social Action*, second edition (Glencoe, Ill.,
1949), pp. 473–87.
[3] Ibid., p. 475.

is the bewildering thing about the example set by Ranke: in his more obvious guise, he was an ultra-conscientious seeker after "facts"; temperamentally, he was a metaphysician—if of a peculiarly vague and unsatisfactory sort; almost never did he "reason" about history in an unambiguously communicable fashion.[4]

If the defining element in the "cultural sciences" was their spiritual character, then the "spirit" of a social or historical institution was obviously what was of central importance. In the idealist tradition, "the unifying concept under which discrete empirical data were subsumed"—as opposed to the general "laws" of positivist theory—"was . . . a particular, unique *Geist*, a specific cultural totality clearly distinct from and incommensurable with all others."[5] These *Geister* were the deepest (or highest?) stuff of which history and society were made, but who could presume to understand them, or to compare them one with another? In their unique individuality, they remained—to use Goethe's expression—"ineffable." Spengler alone pushed this emphasis on the unique to its ultimate absurdity by arguing that the spirit of one civilization was necessarily incomprehensible to a member of another (and even he did not practice what he preached). But for German idealist thought as a whole the problem of how one could possibly arrive at an understanding of human (i.e., spiritual) behavior remained peculiarly vexing. A positivist-type determination of the "causes" of an action clearly would not do. A more flexible procedure, free from mechanistic or naturalistic taint, was urgently required.

The result was the elaboration of the method of inner understanding, or *Verstehen*. This procedure I personally have found to be the most difficult intellectual problem that I have confronted in the present study— the murkiest of the many dark corners in the labyrinth of German social-science method. Dilthey seems to

---

[4] See, in this connection, Theodore H. Von Laue: *Leopold Ranke: The Formative Years* (Princeton, N.J., 1950).

[5] Parsons: *Structure of Social Action*, p. 478.

have been the first to give the procedure a fairly explicit formulation. But it was at Max Weber's hands that its implications for the study of society were most thoroughly elucidated. Hence we may best postpone its further consideration until we come to the work of Weber himself [6]—and after we have analyzed the comparable method that Croce devised in quite a different context.

Meantime it will perhaps suffice to recall that Bergson's recourse to the faculty of intuition had much in common with what his German contemporaries were advocating. Bergson, we may remember, was emphatic in his denial that he meant the same thing by "intuition" as what the Romanticists had sought to convey: he was not attacking, as they had, the claims of reason and of science; he was, rather, trying to supplement and to complete the work of the intellect. Similarly the German neo-idealists of the period from the 1880's to the First World War had a far more sophisticated grasp of the role of natural science than had the original philosophers and historians of the idealist tradition. We may surmise that had Bergson lived in Germany, rather than on the more inhospitable soil of France, he might have found other thinkers who would have understood what he was trying to accomplish. He would perhaps have made the acquaintance of rigorous social theorists who could have tempered his wilder fancies while urging him toward the concrete social applications that Sorel had suggested. In France, unfortunately, he was left to the mercies of the religious enthusiasts who encouraged the turn toward social mysticism that in the end rendered his doctrine so barren of results.

By the 1880's the intellectual situation in Germany was about as follows. Positivism, as we have seen, had made few professed converts. But in a more diffused sense, the positivist mentality had advanced mightily.

[6] See Chapter 8.

The great period of German philosophy was over: to the natural scientists there was accruing the prestige of culture-symbols that had formerly been enjoyed by the philosophers. Similarly the writing of history had apparently seen its best days: Ranke had long outlived his own epoch, and his pupils and the pupils of his pupils had maintained only a part of his inheritance; the spiritual aspect of his teaching had largely been lost, and it was no more than his methodology, with its emphasis on meticulous care and *Sitzfleisch,* that was still held in honor. Indeed, in a pedestrian and unphilosophic sense, a number of the latter-day Rankeans behaved much like positivists.

The problem, then, that the more imaginative thinkers of the era confronted was how to restore the Romantic sense of the historical and ideal world without falling into the errors of the original Romanticists. More particularly, the contemporary situation offered the challenge of engaging the positivists on their own ground—that is, without recourse to the now discredited metaphysics of Romanticism.[7]

By the first decade of the twentieth century, this challenge had been successfully met. The university students were flocking back to historical and cultural studies. "At the turn of the century," Meinecke recalled, "the number of students of . . . history had . . . everywhere sunk to a low figure; after that, however, it mounted again to such an extent that the decade prior to the First World War can rank as a golden age of historical . . . and philosophical study." [8]

We may further recall the thrill of sympathetic participation with which Meinecke had responded to Wilhelm Windelband's "declaration of war against positivism" in the latter's rectoral address of 1894, and his sense of spiritual affinity with the southwest German

[7] Pietro Rossi: *Lo storicismo tedesco contemporaneo* (Turin, 1956), pp. 17–18.

[8] *Strassburg/Freiburg/Berlin 1901–1919: Erinnerungen* (Stuttgart, 1949), p. 22.

school of philosophy. Windelband's address was to
sound in retrospect like the opening shot in the counter-
offensive of German idealism. In actuality, Dilthey's
Einleitung in die Geisteswissenschaften had preceded
it by eleven years. But Dilthey had written too early. It
was not until the 1890's that the educated German public was prepared to listen.

The southwest Germans Windelband and Rickert—
and the philosopher and sociologist Georg Simmel,
whose theoretical work was loosely affiliated with theirs
—have been conventionally labeled neo-Kantians. That
is, their effort to combat the doctrine of positivism has
been viewed as springing from presuppositions handed
down by Kant. Like him, they were trying to determine
categories of thought—and more particularly to distinguish between the categories employed in the cultural
sciences and those characteristic of natural science. In
general, the neo-Kantians located the difference between the two in the *methods* each one employed—
rather than in scientific object or subject matter, which
was one of their points of difference with Dilthey. The
cultural sciences, they argued, were directed toward the
understanding of "particular events" rather than the
formulation of "general laws," as was the case with natural science.

So far this was little more than a truism of historical
thinking in the idealist tradition. Where the neo-
Kantians—and Rickert in particular—refined on that
tradition was in trying to determine more explicitly
how it was possible to explain the world of human history at all. If the cultural sciences did not seek general
laws, in the fashion of the natural sciences, what intellectual operation did they in fact perform in confronting the overwhelming mass of "particular events"?
Ranke, we may recall, had offered little more helpful
than the notion of contemplation. Rickert added the
suggestion that cultural scientists made *choices*—that
is, by their own subjective decision, they chose to examine and to understand one aspect of social reality

rather than another. And such choices necessarily had as their base the investigator's own value-system.

This theory of choice and value was immensely clarifying. It represented a legacy of permanent usefulness for contemporary social study: we shall see later how Weber worked from Rickert's scheme of categories into his own still more fruitful methodological labors. But Rickert's theory had one grave drawback. In putting its whole emphasis on the notion of value, it implied a radically subjective conception of historical knowledge. Value in the social and historical world could not be arrived at by any verifiable process: it could only be "intuited." Hence there was no guarantee of its validity. Ultimately the historian was reduced to an act of faith in his own values.

From this dilemma, the only escape-route was by way of metaphysics. And this was the one that Rickert eventually took. By the logic of his own argument he was driven to an assertion of the absolute validity of the historian's value-system, based on the postulate of a "normal consciousness" in humanity. But such a postulate was nothing if not metaphysical. It implied that values had an independent and transcendental existence outside and above the consciousness of the individual historian.

Thus the neo-Kantians had not really met the positivists on their own ground. In the end, they had been forced, like the Romantics, to have recourse to metaphysics. They had approached with courage and imagination the problem of distinguishing the cultural sciences from the sciences of nature. But they had found no permanently satisfactory solution. The problem remained open.[9]

[9] Rossi: *Storicismo tedesco,* pp. 178–9, 183, 187, 205–7.

II. *Dilthey and the Definition of the "Cultural Sciences"*

Like his contemporary Henry Adams, Wilhelm Dilthey was so old-fashioned that by the end of his life he had become a modern. Like Adams, Dilthey lived in the spiritual world of the eighteenth and early nineteenth centuries; the main part of his own century passed him by; as an old man he found himself rather surprisingly cast in the role of a pathfinder to the thought of the new century that was opening.

Dilthey was born in 1833, five years before Adams, and died in 1911, seven years before the death of his American counterpart. Thus he was already fifty when his *Einleitung in die Geisteswissenschaften* was published. And it was to be another decade before his real influence began. Success came to him suddenly at the end of his life: by the time of his retirement he was lecturing in the largest hall that the University of Berlin could provide.

By that time also he had come a long way from his intellectual origins. The son of a Protestant pastor of the Rhineland, Dilthey had been nurtured on music and liberal theology. His earliest intellectual enthusiasm had been for the Romantic theologian Schleiermacher, and he had originally intended to go into the ministry himself. But his university studies had veered increasingly toward philosophy and history: in Berlin he had encountered Ranke, already venerable, and Johann Gustav Droysen—thirteen years Ranke's junior and of a more Hegelian cast of mind—on whom was to devolve the task of maintaining the tradition of historical idealism during the high tide of positivist influence.

In 1867 Dilthey received his first professorship—of philosophy, rather than of theology or history—at the University of Basel, where he knew Burckhardt and (ironic accident) barely missed meeting Nietzsche. He subsequently lectured at Kiel and Breslau, and, in

1882, was elevated to the chair that had been Hegel's at the University of Berlin. By this time his *Einleitung* was nearly completed, and his own intellectual concerns had been pretty well fixed. These were a curious and rather unstable combination of Kantian memories, strict historical training, a nostalgia for the spiritual world of the Enlightenment, a respect for the aims of positivist investigation, and, still hovering in the background, the misty pantheism of Romantic theology. A gentle and conciliatory spirit, Dilthey was to strive mightily to bring his diverse orientations into some sort of synthesis and to leave behind him a major work of philosophical integration.[1]

This was to be a Critique of Historical Reason. What Kant had done for "pure" and "practical" reason, Dilthey sought to accomplish for the field of history, which the master of German philosophers had neglected. The planned critique of the categories of historical thinking was never completed. Massive fragments of it, however, form a large share of Dilthey's published writings. Essentially what happened was that in the three decades that followed the publication of the *Einleitung*—a mere "introduction," as its title indicated—he kept constantly reworking and changing his ideas, constantly recasting them in the form of new books and essays that he was unable to bring to completion.

In a study like this it is obviously impossible to present any complete analysis of the work of so versatile and complex a thinker as Dilthey. Moreover, he is not a member of our "generation of the 1890's": he is

[1] Biographical details can be found in Otto Friedrich Bollnow: *Dilthey: Eine Einführung in seine Philosophie* (Leipzig, 1936), *passim*; H. A. Hodges: *The Philosophy of Wilhelm Dilthey* (London, 1952), pp. xiii–xv; Hajo Holborn: "Wilhelm Dilthey and the Critique of Historical Reason," *Journal of the History of Ideas*, XI (January 1950), 93; William Kluback: *Wilhelm Dilthey's Philosophy of History* (New York, 1956), pp. 3–51; and the introduction by Georg Misch to Vol. 5 of Dilthey's *Gesammelte Schriften* (Leipzig and Berlin, 1924), pp. vii–cxvii.

rather a great precursor. My purpose is simply to outline the major problems of historical criticism that
Dilthey faced, and to distinguish those among them
for which he offered solutions that have proved to be
permanently useful, as opposed to those problems before which he found himself baffled—and for which his
tentative answers anticipated the more self-confident
labors of younger men such as Croce and Weber.

One may state Dilthey's significance in most general
fashion by characterizing his work as the first thoroughgoing and sophisticated confrontation of history with
positivism and natural science. In this respect he faced
quite a different problem from Kant's, and toward him,
their common master, he displayed more independence
than had Windelband and Rickert. With the publication of his *Einleitung,* Dilthey plunged into what
was to be "both the vocation and the torment of his
whole life: the problem of the scientific value of historical writing."

> In this new field . . . he remained faithful to the
> aversion to every kind of dogmatism that had been
> the dominant note in his mentality from the start.
> According to him, the historical and social sci-
> ences had been hand-maidens to metaphysics right
> up to the end of the eighteenth century; emanci-
> pated through the work of the [German] historical
> school, but without philosophical legitimation,
> they were now, with the appearance of positivism,
> running the risk of relapsing into their former slav-
> ery. To save them he wrote the *Einleitung in die
> Geisteswissenschaften.*[2]

The novelty of this effort lay in the fact that it sought
to combat positivism with its own weapons. Spurning
the help of metaphysics, Dilthey gave explicit recognition to the validity of scientific investigation. Indeed,
one of the most telling observations he directed against

[2] Carlo Antoni: *Dallo storicismo alla sociologia* (Florence,
1940), p. 18.

positivism was the reproach that it was just as meta-physical as the idealist philosophies it had supplanted: the abstractions of positivism were simply implied rather than paraded. With science and the scientific method, Dilthey had no quarrel. His aim, rather, was to dispel the current confusion of the world of nature with the world of human activity. Both realms, Dilthey argued, could be studied in scientific fashion. But it was a different *type* of science from what ordinarily passed by that name that was directed toward the world of culture, society, and history. The *Einleitung* sought to delimit this second type of scientific study.[3]

The distinction between natural and cultural science, Dilthey contended, could be found "on the three-fold planes of difference in fields of research, in forms of experience, and in attitudes on the part of the inves-tigator." [4] The first difference was obvious—although it was one to which Windelband and Rickert paid little attention. The latter two might be epitomized in the simple formulation that knowledge in the field of cul-tural science was derived through some kind of *internal* process—through living experience and understanding—rather than merely externally, as was the case with nat-ural science. Hence meaning in history was not fixed, but changed with the situation in time and culture of the historian himself, and with the active decisions he took in his personal world.[5]

The basic distinction between cultural and natural science Dilthey further refined by distinguishing three classes of statements in the field of cultural study. The first class dealt with reality itself: this was the field of history. The second class consisted of abstractions from

[3] Throughout this discussion one should bear in mind that the German word "*Wissenschaft*" is more inclusive than our word "science"—comprising, in addition to systematic science, what we should call mere "learning."

[4] Rossi: *Storicismo tedesco*, p. 58.

[5] Dilthey: *Gesammelte Schriften*, I (Leipzig and Berlin, 1922), pp. 97, 109.

reality—what we should call social science. Finally
there were the statements that expressed value judgments and "rules," "the practical ingredient of the cultural sciences." For our present purposes, Dilthey's second class of statements is the most interesting. For
these, he maintained, provided historical study with
the analytical tools it required: social science was essential to understanding the historical world. But this
kind of analytical theory could illuminate the investigation only intermittently: the greater part of the time
the historian must rely on something resembling the
"fantasy of the artist." [6]

Theoretically, within Dilthey's schema, the number
of disciplines of the second type could be multiplied
indefinitely. For the creation of a new cultural or social
science, he maintained, did not depend on "staking
out" a new "terrain." It depended, rather, on devising
a new way of cutting into an already existing body of
data. Some of these ways of cutting into the stuff of
historical life Dilthey found over-abstract and tainted
with metaphysics: this he held to be true of sociology,
which—writing as he did before the work of Durkheim,
Weber, and the other founders of the discipline as we
know it today—he could visualize only in the dogmatic
and *a priori* form in which Comte and Spencer had cast
it. It was economics and psychology, rather, that Dilthey fixed on as the models for abstracting sciences in
the cultural world.[7]

Dilthey's encounter with psychology has provoked
more controversy than any other aspect of his thought.
The central position it occupied in his interest is suggested by the fact that the next of his major theoretical works following the publication of the *Einleitung*
was an attempt to establish a "descriptive and analytical psychology." [8] Some critics—particularly those faith-

    6 Ibid., pp. 26, 40.
    7 Ibid., pp. 85, 91–2.
    8 "*Ideen über eine beschreibende und zergliedernde Psy-
chologie,*" *Gesammelte Schriften,* V, 139–240.

ful to the example of Croce—have viewed Dilthey's
effort to ally history with psychology as a capitulation
to positivism. Others—to my mind with more justice—
have seen it as a courageous effort to break loose from
the excessively formalistic psychology of his own day.
Like Bergson, Dilthey sought to shift the basis of psychological theorizing from schematic abstraction to the
"immediate data of consciousness." And he has likewise been alleged to have had an influence on Freud.
For this latter affiliation, I have found no direct evidence. But it is unquestionable that Dilthey's mind
worked in sympathy with that of William James.
When the latter first met Dilthey in Berlin in 1867, he
was much attracted by him and distressed that he could
not see more of him. Three decades later, when *The
Varieties of Religious Experience* appeared, Dilthey
praised it as the great American contribution to the
psychological understanding of religion.[9] Respect between the two was mutual. Indeed, one critic has gone
so far as to call Dilthey "the German William James." [1]

Dilthey's work on psychology was intended as a preparatory study for the second volume of his *Einleitung*.
But this second part never appeared. In the meantime
Dilthey's ideas had begun to shift, and he had become
obsessed by the epistemological problems that his earlier writing had left unsolved. He had discovered that
it was not enough simply to state that the cultural sciences dealt in some sort of inner understanding gained
through sympathetic experience. It was necessary to explain what one meant by that experience and exactly
what processes the mind of the investigator performed
in arriving at an understanding of human culture.

[9] Compare the statements in Antoni: *Dallo storicismo*, pp.
9, 18, and of R. G. Collingwood in *The Idea of History* (Oxford,
1946), pp. 173–5, with those of Holborn in his "Dilthey and
the Critique," pp. 96, 109, 111.

[1] Albert Salomon: "German Sociology," in Georges Gurvitch
and Wilbert E. Moore, editors: *Twentieth Century Sociology*
(New York, 1945), p. 591.

Hence in his last writings Dilthey struggled with the task of defining the relationship among the functions of "experience," "expression," and "understanding"— in brief, how one went about "constructing" the historical world. For it was with a plastic, an architectural metaphor, that Dilthey characterized the task of the historian or social scientist in his last major theoretical writing.[2]

To the problem of historical knowledge, Dilthey gave no conclusive answer. This is the major area in which subsequent writers have preferred Croce's clearer—if excessively simplified—solution, or Weber's pragmatic and relativist approach. Indeed, there is much in Dilthey that from our present vantage-point sounds like an anticipation of Croce. There is, for example, his contention—ultimately derived from Vico—that subject and object, the student and the data, in cultural study are not of a radically different character, as is the case in natural science, but rather belong to the same universe of human history. There is the characterization of the historian's work as a re-living or re-experiencing of the past. There is the assertion that this process of re-experiencing—and more particularly the creative act through which the historian seeks to express the understanding at which he has arrived—partakes at least as much of art as it does of science. And finally there is the recognition that the historian's focus of interest and value-system necessarily spring from his own historical situation.

But it would be unfair to regard Dilthey simply as Croce's precursor. In some respects, Dilthey saw farther than Croce: he grappled with problems that the latter either evaded or denied. Dilthey was more aware than Croce of the intimate relation of history to social science: while the former tried to outline a psychology of the future, the latter cavalierly dismissed the whole sub-

---

[2] "*Der Aufbau der geschichtlichen Welt in den Geisteswissenschaften," Gesammelte Schriften,* VII (Leipzig and Berlin, 1927), pp. 77–188.

ject as the misbegotten offspring of philosophical naturalism. Dilthey's sweep was universal: he strove to reduce to order the multifarious realms of knowledge, the conflicting traditions of cultural study, that he had embraced. Croce more realistically fixed his beacon lights on a few unassailable positions, and from these he surveyed only the areas of human existence on which their beams directly shone.

Thus Dilthey laid out a program that no mortal—and certainly no one whose mind had been formed in the third quarter of the nineteenth century—could hope to bring to completion. Like Weber—and less successfully than Weber—he attempted a synthesis too mighty for the human mind. In the last part of his life, we are told, the torment of his unfinished books kept him from sleeping at night. More particularly he struggled —without success—for an escape from the skeptical and relativist implications of his own thought. "Historical skepticism," he noted, "can be overcome only if the [historian's] method does not need to rely upon the determination of motives." [3] But this "determination of motives" was exactly what his own marriage of history with psychology had implied. If one were to proceed in psychological fashion and try to reach a sympathetic understanding of the motives of historical actors, then there was no fixed ethical standard on which one could call for help. There were no norms against which conflicting values could be judged. And Dilthey scorned to appeal, as the neo-Kantians did, to transcendental values of a metaphysical character.

Yet despite its inconclusiveness, Dilthey's work exerted enormous influence. The distinction he had drawn between natural and cultural science became standard for historians and, to a lesser extent, for social scientists also. After Dilthey historians no longer needed to apologize for the "unscientific" character of their discipline: they understood why its methods could

[3] *"Plan der Fortsetzung zum Aufbau der geschichtlichen Welt in den Geisteswissenschaften," Gesammelte Schriften,* VII, 260.

never be quite the same as those of natural science. And the contemporary tradition of intellectual history—of which Meinecke was to be the most distinguished exponent—grew naturally out of Dilthey's teaching.[4] Indeed, the present study itself, in conception and orientation, has its origins in the canons for the philosophical investigation of society which Dilthey originally established.

III. *Benedetto Croce: From the "First Essays" to the "Historiography"*

"The essence of philosophy," Bergson once said, "is the spirit of simplicity." From whatever point of view we look at it, "we always find that its complication is superficial, its constructions mere accessories, its work of synthesis an illusion: to philosophize is a simple act."[5] Bergson delivered these words in Croce's native land at the philosophical congress held at Bologna in 1911. In that year the French philosopher was at the height of his fame, and his slightly younger Italian colleague was just on the verge of completing the series of systematic studies that were to give him a position of unquestioned pre-eminence among Italian philosophers.

The master of twentieth-century French philosophy and his Italian counterpart had in common the elegant simplicity of their literary style. Croce's, in fact, was even more direct than Bergson's, less burdened with metaphor and more colloquial. In both cases the ease with which his works could be read no doubt contributed to the philosopher's personal ascendancy. And Bergson and Croce had other things in common—notably their reliance on some sort of intuitive faculty. But Croce refused to recognize the association: he in-

---

[4] Holborn: "Dilthey and the Critique," pp. 116–17.
[5] "*L'Intuition philosophique*," *La Pensée et le mouvant: Essais et conférences* (Paris, 1934), p. 139.

sisted that his own procedure had risen to the level of precise concepts, while Bergson's had lingered back in the realm of the non-logical. In the French writer's work he detected "a certain philosophical romanticism" which was repugnant to his limpid Mediterranean mind.[6]

I have been unable to discover any occasion on which Croce deigned to comment on the writings of Freud. Weber likewise fell outside his ken. For although Croce was immensely learned and immensely well read, he did not feel it necessary to keep abreast of all the intellectual innovations of his time: he dealt only with those that seemed relevant to his current interests. Independent, serene, inordinately secure in his intellectual poise and self-esteem, Croce went his own way, untroubled and certain of his course. Only briefly during the First World War did he permit himself to falter. There is something delightfully anachronistic about the spectacle of such self-assurance in our tormented century.

The range of Croce's thought was encyclopedic. The corpus of his writings extends to something over sixty volumes—and this does not include all the miscellaneous reviews published in *La Critica,* the journal of his personal intellectual development which he edited from 1903 on. For half a century he exercised a kind of benevolent dictatorship over Italian literary and philosophical life. Not since Goethe had any single individual dominated so completely the culture of a major European country.

In the non-Italian world, however, Croce exerted his influence primarily as a historian and critical philosopher of history. And it is in this guise that we shall treat him in the present study. Furthermore in this capacity it is perfectly proper to make him the central figure of a chapter in which all the other protagonists are Germans. For Croce's philosophical and historical educa-

[6] Manlio Ciardo: *"Croce e Bergson nel pensiero contemporaneo,"* in Francesco Flora, editor: *Benedetto Croce* (Milan, 1953), p. 384.

tion was very largely German: although he never studied outside his own country—and, in fact, was mostly
self-taught—it was the reading of Germanic theory that
formed his standards of historical scholarship and his
canons of critical interpretation. Along with the Italians Vico and De Sanctis, his philosophical master was
Hegel—and, of course, Karl Marx.

We have analyzed already the Marxian phase of
Croce's intellectual growth. And we have seen how by
1900 he had shaken himself free from this transitory
obsession. We should now retrace our steps to examine
the earlier and more permanent influences that went
into the formation of his mature thought.

Born of wealthy parents in the province of Aquila in
the Abruzzi—the northernmost region of the Italian
south—Benedetto Croce was taken as a child to live in
Naples. And a Neapolitan he remained for the rest of
his life—not merely in the sense of having his residence
in the southern capital, but as a vibrantly sympathetic
participant in its life. For Croce came to love Naples
with a passion—and to love both what was base and
what was exalted in its tradition. Its squalor and noise
did not repel him: he diligently searched its narrow
streets for traces of its past; its popular songs and stories
enchanted him; to the end of his life he laced his conversation with Neapolitan dialect. Similarly he was
proud to succeed to the paradoxical tradition that had
made Naples—whose general cultural level seemed far
below that of the Italian north—a city of philosophers,
and more particularly the home of the founder of the
philosophical tradition in modern historiography, Giambattista Vico.

In 1883, when he was seventeen years old, Croce lost
both his parents in an earthquake on the island of
Ischia. There followed the period of his life that he
was to describe in retrospect as "a bad dream . . . the
darkest and most bitter years" he was ever to experi-

ence. In charitable fashion, the orphaned boy had been
taken into the household of his uncle Silvio Spaventa
in Rome. Spaventa was a man of considerable standing,
a philosopher of repute and a leader of the old Right
in Italian politics, but he seems to have had almost no
influence on the young Croce. The latter's Hegelian
propensities have quite wrongly been ascribed to his
uncle's teaching, and so far as politics was concerned,
he was distressed by the sarcastic fashion in which Spaventa and his friends attacked the government of their
country. In 1876, the old Right, which six years before
had achieved its task of completing the unification of
Italy, had been expelled from the direction of public
affairs. They were never to return to power: frustrated
of practical influence, they could only rail at the mediocre politicians of the Left who had displaced them.
In these judgments the young Croce felt unable to con-
cur. Forty years later, when he wrote the history of his
own time, he undertook to redress the balance—to
grant their due to Depretis and his successors as constructive rulers of Italy.

Thus stranded in Rome with "no friends and no
amusements," Croce did not have the heart to follow in
more than desultory fashion his studies at the university. The only lectures that appealed to him were those
on moral philosophy of Antonio Labriola, who had not
yet begun to discuss the writings of Marx. For the most
part Croce simply studied on his own the topics—
chiefly literary—that happened to interest him: "I used
to pursue researches into subjects chosen by myself, in-
venting my methods . . . as I went along, hesitating,
making mistakes, working too little at some things and
too much at others." After three years of this sort of
existence, he was glad to escape back to Naples. Here
he settled down to the life that was to be his for more
than sixty years—the life of a private scholar, with neither academic degree nor university affiliation, independent financially and independent in the spirit.

In Naples Croce "entered a society of librarians,

keepers of archives, scholars, antiquaries, and such-like
good, worthy, gentle souls, old or middle-aged men for
the most part, not much given to thinking." And for
the six years from 1886 to 1892 he plunged with enthusiasm into the study of the antiquities of his native
city.[7] Unlike so many other philosophers of history,
Croce learned about historical study the hard way,
through the minute investigation of difficult and apparently trivial material. Federico Chabod has given us a
delightful glimpse of the young scholar's manner of life
during this period: from nine in the morning until four
in the afternoon he would work in the state archives,
then shift over to another library until late in the evening, and finally, "after . . . eleven hours of fasting,
dine in a modest eating-house, until at length he would
trot on a donkey's back up the hillside" to his lodging.[8]

In his mature years Croce was to judge with severity
his antiquarian and unphilosophical youth. But we
should be very wrong to follow him too literally in this
negative verdict or to see him in the conventional image of the bloodless scholar. Actually Croce's researches
into the details of the Neapolitan past were suffused
with life and humanity. Unconsciously, perhaps, they
were leading him toward his future concerns, away from
the abstractions of the reigning philosophies and from
the carping spirit that had made his stay in Rome so depressing. They were guiding him toward an assertion
of the values of the imagination and of heroic devotion.
Viewed in this light, every fragment of the past was important, each one bore its testimony of suffering and of
sacrifice. It is revealing to observe that in this period
Croce's favorite historical characters seem to have been
women of ardent temperament, heroines of the spirit
who gave themselves with total generosity either to

---

[7] *"Contributo alla critica di me stesso"* (1918) (reprinted as
an appendix to *Etica e politica* [Bari, 1931]), translated by R. G.
Collingwood as *An Autobiography* (Oxford, 1927), pp. 37–49.
[8] *"Croce storico," Rivista Storica Italiana,* LXIV (1953),
478.

love or to a noble political cause.[9] And it may not be irrelevant to note that the historian himself—until well into his middle years—was sufficiently contemptuous of convention to live quite openly with a woman who was not his wife.

By 1893, however, Croce had grown weary of erudition. Looking around for guides to help him to a more philosophical understanding of his craft, he read for the first time Vico's *Scienza nuova*, he ransacked the works of such Germans as Droysen and Dilthey, he refreshed his memories of the great literary critic and fellow Neapolitan De Sanctis.

> Thus, after much hesitation and a whole series of provisional solutions, during February or March 1893, after a whole day of intense thought, I sketched in the evening an essay which I called *History subsumed under the general concept of Art*. This was a kind of revelation to me of my true self. Not only did it give me the joy of seeing in a clear light certain conceptions which are commonly confused, and tracing the logical origin of numerous false tendencies, but it astonished me by the ease and heat with which I wrote it, as something close to my heart and coming straight from my heart. . . .

The essay created a small sensation when Croce read it to his antiquarian friends at a meeting of the Accademia Pontaniana. As one old scholar subsequently expressed it, Croce had become "a Garibaldi of criticism."[1]

In this, the first of his theoretical writings on history, he had expressed in direct terms a very simple thesis: "Historical writing does not elaborate concepts, but reproduces particular events in their concreteness; and for that reason we have denied it the character of a science. It is therefore easy . . . to conclude that if

[9] Mario Corsi: *Le origini del pensiero di Benedetto Croce* (Florence, 1951) pp. 26, 31, 35, 39.
[1] *Autobiography*, pp. 52–6.

history is not science it must be art." [2] Through this formula, Croce expressed the conviction that had gradually been building up in him during the period of his antiquarian studies—the conviction that his two original loves, literary art and historical erudition, were not two but one. They had in common the same warm, immediate contact with the stuff of life itself. For example, the popular poetry of his native city, whose origins Croce loved to explore, was a source both of artistic joy and of historical enlightenment. Thus the thesis advanced in this first essay represented "the theoretical and systematic solution of what up to that time" had been simply an "ethical conviction" based on the historian's "practical experience." [3]

Already, however, in the explanatory memoranda that he subsequently attached to his main essay, Croce began to move toward a more "conceptual" view of the historian's task. In the first of his systematic volumes, the *Aesthetic* of 1902, Croce stuck to his original definition. But by the time he had completed the final version of his *Logic* seven years later, he had radically shifted his theoretical position. This second position he maintained, with some additions but only minor alterations, until the very end of his life.

In his mature theory of history Croce succeeded in fusing the results of his systematic studies of Vico, of Marx, and of Hegel. And their influence on his thought came in approximately that order. We have seen how he had originally read Vico as preparation for writing his first theoretical essay. Scarcely had the furor created by this little work died down, when Croce was swept into his five-year flirtation with Marxian theory. And it was only when he was through with Marx—when he had incorporated into his canon of historical thinking whatever he had found to be relevant in dialectical ma-

[2] "*La storia ridotta sotto il concetto generale dell'arte,*" *Primi Saggi* (Bari, 1919), p. 24.
[3] Corsi: *Origini del pensiero,* pp. 53–4.

terialism—that he began to give some sustained attention to Marx's philosophical master.

Thus Croce came to Hegel in the reverse of the more
usual and historical order. In his first essay he had mentioned him simply in passing; it was not until 1906 that
he published the results of his more sustained reflections under the significant title "What Is Living and
What Is Dead in Hegel's Philosophy." For the fact
that Croce viewed Hegel as mediated through Marx
gave him a certain detachment and kept him from falling too completely under the former's spell. And of
this there was real danger. After Croce had completed
his *Aesthetic* and written the preliminary version of his
Logic, he "felt that the time had come for a closer acquaintance with this Hegel, whose doctrines" he had
"hitherto rather sampled than studied in their entirety."
And now that he was ready for it, Croce found Hegelianism immensely illuminating. He was frank to recognize that it helped him toward a tighter and more coherent presentation of his own conceptual scheme. The
example of Hegel seems to have had a good deal to do
with Croce's decision to recast his *Aesthetic* and *Logic*
as the first two volumes of his *Philosophy of the Spirit*
and to add to them an analysis of economics and ethics
and a concluding volume on historiography.[4]

Croce always claimed that he had been discriminating in his attitude toward Hegel and had taken from
him only what he strictly required. One of his authoritative expositors has noted that the Hegelian influence
was balanced in his mind by his esteem for the English
philosophy of the seventeenth and eighteenth centuries,
anti-dogmatic like his own, and composed for the most

---

[4] *Autobiography,* pp. 95–101. The work on economics and
ethics (*Filosofia della pratica*) appeared in 1909, the *Logic* in its
revised form in the same year, and the volume on historiography
in 1917, having first been published as articles in 1912 and 1913
and then in book form in German translation in 1915. The first
volume of the series, the *Aesthetic,* remained practically un-
changed in its original form.

part by people who, like himself, were "men of the world and not . . . professors." [5] Certainly it would be a great error to call Croce a Hegelian. But one can argue that Hegel was responsible for the most doubtful features of Croce's thought—its tendency toward a schematic rationalism and its insistence on the pervasive role of a quasi-deity called "the spirit."

From Vico, on the other hand, Croce derived what was most vital and imaginative in his own theoretical work. Vico had been the earliest of his philosophical masters—as he was the first in historical time and geographically the closest to home. But it was not until Croce had completed all but one of the volumes of his *Philosophy of the Spirit* that he attempted a systematic survey of Vico's thought. The resulting book proved to be one of the most influential that Croce ever wrote— marking as it did the beginning of a second wave of Vichian studies. The first had come in the 1820's, after the *Scienza nuova* had lain neglected for almost a century, and formed part of the Romantic revival of interest in the mythical and the non-logical. With Croce's study of 1911, there began a more rigorous process of analysis which has continued right down to the present.

Vico, Croce discovered, had been a philosopher of history in two distinct senses. On the one hand, he had constructed "a typical history of human society"—the earliest secular version of the sort of grand metaphysical designs that Hegel and Spengler were to offer. In this guise, Vico had created a "new science" that was "at once a philosophy of man and a universal history of nations." At the same time, and less obviously, Vico had given to the study of history a new consciousness of its own significance:

> He was bound . . . to rescue history from its condition of inferiority, where it was a mere slave to caprice, vanity, moralising and precept-making,

[5] Giovanni Castellano: *Benedetto Croce: il filosofo-il critico-lo storico*, second edition (Bari, 1936), p. 17.

and other irrelevant aims, and to recognize its own
true end as a necessary complement of eternal
truth. By the same token, philosophy would be
filled with history, suffused with history; and by
this process it would acquire greater breadth and a
more lively sense of the concrete reality demanding
explanation.[6]

It was in this second guise—in this marriage of history
with philosophical method—that the example of Vico
acted as the single most important influence on Croce's
mature theory of historical writing.

By 1913, with the publication of his study of historiography, the "systematic" phase of Croce's career
was over. He was only in his late forties, but now that
his *Philosophy of the Spirit* and his parallel volumes on
historical materialism, on Hegel, and on Vico had been
completed, it might have been supposed that he was
about to close up his philosophical shop. Nothing,
however, was farther from Croce's thought. For he had
never conceived of his series of systematic studies as
constituting a final and inalterable statement of his
views. They were intended, rather, to fill the special and
temporary needs of an Italian educated public that up
to Croce's time had lacked competent guides to the
various fields of philosophical investigation. It was,
moreover, undeniable that Croce "had not yet entirely
liberated himself from the idea of a [philosophical] system in the old sense." [7] With the completion of what
could pass for his systematic work, the remains of such
an illusion dropped away. From this time forth Croce
was to strive for no further syntheses: his subsequent
thoughts ran to volume after volume—but they were

[6] *La filosofia di Giambattista Vico* (Bari, 1911), translated by
R. G. Collingwood as *The Philosophy of Giambattista Vico*
(New York, 1913), pp. 33–4. I have altered the translation some-
what.

[7] Castellano: *Croce*, pp. 29–30.

cast in the form of essays, observations, and miscellaneous reviews.

This change in the character of Croce's writing suggests that the period 1909 to 1913—from the publication of his *Logic* in its final form to the appearance of
his articles on historiography—is the time to mark a
pause and to examine his fully developed theory of
history. In this second—and definitive—formulation,
Croce expressed the view that history was not only
something more conceptual than simply a form of art—
it actually amounted to the sum of human knowledge.
And the conceptual element entered into it through
philosophy, which could be described as the body of
judgments men made on their own history. Thus Croce
did not impose philosophy on history, as Hegel had
done—he *included* philosophy *within* history as the latter's methodology.

The task of the philosopher, then, and the task of
the historian logically became one. The implication of
Croce's theory was that the scholars of the future would
be philosopher-historians like himself. Moreover, this
new definition liberated historical thinking from its
positivist bondage to natural science even more thoroughly than Dilthey's had done. For it went beyond
granting history its autonomy to establish it as the
queen of the sciences. By the same token, Croce depre-
cated the claims of natural science. As against historical
knowledge, he contended, natural science could offer
(in the case of the descriptive sciences) only random
historical data, or (in the case of the analytical sciences)
arbitrary complexes of knowledge, theoretical fictions
constructed for essentially practical purposes.[8] And the
same was true of social science, to the extent that Croce

8 For Croce's view of science, see his *Logica come scienza del
concetto puro* (Bari, 1909), translated from the third edition
(1917) by Douglas Ainslee as *Logic as the Science of the Pure
Concept* (London, 1917), Part II, Chapter 5; Cecil Sprigge:
Benedetto Croce: Man and Thinker (New Haven, Conn., 1952),
Chapter 3; and the discussion by Croce's English disciple R. G.
Collingwood in his *Idea of History*, pp. 197–200.

condescended to talk about it at all. Of the social sciences, the only one in which he showed even a limited interest was economics, and this he again defined as essentially practical in its aim.

Both natural and social science, Croce maintained, dealt only with data externally perceived. History, on the contrary, strove for "internal" comprehension. In this assertion Croce took up the full inheritance of German idealism. But he pushed the idealist line of thinking to a sharper point by arguing that "every true history is contemporary history." By this paradoxical assertion—which became the most celebrated of his dicta—Croce was trying to suggest that the essence of historical knowledge consisted in an imaginative grasp of the great problems of the past, first, as the historical actors themselves had understood them, second, as they took on relevance for the historian's own time. Actually these two aspects of the problem were combined in the historian's mind: he could be said to have understood his material only when he had integrated it with his own consciousness, when he had fused it in his own thought and made it "vibrate" in his "soul."

Thus all true history must be re-lived or re-experienced by the historian: ascertaining "facts" and interpreting or judging them were part of the same process of imaginative re-creation. In the absence of such a process, Croce argued, history could be no more than "chronicle"—"dead history," which had only been "recorded," not "thought" by the historical mind. Croce was severe in judging the work of the chroniclers or "philological" historians, in which category he included most of the specialized historical writers of the nineteenth century. It was his own erudite youth that he was condemning: he knew whereof he spoke. But he granted this sort of history a limited value as a kind of storehouse, where a fund of material lay awaiting the time when a true historian would succeed in rethinking some part of it back into life.

In this view, the rational, the positive could alone be

the subject of history. For this alone was comprehensible. The rest was simply the realm of passive suffering, violence, incoherence. "A fact that seems to be only evil, an epoch that appears to be one of complete decadence, can be nothing but a *non-historical* fact— that is to say, one which has not been historically treated, not penetrated by thought, and which has remained the prey of sentiment and imagination." [9]

Croce's theory of history was in a number of respects a real advance over that of his German predecessors and contemporaries. For one thing, it was stated in a more logical and less mystical form. By welding together philosophy and history, by defining the historian's task in a consistently subjective fashion, by excluding the realm of irrational "sentiment" from historical inquiry, Croce had reduced to nullity some of the problems that had most tormented Dilthey and the neo-Kantians. But these gains had been purchased at the price of an enormous simplification. In reviewing Croce's mature theory, one is tempted to conclude that it was more successful in defining what history was not than in stating exactly what it was.

Croce was a rationalist, if of a rather special sort. Through Vico he had learned to give greater weight to the primitive, the barbaric, than had the more conventional rationalists of preceding generations. But this understanding glimmered no more than fitfully in his mind: as he advanced in years he spoke less and less of those "lives of adventure, of faith, and of passion" that had entranced his youth. Thus the whole realm of illogical sentiment figured only on the periphery of his understanding. But this was precisely the realm with which his contemporaries in the fields of sociology, psychology, and anthropology were most concerned. By his hostility to social science—by his refusal to give any

[9] *Teoria e storia della storiografia* (Bari, 1917), authorized translation by Douglas Ainslee as *History: Its Theory and Practice* (New York, 1921), pp. 12, 19, 24–6, 87–8, 91.

adequate account of the relation of history to its sister-disciplines—Croce simply reinforced the tendency toward rationalist abstraction that was already so strong in his own thought.

But the paradox of the matter was that Croce's theory of historical knowledge was itself far from being coherently rational. In trying to give an account of what precisely the historian did in putting together his data, Croce had come up with nothing more helpful than the metaphor of a "lightning-flash" of understanding. And this was not really much of an advance on Ranke's notion of contemplation. The mystical element in the idealist tradition, which Croce had sedulously tried to purge, came creeping back in the form of a figure of speech.

In elucidating these difficulties, Croce's later work offered a wealth of theoretical elaborations, a supplementary outline of the *content* of history as opposed to its methodology, and the concrete example of major production in the field of straight historical writing.

IV. *Benedetto Croce: The Concept of Ethico-Political History*

In 1910 began what we may call the public phase of Croce's career. In that year he was named a Senator of the Realm—a life position—and four years later he married and began to raise a large family of daughters. Almost simultaneously came the outbreak of the First World War. This event necessarily forced Croce into a more active attitude toward public affairs than his scholarly life and temperament had hitherto permitted. For the campaign for Italy's intervention on the side of France and Britain went against his closest cultural associations: more than any other foreign land, Germany had been his spiritual home. In addition, he correctly saw that Italy had no very good reason for participating in the conflict: he remembered how often in the past his country "had thoughtlessly thrown itself into undertakings in which it had suffered reverses and disasters and acquired only damage and discredit."[1] Thus in the period of Italy's neutrality he argued against intervention. But when the government's decision had gone against him, he duly turned up in the Senate to vote for war, and during the conflict itself he maintained an attitude that was "correct" if something short of enthusiastic. Above all, he strove to maintain intact the idea of an international community of scholars and to combat the tendency among the intellectuals of the warring nations to fall prey to the passions of the masses. "Croce's attitude during the war," as one critic very sharply put it, "can be compared only to that of the Pope, who was the head of the bishops who blessed the German and Austrian arms, as he was of those who blessed the arms of the Italians and French, without there being any contradiction in it."[2]

With the war, however, came a flagging of Croce's creative energies. He took time out to arrange, correct, and revise his earlier work—and to write a brief memoir that was aptly entitled "Contribution to the Criticism of Myself." For the first time since the turn of the century, he felt himself despondent and uncertain of his course.[3] The end of the war brought new anxieties: Italy's first attempt at political democracy was accompanied by the bitterest kind of social strife. In this situation of endemic civil war, Croce yielded to the aged Giolitti's entreaties to join the latter's last ministry. For a full year the Neapolitan philosopher struggled with the unpromising task of directing the Ministry of Public Instruction. In June of 1921 the Giolitti ministry fell; sixteen months later Mussolini was installed in power.

[1] Castellano: *Croce*, p. 88.
[2] Antonio Gramsci: *Il materialismo storico e la filosofia di Benedetto Croce* (*Opere*, vol. 2) (Turin, 1952), p. 174.
[3] *Autobiography*, pp. 114–16.

The advent of Fascism galvanized Croce into new activity. At first he gave Mussolini's regime his qualified endorsement as a revitalizing force in the national life. But by 1925 he had passed over into uncompromising opposition. For the next two decades, his was to be almost the only voice of protest that carried across Italy's frontiers to the outside world.

In the process of intellectual change and growth that Croce himself used to refer to as his "second youth," activity and theory, history-writing and philosophical elaboration, were inextricably entangled. Moral decisions falling within the sphere of Croce's public activity sharpened and altered his abstract notion of politics, while this in turn reacted on his theoretical view of history. By the same token his writing of history itself took on a new shape and dimension.[4] These changes were reciprocal and mutually reinforcing. In the gradual alteration of Croce's thought during the 1920's it is not always possible to say whether action preceded theory, or whether the subterranean process of philosophical reworking had already prepared the way for vigorous assertion in the field of practical activity.

Croce's original view of politics had been skeptical, aloof, elitist—clearly anti-democratic. His respect for the German philosophical tradition and more particularly for Hegel suggests that he shared with the German theorists their scorn for "sentimentality" in politics and their acceptance of a universe of human relations based on force. In the earlier part of his career Croce had been close to the views of his countrymen Mosca and Pareto; with the latter, as we have seen, he maintained a relationship of mutual esteem during the period when they were both working on the critique of Marxism. But when Mosca began to move beyond Pareto toward a more militant defense of liberal institutions and even a grudging endorsement of democracy,

---

[4] *Vittorio de Caprariis, "La Storia d'Italia' nello svolgimento del pensiero politico di B. Croce," in Flora, Croce, p. 291.*

Croce moved along with him.[5] The sympathetic review of the second version of Mosca's *Elementi di scienza politica* which Croce published in *La Critica* in 1923 came as perhaps the earliest sign of a substantial intellectual shift.

Two years later, in his "Manifesto of the Anti-Fascist Intellectuals," Croce broke unequivocally with his country's authoritarian regime. And during the four years from 1925 to 1929, he repeatedly spoke out against the consolidation of the dictatorship. The Chamber of Deputies had been tamed and purged: in the Senate alone a small group of elderly "untouchables" could still make themselves heard in accents of measured protest. To the extent that this group had coherence and leadership, Croce was their chief.

After 1929, the year of Mussolini's pact with the Vatican and his virtually complete triumph over his internal enemies, the little band of dissident senators grew discouraged. Croce himself ceased attending Senate sessions, and from this time forth restricted his defense of liberal inquiry to his books, the columns of *La Critica*, and the numerous acts of kindness with which he aided anti-Fascist intellectuals in a less secure situation than his. By the end of the 1920's, Croce had made his political position so clear that he no longer required a parliamentary forum: he had become the chief symbol and rallying-point for the quiet, nearly stifled minority of those who kept their faith in free institutions during the last decade and a half of the Fascist regime.

It is significant, however, that the years of Croce's activity as the spokesman of the senatorial opposition were also the years when he wrote the four volumes on which his reputation as a practicing historian chiefly rests. With the advent of Fascism, the defining characteristics of Italian history—and of modern European history in general—were again up for discussion. Like other regimes of a militantly ideological origin, Fascism sought to give itself a historical legitimation. New em-

5 See Chapter 7.

phases and partial distortions were the inevitable result. Thus it was incumbent on "liberal" historians of one or another allegiance to re-establish the record and to try to find a solid historical grounding for the values of the free society that Mussolini had destroyed.

In his earlier historical work, Croce had offered detailed studies of the conventional "philological" type. Subsequently he had developed a theory of history that had in effect repudiated these youthful labors. But he had not yet applied his doctrine on a large scale. The crisis of Italian historiography in the 1920's gave him the opportunity to do so—to write major histories of a philosophical sweep and loftiness of tone, and in the process to work out the revised version of his historical thinking which had gradually been maturing in his mind.

In his "tetralogy" of histories published between 1925 and 1932, Croce did two things: first, he resumed the themes of his youthful work, enlarging and recasting them into general interpretive studies of the Kingdom of Naples and of Italy in the era of the Baroque; second, he shifted his focus to a more recent period, sketching in broad outline the history of Europe in the nineteenth century and, in fuller detail, that of his own country from its unification to the First World War.[6] As the publication of these four volumes progressed, it became evident that they were united by a common theme and that this theme in turn would dominate Croce's late theoretical production. The guiding thought was the progress of man's spirit toward self-realization, the unending struggle against natural and human obstacles to organize a free society. In the words of a chapter title from his last major theoretical work, Croce was now writing history "as the story of liberty."

---

[6] *Storia del Regno di Napoli* (Bari, 1925); *Storia d'Italia dal 1871 al 1915* (Bari, 1928); *Storia dell'età barocca in Italia* (Bari, 1929); *Storia d'Europa nel secolo decimonono* (Bari, 1932). All of these except the third have been translated into English. On this whole topic, see Chabod, *"Croce storico,"* pp. 500–14.

Such was the end result of Croce's "ethico-political" definition of the subject matter of history. More than a decade passed, however, between its first tentative statement and its full formulation. We find it initially in a political essay of 1924; it is further elaborated in one of the "marginalia" that Croce added to his work on historiography for the new edition of 1927; [7] by 1938 it forms the central element in the book called in Italian "History as Thought and Action," and somewhat misleadingly rendered into English under a narrower title.[8] For its subject extended beyond "the story of liberty": it included the whole vexed question of the interplay between thought and action in the work of the historical mind.

In this late version of his theory, Croce sought to establish a concept of historical writing that would be universal in scope and yet would avoid the intellectual heterogeneity, the mere running of parallel and unconnected sequences—political, economic, cultural, and the like—that had characterized previous attempts at general history. The unifying concept Croce located in what he called the *"vita morale"* of mankind. By this he meant the whole area of man's highest aspirations, as expressed in art, religion, ethics, and political principles. Most emphatically he did not mean the moralizing type of history that had long been current. And for this reason he chose the term "ethico-political" rather than "moral" to describe what he had in mind.

The result was a fusion of traditional political history with the newer type known as the history of civilization —an invention of Voltaire which had been systematically developed by the positivist historians of the late nineteenth century. Politics, Croce argued, still offered the central theme for historical narrative. But it was

[7] Pages 321–3 of the third and later editions; the English translation does not include these marginalia.

[8] *La storia come pensiero e come azione* (Bari, 1938), translated by Sylvia Sprigge as *History as the Story of Liberty* (New York, 1941).

essential to lift the political account to a higher plane by gathering into it the "moral" elements from the other spheres of human activity. And when this fusion had been made, it would be apparent that the new synthesis naturally grouped itself around the idea of liberty: the record of the past revealed that only when men were free in the spirit were they able to develop to the full their higher political and ethical capacities. Thus freedom was the essence of man's history even in those times—like that which Croce himself was traversing—when its light barely flickered in the surrounding darkness.[9]

Regarded in this fashion, the historian's task suddenly appeared both simple and clear. And the necessarily "contemporary" character of historical writing to which Croce had alluded in his earlier theoretical work was now more fully illuminated. The impetus to historical writing, Croce asserted, arose from a need felt in practical life to understand the past. But historical study was connected with action only as *preparation* for it: it did not dictate solutions to practical problems; it simply served to make action more rational by clarifying the historical origin of contemporary dilemmas and the range through which realistic choice could operate. Similarly, passion was essential to great historical writing: it acted as a necessary spur to the work of creation. But in the final product it figured only in controlled and sublimated form. In thus teaching men to "transfigure" their passions into something rational, the writing of history served to liberate mankind from the tyranny of passion and, by the same process, from the burden of the past.

With regard to history inspired by political partisanship, Croce drew a careful distinction. On the one hand, he held that this was literature based on sentiment or practical purpose which had not yet been refined through the application of the categories of reason. At the same time he took issue with the conventional at-

[9] Ibid., pp. 50–1, 58–62.

titude of refusing to make judgments at all for fear of falling into partisanship. This, he argued, had been the mistake of the nineteenth-century "philological" school, which had had recourse to transparent escape-devices such as arranging diplomatic compromises between points of view that were in fact irreconcilable. Faced with such "pale and bloodless" fare, it was no wonder that the public preferred to read frankly partisan works. For thirty years Croce had been hammering on the point that in historical study the act of judgment constituted an integral part of the process of understanding. And as he had gradually refined his theory, he had come to see that the nub of the problem lay in the *type* of judgments that historians made: did these do no more than reflect the play of petty partisan emotion, or had they been elevated to the plane of universal ethical principle? If the latter was the case, then the writing of history was necessarily "liberal" in character. In his last major theoretical work Croce had finally come to the point where he was ready to state quite simply and flatly that true history could only be liberal history in the broadest sense.[1]

By the time he reached this final position, Croce had completed his tetralogy of historical narratives. And it is significant that the last of them, the *History of Europe in the Nineteenth Century*, went far beyond its predecessors in its simplicity, its abstraction, and in its quasi-religious character. It had had its origin in Croce's anxieties for the future of liberty in the twentieth century: by refurbishing the image of the era in which liberal principles had won their greatest victories, Croce hoped to breathe new life into these values and to encourage those who were opposing the regimes that had destroyed them. Thus his last history has justly been called an "act of faith" [2]—an appeal to the youth of Europe to recover its cultural and ethical heritage before it was too late.

---

[1] Ibid., pp. 17–19, 43–5, 179–87.
[2] Chabod: "*Croce storico*," p. 513.

On the eve of the Second World War, then, Croce had come up squarely against the problem of values. For the better part of his life he had avoided the question that had tormented his predecessors and contemporaries. It was not until he was past seventy that he realized the full implications of his neo-idealist theory. Earlier he had tried to restrict the faculty of *historical* judgment to the realm of abstractions—first of aesthetics, subsequently of logic—through relegating the function of *value* judgment to the lower level of "the practical." But the distinction had eventually broken down. Faced with the advent of Fascism and the destruction of the liberal, parliamentary regime under whose protection he had grown to intellectual maturity, Croce had been obliged to take a political stand. He had been forced to descend into the arena of practical activity in order to defend the institutions and way of life that had provided the preconditions for his creative work. In the process, the line between logical and practical judgment had become blurred: by gradual stages, Croce had evolved—not only in his speeches before the Senate, but in his historical and theoretical writings also—into the advocate of an explicit value-system.

Croce never fully recognized the extent to which his attitude had changed. It was doubtless distasteful to him to observe how far he had gone in the direction of political partisanship. Nor did he admit to himself how much he had come to have in common with the people who had earlier been the targets of his urbane scorn. He was proud to call himself a "liberal" or a "humanist":.the term "democrat" stuck in his throat. But *in practice* he had become an advocate of democracy.[3] His nostalgic gaze might still turn back toward the nineteenth century, when liberal principles existed in their pure state without democratic involvement. But by the 1920's this sort of ideological distinction had be-

[3] Just after the fall of Mussolini, Croce published his main political utterances dating from the Fascist period under the title *Propositi e speranze* (1925–1942): *scritti varî* (Bari, 1943).

come impracticable: the liberal and the democratic traditions were now so completely entangled that to defend one meant to defend the other also. And with his *de facto* acceptance of democracy, Croce had come to accept the inheritance of the Enlightenment in its twentieth-century form. He had at last recognized his true ideological forebears and the direction in which his worship of the rational, his tolerance, his preference for humane solutions, had all along been pointing.

In 1943, with the fall of Fascism, Croce emerged as Italy's leading figure. Paradoxically enough, the Fascist regime itself had contributed toward establishing him in this position. For Mussolini had granted Croce a kind of special license as living proof that free speech in Italy was not totally dead. Thus the fact that he was carrying on his labors under a tyrannical government put Croce on a pinnacle of unchallenged eminence to which no single individual could have attained under a free regime: in the latter case, rivals from among the younger generation would necessarily have appeared; under Fascism the young challengers were unable to come forward—they were not untouchable like Croce.

With the disappearance of Mussolini, all eyes turned toward the Neapolitan philosopher. But "Italy's most revered man and her living symbol of political integrity and intellectual consistency could offer his distressed countrymen little more than paternal counsels of expediency, vague hopes for the future, and eloquent appeals to the individual consciences of those who were called upon for the moral and economic reconstruction of the country." [4] Croce served as minister without portfolio in the first governments of anti-Fascist liberation, he was a prime mover in the reconstitution of the Liberal party, he acted as a source of inspiration to the younger men on whom the active tasks of government had devolved. But in terms of a specific program he

[4] Leonardo Olschki: *The Genius of Italy* (New York, 1949), p. 459.

could offer no guidance. His own influence declined along with the post-war eclipse of the Liberal party, and shortly after the war he retired from politics altogether. Yet he continued his literary labors to the end: death finally overtook him in 1952 at the age of eighty-six.

Croce's failure to give a clear lead in the decisive months after the fall of Fascism suggests the central problem of his career and influence. Not only in the realm of practical life was his example elusive. The same is true of the realm of theory. Croce's prose is limpid; it has the rare charm of sounding like the voice of common sense. As Gramsci put it, Croce was the foremost master of prose that Italy had produced for a hundred years, not because he wrote in a literary tradition, but because his style derived from that of the great scientific writers like Galileo. His unique talent in his own time consisted in expressing "with great simplicity and great vigor all in one, material that ordinarily . . . is presented in a form that is jumbled, obscure, strained, and prolix." His literary style defined an attitude "like that of Goethe"—"an attitude . . . of serenity, self-possession, imperturbable security." [5]

Yet beneath this surface clarity, there are snags and eddies. The flow of Croce's prose is deceptively reassuring: the sentences run too easily into each other; the intellectual difficulties are dismissed in a graceful phrase. With irresistible persuasiveness Croce carries his readers along with him. As we come to the end of a chapter we are both captivated and convinced. But when we subject the same pages to more careful analytical scrutiny, we find ourselves no longer so sure. Too many matters have been left hanging in air, too many questions unanswered. In the end we are driven to ask ourselves in despair: exactly what has Croce said anyway?

An initial clue to these perplexities may be found in

[5] *Lettere dal carcere* (*Opere*, vol. 1) (Turin, 1949), p. 183.

Croce's own image of himself. "Do you know," he once asked a friend, "when I catch myself dreaming, what . . . I discover in the depths of my soul, what is the image in which it bathes and finds rest? A seventeenth-century Neapolitan convent, with its white cells and its cloister, and in its center an enclosure of orange and lemon trees, while outside the tumult of life's ostentation and arrogance is beating in vain against its high walls!" [6]

Croce knew that life was "tumult" and incoherence. But he sought to shut out, or at least to canalize, its passionate strivings by erecting "high walls" of reason and of logic. Yet he was too realistic a thinker to do this consistently: he did not follow his master Hegel in enclosing all human history in a tight framework. The incoherences of life itself constantly broke through the conceptual dikes that Croce had constructed.

Thus his writing of history was not always consistent with his historical theory, and this theory in turn was not always consistent with itself. It has been shrewdly observed that in his applications of his ethico-political concept—in his major historical writings of the 1920's and early 1930's—Croce chose to focus on periods of consent and of intellectual direction: he started his *History of Italy* in 1871, when the tumults of unification were over, and his *History of Europe* in 1815, with the close of the Revolutionary and Napoleonic disturbances. He passed over "the moment of force and of struggle" to concentrate on "the pure ethico-political moment, as though this latter had fallen from the sky" without previous preparation. [7] In addition, Croce assumed so lofty an attitude that the harsher features of his account—and more particularly the economic details—did not stand out with sufficient sharpness. Even as a southerner himself he gave only passing attention to the origins of agricultural poverty, the key problem

---

6 Castellano: *Croce*, p. 86.
7 Gramsci: *Materialismo storico*, p. 192, *Lettere*, p. 187.

of the Italian south. In his *History of the Kingdom of Naples*, he dismissed the geographical and economic limitations of the southern realm as merely physical obstacles to political progress. The failure of the Neapolitan state, he maintained, could not properly be attributed to any such "natural" phenomena: the true reason for failure had to be a moral one.

In thus narrowing his focus onto the ethical issues characteristic of "moments of consent" and the aspiration toward freedom, Croce did not hold true to his own historiographic program as he had originally outlined it. One of the central tenets of the idealist school had been the effort to understand the past in the terms that had had meaning for the contemporaries of the events in question. But in his treatment of the Baroque era, Croce did something quite different: he viewed it as a period of decadence in which the anticipations of subsequent cultural revival were alone of permanent significance. Similarly he violated the idealist canon by formulating the meaning of past epochs in terms of ethical abstractions: in his hands, for example, the history of nineteenth-century Italy was sublimated into the purest exemplification of the liberal ideal.[8]

As this process of abstraction advanced to its climax in his *History of Europe* of 1932 and his theoretical volume of 1938, Croce moved farther and farther from his base in German historical thinking: he increasingly neglected the central principle that the past should be understood *in its own terms*. Instead the abstractions of "reason" and of "liberty" took over. And in entrusting himself to their guidance Croce failed to make clear whether he thought that his own notion of them was eternally valid, as Hegel had assumed, or whether, like all other meanings in history, they were historically conditioned themselves. This latter alternative was the

8 On this whole subject, besides Chabod's "*Croce storico*," see A. Robert Caponigri: *History and Liberty: The Historical Writings of Benedetto Croce* (London, 1955). In my more critical judgments I am differing from both these authors.

implication of Dilthey's philosophy and of the direction in which the German historical school had been heading for more than a century. But it was a line of reasoning that Croce himself did not choose to pursue.

Croce's failure to give an unequivocal answer to the question of whether his abstract categories were absolutely or only relatively valid is the first of the great unsolved problems that his historical thought presents. He himself vigorously repudiated relativism. By "an appeal to the absolute nature of spirit," he sought to ward off its dangers. But this appeal failed "to solve the concrete problem" that existed within his own thinking "of discriminating between more and less accurate historical judgments." Ultimately, whatever Croce himself may say, the implications of his thought are relativist.[9]

Similarly—and with this we come to the second great unsolved problem—Croce's reliance on intuition as a source of historical understanding opened the way to an irrationalism that was in total contrast to his professed aims. We have seen how he tried to distinguish between his own and Bergson's notion of intuition. In his theoretical work of 1938 he enlarged on this distinction by claiming that true history excluded the imagination, except as raw material on which historical thought could feed; "intuition," he added, was valid "only in so far" as it was "reasoned or thought."[1] But this did not really solve the difficulty. Croce never defined in sufficiently precise terms exactly what historical thought did in converting into reason the discoveries reached through intuition or the imagination.

In terms of the idealist conception of history as re-creation—re-living or re-experiencing—intuition and imagination were obviously the ultimate sources of historical knowledge. Then in something that resembled a "flash" of understanding the insights gained through

[9] Maurice Mandelbaum: *The Problem of Historical Knowledge* (New York, 1938), pp. 54–7.

[1] *History as Story of Liberty*, pp. 132, 239.

these apparently non-logical processes were rearranged in a logical and coherent pattern. But Croce did not specify how it was done: in this respect his later work represented no advance over his mature theory of 1909–13. He made it clear that he thought the processes of historical thinking to be quite different from those of natural or social science. And he implied that this difference lay in the more inclusive and certain character of the historian's mental operations. In thus maintaining intact the traditional idealist distinction between history and social science, which Dilthey had already modified beyond recognition, Croce betrayed his failure to recognize the insufficiencies of the idealist canon: he showed that he had not understood the way in which the historian, like the scientist, made arbitrary selections among his data and how history shared with the other social disciplines the uses of inference and of something approaching scientific method.[2] This Weber was to be the first to explain in a rigorous and systematic fashion.

To a skeptical critic, Croce's philosophy offers no satisfactory grounding for historical truth. In the end, one is once more reduced to an "act of faith." This is the ultimate irony of Croce's thinking: what starts as a rationalist theory terminates in a kind of mysticism. But here again Croce was not sufficiently rigorous nor consistent. As he wavered between absolutism and relativism, so he never decisively made up his mind between intuition and the claims of scientific method: in this one respect at least, Bergson proved to be the more consistent thinker. But Croce refused to take his stand either with Bergson's frank mysticism or with Weber's attempt to define a common methodology for history and social science. He tried to have the best of both worlds.

[2] Cf. the analysis in Patrick Gardiner: *The Nature of Historical Explanation* (Oxford, 1952), pp. 40–6, 70–80, 114–39, and W. H. Walsh: *An Introduction to Philosophy of History* (London, 1951), pp. 53–4.

Why was this the case? I think it was because Croce's ambitions for history were too extensive. Starting his theoretical labors as he did in reaction to the claims of positivism, he saw the dangers implicit in the liberation of historical study from positivist method. He recognized that in casting the study of history loose from its scientific attachments, he was running the risk of setting it adrift in a sea of skepticism and relativism. Thus it became his goal to win autonomy for historical study while at the same time retaining the notion of certainty in historical knowledge. And this he could accomplish only by making extreme and paradoxical claims—by denigrating science and establishing history "not in the lowest but in the highest, indeed exclusive rank of knowledge." [3]

Once more we return to the self-image of Croce safely ensconced behind high walls in his cloister grove of orange and lemon trees. For Croce's extreme claims for the virtues of historical study presupposed an exclusion of the most pressing demands of life—that is, of the irrational. Croce had no use for "philosophies of life" or for "the confused utterances of the pragmatists." [4] We have seen how he finally came to find a place in his historical theory for the realm of value. But he continued to define value in rational terms: he failed to recognize the extent to which even his own devotion to liberty was emotional in origin. It was not until emotion had been sublimated into reason that he was willing to accept it as the stuff of historical interpretation.

Thus the problems raised by the non-logical and the primitive, the problems of irrational striving and religious devotion that fascinated Freud and Pareto, Durkheim and Weber, touched Croce only remotely. We feel their direct contact only in his youthful work and in his quarter-century correspondence with Sorel. For Croce religion—the touchstone of twentieth-cen-

[3] *History as Story of Liberty*, pp. 131–2.
[4] *Autobiography*, p. 98.

tury social thought—offered few intellectual difficulties. Although he professed no formal religion himself, he was not an anti-clerical. Toward Catholicism, the religion of his own country, he maintained an attitude of respect, and it must have grieved him when in 1932 his complete works were put on the Index. A decade later he even went so far as to hold out the hand of reconciliation to the Catholics in an essay archly entitled "Why We Cannot but Call Ourselves Christians." But the sense in which Croce applied to himself the name of Christian was hardly calculated to win favor with the religious. For it was only by reinterpreting the Christian tradition to embrace the whole main stream of European culture, including the "godless" Enlightenment itself, that he was able to find a place within it for his own philosophy. "The God of the Christians," he claimed, "is still ours, and our refined philosophies call him the Spirit." [5] To a true believer, this excessively abstract endorsement must have been small comfort indeed.

But such considerations would scarcely have troubled Croce. The depths of religious emotion—the agonies of doubt and the triumphs of faith—were incomprehensible to him. In brief, he lacked a sense of tragedy. In this regard he lagged behind his German contemporaries Troeltsch and Meinecke, who in all other respects were his philosophical inferiors.

v. *Troeltsch, Meinecke, and the Crisis in German Values*

It was in 1896, at a gathering of theologians in Eisenach, that Ernst Troeltsch dramatically burst onto the intellectual scene. One of the most respected of Germany's theological scholars had just completed a "learned, somewhat scholastic lecture." With the open-

[5] *Perchè non possiamo non dirci "cristiani"* (reprint from *La Critica* of November 20, 1942) (Bari, 1944), pp. 18–19, 24.

ing of the general discussion, there sprang "with youthful *élan*" to the rostrum a young professor who began his statement with the provocative words: "Gentlemen, everything is tottering." The older scholars were "appalled." When their spokesman in turn took the floor, he rejected the upstart's line of reasoning as "paltry theology"—at which Troeltsch got up and left, "slamming the doors behind him." The old guard of German theology was doubtless satisfied; but the younger scholars had pricked up their ears.[6]

In this incident the broad outlines of Troeltsch's personality and life goal stand revealed: his contentiousness, his boundless vitality, his untiring search for a firm footing in a situation in which neither theology nor history seemed any longer to offer the notion of an absolute. As Meinecke wrote of him, he was a living incarnation of the words of Heraclitus and Archimedes: "Everything flows. Give me a place where I can stand." Or, put in more theological terms: "Lord, I believe in thee: come to the aid of my disbelief." Troeltsch was like "a thundering mountain stream, whose strength moves mighty burdens as though it were play and threatens to tear away its firm banks and carry them along in its course." His intellectual impatience betrayed itself in his refusal to clarify his thought—in his piling up of abstractions that "press and chase after each other" through his prose.[7] In short, Troeltsch was a force of nature. "Every Heidelberg student who had once seen him tumbling around with youthful frolicsomeness in the waters of the Neckar" knew the peal of his "wonderful . . . laugh."

The son of a Bavarian physician, Troeltsch never lost the Bavarian's surface roughness and carelessness of formal usage. His father had originally intended him for the natural sciences, and from this early exposure he retained a sharp sense for scientific reality, to which

6 Walther Köhler: *Ernst Troeltsch* (Tübingen, 1941), p. 1.
7 "*Ernst Troeltsch und das Problem des Historismus*" (1923), *Schaffender Spiegel* (Stuttgart, 1948), pp. 211, 214–15.

he later added an understanding of Marxist thinking
that was not untinged by sympathy. But he soon felt
an attraction for the "historical world"—and more particularly for theology, where the problems posed by
contemporary culture seemed to present themselves in
their most critical form. So a theologian he became: in
1894, when he was still under thirty, he received a full
professorship at Heidelberg. Here his thought was to
take the most extraordinary and unorthodox course—
until in the end he remained a theologian in little more
than name.[8]

In thus fixing his attention on the spiritual aspects of
man's historical past, Troeltsch began to reap the harvest that Dilthey had sown. And this in two senses—the
one heartening, the other profoundly disturbing. On
the one hand Troeltsch was in a position to profit from
—and to satisfy—the new hunger on the part of the
university students for a return to problems of major
spiritual import. At the same time—and this was the
disconcerting aspect of Dilthey's legacy—the relativist
implications of the philosopher's thought were coming
home to roost: if the historical world was now to be
recovered in its full richness and diversity, where was
one to find a firm foothold, a grounding for truth and
value in the flow of all things human? What defense
was there against the onslaughts of skepticism and relativism? To the end of his life Troeltsch was to struggle
in vain to wrest an answer from history itself. Like Dilthey, he wanted to discover certainty *within* the historical world, not above or beyond it: spurning the aid of
metaphysics or revelation, he accepted the full inheritance of two centuries of Biblical scholarship and the
questionable character of all dogma and church tradition that had been their result.[9]

It was only after the lives of both scholars had passed
the half-century mark that Meinecke's course converged
with that of Troeltsch. But in a sense they had from

[8] Köhler: *Troeltsch*, pp. 4–6, 331.
[9] Rossi: *Storicismo tedesco*, pp. 442–5.

the start been pursuing their intellectual dilemmas
along the same track. Born in 1862—three years before
Troeltsch, and four years before Croce—Friedrich
Meinecke grew up in Berlin in an atmosphere of conservative Prussian orthodoxy. Both his grandfathers had
lived under the rule of Frederick the Great, and his
father had experienced the war of liberation against
Napoleon: to these "long generations" of his forebears,
Meinecke subsequently ascribed his intense feeling for
the past and his sense of being at home in the spiritual
world of the early nineteenth century. At the University of Berlin his historical masters were Droysen and
Treitschke. It was from the former rather than from
Dilthey, whom he encountered only later in his course
of study, that the young Meinecke acquired the notion
of history as thought and as problem. And it was from
him also that he learned to cast Prussia in the provi-
dential role in the history of modern Germany. But in
the Prussian school of historians Droysen ranked as a
moderate. It was Treitschke, rather, whose vehemence
and intolerance made him—both as example and as
warning—the supreme model of the historian turned
propagandist.[1]

With this sort of preparation, it is a wonder that
Meinecke kept his intellectual independence at all.
The young historian matured late: he was diffident and
he had a slight stutter. Yet he had already developed
the intellectual balance, the refined sense for nuance
and ambiguity in history, that give his major historical
works their serenity and cultural sweep. And these
qualities made it apparent that his real master was
neither Droysen nor Treitschke, but Ranke, with whom
he had never studied but whose example he tried to restore in its original spiritual emphasis. Meinecke was
not contentious like Troeltsch or Weber—nor was he
disdainful of his opponents like Croce: he was understanding and conciliatory. At the same time he had

---

[1] Friedrich Meinecke: *Erlebtes 1862–1901* (Leipzig, 1941),
pp. 12–14, 86–8, 90–1, 119, 122–3, 132, 197.

within him a quiet stubbornness, an undramatic variety of intellectual courage that eventually made him the only historian in Europe who could both stand up to Croce and retain the latter's esteem. And like Croce— whose life-span closely coincided with his own—as an old man he opposed with dignity a tyranny that he had the good fortune to outlive.

Meinecke was a great reconciler and synthesizer. And it was through the application of these talents that he was initially able to surmount his personal version of Troeltsch's dilemma. Both were deeply troubled by what Dilthey had called the "anarchy of convictions" characteristic of the contemporary world. Troeltsch encountered the crisis in its religious form: Meinecke faced it as a question of the ethics of national power. How could one, he wondered, follow Ranke and his successors of the German historical school in their endorsement of the power-state as an authentic "spiritual" creation of the historical process itself, and at the same time remain true to the equally German moral imperatives that Kant had taught? Could ethics and power be brought into some sort of harmony, or must they be forever at war for the mastery of the German spirit? [2]

Meinecke's first answer was expressed in a tenuous and difficult synthesis: "Ordinarily the German drama of the nineteenth century is described through the symbolic contrast of Weimar and Potsdam, of the literary and humanistic tradition of Herder, Goethe and Schiller, as against the military tradition of the Great Elector and Frederick II. Meinecke's peculiarity" was that "his heart beat for neither one nor the other of these two poles, but rather for Königsberg, the city of Kant and . . . the fortress of the Prussian recovery" in the Napoleonic era.[3] Or perhaps Meinecke's heart beat for *both* Weimar and Potsdam: in the first of his great trilogy of histories, he sought to prove that the

[2] Rossi: *Storicismo tedesco*, pp. 473–7.
[3] Antoni: *Dallo storicismo*, p. 91.

humanist tradition, far from being crushed by Prussian
dominance, had found its logical culmination and
transfiguration in the unification of Germany under
Bismarck's leadership.

Weltbürgertum und Nationalstaat—cosmopolitan-
ism and the national state—was published in 1908 after
Meinecke had spent fourteen years in the Prussian
archives and seven more as a professor in the German
southwest. In tracing the shift from cosmopolitan to
national values which so sharply separated Goethe's
generation from Bismarck's, Meinecke gave the process
his retrospective blessing. But he did not render this
judgment unreservedly, as his predecessors of the Prussian school had done. With another side of his nature,
he understood and sympathized with the defeated cos-
mopolitans: even this early in his career his attitude
toward the values of united Germany was tinged with
foreboding and nostalgia for a gentler age.

The publication of *Weltbürgertum und Nationalstaat* marked something of an epoch in contemporary
European historiography. As the first major essay in
what Meinecke called *Geistesgeschichte*—the history
of spiritual forces in political life—it started historical
writing on an extremely fruitful course. The aged Dilthey read it and "made long excerpts from it." Croce
welcomed it as the work of a "pure historian," in which
he had "read words . . . that seemed to be" his "very
own." And indeed Meinecke's sort of history was almost identical with what Croce was later to baptize
"ethico-political." Max Weber—whose work on the relation between capitalism and Calvinism had been in
Meinecke's mind as he was writing—came to pay the
historian a congratulatory call. And Weber's colleague
at Heidelberg, Ernst Troeltsch, sent a post card, "in
which he expressed . . . his heart-felt pleasure and
agreement." [4]

So far as I know, this was the first contact between

[4] Meinecke: *Strassburg/Freiburg/Berlin*, p. 102; Croce: *History: Its Theory and Practice*, p. 313.

the two men. Like Meinecke, Troeltsch had found in the German southwest a precarious and temporary balance between the opposing intellectual forces that threatened to tear his thought asunder. Through the influence of his friend Weber, he had reached an initial reconciliation between his religious faith and his critical sense, his respect for tradition and his realistic understanding of the problems of modern society. One day there had come into his hands a book on the "social task of the Protestant church." The work had no merit in itself. Yet, as so often happens in such cases, it inspired the reader to produce something more substantial on a similar theme. Realizing his total ignorance of the subject, Troeltsch threw himself with characteristic energy into the study of the relationship between Christian teaching and the perennial problems of man in society.[5]

The resulting book, the monumental *Social Teaching of the Christian Churches*, was a cruder, more incoherent, and infinitely longer version of the same kind of study of the interplay of economic and religious forces on which Weber was simultaneously working. For all the richness of its thought and scholarship, the book lacked clarity. The intellectual categories were mainly borrowed from Weber. But Troeltsch applied them mechanically, almost as though he had not fully understood them. Weber's carefully articulated analysis of the simultaneous autonomy and interconnectedness of religion and social structure appeared in Troeltsch's work as a mere alternation: the mutual relationship was constantly stated but never satisfactorily explained. And Weber's typology of social phenomena—his most characteristic legacy to subsequent investigation—in Troeltsch's hands seemed forced and artificial.[6]

[5] Antoni: *Dallo storicismo*, pp. 64–5.
[6] See Chapter 8. Large parts of *Die Soziallehren der christlichen Kirchen und Gruppen* (Tübingen, 1912) (*Gesammelte Schriften*, I [Tübingen, 1923]) were originally published between 1908 and 1910 as articles in the *Archiv für Sozialwissenschaft*

Besides the fact that Troeltsch was obviously Weber's intellectual inferior, there was the further difficulty that the former was dealing with material in which his own religious faith, his own value-system, were deeply involved. Unlike Weber, he was in no position to pursue the full relativist implications of his method, to treat Christianity in as detached a fashion as though it were the religion of China. Hence the loftiness of Troeltsch's ethical tone was countered by notes of agonized uncertainty. The synthesis was too precarious. It could not last.

We have seen how in 1914 Meinecke moved to Berlin, having already heard "the thunder of the cannon from Alsace," and how Troeltsch departed for the same destination a year later. In Meinecke's case the reasons for the move were purely professional. In the case of Troeltsch other considerations were involved. Heidelberg had become "too narrow" for him: his position there was too strictly theological, whereas his thought had long ago burst the bounds of traditional theology. Moreover, a "certain coolness" seems to have descended on his relations with Max Weber.[7]

In Berlin, Troeltsch and Meinecke became close friends. In fact, the latter took over from Weber the function of serving as the intellectual guide that Troeltsch evidently required. They took almost daily walks together in the Grunewald—a practice that Meinecke continued for two decades after his friend's death, until in 1943, when he was eighty-one, the Allied bombardments finally forced him to desist. On these rambles they were sometimes joined by the visionary businessman and future statesman Walter Rathenau. Rathenau's presence suggests the turn toward an interest in public affairs which the move to Berlin had entailed. Like Croce, Meinecke and Troeltsch were

und Sozialpolitik. The English translation, by Olive Wyon, was published in two volumes in London in 1931.

[7] Köhler: *Troeltsch,* p. 331.

caught up by the war situation into the main current of
the national life. Earlier neither one had been totally
apolitical. Meinecke, as we have observed, had become
increasingly critical of the Wilhelminian regime and
had made at least one foray into practical politics as a
supporter of Friedrich Naumann.[8] Troeltsch had remained more conformist. But service as the Heidelberg
University representative in the Baden upper house had
given him some practical experience of political activity
at the state level.

In Berlin at war both were swept into the currents
of controversy that separated the conservative majority
from the smaller band of reformers among the German
intellectuals. With these changed circumstances,
Troeltsch followed his friends Weber and Meinecke
into the reforming camp. Like Meinecke he opposed
the war aims of the annexationists and preached the
urgency of democratization before it was too late. Together the two friends joined the circle of moderates
that gathered around the liberal Prince Max of Baden,
and, at the war's end, they helped to found the German
Democratic party.[9] But by that time the war had been
lost. The enormous capital of devotion, of hope for a
purer national life, that had gone into it, seemed all
to have been spent in vain.

Hence there came about an intense crisis of conscience that overshadowed Troeltsch's last years and
broke Meinecke's intellectual life in two. While the
war was still in progress, both had argued that Germany's peculiar tradition of idealist and historically
grounded values gave ethical justification to the national war effort: as opposed to the "mechanistic" philosophies for which France and Britain stood, Germany
fought for a deeper and more spiritual tradition. This
line of argument, of which Thomas Mann was the
most persuasive advocate, was common to German in-

[8] Meinecke: *Strassburg/Freiburg/Berlin*, pp. 123–31, 133,
159–60.
[9] See Chapter 9.

tellectuals in both the conservative and the reforming camps. It helps explain why the latter, for all their opposition to annexation and their insistence on some version of democracy, remained steadfastly nationalist, and how they could still maintain that there was something ethical about Germany's war aims long after it had become evident that at home as on the front it was naked military force alone that mattered.

With the war's end, the conservatives kept to their old line and refused to give any countenance to the new democratic and republican regime. Troeltsch and Meinecke did the opposite. Although they would have preferred some more moderate and "organic" form of democracy than what the Weimar constitution provided, they supported their country's republican institutions. In a spirit of political realism and self-sacrificing patriotism, they accepted the parliamentary type of democracy that they considered an alien importation from the rationalist West. Meinecke, in fact, became the chief symbol of republican loyalty among Germany's historians, in a situation where nearly all the others of equal eminence opposed the Weimar regime. But how could this new allegiance be squared with Meinecke's former emphasis on organic growth and his devotion to historically based thinking? How could he and Troeltsch reconcile their acceptance of the "mechanistic" institutions of parliamentary democracy with their history-minded philosophy?

It is in this context of the lost war and the apparent triumph of Anglo-French values of eighteenth-century derivation that we must view the efforts of the two friends to re-establish the tradition of German historical thinking.[1] The way in which they chose to do it— and, from their standpoint, the only practicable fashion

---

[1] Walther Hofer: *Geschichtschreibung und Weltanschauung: Betrachtungen zum Werk Friedrich Meineckes* (Munich, 1950), pp. 25–6, 341–3; Eric C. Kollman: *"Eine Diagnose der Weimarer Republik: Ernst Troeltschs politische Anschauungen," Historische Zeitschrift*, CLXXXII (October 1956), 306–12.

—was by making a radical distinction. *Pragmatically,* they had become Western-type democrats. From a theoretical and philosophical standpoint, they remained true to German historical thought, to the tradition of *Historismus.* By subjecting this tradition to a careful review, they sought to rescue it from the discredit it had suffered through Germany's defeat in battle, and the further opprobrium that had fallen upon it when Spengler's *Decline of the West* had carried off the postwar reading public on an intoxicating wave of meta-historical prophecy.[2]

Already during the war years Troeltsch had been at work on the theoretical study—of which only the first volume was ever completed—entitled *Der Historismus und seine Probleme.* As the first of his major books had been a tribute to Weber's influence, so this second work reflected his intellectual dependence on Meinecke. In the form in which it was published in 1922, it was at least as inconclusive as his *Social Teaching.* By an exhaustive search through the major literature of historical thinking from Kant to Croce, Troeltsch tried to explain how it was that *Historismus,* which had once been a force of "liberation and uplift," had in the contemporary world become a "burden" and a source of "perplexity." He found his answer in the relativist implications of the work of Nietzsche and Dilthey, Rickert and Weber, Bergson and Croce—to all of whom he gave close and sympathetic attention. Dilthey he characterized as "the most intellectually gifted, the finest and the liveliest representative of pure *Historismus.*" From Rickert, he drew his analysis of the role of value-judgments in the processes of historical thinking. Bergson and Croce he contrasted as the leading speculative thinkers of their respective countries. And of the two he found that it was the French philosopher who had seen more deeply into the nature of historical process. For Bergson alone responded to the

[2] See Chapter 9.

great "challenge" of contemporary thought by providing a "pure analysis of movement . . . free . . . from all prejudices of . . . rationalism." [3] Once more we find that the notion of "flow" is central to the understanding of Troeltsch's thought.

And once more—through this very infatuation with the flow of historical phenomena—we find him unable to gain a firm foothold. In the introduction to his published volume, Troeltsch proposed to seek a way out of the morass of relativism through a dynamic synthesis of the major values that had contributed to the shaping of the European tradition. But this synthesis he was unable to accomplish himself. Presumably it would have been the subject of the unwritten second volume of his *Historismus*. In his published work he restricted himself to the sibylline utterance: "The essential and individual identity of the finite spirits with the infinite spirit and . . . their intuitive participation in the latter's concrete content and mobile unity of life—that is the key to the solution of our problem." [4]

Death carried Troeltsch off in February 1923 on the eve of a lecture trip to England, which—like so many other "good" Germans—he had always admired and always wanted to visit. His literary executors published the manuscripts of the lectures that he had intended for his English audience under the title *Der Historismus und seine Überwindung*—thereby implying that in some fashion the author had "overcome" the crisis in historical thinking. But a reading of the lectures themselves suggests the contrary. It clearly reveals that just before his death Troeltsch was as much at sea as ever. He had found no other way out of his difficulties than an appeal to higher—and ultimately metaphysical—values. "Scepticism and relativism," he wrote, "are only an apparently necessary consequence of modern intellectual conditions and of Historicism. They can be

[3] *Gesammelte Schriften*, III (Tübingen, 1922), pp. 10, 528, 559–65, 630–2.
[4] Ibid., pp. vii–viii, 677.

overcome by way of Ethics, and by way of the ideal forces emerging from history itself, which are only mirrored and concentrated in Ethics."[5] But surely Troeltsch knew that the study of history provided no unequivocal ethical guide: he had long ago outgrown the illusion that he could find a moral code imbedded in the data of history itself. His last work was, rather, a confession of failure—an admission that it had proved impossible to discover stable values *within* the flow of the historical process. In effect, Troeltsch had come back to his starting-point—to revealed religion and faith in things unseen.[6]

Thus Troeltsch died *en pleine crise*. Even as a theologian, he had been supplanted by his juniors: in 1918 Karl Barth had launched the neo-orthodox movement that was to reject with scorn the sort of tolerant, historically based religion of which Troeltsch was the last great representative. It remained for Meinecke to pick up the pieces of the endeavor on which he and his friend had jointly embarked and to try his own hand at a rehabilitation of *Historismus*.

Like Troeltsch, Meinecke faced the problem in a double guise—as a question of abstract historiographic theory and as a question of applied values. His initial solution was once more to separate out the value element from the abstractions of historical philosophy, as he had already done by implication in his acceptance of the Weimar republic. In the review he wrote of Troeltsch's last work, he gave full credit to his friend's immense scholarship and the integrity of his search. But he argued that Troeltsch had made a fundamental error in trying to find an ethical absolute in history. In so doing he had ventured onto metaphysical ground, where *Historismus* did not properly belong. In questions of metaphysics, Meinecke maintained, historical

[5] *Der Historismus und seine Überwindung* (Berlin, 1924), translated under the direction of Baron F. von Hügel as *Christian Thought: Its History and Application* (London, 1923), pp. 106–7.
[6] Rossi: *Storicismo tedesco*, pp. 502–21.

thought must content itself with "general presentiment and intimation. What . . . from the scientific standpoint is its strength becomes its weakness from the standpoint of ethics and practice. . . . With respect to the highest values of life . . . it can say nothing definite and palpable . . . nothing of universal validity . . . that can charm the masses."

Thus Troeltsch had been wrong, Meinecke concluded, to reproach him—Meinecke—for restricting his thought to "pure contemplation." Actually this was the true historian's only recourse. If one tried to "draw up . . . a . . . cultural program," as Troeltsch had done, the result would be to "burden" historical thought with "practical tendencies" that might "disturb its pure striving for the truth." [7] This—in far cruder form—had been Spengler's error; it had been one of the sins of the positivists; in short, in trying to defend *Historismus*, Troeltsch had fallen into the mistakes of its enemies. And Meinecke in turn, in striving to preserve historical thought from practical entanglement, was speaking with the voice of the Croce of the pre-war era.

Yet, like Croce himself, Meinecke was very soon to be forced by circumstances to apply his historical thinking to the area of political value-judgments. In the second of his trilogy of major writings—*Die Idee der Staatsräson in der neueren Geschichte*—which appeared in 1924 a year after his article on Troeltsch, Meinecke grappled once again with the problem of the ethics of power and reason of state.[8] What in his *Weltbürgertum* he had treated in an exclusively German context, he now extended to the whole course of modern European history. And where in his earlier work he had tried to bring ethics and power into a precarious synthesis,

---

[7] *"Troeltsch und Historismus,"* pp. 226–7.

[8] It was not until 1957 that this, the only one of Meinecke's major works to be translated, appeared in London in an English version by D. Scott entitled *Machiavellism: The Doctrine of Raison d'état and Its Place in Modern History.*

he now came to the regretful conclusion that the two were ultimately irreconcilable. The experience of his country at war and the resulting collapse of Bismarck's handiwork had convinced Meinecke of the artificiality of his earlier reconciliation.

Within less than a decade the course of German political history confirmed his negative conclusion. The advent of Hitler brought Meinecke into no personal danger: he had already retired from his professorship at Berlin, and he was too old for active controversy. The Nazis restricted themselves to depriving him of his editorship of the *Historische Zeitschrift*, which he had directed for forty-two years, and then left him alone. Meantime Meinecke got on with his historical labors. The concluding work in his trilogy, *Die Entstehung des Historismus*, appeared in 1936, three decades after he had first undertaken his work of synthesis in the ethico-political field.

This last study, which traced the rise of historical thinking since the eighteenth century, was the most serene and the widest in its compass of all Meinecke's works. The problem that had worried him since his earliest ventures in scholarship he had now pushed to its ultimate limits. His thought had spread in concentric circles: what had begun within the framework of the ethico-political history of Germany and had subsequently been extended to a Europe-wide sphere, Meinecke now undertook to treat in the context of historical thinking itself. Indeed, the subject was so ramifying and difficult that the elderly historian—who had by now reached his mid-seventies—was obliged to give up the hope of bringing it to completion. He was unable to carry his account beyond the work of Goethe: he simply indicated what would have been its logical conclusion by appending to his book a lecture on Ranke that he had prepared for the fiftieth anniversary of the historian's death.

Despite its unfinished form, Meinecke's line of argument was sufficiently clear. As he had already suggested in his essay on Troeltsch, he was taking his stand with the "pure" tradition of German historical thinking—a tradition from which relativism could be regarded as a "shallow" aberration. He had gone back behind Troeltsch, behind Dilthey, to the spiritual world into which he had been born, the world of late eighteenth- and early nineteenth-century idealism. He had gone back to his beloved masters, to Herder, to Goethe, and to Ranke. Faced with the National Socialist destruction of civilized values, he had sought refuge, like so many others of his more sensitive countrymen, in an ideal world of the spirit. Ultimately he had succumbed to his own vaporous brand of metaphysic. What he had earlier called mere "presentiment and intimation" had now come into the center of his thought. As his personal response to the challenge of relativism, he followed Goethe in declaring his "faith in final absolute values" for which he could offer no validation beyond the voice of his own "soul."

In so doing, Meinecke retracted nothing of what he had written earlier. He entitled the second volume of his study "The German Movement," and he described the development of historical thinking as, alongside the Reformation, the second of Germany's "great deeds" in the service of civilization.[9] But this intellectual contribution he refrained from relating in any fashion to his country's political achievement. The pragmatic separation between the sphere of ideas and the sphere of politics which had become increasingly explicit in his post-war writings he had now delineated even more sharply. Meinecke's last great work was full of quiet but unmistakable references to Nazism. By implication at least, it condemned the whole course of German nationalist policy that had ultimately led to Hitler. At the same time, since the analysis did not extend beyond the early nineteenth century, Meinecke was not obliged

[9] *Die Entstehung des Historismus* (Munich and Berlin, 1936), I, 2, 4–5, II, 626–7.

to assess the responsibility of *Historismus* itself for what had occurred in his own time.

There remained only this one further step to take. With the end of the Second World War, with the ruin and partition of his country, Meinecke—now over eighty—once again tried to make an intellectual adjustment to an even more complete catastrophe than that which had overwhelmed him a quarter-century earlier. In a little book of retrospect published in 1946, he revised his views in a fashion that was unprecedented for a historian of such age and eminence. One by one he sacrificed his earlier idols. Now not only Hitler stood condemned: Bismarck was also brought into question "as a borderline case." Indeed, the whole process of German unification appeared in the perspective of 1946 as of doubtful ethical merit. In Meinecke's spirit Weimar had at last definitively triumphed over Potsdam, and Goethe over Bismarck. Even the gentle Ranke was caught up in the process of re-evaluation. Alongside the master of German historians, who had surrounded the realities of power with the euphemisms of "the spirit," Meinecke was now prepared to place the Swiss Burckhardt, who, "more clear-sighted than any other thinker of his time," gave warning of the despotisms to come.[1]

In 1954, when Meinecke died, having lived to even more than Ranke's ninety years and having rendered a last service to scholarship by lending his name as honorary rector to the newly established Free University of Berlin, he had moved a long distance from the gods of his youth. He had not granted in so many words that the Anglo-French empiricists had been right all along in their distrust of German idealism and historical thinking. To have done so would have been to sacrifice

[1] *Die deutsche Katastrophe: Betrachtungen und Erinnerungen* (Wiesbaden and Zürich, 1946), translated by Sidney B. Fay as *The German Catastrophe: Reflections and Recollections* (Cambridge, Mass., 1950), pp. 1–2, 13–14. On the course of Meinecke's intellectual change from 1918 to 1946, besides Hofer's *Geschichtschreibung und Weltanschauung*, see Rossi: *Storicismo tedesco*, pp. 492–501, 521–42.

all the enrichment of understanding that had come out of nineteenth-century Germany. But in appealing beyond Ranke to Goethe himself, Meinecke had tried to go back to a time when the idealist tradition was still unencumbered by mystical abstractions and association with the power-state. He had gone back to the late eighteenth century, when Germany had not yet diverged from the Western European norm, and when men like Goethe and Kant were still working within the assumptions of Anglo-French thought to raise this common intellectual heritage to a higher level of intuitive grasp. In short, he had gone back to the last and greatest of the products of the Enlightenment.

Neither Troeltsch nor Meinecke was a particularly coherent historical thinker. While the former was frankly confused and never attained to a full mastery of his materials, Meinecke unquestionably possessed a talent of a high order. "With extreme finesse he knew how to pick out" what was vital and "with the scrupulousness of a goldsmith" to assign to each historical element its proper place in his account. But when he turned from being a historian to play the philosopher, when "rigor of argument" should have taken over from "finesse of interpretation, . . . this very richness of points of view, this . . . capacity for psychological empathy," became "a weakness." [2] Meinecke had an enormous gift for historical "intuition." But, like his master Ranke, he was incapable of reasoning about history in any unambiguous fashion.

This was Croce's complaint when he came to review the *Entstehung des Historismus*. Although he granted at the start that much could be learned from the "difficult argument" of a book which "in doctrine, acumen and thoroughness" was "altogether worthy" of its author, he differed sharply with Meinecke's central contention. For Meinecke historical thinking seemed to

[2] Antoni: *Dallo storicismo*, p. 97.

consist in making a place for the "irrational in human life." But this, Croce argued, was not at all what *Historismus* actually did. Properly regarded, German historical thinking had criticized and overcome the "abstract rationalism" of the Enlightenment only *"in so far as"* it was *"more profoundly rationalistic"* than the Enlightenment itself.[3] Thus the issue between the two historians was squarely joined. As Meinecke said in his rebuttal, Croce had taken his stand with Hegel while he himself remained true to the example of Ranke.[4]

But the issue was not quite so simple as that. Croce, as we have already observed, was far from being an out-and-out Hegelian, and Meinecke was eventually to become more critical of his beloved Ranke. Actually, in their view of historical study as a whole, the two were united in more ways than they were separated. They had both come out of the tradition of German idealism: they had in common the lessons of Droysen and of Dilthey. Both of them, from the severe critics of the Enlightenment that they had been in their youth, arrived as old men, by quite different pathways, at a wry and guarded endorsement of the philosophy they had scorned.

What separated them, rather, was a divergent interpretation of Dilthey's intellectual legacy. Croce had tried to discipline it by making it more logical and precise. Meinecke had gradually led it back to its origins in late eighteenth-century idealism. Each had ended in a position that was far more *committed*, from a political standpoint, more tied to the world of practical action, than what Dilthey had taught or what the historian himself had originally intended. Moreover, both had narrowed their common inheritance: neither had grasped the full import of Dilthey's analysis of the in-

---

[3] *History as Story of Liberty*, p. 66.
[4] *"Zur Entstehungsgeschichte des Historismus und des Schleiermacherschen Individualitätsgedankens,"* Vom geschichtlichen Sinn und vom Sinn der Geschichte, fourth edition (Leipzig, 1939), pp. 96–7.

terrelationships among the different branches of human study, nor had resumed the attempt to bring history into a dynamic accord with social science; each was too exclusively absorbed in preserving the newly won autonomy of historical study. Finally, both had failed to see that the relativist implications of Dilthey's thought might not necessarily threaten the whole notion of *Historismus*: it did not occur to them to revise the idealist theory of values within a frankly relativist framework. These were the great tasks that still remained if the intellectual revolution of the 1890's was to be pushed to its furthest limits.

The Heirs of Machiavelli:
Pareto, Mosca, Michels

IN September 1917 Benedetto Croce, in introducing to the public a new edition of his essays on historical materialism, declared that the study of Marx had brought him back "to the best traditions of Italian political science, thanks to the firm assertion of the principle of force, of struggle, of power, and the satirical and caustic opposition to the anti-historical and democratic insipidities of natural law doctrine—to the so-called ideals of 1789." [1] For Croce, such a statement was on the periphery of his main interests. It recalled a quasi-Marxist position that he had long ago outgrown and a skeptical attitude toward politics that his future opposition to the Fascist state would definitely transcend. But at the same time it pointed to the central concerns of a group of contemporary Italian thinkers for whom Croce professed great respect and more than

[1] *Materialismo storico ed economia marxistica*, ninth edition revised (Bari, 1951), p. xiii.

a little ideological sympathy. Although he did not mention it in so many words, his preface of 1917 might well have recalled the publication in the previous year of Vilfredo Pareto's *Trattato di sociologia generale*—the most elaborate exposition of a line of thought that has quite properly been called "Machiavellian." [2]

The Italian and semi-Italian representatives of the Machiavellian school—Vilfredo Pareto, Gaetano Mosca, and Robert Michels—do not rank among the most creative minds of the early twentieth century. In terms of wide-ranging imagination and a sophisticated understanding of the categories of social thought they cannot be placed alongside Freud or Weber or their countryman Croce. Yet the very limitations of their thinking gave it a sharper outline than characterized the work of their greater contemporaries, and brought it a more immediate public response. In their anti-metaphysical, intensely practical bent Pareto and Mosca were heirs to an authentic Italian tradition. They codified in a readily comprehensible and ostensibly scientific form the newly rediscovered political doctrines that Sorel and Spengler enunciated in intentionally provocative fragments, and at which a gentler spirit like Croce had no more than hinted.

Pareto, as we have seen earlier, maintained with Sorel a literary friendship of long standing. And he believed that his own theories and Sorel's had to a large extent run parellel. On the latter's death he noted that in his *Trattato* he had "tried to accomplish, with general theories drawn exclusively from experience, what Sorel was doing in other fields." Sorel's "celebrated theory of the *myth*," he added, was only a "particular case" of his own "theory of *residues*." [3]

Similarly Michels had known Sorel in Paris in the period just before the publication of the *Reflections on*

[2] See, for example, James Burnham: *The Machiavellians: Defenders of Freedom* (New York, 1943).

[3] Vilfredo Pareto: "*Georges Sorel*," *La Ronda*, IV (September and October 1922), 542.

Violence, and, while differing with him on the virtues of the syndicalist leaders, had responded warmly to his brutal critique of ideological rhetoric. He was also a friend and protégé of Weber—indeed, in the first decade of the century he served as one of the rare points of contact between French and German social thought.[4] A synthesizing mind rather than a notably original thinker, Michels was to draw together in a coherent doctrine of political leadership elements derived from nearly all the major social theorists of the generation just prior to his own.

Unquestionably, then, Michels was the most cosmopolitan of the leading intellectuals of the early twentieth century—German through his father, French (like Pareto) through his mother, and Italian by a mixture of necessity and choice. When his early Socialist associations had debarred him from academic preferment in his native Germany, he accepted a foreign teaching appointment, first in Italy, then in Switzerland, finally —and permanently—in his beloved Italy. The classic work on political parties for which he was to be chiefly remembered derived much of its authenticity from the lively fashion in which it reflected the author's firsthand experience with the Socialist parties and trade-union movements in all three of the great nations of the West European continent. And when he wrote in it of the personal sacrifice of family associations and professional opportunities which so many Socialist intellectuals of middle-class origin had made, it was doubtless his own case that he had in mind.[5]

Thus both Pareto and Michels formed part of that

[4] "Georges Sorel: Apostle of Fanaticism," *Modern France: Problems of the Third and Fourth Republics*, edited by Edward Mead Earle (Princeton, N.J., 1951), pp. 267, 285; Marianne Weber: *Max Weber: Ein Lebensbild*, new edition (Heidelberg, 1950), pp. 395–6, 402, 408, 526–7.

[5] See, e.g., p. 326 of *Political Parties* (New York, 1915), translated by Eden and Cedar Paul from the Italian edition of *Zur Soziologie des Parteiwesens in der modernen Demokratie* (Leipzig, 1911).

Franco-Italian circle of intellectuals—seeing each other only rarely if at all and held together by no more than correspondence and an intense exchange of ideas— which had Sorel as its central figure. And, like Pareto, Michels came to sociology by way of socialism. Of the trio of neo-Machiavellians, Mosca alone stood aloof from Marxist theory, toward which he displayed an unrelenting hostility based at least in part on misinformation. Likewise he remained untouched by the almost magical attraction of Georges Sorel. As compared to his contemporaries of a similar turn of mind, Mosca never strayed from the path of respectability. Both Pareto and Michels in their different ways at one time or another defied the conventions of upper middle-class society. Mosca—for all the shockingly paradoxical form in which he cast his doctrines—maintained an outward existence that was a model of decorum. Through a life of more than eighty years, as professor, deputy, senator, and minister, he never departed from an attitude of serene competence and of passion held firmly in check: even his opposition to Fascism had something restrained about it. Of the three he alone was to survive into the Second World War and to see the beginning of the breakdown of the regime that he had opposed with both moderation and firmness.

Moreover, Mosca alone worked out his theories in an exclusively Italian setting. His Sicilian birth and the fact that he had passed his whole youth in the Italian south gave the decisive steer to his political thinking. Although he moved to Rome in 1887, when he was just under thirty, and spent the remainder of his life either there or in Turin—where, in the early 1900's, he encouraged and befriended Robert Michels—he never shook off an early skepticism toward representative institutions derived from first-hand experience of the unabashed violence and corruption of Sicilian politics.[6] For Pareto and Michels disillusionment came later. It

[6] Mario Delle Piane: *Gaetano Mosca. Classe politica e liberalismo* (Naples, 1952), pp. 374–5.

was only when the former had lost his battle for a liberal economic policy in his native country, and after the latter had discovered that Socialist parties were just as oligarchical as their conservative enemies, that Pareto and Michels reached the disabused conclusions that we now associate with their names. It was only after they had been disappointed in the hopeful doctrines of the French Enlightenment that they were willing to acknowledge the Italian Machiavelli as their master.

Indeed, the fact that Mosca had never been anything but skeptical—that he had never experienced the shock of disillusionment—may have a good deal to do with the relatively favorable attitude toward representative democracy at which he eventually arrived. On the contrary, Pareto and Michels steadily evolved toward a more critical and even quasi-fascist view. These differences, however marginal they may seem today, are actually of crucial importance in judging the work of these three theorists. The main outlines of Mosca's and Pareto's thought may be similar: in both cases it suggests aristocratic fastidiousness and a distrust of mass democracy; in both cases it unmistakably reflects the political circumstances of the 1880's and 1890's—perhaps the least attractive era of the Italian parliamentary regime. Yet the form of Pareto's and Mosca's works and the methodological presuppositions behind them differed sharply, and these differences, despite the most curious overlappings and internal contradictions, help explain the ultimate divergence that brought Pareto down on one side of a major political divide and Mosca on the other.

As speculative sociologists Pareto and Mosca and Michels were alike Machiavellians in their insistence on the sharp separation between rulers and ruled, on the necessary role of force and fraud in government, and on the inevitable degeneration of all political groups and institutions. With these pessimistic doctrines they coupled—in only apparent disharmony—an equally Machiavellian longing for freedom.

It is through them primarily that contemporary political science and sociology have derived the now standard notion of a political and social élite. It was around this concept that they organized their critique of political ideologies—an analysis that completed the work of Marx by subjecting to his own sort of treatment the socialist aspirations and the socialist view of history that the founder of dialectical materialism had respected as the sole ideology worthy to survive.

We have seen how Pareto's critique of Marxism in his *Systèmes socialistes* had led naturally into a definition of the role of élites in history.[7] His notion of their origin and constitution was pretty crude as compared with our contemporary understanding of the formation of leading groups. For Pareto—like Mosca and Michels also—simply assumed that "superiority" in individuals was something innate and undifferentiated. He failed to recognize the importance of systematic training in the fostering of superior skills, and the differentiation among these skills which might assure success in one situation and bring on catastrophe in another. Moreover he took it for granted that superior individuals craved power: he made insufficient allowance for the other motivations that so often in the past had reduced a power drive to nullity. Yet Pareto's central assumption has stood firm. Again and again contemporary political scientists and sociologists have returned to his major principle that political movements could never be more than the work of active minorities, and that the mass of mankind would remain passive instruments in the power struggle, however "popular" the form of government under which they lived.

This major assumption offered the point of departure for the political portions of Pareto's *Trattato*. But it was actually Mosca—although he was Pareto's junior

[7] See Chapter 3.

by ten years—who first enunciated the concept of a
ruling minority. Mosca's *Teorica dei governi* [8] had formulated the theory of a "political class" nearly two
decades before Pareto hit upon roughly the same idea.
And the fuller exposition of this concept which Mosca
gave in the first version of his *Elementi di scienza politica* [9] still antedated by more than half a decade Pareto's initial formulation. Thus, Mosca was undoubtedly justified in insisting with some vigor on his own
right of priority.[1] And Michels found himself in a difficult position when he tried to give credit to both men,
whom he alike respected as intellectual mentors.

Within this common agreement on the theory of
governing minorities, each of the three thinkers placed
his emphasis in a different fashion. Mosca's formulation was the first and most general. Yet it was in a
characteristically political context—it did no more than
hint at the extension of the doctrine to society as
a whole. For the Sicilian theorist's primary concern
was directed toward the functioning of parliamentary
bodies and the behavior of informal political groupings.
It was for this sort of study that his personal experience
had equipped him, and it was in the definition of parliamentary oligarchies that he excelled. His *Teorica* and
his *Elementi* presented in persuasive form a view of the
political process as managed by narrow and self-perpetuating cliques—a situation in which the presumed
representative of "the people" was not in fact elected
by his constituents but "had himself elected" by impos-
ing his own candidacy.

Yet below the surface of his political reasoning,
Mosca suggested a wider social application. When he

[8] Originally published in Turin in 1884. A second edition was
published in Milan in 1925.

[9] Originally published in Turin in 1896. This book, plus the
second volume that Mosca appended to it in 1923, has been
translated by Hannah D. Kahn, under the editorship of Arthur
Livingston, as *The Ruling Class* (New York, 1939).

[1] Alfonso de Pietri-Tonelli: "*Mosca e Pareto*," *Rivista inter-
nazionale di scienze socali*, VI (July 1935), 468–93.

spoke of the "social forces" that in a properly functioning representative system should all have the opportunity to play their part, he was coming fairly close to a theory of politics based on economic classes. For by social forces he meant the major public interests constituted by businessmen and agriculturists, intellectuals and the military. And of these it was his own "force"—the intellectuals of middling income—for which he served as the "unconscious . . . spokesman." When he characterized "disinterested" public servants as a second stratum of the political class that gave it both competence and continuity, it was people like himself that he had in mind. Their recruitment, he implied, came from the inert mass of the population itself. Thus there was in Mosca a kind of "crypto-Marxism"—as there was a "crypto-democracy" that would eventually land him in a wry acceptance of popular government itself.[2]

It was left for Michels to extend Mosca's theories to the mass organizations characteristic of our own time—organizations that were not yet in existence when the latter first devised his notion of the political class. In the study entitled *Political Parties*—published more than a quarter-century after Mosca's *Teorica*—Michels applied the concept of élites to the Socialist parties and trade unions which had grown up in the meantime and with which he was so well acquainted. What he baptized the "iron law of oligarchy" was a codification of a practical truth that he had discovered through personal experience—the hard-won conviction that political organizations, through the internal necessities of discipline and administrative continuity, inevitably became closed and self-perpetuating oligarchies.[3]

As for Pareto, in his hands the theory of élites eventually was relegated to the position of a subordinate

[2] James H. Meisel: *The Myth of the Ruling Class: Gaetano Mosca and the "Elite"* (Ann Arbor, Mich., 1958), pp. 60–1, 218, 303.

[3] *Political Parties*, pp. 11, 401.

and contributory element in a still more general hypothesis. Alone of the three, Pareto went beyond the facts of political manipulation on which they all agreed, to attempt a definition of those basic human impulses that offered the raw material for mass leadership. His celebrated theory of "residues" and "derivations" applied the common fund of political knowledge to the other aspects of society—more particularly war and religion. In this schema, the residues represented what was unvarying, or at least what changed only very slowly, in human conduct, the derivations the constantly varying explanations and rationalizations of such behavior. Customarily it had been the latter that had occupied the foreground of history: in the future, if Pareto's precepts were to be followed, it would be the residues on which students of society would focus their attention.

Actually, Mosca had come close to a similar formulation when in his first book he had asserted that each political class rationalized its rule in terms of a convenient "political formula"—liberalism, democracy, and socialism being the obvious contemporary examples. But Mosca had not pursued this discovery any farther. He had not gone on to suggest, as Pareto did, that a political formula was simply one example of a more inclusive category of rationalizations: he had not elaborated his hypothesis by pointing to the moral or pseudo-rational "derivations" with which mankind sought to justify the most varied kinds of activity. In this sense Pareto completed Mosca's original insight.

In this same sense the learned world has been right in treating Pareto as the more important figure. Yet we should accept such a judgment only with the strongest reservations. As an empirical worker Pareto was Mosca's inferior: through eight years of parliamentary reporting and his subsequent career as a deputy, the latter acquired an intimate, first-hand knowledge of Italian politics to which Pareto, isolated as he was on the shores of the Lake of Geneva, could never attain. Indeed, of the three it was Michels who marshaled his

evidence most carefully and whose writings come closest to contemporary standards of scientific investigation. Moreover, if Mosca attempted less than Pareto,
he succeeded better in what he actually tried to do. His
Elementi in their final form constitute a clear, graceful,
and classic expression of a theory of politics that has
by now gained wide acceptance. Its good humor and
moderation have won it adherents even in the democratic camp: Mosca's insistence on free competition
among political minorities as the surest guarantee of
liberty has appealed to a number of democratic theorists as a realistic substitute for the traditional arguments from majority rule.[4] We shall find the ultimate
irony of Pareto's relation to Mosca when we observe
that the former's work has stood up best in those very
respects in which it most resembles the writings of his
younger countryman.

One further comparison is in order. Mosca and
Michels were not particularly interested in analyzing
or criticizing the philosophical presuppositions on
which their theories were based. Indeed, in Mosca's
case, the positivist position from which the author
had approached his work remained unaltered through
nearly sixty years of intellectual activity. Or at least
its explicit statement never changed, however much
Mosca's increasing experience of the ambiguities of history might alter it in practice.[5] Pareto too had started
from positivist presuppositions. But, as a more rigorous
thinker than Mosca, he did not rest content with the
bald enunciation of certain fairly obvious principles of
social-science method. Nearly a quarter of his *Trattato*
he devoted to an elaborate exposition of the subjective
and epistemological problems that he had encountered
in his work. In the course of this analysis, Pareto—by

[4] See, for example, Robert A. Dahl: *A Preface to Democratic
Theory* (Chicago, 1956), pp. 54–5, 132.

[5] For elaboration on this theme, see my essay, "Gaetano Mosca
and the Political Lessons of History," in *Teachers of History:
Essays in Honor of Laurence Bradford Packard*, edited by
H. Stuart Hughes (Ithaca, N.Y., 1954), pp. 146–67.

implication at least—was to burst the bounds of his positivist framework. By the same process he was to land himself in inextricable difficulties. This heightened philosophical awareness suggests that we should examine Pareto's method and conclusions in greater detail than seems warranted in the case of Mosca and Michels. In so doing we may perhaps be able to find an explanation of why Pareto's work, after the enormous vogue it enjoyed in the 1920's and 1930's, is comparatively little regarded today—why it has not become the "point of departure for the very fruitful researches" which his most authoritative expositor had confidently anticipated.[6]

Initially we should recall Pareto's intellectual origins. In his early education, natural science and classical studies were the decisive influences. The latter he left dormant for the four central decades of his life—to return to them in his later years when he drew from the history and mythology of Greek and Roman antiquity the curious examples that enliven his *Trattato*. From natural science he never departed very far. By training and original profession an engineer, he retained the technician's cast of mind throughout his subsequent evolution to mathematical economics, the critique of socialism, and, finally, systematic sociology.

I have said that Pareto was a positivist. I should modify this statement by adding that his positivism was not of a crude or unreflective variety. He struggled hard—without complete success—to free himself from the influence of the Social Darwinism that had captivated his youth. He was hostile to the ideas of William James: unlike so many of his contemporaries, he refused to be dazzled by the scientific paradoxes of philosophical pragmatism. But his own notion of science came close to the teachings of Mach and Poincaré: in

[6] G. H. Bousquet: *Vilfredo Pareto: sa vie et son œuvre* (Paris, 1928), p. 212.

this sense it was far more sophisticated than that of most positivists.[7]

In none of his capacities did Pareto function as an empirical investigator. He was a book-bound scholar: he closed himself up in his well-stocked library and from this safe haven viewed the world with Olympian detachment. He was not tempted to engage in unconventional or on-the-spot researches. The elaboration of theories based on extensive reading sufficed. Hence, however much Pareto himself would have objected to the term, I think we must classify his work as "speculative sociology." We must treat with some skepticism his own claims to "logico-experimental" method. Logical it may have been, but not experimental.

A second clue to Pareto's intellectual presuppositions may be found in the personal prejudices with which he approached his work. His father had been a Mazzinian liberal who had gone into exile for his political beliefs—hence the residence in France which, along with the inheritance from his mother, had made the younger Pareto bilingual. Toward his paternal tradition he was obviously divided in mind. One part of it he had retained without question—another part he had cast off in violent fashion. A liberal Pareto remained all his life, more particularly in economics, but also in his insistence on freedom of speech and teaching. Yet the humanitarian and democratic aspects of the Mazzinian inheritance he rejected with an excessive scorn that strikes one as highly suspect: one wonders how many traces of this way of thinking remained lurking in his semi-conscious. For humanitarians Pareto reserved his sharpest taunts: he characterized them as a "baneful

---

[7] Ibid., p. 205; Vilfredo Pareto: *Trattato di sociologia generale*, 2 vols. (Florence, 1916), translated by Andrew Bongiorno and Arthur Livingston under the editorship of the latter as *The Mind and Society*, 4 vols. (New York, 1935), Paragraphs 69, 828, 915 (the paragraph numbering is the same in all editions); Talcott Parsons: *The Structure of Social Action*, second edition (Glencoe, Ill., 1949), p. 181.

animal pest" worthy only of extermination. Professional prudes were his other favorite target. And in the roster of his pet hatreds the demagogues and profiteers of "plutocratic" democracy came only a short distance behind. Again we find a psychological contradiction: in his view of public morality Pareto was extremely rigorous—in his ideas on private morality he was playfully permissive.[8]

A final clue lies in his sense of failure. Despite the free trade polemics to which Pareto had devoted his best energies in the period of the 1880's, protectionism had triumphed in his native land. And under this regime not only Italy but other countries that had followed a similar course had survived and even prospered. Something, Pareto surmised, must have gone wrong with his own reasoning. As an economist he was still sure that he was right. Economics—the science, *par excellence*, of the logical—could not err if its logical processes had been correctly followed. But it was always possible that the calculations of mathematical economics had left something out. Evidently this was what had happened to Pareto. It was this "something" for which he was searching as he embarked on the composition of his *Trattato*.[9]

The non-logical, then, became the subject of Pareto's sociological investigation. As he had defined it, it was simply a "residual category."[1] It was what was left over as incomprehensible after the realm of the logical had been delimited and understood. The very word "residue" with which Pareto classified its manifestations betrayed its character as a mere remainder. This dubious pedigree of the non-logical is central to the understanding of Pareto's speculative sociology. It suggests the

[8] Franz Borkenau: *Pareto* (New York, 1936), pp. 11, 17, 156; *Mind and Society*, Paragraphs 301–4, 2191.

[9] See his jubilee address of 1917, published in abbreviated form in P. M. Arcari: *Pareto* (Florence, 1948), pp. 43–8; also *Mind and Society*, Paragraph 2079.

[1] Parsons: *Structure of Social Action*, p. 192.

hesitation, indeed bewilderment, with which he approached this new material that was so alien to his intellectual preparation. At an age at which most men have permanently cut off their receptivity to new ideas, Pareto set out on the most perplexing quest of his whole long career.

He had sensed that there were some basic persistences in human conduct. But he was at a loss to know how to get at them. Things might have been quite different if he had happily jumped right into the middle of the non-logical—if he had *started* with it, rather than coming to it late in time as a puzzling and annoying remainder. As it was, he was debarred from following either of the two promising avenues of approach that opened before his contemporaries. A prisoner of his own categories of thought, he was not free to explore the lines of investigation that were to prove so illuminating to others.

The first possible path lay through empirical or clinical psychology. It was by this route that Freud had stumbled upon the knowledge that was to revolutionize the twentieth-century study of man. But Pareto explicitly foreswore any psychological probing; he would limit his investigation, he announced, to the *manifestations* of "sentiments and instincts." He would examine non-logical conduct only from the outside, without trying to reach any "internal" understanding. Moreover, even if he had attempted something of the sort, it is extremely doubtful how successful he would have been. The theory and practice of psychoanalysis were unknown to him. Although Freud was only eight years his junior, and although a number of passages in the *Trattato* reveal an acute understanding of "Freudian" sexual connections, Pareto was totally ignorant of the work of his great contemporary—in part for the simple reason that he could not read German. If Pareto had been familiar with the major writings of Freud—nearly all of which had been published prior to the *Trattato*—he might have cast his own work in quite a different form. He might have subsumed a number of aspects of his first five residues under Residue VI, entitled simply "Sex," which, as the *Trattato* was actually composed, figured as a loosely attached and not entirely appropriate appendage to Pareto's main classifications.[2]

From a second path, that of "intuition," Pareto was similarly debarred. He could not permit himself to follow Bergson in accepting intuition as a category of investigation: no self-respecting social scientist of the period—even among the anti-positivists—was willing to go that far. But even the more "scientific" procedure of Max Weber and his school—the sympathetic effort to grasp the immanent logic of the relations among non-logical phenomena—Pareto rejected by dismissing these phenomena as essentially arbitrary rationalizations or "derivations." Here also his ignorance of German, and hence of Weber's sociological work, is obviously relevant. But once again, even if he had known of Weber, the result would probably not have been very different. The whole procedure, derived from the German idealist tradition, of internal understanding, or *Verstehen*, was incompatible with Pareto's positivistically based categories of thought. For it implied a concern with values—and these also Pareto had explicitly refused to discuss, except for the doubtful and quasi-logical category of "social utility."[3]

One of Pareto's most probing critics has correctly suggested that things would have been clearer if the author had subdivided his residues into first, instincts—an at least partially biological category—and second, values—or ideal ends.[4] As it is, the residues suffer from inadequate definition. They hover in a limbo from which positivist reasoning is powerless to release them. Sometimes they appear to be simply biological instincts (and Pareto now and then slips into an ambiguous and

[2] Borkenau: *Pareto*, pp. 39–40, 166; Bousquet, *Pareto*, p. 204; *Mind and Society*, Paragraphs 875, 1202, 1330–2, 1356.
[3] *Mind and Society*, Paragraphs 2111–55.
[4] Parsons: *Structure of Social Action*, p. 225.

loose usage of this very word [5]); sometimes they look like clarifying abstractions in the realm of values—what Weber would have called "ideal types."

The result is an impression of a certain arbitrariness. Pareto ruthlessly criticized the work of Comte and Spencer—but in the end he produced a formal sociology that was not so very different from theirs. Like them, he operated by a kind of reduction from the top down: he squeezed the life blood out of human behavior until finally little more than a listing of hollow categories was left. And why, we are tempted to ask, are there these particular categories and not others? Why are there exactly six residues, defined in capricious fashion in accordance with Pareto's rather special tastes and vocabulary? Pareto himself has said, and his most authoritative commentator has confirmed the assertion, that the residues are not intended to be permanent groupings; they are only provisionally defined.[6] But here Pareto's language again betrays him: his dogmatic tone suggests that the residues have a "real" rather than a merely abstract existence. And the impression of arbitrariness is confirmed by the way in which the supporting data are related to the generalizations. These latter do not appear to grow out of the data, according to accepted empirical procedure. Rather the data are simply appended to the generalizations as *examples*—sometimes many, sometimes only one or two—in mechanistic eighteenth-century fashion.

It is not surprising, then, that two social thinkers of such diverse intellectual origins as Benedetto Croce and Karl Mannheim should have protested against the excessively mechanistic character of Pareto's method.[7] Here once again the author of the *Trattato* defended

---

[5] See, e.g., *Mind and Society*, Paragraph 1218.

[6] Ibid., Paragraph 1690; Bousquet: *Pareto*, p. 136.

[7] See Croce's two letters to Pareto, dating from the year 1900, added to the second (1906) and later editions of *Materialismo storico*, pp. 227, 233, 238, 240; Karl Mannheim: *Ideology and Utopia* (expansion and translation of *Ideologie und Utopie* [Bonn, 1929]) (London and New York, 1936), p. 123.

himself by maintaining that the mechanistic language was merely an "analogy." [8] But the defense is only partially convincing. Surely the *kind* of analogies, of metaphors, that a writer chooses, is not a casual nor unimportant matter. It suggests how his mind works— from what realms of thought and activity he has derived his method of dealing with problems. And Pareto the engineer could scarcely help drawing his "latent presupposed metaphysic" (to use Croce's phrase) from the field of mechanics that he knew so well.

Or, to put it another way, the result of Pareto's purely external consideration of non-logical conduct was a kind of sterile behaviorism. Pareto, as we have seen, refused to inquire into the content of his residues. He established them as the mere "givens" of human behavior, varying "but slightly and but slowly" through history, and essentially inexplicable.[9] Hence it is not unfair to conclude that Pareto left his main problem unsolved. He failed to explain non-logical conduct—he merely tried to delimit it.

Quite obviously, then, what little he had learned about it could be briefly expressed. And indeed what we find is that the bulk of the two-thousand-page *Trattato* consists of illustrative examples. More specifically, we find a complicated methodology only tenuously connected with an entertaining catalogue of *faits divers*. It is these latter that give the *Trattato* its verve and perennial appeal. They come from the most varied sources—classical literature and the daily newspapers are the most frequent—and their relevance is not always immediately apparent. We suspect that Pareto simply smuggled some of them in because he wanted to—because they illustrated one of his persistent predilections or hatreds. Indeed, we find that on the whole these examples do not so much explain his residues as reveal the folly, ignorance, and error of mankind. They constitute an eighteenth-century-type compendium in

---

[8] *Mind and Society*, Paragraph 128.
[9] Ibid., Paragraph 2410; Borkenau, *Pareto*, pp. 43, 48.

the tradition of Bayle or Voltaire. And this impression of Pareto as a belated French *philosophe* is confirmed when we learn that Bayle's *Dictionnaire historique et critique* was his favorite bedside reading.[1]

Pareto professed to be free of logical prejudices. At the beginning of the *Trattato* he proposed to disregard the question of the "experimental truth" of a "derivation" and to judge it solely on the basis of its social usefulness. The most absurd practice or belief, he asserted, could still have beneficial consequences.[2] Moreover, through recognizing the importance of ritual in human society, he at least glimpsed the role of value elements that implied the insufficiency of his positivist categories.[3] But this was only in his moments of maximum awareness. The greater part of the time he operated on a less sophisticated intellectual plane. Generally, in Pareto's encounters with the non-logical, it was an attitude of mockery that dominated.

Thus he found himself in a most paradoxical position. While professing a complete agnosticism on political and religious questions, he actually voiced the strongest prejudices. While laying claim to total scientific detachment, he was in fact deeply engaged by the issues of his day. Hence his work could not properly figure as social science. Nor was it sufficiently imaginative to rank as first-rate speculation. By his stubborn adherence to an outmoded philosophical position, Pareto had denied himself a claim to greatness both as a scientist and as a speculative thinker.

Something at least of this unfortunate situation he seems to have sensed himself. Throughout the *Trattato* there runs a thread of methodological defeatism. In one of his guises Pareto was the last of the system-builders, the residuary legatee of Comte and Spencer.

---

[1] Giuseppe La Ferla: *Vilfredo Pareto filosofo volteriano* (Florence, 1954), pp. 32–3, 68–9, 73, 140; Bousquet: *Pareto*, p. 205; Borkenau: *Pareto*, p. 69.

[2] *Mind and Society*, Paragraphs 72–3.

[3] Parsons: *Structure of Social Action*, pp. 209–10.

In trying to establish what could properly be accomplished by their method—which I have chosen to call a method of "reduction"—he had indeed proved how very little that was. He was a sufficiently penetrating critic to point out where Comte and Spencer had gone astray—but he was unable to recognize that it might be their whole approach that was radically at fault.

A transition figure, too old to learn a new method, Pareto, like Sorel, could find no way out of his difficulties. He could not understand that one might get farther by building up theory gradually from a base in specific, delimited empirical studies, as his contemporaries Durkheim and Weber were doing, rather than by trying once for all to establish a structure of general sociology. He could not see that it was through an explicit recognition of values—including one's own—that the way to an understanding of the non-logical lay, and that this very recognition provided the best assurance that one's personal prejudices would not worm their way back into the argument in disguised form. In brief, he was unable to realize that the "derivations," far from being mere rationalizations, were actually the key to the whole problem.

When this has been said, we may well ask: why bother with Pareto at all? Why, despite all his failings, do we still come away from reading him with a sense that he has at least partially established what he undertook to prove?

Initially we should recall the polemical success of the *Systèmes socialistes*. It was here, rather than in the *Trattato*, that Pareto's superb critical intelligence appeared to best advantage. For in his book on socialism he combined most effectively the analytical tightness that characterized his original economic studies with the literary verve that his subsequent sociological work was to display. The *Systèmes socialistes* had a narrower theme than the *Trattato* and expressed the author's personal predilections more explicitly. Perhaps for this very reason it accomplished its purpose better: the theory grew out of the polemic in a readily observable relationship to empirical fact.

This theory constituted the initial statement of Pareto's doctrine of the élite. And to it he returned in the last part of the *Trattato*, bringing to bear on it his complicated paraphernalia of residues and derivations. This last section by general consent ranks as the most satisfactory part of his sociology, indeed the only part that has exerted much permanent influence. The irony of the relationship of the elderly Pareto to his earlier incarnation was that his sociological theories succeeded best where they most resembled his more polemical and less systematic efforts—or where they echoed the words of Mosca. Pareto's residues took on reality and relevance only after they had received a specifically political application.

But this was at the price of a radical simplification. In the last part of the *Trattato* the derivations lead only a shadow existence. And the residues, originally six in number, are in practice reduced to two.[4] As the work draws to a close, the whole vast scaffolding that Pareto has earlier constructed is progressively dismantled down to a theory of the alternation through history of two contrasting and complementary attitudes toward the wider aspects of political life.

The recognition of these attitudes is once again a legacy from Machiavelli. "Lions" and "foxes"—the classic contrast suggests that Pareto's original concept may have been an extremely simple "intuition." As has happened so often in the history of social thought, the theorist spent a decade of his life and two thousand pages explaining with pseudo-empirical arguments an early flash of imaginative insight. Residue I—"instinct

---

[4] Residues III ("need of expressing sentiments by external acts") and VI ("sex") virtually drop out, while Residues IV ("sociality") and V ("integrity of the individual and his appurtenances") tend to group themselves under Residue II. See Borkenau: *Pareto*, p. 72.

for combinations"—is simply the metaphor of the fox spelled out in detail. Or this at least is what we realize, once the original definition of the residue—which is excessively abstract and based largely on historical examples—is given a contemporary application. Similarly, Residue II—"persistence of aggregates"—explains the symbol of the lion. It is here that Pareto demonstrates his virtuosity in most convincing fashion. The first residue is not difficult to establish: to Italians at least, the word *combinazioni* in itself is sufficient to convey a clear and widely ramifying meaning. "Persistence of aggregates," however, is a subtler complex, grouping under one heading such diverse manifestations as conservative ideals, revolutionary ardor, and religious zeal. Its definition as an abiding element in human society is perhaps Pareto's single greatest contribution to contemporary political speculation.

Nothing, then, would be more inaccurate than to conclude as some hasty readers have done, that the two key residues stand respectively for conservatism and dissent. Indeed, one of the great virtues of Pareto's schema is that it cuts across the conventional left-right cleavage. Thus—to take an example close to Pareto's own experience—it offers an imaginative explanation of the bewildering ideological shifts of a Mussolini. Whether a revolutionary Socialist or the darling of the Italian propertied classes, the Duce in one sense always remained true to himself: he was never anything but a lion.

To chart the vicissitudes of these two attitudes through more than two thousand years of Western history was Pareto's final achievement. The assessment of how much of each residue characterized the successive élites of history—and how the contradictory attitude manifested itself either through the progressive infusion of new elements into an old ruling class or through the violent overthrow of one élite by another—this estimate of the "social equilibrium" called forth Pareto's most pungent and telling commentary. It is unquestionable that his personal sentiments were deeply involved in the discussion. For his own time, at least, he was convinced that a reaction was in order. The Western world, he argued, was reaching the end of a cycle of "demagogic plutocracy": the foxes held nearly unchecked sway, and unless the ruling classes produced their own lions to restore the balance, the lions already visible among the lower orders would sweep the present élite into the scrap-heap of history.[5]

Like Sorel, Pareto saw the contemporary need for a restoration of heroic values. Yet his attitude was not a simple one of political militancy. On the contrary, he was enough of an Italian skeptic to find a good deal of the fox in himself. He had the tolerance for ambiguity of the born historian. A saving ambivalence underlay his contradictory prejudices, and he revealed the span of his sympathies by the way in which he fashioned the definition of his two historical persistences. His debt to Machiavelli he acknowledged with gratitude—toward Vico he was more churlish.[6] Yet it was obviously from the latter as well as from Machiavelli that he had derived his cyclical view of history. More systematically than Mosca, Pareto had drawn on one of the oldest traditions of Italian thought to bring the revivifying breath of skepticism to the musty chambers of social theory.

And so we are left with the ultimate question: can the neo-Machiavellians in any verifiable sense be held responsible, even in part, for the advent of Fascism in Italy? Should we count them among the gravediggers of early twentieth-century democracy? Such a question obviously permits of no complete answer. All we can do is to suggest a few critical distinctions that may reduce it to manageable proportions.

Initially we may repeat the conventional but still

---

[5] *Mind and Society*, Paragraphs 2025–59, 2178–9, 2340–1, 2386–7, 2392, 2480, 2553; Arcari: *Pareto*, p. 271.
[6] *Mind and Society*, Paragraphs 1975, 2166, 2330, 2532.

valid observation that the neo-Machiavellian current of thought in Italy contributed to that anti-parliamentary atmosphere from which Mussolini was eventually to profit. Pareto in particular, by his violent attacks on the personnel and functioning of parliamentary democracy, undoubtedly helped to discredit in the minds of that minority of educated Italians who read his work the institutions of the pre-Fascist state. And when Mussolini had at length achieved power, Pareto recognized the new dispensation as the fulfillment of his earlier predictions. He accepted the senatorship that the Duce offered him—although he never actually took his seat—and during the ten months that elapsed between the March on Rome and his own death he ranked as at least a qualified supporter of the Fascist regime.

The fashion, however, in which he qualified his allegiance, was of more than incidental importance. For it recalled the original ambivalence that Pareto had displayed toward his Mazzinian inheritance. The anti-humanitarian in him applauded Mussolini's hardness and realism. The liberal deplored the Fascist measures that curbed the citizen's freedom of expression. Hence it was psychologically appropriate that Pareto's last published statements should have been pleas for the preservation of liberty of the press and of teaching.[7]

Mussolini himself in his customary fashion took pleasure in citing Pareto as one of his masters. Here, at least, the future Duce's personal association with the author in question was not quite so remote as was usually the case with these unsought-for expressions of esteem. In the summer of 1904, when Mussolini was living as a draft-evader in Switzerland, he enrolled for two of Pareto's courses of lectures at the University of Lausanne—yet it is by no means clear that he actually attended them. In the same year he praised the *Systèmes socialistes* for its "precision," "clarity," and "frankness," and subsequently characterized the idea

[7] La Ferla: *Pareto*, pp. 169–70; Bousquet: *Pareto*, pp. 189–94.

of the élite enunciated in that book as "probably the
most extraordinary sociological conception of modern
times." Apparently, then, he had read at least this
much of Pareto's work. But there is no evidence at all
that he was familiar with the *Trattato*.[8]

So far as I know, Mussolini never bestowed a similar
accolade on the work of either Mosca or Michels. In
the case of the latter, the oversight was quite natural:
Michels was younger and less well known in Italy than
the two rival creators of the theory of élites, and the
Duce may simply not have heard of him. In point of
fact, however, Michels adapted himself quite easily to
the Fascist regime, and his later writings contain references to Mussolini's rule that are unmistakably respectful in tone.[9] There is a quaint justice in the fact that it
was the least original among the trio of neo-Machiavellians who found Fascism the least troubl'ng.

In Mosca's case, however, Mussolini was well advised
to maintain silence. Already in the second edition of
the *Elementi*, which had gone to press just before the
March on Rome, Mosca had taken a far more affirmative position toward parliamentarism and democracy
than had characterized the book in its original form.
And after Mussolini's accession to power, Mosca joined
his fellow senator Croce in a dignified stand against the
growing arbitrariness of the Duce's authority. Mosca
was never outstanding for anti-Fascist militancy: political militancy as such was abhorrent to him. But he
ranked among the small band of senators who in the
late 1920's were almost alone in Italy in openly voicing
their opposition to Mussolini's rule.[1]

[8] Gaudens Megaro: *Mussolini in the Making* (London, 1938),
pp. 112–17.
[9] See, for example, the *Corso di sociologia politica* (Rome,
1927), translated and edited by Alfred de Grazia as *First Lectures
in Political Sociology* (Minneapolis, 1949), pp. 113–15, 119,
126, 128, 131, 137, 153.
[1] See the introductory essay by Gaetano Salvemini to A. William Salomone: *Italian Democracy in the Making* (Philadelphia,
1945), pp. xv–xvi.

Both Pareto and Mosca distinguished sharply between the liberal and the democratic traditions. Both of them espoused the former and called the latter into question. Both held to the nineteenth-century view that free institutions were compatible rather with oligarchy than with popular government. But in the ultimate confrontation with the destroyer of liberalism and democracy, they took divergent courses. Pareto, like most Italian liberals, acquiesced in the sacrifice of freedom to order. Mosca, like Croce and a handful of others, found his way to a grudging acceptance of democracy. And, like Croce, he found it through recognizing that in the twentieth century the fate of popular government and the fate of liberalism were inextricably entangled, and that the two must stand or fall together.

Why this crucial difference? One explanation would be that Mosca lived long enough to experience Fascism in its fully developed form: Pareto died before the new regime had had time to display a number of its more sinister features. But this explanation is obviously insufficient. It fails to take account of the reorientation in Mosca's thought that had occurred even before Mussolini's accession to power. What this reorientation betokened was, rather, a deep-seated divergence between Mosca's and Pareto's whole approach. For all their apparent similarity, the two men's minds worked quite differently. Pareto sought for formulas in mechanistic fashion. Mosca—despite his positivist language—let his mind play easily over possibilities and hypotheses. Pareto's intellectual manner was cold and scornful—Mosca's warm and good-humored. Both were skeptics. But in Pareto's case the skepticism reflected the bitter disillusionment of political defeat—with Mosca it derived from the urbane knowledge of human nature congenital to the Italian south. Both were children of the Enlightenment. But in Pareto it was the negative, mocking aspect of the eighteenth-century inheritance that dominated—in Mosca it was the willingness to subject all human institutions to dispassionate scrutiny and to learn from mankind's mistakes how to make future generations a trifle less unhappy than their predecessors. Once more we find that it is the style and tone of a man's thought, his scarcely articulated presuppositions and aspirations, to which we must look for the clue to his vision and his blindness, his intellectual triumph and failure.

Postscript: Alain and the Restatement of Radicalism

At first regard, nothing could seem more alien to the thought of Pareto and Mosca and Michels than the work of the modest French *lycée* professor and essayist Emile-Auguste Chartier, usually known by his pen-name, Alain. For Alain sounded like a voice from the remote past. He was not only old-fashioned—he was ostentatiously provincial.

> Everything is obvious about him, and everything is strange. A philosopher writing daily "columns" in a provincial newspaper, and by imperceptible steps establishing himself as a power in French thought and literature; a political theorist wearing without shame the outmoded and almost seamy garb of the small-town radical, and maintaining stubbornly his position against the mighty hosts of Maurrasian reaction on the right and Marxism on the left; a profoundly religious man, a catholic in the fullest sense, who also professed to be a free-thinker and a determined anticlerical—Alain is the most improbable of chimeras.[2]

As the self-constituted keeper of the conscience of the French Radical party, he was unavoidably a doctrinaire democrat. He stood for the rights of the elector, he struggled against the power of the bureaucracy, he distrusted the corruptions of Paris—in short, as a rather

  [2] Albert Guérard: "The Enigma of Alain," *Fossils and Presences* (Stanford, Calif., 1957), p. 171.

naïve "incorruptible" he represented all the things at which Pareto railed and Mosca smiled. Why, then, do we consider him along with them—even if only as an appendage?

Actually, Alain was not as unsophisticated as he seemed. His political memory was elephantine, and the short daily columns in which he voiced his opinions can still be read with profit as pungent commentaries on the France of the decade immediately preceding the First World War and of the half-decade that followed it. Ten years younger than Mosca, he had already lived through a good deal of history when he first began to write his articles, and he had developed a nearly infallible sense for what was really important in political life. The Dreyfus case had given him the first elements of a political education. It was this that had spurred him to enter the field of journalism and to help in organizing those "Popular Universities" for the enlightenment of the poor which were the targets of Sorel's particular scorn. A decade and a half later the First World War completed the lesson. Enlisting as a private soldier at an age at which most of his contemporaries were safely behind desks, Alain saw four years of service at the front. The experience both hardened him and made him more humane. When on his return to civilian life he resumed his newspaper columns, it was apparent that a passionate revulsion against war had been added to his former hatreds—and with it a new and deeper pity for *la condition humaine*.[3]

Thus Alain was far from being what he often seemed —a stubborn little professor without experience of the great world. There was only one side of him that was doctrinaire—the side that descended from Rousseau and never doubted for a moment the dogma of universal suffrage. It is his other side, the incarnation in which he was as "tough" and realistic as Pareto or Mosca, that is of interest to us now.

---

[3] Ibid., p. 175.

Alain understood to perfection the fashion in which French government and politics actually worked. He had few illusions about democracy. He was just as convinced as Mosca or Pareto that it was an élite or oligarchy—he used both terms—that was the real master of the state. And he charted with rare precision the fashion in which the oligarchs employed the arts of "politeness and cordiality" to disarm their foes. In terms strikingly reminiscent of Michels he noted how political parties inevitably succumbed to their own organizational needs. Even the sacred doctrine of universal suffrage he subjected to critical scrutiny: unquestionably "the people" could err. "A tyrant can be elected by universal suffrage and be no less a tyrant for that." Indeed, there is something curiously negative about Alain's whole doctrine. "Many people," he notes, "say that the important thing is to advance; I think rather that the important thing is not to retreat." [4] The best that the citizen—or the deputy—can do is to "control" the action of the permanent officials. A steady, unremitting, indefatigable resistance to injustice and oppression—that is the substance of Alain's political credo.

A Norman and a man of modest origin like Sorel, Alain had something of Sorel's downrightness and almost peasant simplicity. But, unlike Sorel, Alain had passed through the conventional selecting-ground of the French literary and philosophical élite, the Ecole Normale Supérieure. He differed from such other *normaliens* as Durkheim and Bergson, however, in never attaining—or apparently seeking—the highest academic honors. He remained all his life a secondary-school teacher—and proud to be one—proud to be in opposition to the Sorbonne and to the constituted powers of the university, as he was in opposition to all other constituted authority. "The rebel," he wrote of himself in reviewing nearly eighty years of his life, "took on

[4] *Eléments d'une doctrine radicale* (Parks, 1925), pp. 111, 124, 152, 180.

only the garment" of respectability. "Even today I think with the movement of a horse that resists the rein." [5]

Alain occupied a position somewhere between Sorel's uncompromising rejection of bourgeois culture and the substantial acceptance of the *status quo* characteristic of his contemporaries, both French and Italian, who held major university chairs and enjoyed flattering public honors. Hence he was qualified—as Sorel obviously was not—to bring into the democratic tradition the essentials of the political doctrine that Pareto and Mosca had enunciated from the standpoint of an aristocratic conservatism. Alain, like Sorel, had seen a number of the same things they had. But he was congenitally opposed both to Sorel's or Pareto's attitude of scorn and to Mosca's urbane tolerance of folly. A robustly optimistic temper kept him alike from skepticism and from catastrophic social protest.

The neo-Machiavellians—like Machiavelli himself— viewed political life from the standpoint of the rulers. Alain unquestioningly took his stand with the ruled. Here lay the nub of the difference.

---

[5] "*Avant-propos à des morceaux choisis*" (hitherto unpublished manuscript dating from 1946), *La Nouvelle Revue Française: Hommage à Alain* (Paris, 1952), p. 305.

Max Weber and the Transcending
of Positivism and Idealism

Preamble: Durkheim and the Positivist Remainder

AGAIN AND AGAIN in the course of the present study
we have followed the process of slow revision that
led one or another thinker away from the assumptions
of his youth toward new definitions of the nature of
experience in society. We have seen it quite explicitly
in the case of Meinecke—more quietly and by implication only in the work of Mosca and Freud. With Emile
Durkheim we come to the single most dramatic instance of such a change: from being the most positivistically minded of the protagonists of this study, Durkheim gradually evolved toward a standpoint that was
idealist in all but name. This is the perplexing thing
about his work: while its ultimate implications are
"spiritual" in the extreme, its explicit methodology
remains positivist and even mechanistic. Durkheim
never realized quite how far he had come: he died be-

fore he had had time to make a full and coherent statement of his final position.

We have met Durkheim already as Bergson's contemporary at the Ecole Normale Supérieure and as the
author of a tantalizingly incomplete critique of socialism. By the time he delivered the lectures on which
this posthumous book was based, Durkheim had just
about won his battle for personal recognition and for
recognition of sociology as a field of study in the academic world. Earlier his course had been a difficult one.
In contrast to the brilliant Bergson, he had made only
a mediocre record at Normale, and in the *agrégation* of
1882 he placed next to the bottom. This undistinguished showing, however, may simply reflect the fact
that he had been obliged to take his examinations in
philosophy—since the formal study of sociology did not
yet exist. And it was as a *lycée* professor of philosophy
that he earned his living during the next five years.

Durkheim's reasons for becoming a sociologist immediately suggest the nature of his intellectual assumptions and value-system. In the first place, although he
respected at least one of his philosophy teachers at
Normale, he was radically dissatisfied with the mystical
abstractions, the literary and *dilettante* character of the
philosophy to which he had been exposed as a student.
In its place, he wanted to establish an intellectual discipline that would be more concrete and would refer
more directly to social reality. And in so doing he was
not ashamed to call himself the heir of Auguste Comte,
and to subject himself to the influence of Herbert
Spencer. But he soon balanced this positivist emphasis
through a systematic survey of the German intellectual
scene: in the year 1886 he made a journey of explora-
tion to Germany, from which resulted two thorough re-
ports that first established his reputation as a social
thinker.

The French state rewarded him by entrusting him
with a course in social science at the University of Bordeaux—which marked the earliest official recognition in

France of the new discipline of sociology. Nine years later, in 1896, the first French chair of social science was created for him, again at Bordeaux, and in 1902 he received the call to Paris. A loyal servant of the French state Durkheim remained throughout his life. Indeed, the second of his reasons for undertaking the study of sociology at all had been "his desire to contribute to the moral consolidation of the Third Republic." Almost alone among the major thinkers we have been studying, Durkheim never wavered in his militant advocacy of democratic and humanitarian values: he stood for all the things which Pareto scorned and which Croce and Mosca regarded with detached skepticism. In Durkheim's mind, science reinforced democracy, and democracy science: he was a true child of the Enlightenment.[1]

These loyalties place Durkheim in a somewhat special position *vis-à-vis* his contemporaries. Bergson and Freud, in a very general sense, agreed with him, but they were more detached from the immediate problems of society. It is only in his anthropologically oriented studies that we find Freud making specific reference to Durkheim's work.[2] Sorel's attitude, as we saw earlier, was marked by ironic deference: Durkheim, he noted, was by far the "cleverest" sociologist in the French educational system, and he cited the latter's *Suicide* with approval.[3] Despite their radically contrasting attitudes toward their country's political institutions, the two men had certain important things in common: they were science-minded, and they were interested in the

[1] Harry Alpert: *Emile Durkheim and His Sociology* (New York, 1939), pp. 15, 17–21, 23–33, 38–42, 61; Talcott Parsons: *The Structure of Social Action*, second edition (Glencoe, Ill., 1949), p. 301.
[2] *Totem und Tabu* (Leipzig and Vienna, 1913), translated from the fifth edition (1934) by James Strachey as *Totem and Taboo* (*Standard Edition*, XIII, 1–162) (London, 1955), pp. 113, 116, 120, 124.
[3] "*Avenir socialiste des syndicats*" (1898), *Matériaux d'une théorie du prolétariat* (Paris, 1919), pp. 83, 124–8.

practical aspect of scientific discovery. Indeed, in Durkheim's late work we encounter a theory of knowledge that is almost Sorelian in its specifically practical origin.[4] Within France, Durkheim enjoyed for the whole latter part of his life a steadily growing reputation: to a far greater extent than was the case with any German or Italian thinker, he was able to lead virtually the whole study of social science in his own country into the channels that he had marked out for it.

Yet this very intense concentration on the future of *French* social science tended to separate him from the world of German-Italian intellectual exchange. Neither Croce nor Weber paid any attention to him. Nor did he occupy himself with the problems of understanding mankind *in the historical world*, which were their main concern. For purposes of our present study, Durkheim is a peripheral figure.

Among the strong points of Durkheim's approach to social study, the first and most obvious was his militant refusal of all forms of metaphysical argument. Like Croce, he classed himself as an unrepentant rationalist. But he differed from Croce in having no Hegelian nor neo-idealist propensities. Since sociology, he noted,

had its birth in the great philosophical doctrines, it has retained the habit of relying on some philosophical system with which it has . . . become closely bound up. It has thus been successively positivistic, evolutionary, idealistic, when it should have been content to be simply sociology. . . .

Sociology does not need to choose between the great hypotheses which divide metaphysicians. It needs to affirm free will no more than determinism. All that it asks is that the principle of causality be applied to social phenomena. And even this

[4] *Les Formes élémentaires de la vie religieuse* (Paris, 1912), translated by Joseph Ward Swain as *The Elementary Forms of the Religious Life*, new edition (Glencoe, Ill., 1947), pp. 18–19.

principle is enunciated . . . not as a rational necessity but only as an empirical postulate, the product of legitimate induction.[5]

If we need a brief formula, we may term Durkheim's
initial position a moderate and sophisticated positivism.

Secondly, Durkheim was able to maintain, in a fashion that was unknown in other countries, a characteristically French alliance between sociology and anthropology. His students could be found in both fields, and
his own last major work could be considered a contribution to both disciplines. And this linkage he made possible through the markedly empirical character of his
own labors. As opposed to Comte and Spencer—and
Pareto after them—with their ambitions to encompass
the whole of sociology in one mighty work, Durkheim
concentrated his attention on discrete problems of
manageable proportions. Of the four main books for
which he is known, only one is programmatic—*The
Rules of Sociological Method,* which is a slim and modest affair compared to Pareto's vast elaboration of principles. The other three—on the division of labor, on
suicide, and on aboriginal religion—are all empirical
studies serving as adequate springboards for relatively
restrained flights into theory.

This empirical focus constitutes a third strong point
of Durkheim's approach. Finally, we might add his concern for what he called the *moral* element in society. It
is in this guise that Durkheim most obviously ranks as
an heir of the Enlightenment. From the start—even
when he was dealing with apparently narrow and technical problems such as suicide and the division of labor—he was in fact concentrating his attention on the
central values of life in society. It was in these early
works, for example, that he first defined the concept of
anomie—a state of social disequilibrium in which the

---

[5] *Les Règles de la méthode sociologique* (Paris, 1895), translated from the eighth edition by Sarah A. Solovay and John H.
Mueller as *The Rules of Sociological Method* (Chicago, 1938),
p. 141. I have altered the translation somewhat.

hierarchy of values disintegrates and "all regulation is lacking." [6] Durkheim's *anomie*, like Pareto's *élite* or Weber's *charisma*, has passed into the standard vocabulary of contemporary social discussion. As a term for describing an intangible and essentially spiritual aspect of society, it suggests that even in his early work Durkheim was by no means bound to a merely mechanical view of the social universe.

Yet here lies the very problem. Durkheim realized from the start that the defining characteristics of society were of a subjective order. The *sense* of being a member of a social unit he knew to be the decisive consideration. But he found it almost impossible to find suitable terms in which to express this understanding. In his first book he quite consciously employed a mechanistic vocabulary in an effort to give his work a scientific tone: later it became largely a matter of intellectual habit. Thus in this early work Durkheim most inappropriately referred to social factors as "things"— thereby suggesting that there was something tangible and external about them. Concomitantly he experimented with such non-mechanical terms as "collective consciousness" and "collective representations." None of these, however, proved adequate to express his sense of the symbolic and moral aspect of social solidarity. Like Freud or Pareto, he was handicapped to the very end of his life by a vocabulary in which terms borrowed from mechanics came most naturally to hand.

In the academic year 1894–5 Durkheim for the first time offered a course on religion. The study of this new subject came as a "revelation" to him. "The course of 1895," he wrote, "marks a line of demarcation in the development of my thought; so much so, that all my previous researches had to be taken up again with re-

---

[6] *Le Suicide: étude de sociologie* (Paris, 1897), translated from the edition of 1930 by John A. Spaulding and George Simpson as *Suicide: A Study in Sociology* (Glencoe, Ill., 1951), pp. 252–3.

newed efforts in order to be placed in harmony with
these new views." [7]

As we have already seen with Bergson and Sorel and
Pareto—and as we shall very shortly observe in the case
of Weber—a confrontation with religious phenomena
has repeatedly been an experience of decisive importance in the unfolding of twentieth-century social
thought. In Durkheim's case it marked the beginning
of a slow transition to a new and deeper understanding
of his subject matter. But this transition was completed
too late for him to carry out in thoroughgoing fashion
the revision of his previous researches that he had
planned. When the work that marked the culmination
of this late phase—*The Elementary Forms of the Religious Life*—was published, the war was only two years
away; and the conflict was to involve Durkheim in a
turmoil of activity and suffering that eventually cost
him his life.

In approaching the sphere of religion, Durkheim—
the rabbi's son turned unbeliever—adopted an attitude
not dissimilar to that of William James, whose father
had also been of the clergy. And in this attitude both
James and Durkheim were innovators. Until the very
end of the nineteenth century the scholarly discussion
of religion had conventionally reflected the personal
belief or disbelief of the individual scholars: those who
were religious themselves had written of the phenomenon with affectionate respect; the freethinkers had
used religious history and ethnology as "a weapon
against religion." Durkheim proposed to do neither.
Unlike Pareto, he kept his own disbelief strictly out of
the discussion by adopting a stand that made the whole
question irrelevant. It was not important, he argued, to
inquire whether one or another doctrine was "true" or
"false." Depending on how one chose to consider it, all
religion was *both* true and false. Its specific "beliefs and
practices" were "undoubtedly . . . disconcerting." But
even "the most barbarous and the most fantastic rites

[7] Alpert: *Durkheim*, p. 67.

and the strangest myths" corresponded to some deeper "social . . . need."

In reality, then, there are no religions which are false. All are true in their own fashion. . . . . The reasons with which the faithful justify them may be, and generally are, erroneous; but the true reasons do not cease to exist, and it is the duty of science to discover them.[8]

These "true" reasons Durkheim eventually located, not where both believers and unbelievers had earlier assumed them to be—in the dogmas of organized religion —but in religious practice, in what the French call the cult. It was in the *practice* of religion, as James had discovered, that the scientific reality of religious experience lay. And this reality was a *social* reality. The practice of religion produced a sense of solidarity, of personal reinforcement through the group—in short, a sense of society itself. Thus Durkheim was led to define society as religious in origin. Religion *created* society: that was its true function from the standpoint of positive science.[9]

By the same token, Durkheim was led in effect to the assertion that society existed "only in the minds of individuals. . . . In escaping from the toils of positivism" he "overshot the mark" and went "clean over to idealism." If religion in the end proved to be a social phenomenon, so also society turned out to be a religious phenomenon.[1] An ironical conclusion for one who had first tried to define society in terms of "things."

The outbreak of the war swept Durkheim into a fever of public activity. As a Jew and an Alsatian, he was a more than normally patriotic Frenchman. And he felt no incompatibility between his role as a man of science and what he conceived to be his duties as the citizen of

---

[8] *Elementary Forms*, pp. 2–3.
[9] Ibid., pp. 416–19.
[1] Parsons: *Structure of Social Action*, pp. 427, 442, 445.

a nation at war: his wartime writings largely consist of propagandist tracts directed against a Germany defined as both an intellectual and a national enemy. In addition Durkheim was indefatigable in the work of the numerous academic committees that strove to reinforce the French war effort.

Gradually all this activity sapped his strength. And the news of the death of his son—who had at the same time been one of his most promising students—inflicted a blow from which he never recovered. In the autumn of 1917 Durkheim died, still under sixty, and with his new view of the social universe still only in outline form.[2]

He left behind him a personal example and a series of methodological precepts that have proved to be fundamental to the development of contemporary social science. But in a more philosophical sense, his teaching gave no clear lead. To the very end, a central contradiction remained. On the one hand, there was the positivist vocabulary, the striving for a system of "imperative rules" in which critics have seen the last traces of the Comtian metaphysic.[3] And with it there went a hankering after simple and unilateral explanations. At the same time, there was the sweepingly spiritual definition of social reality, whose implications were obviously idealist, permissive, and pluralistic. These two aspects of his doctrine Durkheim never brought into any conclusive synthesis.

Finally, we should note the unhistorical character of Durkheim's thought. His formulations were more static than dynamic; they were cast in terms of structure rather than of process. He had succeeded in marrying sociology to anthropology under quasi-positivist auspices. In similar fashion the German neo-idealists were virtually fusing the world of social science and the world of historical experience. These two systems of al-

[2] Alpert: *Durkheim,* pp. 72–7.
[3] Roger Lacombe: *La Méthode sociologique de Durkheim: étude critique* (Paris, 1926), pp. 164–6.

liances had not yet met. And their meeting was to be Max Weber's great achievement. To combine the Germanic sense for history and philosophy with the Anglo-French and positivist notion of scientific rigor was the task that Weber set himself—a task that he, more than any other of his contemporaries, was qualified by temperament and training to confront.

1. *Intellectual Origins and Early Production*

Durkheim and Weber are conventionally held in honor as the two most important founders of the discipline of sociology as we know it today. And it has on occasion proved possible to find in their leading concepts a wide area of agreement. This reconciliation, however, has been a kind of *tour de force*—a dramatic illustration of the extent to which early twentieth-century social thought was heading in a single direction, despite the most extraordinary personal and intellectual divergences among its creators.[4] From the more general standpoint of intellectual history, the dissimilarities between the two have remained unresolved.

To recall that Durkheim was French and Weber German, that the former was Jewish and the latter the offspring of the Prussian upper middle class—and that both were more than usually patriotic—is only to begin to sketch their differences. Obviously it is relevant to add that while one came out of the positivist tradition, the other was by origin a German idealist. And this idealist pedigree suggests the whole intellectual atmosphere that has differentiated French sociology from German—Durkheim's tradition from Weber's. In France, as we have repeatedly observed, the dominant temper was rationalist, science-minded, anti-clerical—in short, inspired by a sober confidence in modern society and the works of man. In Germany there had lingered on from the early nineteenth century a non-

[4] Parsons: *Structure of Social Action*, pp. 13–14.

dogmatic religiosity, an emphasis on the spiritual and a distrust of the material world. German social thinkers characteristically came from conservative, religiously oriented families: clergymen's sons were not infrequent. In this tradition it seemed natural to set emotion against reason, community sentiment against technological change, and to protest, either directly or by implication, against capitalism and the rationalized society.[5]

To put the difference in personal terms, Durkheim does not strike one as a particularly troubled individual. Indeed, his chief intellectual weakness was a tendency to dogmatism. Weber, for all the intemperance of his polemical style, was hesitant, self-divided, and enormously troubled. For that very reason he is the key figure of our study. He stands at more decisive meeting points than any other thinker. To begin to list these confrontations is to suggest his range and the ambiguous nature of his achievement: idealism and scientific method; economics and religion; Marxism and nationalism; political commitment and an insistence on "objectivity" in social science. He was both a democrat in his personal convictions and a contributor to that radical critique of democracy which Pareto and Mosca had launched. He was skeptical about the viability of the Enlightenment under twentieth-century conditions, yet his temperamental reaction to events was more often than not of an "enlightened" character. Even in his contributions to the terminology of social science his contradictions and ambivalences are mirrored.

As we associate Durkheim with the concept of *anomie,* so we think of Weber in connection with the linked notions of bureaucracy and *charisma*. These concepts contradict and balance each other, and Weber's

[5] Raymond Aron: *La Sociologie allemande contemporaine* (Paris, 1936), translated from the second edition (1950) by Mary and Thomas Bottomore as *German Sociology* (Glencoe, Ill., 1957), pp. 114–15.

attitude toward them is in turn one of attraction and repulsion. On the one hand he was convinced that the deepest tendency of the contemporary Western world was toward a bureaucratization of all phases of public activity: this was the tangible manifestation of that more general process of rationalization which had distinguished the West from all other known civilizations. As a rationalist himself, as an heir to "the Protestant ethic," Weber with one part of himself applauded this tendency. At the same time he fully appreciated the dangers that bureaucracy presented for personal and intellectual freedom—which was another of his deeply cherished values.

In this situation, he surmised, "charismatic" leadership might offer a way out. With one side of his nature, Weber always responded to the notion of a "chief": he himself, had he chosen to exert his talents in this direction, could have been an incomparable leader of men. But here also the danger to liberty was acute. In his very definition of his new term, Weber suggested all that was primitive and threatening about it:

> "Charisma" shall be understood to refer to an *extraordinary* quality of a person, regardless of whether this quality is actual, alleged, or presumed. "Charismatic authority," hence, shall refer to a rule over men . . . to which the governed submit because of their belief in the extraordinary quality of the specific *person*. The magical sorcerer, the prophet, the leader of hunting and booty expeditions, the warrior chieftain, the . . . "Caesarist" ruler . . . are such types. . . . The legitimacy of charismatic rule thus rests upon the belief in magical powers, revelations and hero worship. . . . Charismatic rule is not managed according to general norms, either traditional or rational, . . . and in this sense . . . is "irrational." It is "revolu-

tionary" in the sense of not being bound to the existing order.[6]

Partly because he possessed so much *charisma* himself—because he himself was so profoundly shaken by the "demonic"—Weber distrusted it and held it at arm's length. In the same fashion he was aware of the lurking danger within his own thinking: he saw how dissolving and destructive were its implications, and he refused the role of an intellectual guide. In Weber's thought, the whole vast ambiguity of our century was held for one brief moment in a desperate synthesis. As his widow put it, he took it upon himself "to bear" without flinching "the *antinomies* of existence"—to live without illusions and at the same time in accordance with his personal ideals. When he was once asked what his learning meant to him, he answered quite simply: "I want to see how much I can endure." [7]

In facing his intellectual problems, Weber enjoyed the dubious advantage of having the contradictions of his world built right into his family inheritance and personality. His mother's family were Rhineland liberals, to whom intellectual and spiritual concerns were second nature. His father came of a line of merchant patricians, orderly, disciplined, hard-working men, on whose image Weber was to draw when he began to analyze the "spirit of capitalism." The elder Weber had become a lawyer: during Max's boyhood he sat in the Reichstag as a National Liberal deputy—one of those "realists" who had followed when Bismarck called the turn. Between father and mother, there was

[6] "*Die Wirtschaftsethik der Weltreligionen: Einleitung*" (1915), *Gesammelte Aufsätze zur Religionssoziologie*, I (Tübingen, 1922), pp. 237–75; translated by H. H. Gerth and C. Wright Mills as "The Social Psychology of the World Religions," *From Max Weber: Essays in Sociology* (New York, 1946), pp. 295–6.

[7] Marianne Weber: *Max Weber: Ein Lebensbild*, new edition (Heidelberg, 1950), p. 731.

an ever-widening spiritual gulf: she was religious, high-minded, devoted to the poor, generous in projects of social welfare; he was shrewd, good-humoredly authoritarian, conventional and superficial in his interests, and self-indulgent in his personal habits. The son was to suffer greatly from this temperamental misunderstanding as its full import gradually dawned upon him.

He himself eventually sided with his mother. But throughout his life, traces of the paternal influence remained. Although he grew to be ashamed of his student beer-drinking and dueling days, even as a mature man he would challenge his antagonists to a duel when he thought that honor was involved, and he took a strictly conventional pride in his rank as a Prussian reserve officer. His father's politics he never adopted: he started to the right of him, as still more conservative and nationalist, and ended far to the left as a most eccentric sort of democrat. But he betrayed what he owed his father by the imperious—indeed, brutal—quality of his political utterances, and by the uncompromising fashion in which he insisted on Germany's national greatness right down to the day of his death.

Similarly, on the eve of his death he was still not sure what was the true purpose of his life. As a young man he was attracted to politics. In the early part of his scholarly career he maintained this interest as an avocation parallel to his professional labors; it was only when he had become crippled by psychic illness that he abandoned the thought of public life and devoted his full energies to scholarship. With the war, however, Weber—like so many others—was drawn into active political partisanship, and for a brief period in 1919 it looked as though he would play a leading role in the new German republic. This expectation came to nothin—but the vague hope lingered on. Weber never thought of himself as a "true scholar" in the usual sense.[8] It was perhaps for this reason that he insisted

[8] Ibid., pp. 192, 723.

so strongly on a radical separation between the vocation of science and the vocation of politics: he feared the dual allegiance in his own soul.[9]

Today we think of Weber primarily as a sociologist. But this was only the last of a succession of disciplines with which he was professionally associated. He began his scholarly life as a student of the law, and it was in this field that he received his first teaching appointment in 1892, when he was just turning twenty-eight. His legal researches, however, were already directed toward economic and social history, and when he was called to a university chair, at Freiburg in 1894, it was as professor of economics. And it was in the same field that he received the invitation to Heidelberg three years later. It was only at the end of his life, when he taught as a visiting professor in Vienna and subsequently accepted a chair at the University of Munich, that he began to lecture specifically on sociology.

Similarly, in terms of an intellectual progression, we may trace Weber's course from law through economic history to the general methodology of the social sciences, and then, after a series of preparatory labors in the sociology of religion, to systematic sociology itself. From one standpoint, we might adduce this series of shifts as further evidence of Weber's intellectual contradictions. At the same time—and more profoundly—it suggests his heroic efforts to bring his diverse interests into some sort of synthesis. For when we look at them more closely, we discover that all these concerns are dominated by one overriding problem—the problem of rationality in Western society.[1]

[9] See the parallel lectures, delivered before student audiences in Munich in 1918: *"Wissenschaft als Beruf," Gesammelte Aufsätze zur Wissenschaftslehre,* second edition (Tübingen, 1951), pp. 566–97 ("Science as a Vocation," *From Max Weber,* pp. 129–56), and *"Politik als Beruf," Gesammelte Politische Schriften* (Munich, 1921), pp. 396–450 ("Politics as a Vocation," *From Max Weber,* pp. 77–128).

[1] Introduction by Talcott Parsons to Weber's *The Theory of Social and Economic Organization* (translation of Part I of

In his efforts to reach a synthesis, Weber held on to a number of the characteristic presuppositions of the intellectual tradition that had produced him. Although he was eventually to subject his masters to the most searching sort of criticism, he retained throughout his life the traces of their beneficent influence. The weaknesses of the German social science tradition are already familiar to us—its penchant toward metaphysical speculation and its infatuation with "the spirit." We might add the German practice of teaching economics in terms of history alone and of disparaging the claims of theory—an attitude that infuriated Pareto, himself a convert, like Weber, from economics to sociology, but from a very different economic school: Pareto, as a rigorously classical and mathematical theorist, was outraged by what he regarded as the slipshod quality of German economic thinking.

Yet when all this has been said, the enormous merit of German social thought was that it dwelt *in the historical world*. History was one subject that Weber never specifically studied or taught. But his whole intellectual life was suffused with historical thinking. Law, like economics, was taught in Germany as a historical discipline. Sociology was being cast in a similar mold. And philosophy, as we have seen, had posed as one of its central problems the elaboration of the categories of historical thought. It was from the philosopher Rickert, who was his colleague and friend at the University of Freiburg, that Weber first learned to formulate the question of value-judgments in the methodology of social science.

More directly, the professors whom Weber had respected in his university days had been the economic historians Wilhelm Roscher—Ranke's former pupil—at Berlin, and Karl Knies, whom he was eventually to succeed at Heidelberg. From them he learned a brand of economics that embraced virtually the whole field of social science and that was energetically committed to ethical judgments and practical applications. For in Germany the study of economics was intimately involved in social reform, and the professors who were facetiously called "socialists of the academic chair" devoted their talents to the problems of the relations between capital and labor in their newly industrialized nation. In 1873 they had founded the *Verein für Sozialpolitik,* of which Weber became an active and enterprising member. Thus at the very start of his academic career he was prepared for the inevitable confrontation with Marx: to achieve by more conservative means the social justice at which the Marxists aimed had become the major purpose of the *Verein.* In its very effort to counterbalance the influence of Marx, it betrayed how much it owed him.

As a self-conscious younger generation of economic historians, Weber and his friends tried to free themselves from those parts of their intellectual preparation that they felt to be old-fashioned and confining. In particular, they wanted to formulate in more specific terms than their elders had proposed the pervading "spirit" of economic institutions. The young Werner Sombart's approach was boldly impressionistic: Weber was more careful and more concerned with conceptual rigor. Almost alone of the German historical school, he was ready to grant a limited validity to the theoretical schema of classical economics.

Yet Weber's early writings showed few signs of exceptional intellectual independence. They were detailed, learned, immensely competent—quite conventional in their characteristically German combination of historical erudition, nationalism, and concern for the welfare of the laboring classes. Already, however, these youthful studies were beginning to point toward the interests that occupied their author's mature years. This was particularly the case with the survey of the situation of agrarian labor in eastern Germany which Weber undertook on behalf of the *Verein für Sozialpolitik* in 1891. Here for the first time he found himself face to face with a major conflict between national values and economic rationality. For he soon discovered that the central point in question—the replacement of German workers by Poles in the great estates east of the Elbe—could not be approached in purely economic terms. From the economic standpoint, the issue was simple: Polish labor was cheaper than German. But from the standpoint of national interest, this was proving to be a dangerous solution, since it increasingly exposed Germany's vital eastern frontier to Slavic penetration. And Weber finally felt that he had understood the crux of his problem when he came to the realization that it was the same East Elbian aristocrats who in their political and military capacity were irreproachably loyal to national values, who in their economic role were pursuing a thoroughly anti-national course.

The ambiguities of value-judgments—the conflicts of allegiances and of planes of understanding—all these riddles that were to torment Weber's maturity were implicit in this first major study. More immediately, it produced in his mind a vast disillusionment with his country's governing classes. Now that he had understood that they were incapable of living up to their national professions, he was ready to look for a new and more broadly based élite—hence his interest in Naumann's Christian-social aims. But Weber's reasons for passing over into the opposition were quite different from those that usually inspired such apostasies: his originality consisted in "directing against the Wilhelminian monarchy not the customary attacks based on principle, but rather those very arguments of which it —[the monarchy]—made itself the guardian and proponent: the interest and power of the state, and the vigor and authority of its political direction." To Weber, the more usual arguments about "state forms"—monarchy, democracy, and the like—seemed merely secondary issues of "techniques" and "mechanisms." [2] It was the strength of the nation alone that really counted.

Thus his early professional studies had already shaken Weber out of his original political allegiance. They had only begun, however, to disrupt the categories of his abstract thought. This latter reorientation was to be the indirect product of an unexpected disaster that very nearly ended his intellectual life altogether.

II. *The Methodological Phase*

In early 1898, when Weber had been only a year in Heidelberg, "an evil something out of the subterranean unconscious . . . grasped him by its claws" and deprived him of all power to teach or study.[3] For the next four years he was sunk in a depression of extraordinary severity. He felt unable to read, to interest himself in living—he barely existed. It was only during the winter of 1901–2, which he and his wife passed in Rome, that he gradually began to recover his intellectual powers.

To search out the origins of Weber's ailment is a task for the psychiatrist rather than the historian. Even the psychiatric amateur, however, may speculate on the elements in Weber's earlier life that contributed to it. Most obviously there was the enormous burden of work involved in the shift-over/from law to economics and in the combination of academic pursuits with semi-public activity. There was also the spiritual cleavage between his mother and father: it is significant that Weber's collapse followed shortly upon a violent scene with his father, in which the son's pent-up animosity had for the first time burst forth—and which was in turn succeeded by the father's death a few weeks later. So far as we can tell, the vulnerable point in Weber's

[2] Carlo Antoni: *Dallo storicismo alla sociologia* (Florence, 1940), p. 135.
[3] Marianne Weber: *Max Weber*, p. 269.

psychology was his doubt of his own ability to play the role of husband and father. Concomitantly, he had a strong attachment to his mother, whose pride in and ambition for Max, her first-born, revealed the familiar search for compensation of a strong-willed woman disappointed in her own marriage.

Weber's wife, Marianne, resembled her mother-in-law in the loftiness of her ethical goals and the strength of her will. Reading between the lines of the former's vastly informative and sensitive biography of her husband, we may surmise that the two women early struck up a tacit alliance directed toward the goal of making a great man out of the individual whom they cherished in common. Before his marriage Weber had had a five-year relationship with a distant female cousin, a gentle, vaguely ailing neurotic: this sad, unexpressed, unfulfilled love left him with a deep sense of remorse and the "enigmatic feeling that he did not have it in him . . . to make a woman happy." He entered marriage "encrusted" with "guilt feeling, renunciation, and repressions of all kinds"; the marriage remained childless; yet between husband and wife there seems to have been established the sort of spiritual communion that had been so notably lacking in the case of Weber's parents.[4]

In brief, "one may certainly infer an inordinately strong Oedipus situation."[5] There is a grim appropriateness in the fact that the only rival of Freud for the title of the leading social thinker of our century should have been a classic example of the latter's most famous theory—that he should have lain crippled by mental suffering at the very moment when *The Interpretation of Dreams* was appearing in print—and that he should have undergone the ministrations of a series of psychiatrists, none of whom helped him at all, while remaining in total ignorance of the work of the one physician who might have cured him.

Weber did not come into contact with Freud's theo-

[4] Ibid., pp. 186, 208.
[5] Introduction by Gerth and Mills to *From Max Weber*, p. 29.

ries until about 1907, when a self-styled disciple of the
Viennese physician appeared in Heidelberg and—so far
as we can tell from Frau Weber's account—began to
preach the doctrine of free love. Thus it was in this
highly partial and sensationalized form that Weber first
encountered the teachings of psychoanalysis. His first
reaction was repugnance: he and his wife held to a concept of the relationship between the sexes that was
"pure" in the extreme. But as he came to devote closer
attention to the problems of personal morality in modern society, Weber reached a more tolerant conclusion.
Even a breach of the principle of monogamous marriage might be understandable, he reasoned, if the new
tie were based on "responsibility." In this formula, we
encounter one of Weber's most characteristic ways of
thinking. And we find another of them in his eventual
verdict on Freud's work: it was unquestionably of scientific importance, but from it, no more than from any
other scientific doctrine, could one derive a *Weltanschauung*—as Freud himself was to try to do in the
speculative writings of his later years.

Weber's widow tells us that her husband "plunged
into Freud's teachings." [6] Presumably this means that
he read widely in the latter's works. But we know very
little of the result. Weber did not comment on nor
analyze the theory of psychoanalysis in his own sociological writings. Nor did he and Freud ever meet in
person. In all the essentials the two followed separate
paths: the intellectual confrontation that held the
greatest possibilities for our era never occurred. We are
left with the paradoxical suspicion that the most probing social theory of our time was the indirect sequel of
an *unresolved* neurosis of a classic Freudian type.

To the extent that Weber ever was cured, he cured
himself without medical help. In early 1902, for the first
time in nearly four years, he found himself able to read
a book—a book of art history. This choice reflected the

---

[6] Marianne Weber: *Max Weber*, pp. 413–21, 429–31.

basic necessity of his intellectual restoration. It was the mental overload, the pressure of *professional* labor, he felt, that had undone him, and during the first part of his recovery, he refused to read any books in his own field. It was only gradually that he worked his way back to them. And even then he felt permanently unable to carry out any intellectual assignment to which a deadline was attached. Hence, on his return to Heidelberg in 1902, after a few unsuccessful efforts to resume teaching, he gave up the attempt entirely: for the next fifteen years he was simply an honorary professor without teaching responsibility.

During the decade from 1903 to the outbreak of the war—the most productive period of his life—Weber lived on the careful regime of a semi-invalid. He always feared a recurrence of his malady, and on at least two occasions he went into a moderately severe relapse. But in general he found that frequent trips—preferably again into the Italian sun—restored him sufficiently to permit him to resume his work. At home in Heidelberg he followed a strict schedule: a working-day limited to six hours, a carefully regulated amount of contact with his friends and a minimum of general social life, no public speaking—above all, no evening activity that might disturb his precarious sleep.[7] He suffered and grumbled mightily over his intellectual production; it seemed to progress with appalling slowness; but as the years passed it began to mount to a most impressive total.

In all this I think we may properly discern the egocentric, infinitely painstaking labor of the neurotic of genius—we are reminded of Proust—to provide the external circumstances that will alone make his work of creation possible. Like Proust, Weber was setting up artificial walls, apparently senseless barriers and taboos against the intrusion of the irrelevant. Unconsciously exploiting his illness for his own intellectual purposes,

[7] Ibid., pp. 287–94, 298–300, 514–16.

he used it ruthlessly to strip down to the essentials all the meaningless paraphernalia of existence.

Similarly, at the level of the intellectual life itself, Weber was able to make a virtue out of his misfortune —to find the spur to creativity in his neurosis itself. His four years of intellectual paralysis were only apparently wasted. Actually Weber seems to have been thinking— and thinking hard—a good deal of the time. Indeed, one subsidiary reason why he may have felt unable to read and write was that he was digging into a new sort of problem for which the conventional methods of his youth were proving quite inadequate. Obviously, Weber's four-year absence from scholarly labor provided the intellectual advantage of a clean break (and we may note that the years he lost were the very years of the great critique of Marxism in the Western European world: Weber thus missed the main phase of criticism —but only to resume the work of Pareto and Croce and Sorel a few years later and in a still more rigorous form). Above and beyond that, Weber's impatience with the literature of his own discipline turned him to broader concerns. From now on, he was to be satisfied only with what was most troubling and difficult in the profession of social science—the philosophy and meth- odology of that science itself: the net result of Weber's psychic collapse was that he decided to worry in a systematic fashion about the really worrying issues of social theory.

This new phase started in 1903, when Weber was just under forty, with the desperately slow composition of a long and inordinately difficult critique of the work of his economic masters Roscher and Knies.[8] It proved

8 *"Roscher und Knies und die logischen Probleme der his- torischen Nationalökonomie,"* after having been published in three installments between 1903 and 1906 in *Schmollers Jahr- buch,* XXVII, XXIX, XXX, was republished as pp. 1–145 of the *Gesammelte Aufsätze zur Wissenschaftslehre.* It is one of two important methodological essays that have not been translated

to be the first of the series of essays on methodology to which, more than to any other of his writings, Weber owes his great contemporary influence. These essays make extremely heavy reading. In composing them Weber quite frankly paid no attention to style: it was sufficient for him if his thought had been expressed with rigor and precision. One suspects that it was only by making some such self-limitation that he succeeded in completing them at all. It is part of the irony of Weber's career that he, who was one of the most forceful speakers of his time, should have been condemned to sixteen years of silence and to the torment of a wretched literary style.

In the following year, 1904, two external events provided Weber with the stimulus to renewed labor that he required. The first was a trip to the United States, which he enjoyed thoroughly and which seems to have had a tonic effect on his spirits. The second was his assumption of the co-editorship of the *Archiv für Sozialwissenschaft und Sozialpolitik*, which in his hands and that of his colleagues Sombart and Jaffé became the most distinguished social-science review of the day. Now that he was no longer teaching, the *Archiv* provided Weber with precisely the vehicle he needed—a definite but not overtaxing job, a link with the work of his peers among contemporary social scientists, and an outlet for his own scholarly production. For the next decade Weber was to publish almost exclusively in the form of long articles in the *Archiv*. While this practice restricted him to a scholarly audience, it had the advantage of flexibility and the absence of the sort of pressure associated with the publication of a book.

Besides the essay on Roscher and Knies, Weber's methodological reflections may be found first and foremost in his programmatic pronouncement on " 'Objectivity' in Social Science and Social Policy," with which

into English. On this whole phase of Weber's writing the standard work is Alexander von Schelting's *Max Webers Wissenchaftslehre* (Tübingen, 1934).

he launched his editorship of the *Archiv* in 1904, and
in only slightly less important form in the essays entitled "Critical Studies in the Logic of the Cultural
Sciences" (1906) and "The Meaning of 'Ethical Neutrality' in Sociology and Economics" (1917–18).[9] To
them one might add the article published just before
the war in which Weber outlined the method of *Verstehen* in the elaboration of sociological concepts.[1]

In composing these essays, Weber's standpoint was
almost invariably polemical. He was fighting what was
at least a two-front war—on the one hand against the
superficialities of positivism or "naturalism" (although
he was himself not infrequently accused of being a positivist), on the other hand against the conventional
canons of idealist thought, and more particularly its
denial of the possibilities of scientific work in the field
of human culture. Within the framework of the present study, Weber's analysis of idealism is the more interesting of the two. For it documents his struggle for
liberation from his own intellectual past. It reveals him
as a vigorous critic of both the main forms in which
idealist social thought had been cast—the historical
erudition of what Croce called the "philological"
school, and the large speculations of the metaphysicians. From this double (or threefold) critique it eventually emerges that Weber's goal was to establish a
"middle" level of empirically derived conceptualization: he was trying to introduce conceptual rigor into a

[9] These three essays have been translated by Edward A. Shils
and Henry A. Finch as *Max Weber on the Methodology of the
Social Sciences* (Glencoe, Ill., 1949). They can be found in their
original form in the *Gesammelte Aufsätze zur Wissenschaftslehre*
under the following titles: *"Die 'Objektivität' sozialwissenschaft-
licher und sozialpolitischer Erkenntnis,"* pp. 146–214, *"Kritische
Studien auf dem Gebiet der kulturwissenschaftlichen Logik,"* pp.
215–90, *"Der Sinn der 'Wertfreiheit' der soziologischen und
ökonomischen Wissenschaften,"* pp. 475–526.

[1] *"Über einige Kategorien der verstehenden Soziologie,"* Logos,
IV (1913) (*Gesammelte Aufsätze zur Wissenschaftslehre*, pp.
427–74). This is the other important essay that has not been
translated.

tradition where either intuition or a naïve concern for the "facts" had hitherto ruled unchallenged.[2]

Weber's initial task was quite obviously to free himself from the influence of his immediate predecessors as historically oriented economists. And this in turn involved him in a multiple conflict. For the German tradition of economic history represented a curious hybrid of a kind of crypto-Marxism and a romantic notion of the "spirit" of human communities derived in part from Ranke. With the Marxist aspect of this tradition Weber was to deal more specifically in his studies of religion. His critique of the romantic aspect was already apparent in his first methodological essay: his old master Knies, he protested, had advanced a theory of personality that was "entirely in the spirit of romanticism"; and Knies's notion of a "folk soul," when critically scrutinized, proved to be a "metaphysically paler version of Roscher's pious belief that the 'souls' . . . of peoples originate directly from the hand of God." [3]

Thus Roscher and Knies had in effect smuggled a value element into an analysis that laid claim to methodological exactitude: [4] by their implicit endorsement of individual "spiritual" entities they had linked the tradition of precise historical investigation with the other branch of idealist social thought that dealt in values and abstractions. And this confusion of method they had justified by the well-worn argument that the world of man was radically different from the world of nature—that the former was a realm of freedom in which the usual type of scientific explanation in terms of causes or laws did not apply: into this realm of "irrationality" social scientists were obliged to feel their way by imprecise, intuitive methods that defied exact description.

[2] Parsons: *Structure of Social Action*, pp. 580–1.
[3] "Roscher und Knies," *Gesammelte Aufsätze zur Wissenschaftslehre*, p. 143.
[4] Pietro Rossi: *Lo storicismo tedesco contemporaneo* (Turin, 1956), pp. 283–7.

As Weber during his months of psychic paralysis had pondered on the lessons of his own intellectual forebears, he had discerned a kind of mystic obfuscation that lay at their very center. He had begun to see that the positivists had not been totally wrong in their science-minded assertions. They had simply chosen one horn of a great dilemma and the idealists another. Neither party had properly understood the terms they employed (or refused to employ). Neither had had a satisfactory notion of the nature of "law" and "cause," "objectivity" and "value," in the social or cultural studies. They had not defined these terms with sufficient care, nor had they delimited with any rigor the range through which they could be employed. To do so was the underlying purpose of Weber's own methodological essays.

First in logical order came the notion of law. Human behavior, Weber argued, was just as lawful as events in the natural world. For if it was capable of rational explanation at all—and social theorists of all schools agreed that to some extent or other it *was* rationally explicable—then there must be something lawful about it. And this lawful aspect lay in its predictability. Indeed to call a certain type of behavior "crazy" meant to suggest that it was "incalculable." Viewed in this fashion, the truth about the world of human beings was just the opposite of what the idealists had imagined. The realm of human freedom was the reverse of a realm of irrationality: man never felt so free as when he was acting rationally:

> The error in the assumption that any freedom of the will—however it is understood—is identical with the "irrationality" of action, or that the latter is conditioned by the former, is quite obvious. The characteristic of "incalculability," equally great but not greater than that of "blind forces of nature," is the privilege of—the insane. On the other hand,

we associate the highest measure of an empirical "feeling of freedom" with those actions which we are conscious of performing rationally—i.e., . . . in which we pursue a clearly perceived end by "means" which are the most adequate in accordance with the extent of our knowledge, i.e., in accordance with empirical *rules*.[5]

These "rules," in a narrower sense, could also be termed "causes." It was in his discussion of causal explanation that Weber most explicitly came into conflict with the idealist tradition. Croce, we may note, had eliminated from historical explanation the notion of cause, as a mechanical concept applicable only in the natural sciences. With this theoretical position, Weber did not disagree totally. In his methodological essays he cited Croce more than once, and sometimes with approval: he was at one with Croce in his scorn for the procedure of drawing up "statesman-like" compromises between opposing points of view, and in maintaining that "values," particularly those of an ethical character, were subjective in origin and could not be derived through any empirical procedure. But he differed sharply with Croce on the criteria of historical explanation: Croce's exclusively aesthetic and logical categories he found quite insufficient; the employment of such terms as "intuition" and "re-experiencing" he rejected as unsatisfactory; some version of causal explanation, he argued, must be devised to take their place.[6]

It is unfortunate that in his methodological essays Weber refers only to Croce's work published before 1909—before the latter's major change from an aes-

[5] *"Roscher und Knies," Gesammelte Aufsätze zur Wissenschaftslehre*, pp. 67, 136–7; "Logic of Cultural Sciences," *Methodology*, pp. 124–5.

[6] "Meaning of 'Ethical Neutrality,'" *Methodology*, p. 10; "Logic of Cultural Sciences," Ibid., pp. 148–9n.; *"Roscher und Knies," Gesammelte Aufsätze zur Wissenschaftslehre*, pp. 108–10, 122–3.

thetic to a philosophical definition of the character of historical study. But even if he had dealt with Croce's subsequent writings, there would have been no real meeting of minds. Weber was ready to go along with Croce and the idealists in severely limiting the range of causal explanation in the historical and social world. But he was not willing to eliminate it altogether. The essential difference between the natural and the human world, he contended, lay in the fact that in the latter realm it was impossible to arrive at laws—or causal explanations—that would in any sense give a satisfactory or exhaustive explanation of even the simplest human action. The problem, then, became one of devising a method of arriving at *partial* explanations of a causal character—explanations that for all their patent one-sidedness would be somewhat more rigorous than the conventional procedure in terms of "re-experiencing," "intuition," or "feel."

As his own answer to this problem, Weber devised a most ingenious schema of *hypothetical* analysis. It was based on the conviction that in the study of human affairs the best that a causal explanation could do was to locate the factor which, when removed, would make the decisive difference in a given sequence of events— the factor, that is, which, when thought away, would not permit us to conceive of the event in question as occurring. As applied in a few sample cases, this procedure proved only moderately convincing. But it opened the way to Weber's extremely instructive reflections on "objectivity" and "value."

In proposing his method of hypothetical causal explanation, Weber was careful to specify that the decisive factor in question could be described as decisive only *from the standpoint of the individual investigator.* And this in turn meant that the selection of this factor was based, ultimately, on some explicit or implicit value-system.[7] The inevitable *choices* among their data

---

[7] " 'Objectivity' in Social Science," *Methodology*, p. 78; "Logic of Cultural Sciences," Ibid., pp. 166, 180–1.

that historians and social scientists made faithfully reflected the values they personally cherished: as an individual acting in the world of practical reality, the investigator of society developed an attitude toward life that
was subsequently mirrored in his scientific production.

Thus far Weber's argument closely followed that of
Rickert, to whom he freely acknowledged his debt.
Where Weber diverged from Rickert, however, was in
refusing all metaphysical support for his own values and
in trying to maintain—despite its ultimate psychological impossibility—the claims of "objectivity" or
"ethical neutrality" in scientific pursuits. The characteristic German professor, Weber maintained, was a
propagandist, whether open or covert: he preached
some kind of social message from his academic chair.
And this situation was intolerable. "The professor
should not demand the right as a professor to carry the
marshal's baton of the statesman or reformer in his
knapsack. This is just what he does when he uses the
unassailability of the academic chair for the expression
of political . . . evaluations." In short, the German
professors were abusing their privileged status when
they pontificated *ex cathedra* on public matters without fear of contradiction from students or colleagues.
In insisting thus strongly on the need for academic
self-restraint, Weber evidently had in mind the example of the great historian-propagandist Heinrich von
Treitschke, whose lectures he had attended during his
own student days in Berlin.[8]

A heroic effort was required, then, if the professor
was to separate his scientific from his public role. And
the struggle was particularly acute in the case of Weber
himself, who, as we have seen, was a man of passionate
political and social conviction. These convictions
Weber had no intention of repressing. He did not argue that it was necessary to combat them in one's own
soul. On the contrary, he implied that they were essen-

[8] "Meaning of 'Ethical Neutrality,'" Ibid., p. 5; Marianne
Weber: *Max Weber*, p. 138.

tial to creation in the social-science field: it was only
through a kind of sublimation of these very convictions
(we are reminded of the later Croce) that significant
scientific choice became possible. "An *attitude of moral
indifference*," Weber insisted, "has no connection with
scientific 'objectivity.' " [9]

Thus in Weber's hands the relationship between scientific objectivity and value-judgment was developed
into a peculiarly subtle process of mutual interaction.
On the one hand, scientific investigation took its departure from some standpoint in the realm of values.
Subsequently this investigation in turn began to illuminate the range of value choices. It could demonstrate
what values were consistent or inconsistent with each
other; it could determine the consequences or implications of a proposed course of action; it could estimate
what "the attainment of a desired end" would " 'cost'
in terms of the predictable loss of other values." But
it could not make "the act of choice itself": that was
the sole responsibility of "the acting, willing person";
he was obliged to weigh and choose "from among the
values involved according to his own conscience and his
personal view of the world." In short, "an empirical
science" could not "tell anyone what he *should* do—
but rather what he *can* do—and under certain circumstances—what he wishes to do." [1]
Ultimately, however, it was only the values entertained by individual human beings that gave "meaning"—in the double sense of comprehensibility and
purpose—to the existence of man in society. And this
meaning was established through what we call culture.
"Culture," Weber asserted, could be regarded as "a
finite segment of the meaningless infinity of the world

[9] " 'Objectivity' in Social Science," *Methodology*, p. 60.
[1] "Meaning of 'Ethical Neutrality,' " Ibid., pp. 20–1; " 'Objectivity' in Social Science," Ibid., pp. 53–4.

process, a segment on which *human beings* confer meaning and significance." [2]

The statement sounds like a quotation from Dilthey. Very frequently in Weber's writings we come across expressions that call Dilthey to mind—for example the insistence that "a new 'science' emerges where new problems are pursued by new methods and truths are thereby discovered which open up significant new points of view." But the agreement may be only accidental: one of the perplexing things about Weber's methodological essays is the absence of any sustained analysis of Dilthey's teaching, although the references suggest familiarity with it. [3] In practice, however, Weber combined what was viable in Dilthey with the lessons derived from his own philosophical master Rickert—while at the same time demonstrating the unreality of the problems that had both baffled them and kept them apart.

To put it very simply, Weber maintained that in the social or cultural sciences the method and the object, the precepts for investigation and the theory of knowledge, were simply different aspects of the same thing. The great quarrel that had separated Dilthey from Windelband—and later from Rickert—over whether the cultural sciences were distinguished from the natural sciences by the object they investigated, or rather by the method they pursued, Weber found to be irrelevant. In practice, he argued, the object of investigation *defined itself* through the very method that was directed toward it. It was immaterial whether one chose to emphasize the object or field of study, or whether one decided to lay the stress on the method of such study. The question could be settled on *pragmatic* grounds: as with all similar problems, the answer depended on where and how one chose to cut into it.

[2] Ibid., p. 81.
[3] Ibid., p. 68. Specific references to Dilthey occur only in the essay on Roscher and Knies.

Thus the whole philosophical debate about the validity
of our knowledge of the historical or social world simply
fell to the ground. "Philosophy cannot define what historicity is: *it can only tell us how historical and social
phenomena are investigated.*" [4]

In refusing to recognize anything absolute about
value-judgments—in abandoning all metaphysical support for ethical or practical norms—Weber had taken
his leave of Rickert and come close to the world of
twilight relativism in which Dilthey had dwelt. He had
ended in a universe of mutual conditioning—an infinitely complex view of human affairs in which pluralism was as inevitable philosophically as a succession of
unilateral approaches was a practical necessity. In brief,
he had arrived at a "fictional" viewpoint not unlike
that of Vaihinger.[5] In the social and cultural world, he
had found, a fixed reality was undiscoverable. All that
was sure was that human beings held to ethical and
cultural values whose origin and ultimate meaning were
veiled in mystery, and that the investigation of these
values was alone made possible by the pursuit of certain frankly arbitrary methods that *in practice* gave
comprehensible results.

In order to understand more adequately both Weber's philosophical pluralism and his fictional approach,
we should give some final attention to the two specific
methods most frequently associated with his name—
the procedure called Verstehen and the elaboration of
"ideal types."

The first of these was a vestigial remnant of Weber's
idealist past. Crudely put, Verstehen—"understanding"
—can be characterized as the German formula for giving philosophical standing and dignity to a source of
knowledge that in the Latin world was either called
"intuition" or simply accepted as something inexpli-

⁴ Rossi: *Storicismo tedesco*, pp. 302, 334, 337.
⁵ Parsons: *Structure of Social Action*, p. 593.

cable. It was a method that all investigators of society employed—the historians and philosophers with a perfectly good conscience, the social scientists more covertly and ashamedly. It was at the origin of Dilthey's "re-experiencing" and Croce's "re-thinking." In short, it was the effort to "feel oneself into" a historical or social action by putting oneself in the place of the actor or actors. It was a method of psychological sympathy—the method that most sharply distinguished the "inner" investigation of the human world from the merely external investigation of the world of nature.

Weber accepted this procedure without modification from his Germanic forebears. As opposed to Durkheim and the positivists, he recognized that some such intuitive method was unavoidable if the study of human behavior was not to be limited to mere observing and counting—and no contemporary social scientist was in practice doing only that. But where he differed from his idealist teachers was in recognizing the dangers of relying exclusively on "understanding." He sought to limit its range and to combine it with causal explanations of a quasi-positivist type. "*Verstehen*," he asserted, "must . . . be controlled so far as possible by the . . . usual methods of causal imputation, before even the most evident interpretation can become a valid 'intelligible explanation.' " [6] To achieve scientific validity, the knowledge derived from *Verstehen* must be verified by empirical tests.

Our immediate intuitions of meaning may be real and, as such, correct. But their interpretation cannot dispense with a rationally consistent system of theoretical concepts. Only in so far as they measure up to such criticism can intuitions constitute knowledge. And without such criticism the door is opened to any number of uncontrolled and unverifiable allegations. Weber had a very deep and

[6] "*Kategorien der verstehenden Soziologie*," *Gesammelte Aufsätze zur Wissenschaftslehre*, p. 428.

strong ethical feeling on this point; to him the intuitionist position made possible the evasion of responsibility for scientific judgments.[7]

Thus he retained from this position only what he believed could stand the test of rigorous scientific proof.
In effect, he reduced it to the "source of 'hunches,'
which help us in the formulation of hypotheses."[8]
Limited and controlled in this fashion, some sort of
Verstehen procedure—whether or not it be dignified by
this rather special term—has passed over from the writing of history to become an accepted part of social-
science method.

The causal type of explanation that was to check and
correct the operation of "understanding" was, as we
have already observed, both partial and incomplete. It
consisted of a series of cross fires, of alternative sequences of causation, whose sum did not exhaust the
explanatory possibilities inherent in any given situation.
Of necessity it had something arbitrary about it. It was
frankly and unashamedly a construction of the human
mind.

Closely related to this notion of cause was Weber's
definition of the "ideal type." Indeed, an ideal type
might be thought of as a unilateral complex of causal
explanations. As such, it was close to what Sorel had
called a *diremption*. "An ideal type," Weber asserted,

is formed by the one-sided *accentuation* of one or
more points of view and by the synthesis of a great
many diffuse, discrete, more or less present and
occasionally absent *concrete individual* phenomena, which are arranged according to those one-
sidedly emphasized viewpoints into a unified *ana-*

---

[7] Parsons: *Structure of Social Action*, p. 589.
[8] Theodore Abel: "The Operation Called *Verstehen*" (*American Journal of Sociology*, LIV [1948]), reprinted in *Readings in
the Philosophy of Science*, edited by Herbert Feigl and May
Brodbeck (New York, 1953), p. 687.

lytical construct. In its conceptual purity, this mental construct cannot be found empirically anywhere in reality. It is a *utopia*. . . .

It has the significance of a purely ideal *limiting* concept with which the real situation or action is *compared* and surveyed for the explication of certain of its significant components. Such concepts are constructs in terms of which we formulate relationships by the application of the category of objective possibility. By means of this category, the adequacy of our imagination, oriented and disciplined by reality, is *judged*.

Thus these ideal types might be of all sorts and of all levels of abstraction. They might be "class or generic concepts (*Gattungsbegriffe*) . . . —ideas in the sense of thought-patterns which actually exist in the minds of human beings . . . —ideals which govern human beings . . . —ideals with which the historian approaches historical facts—*theoretical* constructs using empirical data illustratively—*historical* investigations which utilize theoretical concepts as ideal limiting cases"— indeed, a whole continuum of "various possible combinations" that might be multiplied indefinitely.[9] In general, however, the concrete examples that Weber gave were of two main types. In the first place, they were generic concepts—classes of social phenomena such as "state" or "church." In the second place, they were "idealized" individual complexes of phenomena—"capitalism," for instance—of which only one pure type was presumed to exist.

In employing the term ideal type—which he had actually found in the writings of the legal scholar Georg Jellinek—"Weber did not mean to introduce a new conceptual tool. He merely intended to bring to full awareness what social scientists and historians had been doing when they used words like 'the economic man,'

9 " 'Objectivity' in Social Science," *Methodology*, pp. 90, 93, 103.

'feudalism,' 'Gothic *versus* Romanesque architecture,' or 'kingship.' " [1] Nor did he regard his own constructions as permanently valid. On the contrary, he thought of them as mere devices for understanding, artificial tools that were destined to be supplanted by new concepts of better fabrication. "The history of the social sciences," he reasoned, "is and remains a continuous process passing from the attempt to order reality analytically through the construction of concepts—the dissolution of the analytical constructs so constructed through the expansion and shift of the scientific horizon—and the reformulation anew of concepts on the foundations thus transformed." [2]

Yet even in the tentative form in which he cast it, Weber's definition of the ideal type has proved to be one of his most influential contributions to the methodology of social thought. Such scholars as Joseph Schumpeter, Weber's greatest successor in the role of an economic sociologist, have delineated the concept more precisely under the new term of "model." And on this new basis "models" have become an enormously popular stock-in-trade among social scientists. In complex logical and mathematical forms that Weber never dreamed of, model-building has attained to a high degree of precision and has encompassed a variety of new applications. Yet Weber remains in honor as the original model-builder—the man who first made explicit the procedure of abstract theoretical construction that alone renders possible the rational understanding of the human world.

III. *The Studies of Religion*

Weber's own chief application of his ideal-type method was to the study of religion—which also constituted the main focus of his empirical labors in the decade and a

[1] Introduction by Gerth and Mills to *From Max Weber*, p. 59.
[2] " 'Objectivity' in Social Science," *Methodology*, p. 105.

half following his psychic collapse. This series of studies he first undertook in 1904, and he continued to work on it nearly up to the time of his death in 1920. Thus the religious phase overlapped the phase of methodological analysis—but it was the latter that necessarily offered the presuppositions for this new variety of empirical study.

Besides being the first *conscious* application of the ideal-type procedure, Weber's studies of religion are significant for his intellectual development in two other important respects. First—as with Pareto or Durkheim —they offer the crucial test case in his confrontation with the non-logical world. Second—and again as with his great contemporaries in Italy and France—they document his encounter with Marx. But in Weber's case, as opposed to that of Pareto or Durkheim, the reckoning with religion did not come *after* the settling of accounts with Marx, as the consequence of a further maturation of thought. The two went on simultaneously: their effect was interacting. As a result, Weber was able to see farther and more clearly in both respects than was possible for his contemporaries from the Latin world.

Weber's widow has suggested that his lasting interest in the sociology of religion represented the transmuted "form in which the genuine religious sentiment in his mother's family lived on in him." He himself had no defined religious belief. "I am . . . absolutely unmusical in religious matters," he wrote in 1909, "and I feel neither the need nor the capacity to raise up in myself any sort of spiritual edifices of a religious character. Yet after careful self-examination I find myself neither antireligious *nor irreligious*." This quality of suspended judgment in spiritual matters constituted one of Weber's great assets. As opposed to the militantly antireligious Freud and Pareto, the skeptical and rationalist Durkheim, or the avowedly mystical Bergson, Weber was almost alone among the major social thinkers of his time in remaining open to religious impressions while succumbing to no specific dogmatic teaching. Like Sorel—but more systematically and analytically than Sorel—Weber gave to religion his full respect without letting it catch him in its toils.

Moreover, under the intentionally dry and "scientific" style of his religious studies, we can catch glimpses of Weber's own spiritual commitment to his subject matter. We may detect the surging of deeply experienced emotion at the enigmas and paradoxes of human destiny that the study of religion disclosed. And we may also surmise that in the "sublime figures of heroic Puritanism" which he presented in his work on the Protestant ethic, "certain of his own traits" stand revealed. In this earliest of his religious studies, Weber seems to have felt himself into the role of a Calvinist leader of iron resolve—a man who had conquered the demon in his own soul and chained himself to the wheel of duty. Subsequently—like Freud—he was to see himself in the image of a Hebrew prophet. During the war years, he was to warn his people in the tones of a Jeremiah of their political irresponsibility and of the dangers to the nation that lay ahead.[3]

In Weber's view, all social theories or ideologies could be classified as ideal types. And of these, Marx's had obviously been a particularly suggestive and influential specimen. Like Croce, Weber granted a "relative legitimacy to the materialist conception of history," that is, if it were understood "not as a general interpretation of history but as a *heuristic principle*"— a path to understanding—whose "unilateral character" was "inherent in any point of view that tries to delimit its own field of investigation." [4] In common with Croce, Weber saw that the very partiality of the Marxian analysis gave it a sharper edge: it cut cleanly into an area of life in society that earlier theories had neglected. But, unlike Croce, Weber did not stop when he had

[3] Marianne Weber: *Max Weber*, pp. 370, 382–3, 385, 639.
[4] Rossi: *Storicismo tedesco*, p. 345.

incorporated what he had found valid in Marxism into the canon of his own thinking; he went on to relate the one-sidedness of historical materialism to the unilateral character of all social theory, and to give to Marxism a new dimension by running another unilateral sequence of his own.

Of all the critiques of Marxism that came out of the generation of the 1890's, Weber's was the most subtle and the widest in range. This last critique, as we have seen, partly for accidental reasons followed the others by half a decade, and the fact that it was presented in the context of the sociology of religion gave it a special point and relevance. Furthermore, as opposed to Pareto or Croce, to whom Marx's way of thinking was basically distasteful, Weber had much in common with the founder of dialectical materialism. Once more he recalls Sorel in his intuitive understanding for the way in which Marx's mind had worked.

The two had in common the *radical* character of their analysis of society—radical, that is, not in the ordinary political sense of being "on the left," but in the original philological meaning of a concern with the roots of social difficulties. Both were impatient men— and more particularly impatient with the verbal superficialities and euphemisms that customarily concealed harsh reality. And both attempted a kind of philosophical sociology of contemporary man: what Marx called the "alienation" of the workers from the means of production, Weber broadened into the more inclusive category of the rationalization of modern life. Weber "relativized" Marx's theory by fitting it into a wider hypothesis as a "special case" that the latter had "dramatized" with telling effect.[5]

But in following—or better, paralleling—Marx in these respects, Weber made a basic alteration in emphasis. In Weber's hands, "capitalism" was enlarged

[5] Karl Löwith: *"Max Weber und Karl Marx,"* Archiv für Sozialwissenschaft und Sozialpolitik, LXVII (1932), 54, 60-2, 80; Introduction by Gerth and Mills to *From Max Weber*, p. 50.

into an even more ramifying conception than it had been for Marx; indeed, it became questionable whether such an economic term was adequate to cover at all what Weber was talking about. Viewed in the context of the rationalization or bureaucratization of living, the distinction between capitalism and socialism ceased to be of major importance; in effect, Weber emphasized their continuity. Still more important, and in line with his inheritance from the neo-idealists, Weber held that an "indispensable . . . element in the explanation" of a phenomenon like capitalism "lay in a system of ultimate values and value attitudes." [6] Thus he refined on Marx's notion of a class by adding to it a new category in which the value aspect of group relationships would stand out in sharper fashion: a class, he asserted, was an economic category of people united by material interests; a status group (*Stand*) could be defined as one in which considerations of prestige and honor were paramount.

Already in his early agrarian studies, Weber had come to the conclusion that in the large-scale flight from the land of German rural workers east of the Elbe, ideal and spiritual motives had at least as great an influence as material considerations. And his subsequent reflections had simply deepened this conviction. A decade after his agrarian survey, when he undertook his studies of religion, it was with the express intention of documenting through systematic empirical findings the interlocking action of economic and spiritual factors in producing the great social transformations of the past.

The first of these studies, *The Protestant Ethic and the Spirit of Capitalism*, early became the most widely read of Weber's writings.[7] And this popularity was un-

[6] Parsons: Introduction to *Theory of Social and Economic Organization*, p. 79, *Structure of Social Action*, pp. 509–10.
[7] Translation by Talcott Parsons (New York and London, 1930). After having originally been published as articles in vol-

questionably justified. Despite all the criticism to which it has been subjected, and the corrections of detail that it has undergone,[8] *The Protestant Ethic* remains one of the great works of the social thought of our time—an almost unique combination of imaginative boldness in its central hypothesis and meticulous scholarship in its documentation. In its careful balancing of the material and spiritual, it pursues an argument of a subtlety that has frequently thrown the overhasty reader off the track.

Weber's critics could have been spared most of their pains if they had pondered more carefully two of the author's guiding pronouncements. In the first place, he carefully specified that he was not arguing that Protestantism had "caused" the rise of capitalism. "We have no intention whatever," he wrote,

> of maintaining such a foolish and doctrinaire thesis as that the spirit of capitalism . . . could only have arisen as the result of certain effects of the Reformation, or even that capitalism as an economic system is a creation of the Reformation. . . . On the contrary, we only wish to ascertain whether and to what extent religious forces have taken part in the qualitative formation and the quantitative expansion of that spirit over the world, and what concrete aspects of our capitalistic culture can be traced to them. In view of the tremendous confusion of interdependent influences among the material basis, the forms of social and political organization, and the ideas current in the time of the Reformation, we can only proceed by investigating whether and at what points certain correlations between forms of religious belief and

---

umes XX (1904) and XXI (1905) of the *Archiv für Sozialwissenschaft und Sozialpolitik, "Die protestantische Ethik und der Geist des Kapitalismus"* was reprinted in the *Gesammelte Aufsätze zur Religionssoziologie*, I, 17–206.

[8] Notably by R. H. Tawney in his *Religion and the Rise of Capitalism* (London, 1926).

practical ethics can be worked out. At the same
time we shall as far as possible clarify the manner
and the general *direction* in which, by virtue of
those relationships, the religious movements have
influenced the development of material culture.[9]

Or, as Weber put it in another place, "the 'world
images' that have been created by 'ideas' have, like
switchmen, determined the tracks along which action
has been pushed by the dynamic of interest": at certain
decisive points in history, a spiritual program and the
pressure of a material-interest group have converged.
Obviously Weber was not trying to chart a simple
causal sequence. He was attempting the infinitely more
complex task of delineating the "elective affinity" between capitalism and Protestantism—the largely unconscious similarities of outlook that led the second
and third generations of Calvinists to put their stern,
self-denying, ascetic capacities into the service of God's
purposes on earth and, in the process, to give a new
rationality and dynamism to the techniques of expand-
ing capitalism.[1] He was trying to show how an ethic
originally devised for other-worldly purposes became
transmuted into a marvelously efficient stimulus to material gain.

In the second place—and this was simply another
way of phrasing the first pronouncement—Weber denied any intention of "refuting" Marxism or the materialist interpretation of history. It was not his aim,
he wrote, "to substitute for a one-sided materialistic
[interpretation] an equally one-sided spiritualistic
causal interpretation of culture and of history." He was
simply trying to show what would happen when one
treated "only one side of the causal chain." Marx had
run the causal sequence in one direction, i.e., from

---

[9] *Protestant Ethic*, pp. 91–2. I have altered the translation
slightly.
[1] "Social Psychology of World Religions," *From Max Weber*,
p. 280; Introduction by Gerth and Mills, *Ibid.*, p. 62–3.

economic to spiritual factors. Weber wanted to run it
in the reverse order as a complement to what Marx had
done. Each method, he argued, was "equally possible."
Both of them—and others besides—were perfectly per-
missible. But neither was exhaustive: each could serve
only "as the preparation," not "as the conclusion of
an investigation." [2] Actually, according to Weber's
own methodology, such a conclusion could never be
achieved. But it could be approached more closely
through combining a number of *alternative causal sequences* of the sort that he himself and Marx had run.

In his study of Protestantism Weber drew, as so
many of his contemporaries had done, on the scholarship and example of William James. On his trip to the
United States—which in fact interrupted the composition of this work—Weber not only met James but
also derived some of the first-hand impressions that
enliven his discussion of the more eccentric of the
Protestant sects.[3] The sects offered a curiosity-shop of
extravagant and apparently irrational religious behavior.
Yet, as Weber soon discovered, the same individuals
who in their religious capacity endorsed these practices,
in their role as American businessmen were the epito-
mes of rational and ordered living. Here lay another of
the paradoxes in the relationship between Protestantism and capitalism. In most respects, however, Weber
found that the United States offered an extreme case
of the rationalization of existence. It seemed to mark
the farthest point yet reached on the path along which
the Western world as a whole was apparently heading.
It was in America that the fusion of the Protestant and

[2] *Protestant Ethic*, pp. 27, 183; Löwith: "*Weber und Marx*,"
pp. 210–11.
[3] See the shorter essay, dating from 1906, that supplements
the main study of the Protestant ethic: "*Die protestantischen
Sekten und der Geist des Kapitalismus*," *Gesammelte Aufsätze
zur Religionssoziologie*, I, 207–36 ("The Protestant Sects and the
Spirit of Capitalism," *From Max Weber*, pp. 302–22); also
Marianne Weber: *Max Weber*, pp. 316–45.

the capitalist ethic had been most complete, and that
society came closest to that uniform, soulless efficiency
that loomed up as the model of the future.

Throughout the foregoing discussion it has doubtless
become apparent that Weber thought of capitalism as
a complex of rational procedures. In this respect he
differed sharply from Marx's insistence on its contradictions. For Weber, capitalism—like bureaucracy—
was simply another of the major manifestations of that
all-embracing process of rationalization that concerned
him most profoundly in the history of the Western
world. Why, he asked himself, had this process occurred to its full extent in the West alone? Why had
it stopped short in India, in China, in all the other
parts of the world that were the equals of the West in
religious and humanistic culture? In these civilizations
also there existed a kind of capitalism; but it had not
pursued the same course as in the West. Why did "the
capitalistic interests" of China and India not find their
way to the full rationalization of life? "Why did not
the scientific, the artistic, the political, or the economic
development there enter upon that path . . . which
is peculiar to the Occident?" [4] This was the deepest of
the riddles that had inspired Weber to undertake his
studies of religion. Beyond the confrontation with
Marx, beyond the reckoning with the spiritual world,
Weber was interested above all in seeking out the reasons for the historical uniqueness of his own civilization.

In *The Protestant Ethic* he had reached an initial
solution. He had come to the conclusion that it was
the dynamic force of Protestantism, and more particularly of Calvinism, that had made the decisive difference. In the studies of the great Asian religions that
succeeded it, he tried to work the proof in reverse. He
attempted to show what was lacking in Buddhism or
Hinduism—namely, an ethic that endorsed and encouraged the life of rationally oriented business activ-

---

[4] *Protestant Ethic*, p. 25.

ity. Thus these subsequent studies had a broader range than the original work on Protestantism. In his effort to establish the economic mentality of the Asian cultures, Weber found it necessary to run more than one causal sequence: he not only traced the influence of religion on economic life; he searched out the geographic and material conditions that had helped to direct religious thought itself into certain well-defined channels.

As the publication of these studies proceeded, Weber clearly revealed his personal commitment to the rational values of his own society. His profound concern for reason—his distress at the paradox that made it both the highest achievement of the West and the source of the "soullessness" of contemporary life—inspired him to subject the culture of rationality itself to searching examination. This concern for the status of reason in contemporary society emerges with particular clarity in the last phase of Weber's life and work.

IV. *Sociology and History*

Eventually even Weber succumbed to the temptation to write a general treatise. In 1909 he started to plan out a summary essay that would serve as the central part of a collaborative compendium of economic sociology. It constantly grew in scope as the years passed, its publication was delayed by the war, and when it finally appeared after Weber's death under the title *Wirtschaft und Gesellschaft*—economics and society—it was still in unfinished form. But the first part, which was devoted to theory, had been completed, and the outlines of the rest were clear enough to give an adequate idea of the structure that Weber had in mind.

Was *Wirtschaft und Gesellschaft* the crowning achievement of Weber's career, or was it a vast mistake, an unwarranted departure from the program of building up theory in modest fashion from specific empirical studies that had distinguished his own earlier work and Durkheim's from that of Pareto? Unquestionably it marked a sharp change in approach. Even in style it was quite different from the methodological or religious studies. Where in these works the writing had been clumsy and involuted, in *Wirtschaft und Gesellschaft* the characteristic sentences were short declarative statements, following one on another in a clipped, martial rhythm, without modifiers or qualifications. A great deal of it Weber wrote "off the top of his head," and he left it bereft of footnotes and the other customary scholarly paraphernalia.[5]

For the most eminent American authority on Weber, *Wirtschaft und Gesellschaft* is "a tremendous 'architectonic' panorama, . . . the finest product of the historical relativism of the idealistic tradition"; it reveals a "knowledge of comparative institutions which is perhaps unique in the history of the social sciences." To an Italian scholar of similar stature, it is merely a "terminology" applied to the study of history, "a series of abstractions relatively devoid of content." Certainly the procedure of lining up ideal types in serried ranks is the most doubtful feature of the work. Even Weber's American expositor has granted that it suggests a " 'mosaic' theory of concrete society": the pieces are fitted together, but neither their interconnections nor their tentative and "fictional" character are sufficiently established. "History then becomes a process of shuffling ideal types, as *units*." It becomes something more fixed than what Weber had conceived in his moments of maximum awareness.[6]

In my own study of Weber, I have found myself drawing less often on *Wirtschaft und Gesellschaft* than on any other of his major works. This suggests its cen-

[5] Marianne Weber: *Max Weber*, pp. 462–3, 728.

[6] Parsons: *Structure of Social Action*, pp. 626, 653, Introduction to *Theory of Social and Economic Organization*, p. 83; Antoni: *Dallo storicismo*, p. 181.

tral difficulty: it offers a vastly impressive array of sociological learning, but only a small number of immediately relevant insights. In practice, only a very few
of the ideal types that Weber outlined in it have
proved susceptible of concrete application. And most of
these—like his definitions of class and status group,
charisma and bureaucracy—had their origin in his earlier empirical studies.

It would be wrong, however, to leave the impression
that *Wirtschaft und Gesellschaft* was simply a German
version of Pareto's treatise, with which in composition
it was almost exactly contemporary. This was far from
being the case. Weber had made a complete and permanent break with the positivist practice of seeking
general sociological "laws." Indeed, the difficulty in his
own systematic work was quite the reverse: in its emphasis on the free-standing character of social entities,
Wirtschaft und Gesellschaft suggested a reversion to
the idealist notion of the "spirit" of institutions. But
this idealist residue was also its strength. Weber's type
of sociology was firmly lodged within the framework
of history. "The systematic elaboration of sociology"
remained "subordinate to the procedures of historical
knowledge," offering as it did "a conceptual apparatus"
designed "to make possible the understanding of human behavior in the concrete 'becoming' of . . . individual events" in the world of history.[7]

For Weber the outbreak of the war, as with most of
his contemporaries, brought about a radical alteration
in his manner of living. But in Weber's case the change
was far more dramatic. From a semi-invalid, living on
the strict schedule dictated by the demands of his eccentric version of psychic hygiene, he was transformed
practically overnight into an active, "normal" being.
For more than a year, in his capacity as a reserve officer,

[7] Rossi: *Storicismo tedesco*, pp. 360–1.

he ran a military hospital with energetic efficiency. Subsequently he threw himself into political polemics, into
anxious consultations about the conduct of government
and Germany's war aims—all the time continuing to
work on his sociological writing, both religious and systematic. He found himself traveling constantly, meeting new people, even speaking in public. In brief, he
seemed "cured."

In the spring of 1918, as the war was drawing to a
close, he went to Vienna as a visiting professor. Here
he was a sensational success. His lectures were held in
the largest available auditorium, where "about a third
of his listeners consisted of mature men: politicians,
officials, teachers." A description from a contemporary
newspaper suggests the compelling quality of his plat-
form personality:

> Tall and fully bearded, this scholar resembles one
> of the German stone masons of the Renaissance
> period; only the eyes lack the naïveté and sensu-
> ous joy of the artist. His gaze is from the inner-
> most, from hidden passages, and it reaches into the
> greatest distances. His manner of expression cor-
> responds to the man's exterior; it is infinitely plas-
> tic. We meet here an almost Hellenic way of see-
> ing things. The words are simply formed, and, in
> their quiet simplicity, they remind us of Cyclopean
> blocks. When, however, an individual personality
> is introduced into the discussion, then it immedi-
> ately becomes monumental; each trait is chiselled
> as though in marble and put in the clearest light.
> Now and then the words are emphasized by a
> slight motion of the hand. . . . It is by no means,
> however, rhetorical mastery . . . alone that calls
> forth this extraordinary power of attraction, nor
> even the original and strictly factual character of
> the thought, but rather . . . the ability to awaken
> feelings that slumber in the souls of others. From
> each and every word it is clearly apparent that he

feels himself to be the heir of the German past and that he is governed by the consciousness of his responsibility toward posterity.[8]

In his sixteen years of self-imposed silence, Weber had slowly and rather unexpectedly grown famous. Now he had suddenly emerged as a public figure. The image he evoked among the younger generation was that of a half-mythical, enigmatic, vaguely "Satanic" figure who refused to give the word of guidance to those who were thirsting for intellectual and spiritual direction. And Weber was thoroughly conscious of the expectations vested in him. As national defeat approached, he held himself in readiness to serve his country. Naturally he wanted to be among his own people in their hour of difficulty. For this reason he declined the offer of a permanent chair in Vienna and returned to Germany just as the initiative was decisively passing to the enemy on the battlefields of France.

In the immediate post-armistice period, Weber seemed marked out for a leading political role. His polemics against his country's wartime regime had made a widespread impression; he participated in the foundation of the Democratic party; he was locally selected as a candidate for a seat in the constitutional assembly that was to meet at Weimar. But this first direct venture into politics came to nothing; the higher party leadership substituted for Weber a straight organization candidate. Weber's contribution to the founding phase of the German republic was restricted to participation in the advisory committee of experts that worked out an initial draft of the constitution—where he was mainly responsible for the provision of a presidency based on popular election that subsequently was to prove so dangerous to German democracy.

[8] Marianne Weber: *Max Weber*, pp. 652–5. I have taken the translation of the first part of this passage from Gerth and Mills's Introduction to *From Max Weber*, p. 26.

It was as yet too early, Weber concluded, for him to devote his full talents to statesmanship. Hence he decided to continue in his capacity as a scholar, and among the various flattering offers that had followed his return to active teaching, he settled on a chair in Munich. But even here his activities were far from being purely academic. He engaged in informal discussions with students of the most varied political leanings. He made an appearance in court to vouch for the ethical integrity of the inexperienced leaders of what had been for a brief period the Bavarian Soviet Republic. He held a measured exchange of views with the new historical messiah Oswald Spengler. Most characteristically, he outlined in his parallel lectures on "Science as a Vocation" and "Politics as a Vocation" his familiar distinction between value-spheres and his ethic of responsible choice.

In Munich, as in Vienna, Weber's lectures created a sensation. Into the more advanced of them he poured the systematic sociological theory that was taking form as *Wirtschaft und Gesellschaft*. And he labored mightily to fashion both this work and his collected essays on the sociology of religion into their final version. Meantime new demands on his time were pressing upon him —further scholarly projects and speaking engagements of all sorts. To these intellectual responsibilities there were added unanticipated family cares. In the autumn of 1919 Weber's mother died: we can only guess at how profoundly this loss affected him. A few months later came the death of his sister: her husband had fallen in battle in the first weeks of the war, and she left four orphaned children. In a wave of generous emotion, Max and Marianne Weber decided to adopt them. The inevitable second thoughts followed: had they become too accustomed to their life without children?—was it too late to begin in their fifties to play the role of parents? Weber tortured himself with the question: would he succeed in being a father?

There followed a relapse into severe nervous depression. By the end of April, however, he had pulled himself out of it and was talking of how "the scientific tasks that he saw before him would stretch to a hundred years." But still his wife delayed the actual arrival of the children in her house. In early June, Weber caught cold—it was apparently a trivial ailment. Yet by the time it was diagnosed as a deep-seated pneumonia, it was too late. Weber proved a cheerful patient: he did not fight the illness. In mid-June 1920 he lay dead.[9]

Weber's sudden death is conventionally described as a career cut short at its very height. In terms of professional accomplishment this is doubtless true—although we may question whether the new course marked out in *Wirtschaft und Gesellschaft* represented the best possible employment of his talents. But in personal terms, the matter is more perplexing. Did Weber have a sense that his new responsibilities were threatening to overwhelm him?—was he in his last months living in dread of a relapse into his earlier malady, to which anything, even death, would be preferable? Did he unconsciously long for release from his sudden eminence? At this very moment, Freud was publishing his speculations on the "death instinct" in human beings. We can only wonder.

In Weber's last phase of work and thought, the unbearable antinomies that had been apparent in his earlier writing were by no means resolved. On the contrary they were intensified. The problematic character of rationality in the Western world came to torment him ever more profoundly. Here also we may be led to suspect a kind of world-weariness: Weber's intellectual struggle had become intolerably intense. The value-spheres that he had delineated he had eventually found irreconcilable. As the individual, Weber argued, must

[9] Marianne Weber: *Max Weber*, pp. 642–7, 686–95, 711, 720–7, 740–54; J. P. Mayer: *Max Weber and German Politics* (London, 1943), Chapters 4, 5, 6.

make a clear choice between a career in scholarship and a career in politics, so he was obliged to opt for one or another ethical system. If he chose the "ethic of ultimate ends" of the Sermon on the Mount, then he could not participate in the life of the world. This was an ethic fitted only to sainthood; it did not pose the question of the practical consequences of actions. But if a man chose to become an active participant in public affairs, then he was condemned to an "ethic of responsibility" that might well violate his personal standards of morality. To serve the public good, he would be obliged to commit acts at which his soul recoiled— like those citizens of Florence immortalized by Machiavelli "who deemed the greatness of their native city higher than the salvation of their souls." [1]

Unlike Freud, whose faith in reason was unshakable, and who found that ethics presented no problem—unlike Croce, with his serene disregard for the ultimate riddles of existence—Weber never skirted a moral or intellectual issue. He met them all head on. Indeed, with a kind of perverse vocation for self-torment, he pushed all the contradictions to their point of maximum lucidity: here, in a wider sense, we may find another manifestation of his ideal-type procedure. It is for this reason that Weber sums up, more than any other single figure, the major themes of the present study.

Unquestionably Weber's chief intellectual weakness lies in the field of psychology. His "isolation of rationality" and his "treatment of affect as *only* a factor of deviation from rational norms is clearly incompatible with the findings of modern psychology, which rather point definitely to the integration of affective and rationally cognitive elements in the same action." [2] We-

---

[1] "Politics as a Vocation," *From Max Weber*, pp. 120–7; Rossi: *Storicismo tedesco*, pp. 368–72.
[2] Parsons: Introduction to *Theory of Social and Economic Organization*, p. 27.

ber, like Croce or Pareto, was *directly* interested only
in what was rationally understandable. The illogical,
the affective, remained for him no more than a residual
category.

A second weakness—and perhaps the one instance of
intellectual faltering in his whole theoretical production—was his refusal to recognize the implicit relativism
of his own thought. We have seen that none of Weber's predecessors or contemporaries consented to call
himself a relativist. And Weber was no exception. He
rejected relativism as the "crudest misunderstanding"
of his point of view.[3] In the sense of a radical skepticism—in the sense of a philosophy which questions the
whole notion of responsible choice—Weber was certainly not a relativist.[4] But in the sense of a point of
view that denies any metaphysical certainty—whether
of ethics or of historical truth—Weber can properly
be characterized by this term. He frankly recognized
the personal, affective origin of his own convictions:
he found no ultimate grounding for them. But he grew
dizzy at the abysses that this line of reasoning seemed
to open. We of the generation of his grandchildren,
who have grown up in an atmosphere of intellectual
and moral relativism, may find ourselves less frightened.

There was thus a kind of desperation about Weber's
own choices. He held to them with a passion for which
he could offer no philosophical justification. He had,
for example, a profound belief in the value of human
freedom. But he saw how problematical was the future
of freedom in a society that seemed inexorably headed
toward rationalization and bureaucratization. At the
same time, he realized, the process of rationalization
itself could not be rejected out of hand. As the direct
product of disciplined reason, it necessarily received his

[3] "Meaning of 'Ethical Neutrality,'" *Methodology*, p. 18.
[4] The contrary, however, has been persuasively argued by Leo
Strauss in his *Natural Right and History* (Chicago, 1953), Chapter 2.

intellectual endorsement. And reason itself, Weber had always argued, was at the source of human freedom. Hence, he was obliged to affirm as best he could the values of freedom *within* the framework of a rationalized society.

The vistas of the future that opened out before him were bleak in the extreme. What he often called—after Schiller—the "disenchantment of the world" seemed its most profound tendency. This was approximately the same process that Pareto had charted as a transition from a society in which the residue of "persistence of aggregates" was dominant, to one in which "instinct for combinations" ruled, or Durkheim's corresponding progression from social integration to *anomie*. "The ultimate and most sublime values," Weber declared, "have retreated from public life either into the transcendental realm of mystic life or into the brotherliness of direct and personal human relations. It is not accidental that our greatest art is intimate and not monumental, nor is it accidental that today only within the smallest and intimate circles, in personal human situations, in *pianissimo*, that something is pulsating that corresponds to the prophetic *pneuma*, which in former times swept through the great communities like a firebrand, welding them together." The days of great philosophical and religious creation were apparently over. "Not summer's bloom lies ahead of us, but rather a polar night of icy darkness and hardness." [5]

In a less extreme and apocalyptic form, Weber's vision of the future bears disconcerting resemblances to Spengler's. Like the author of *The Decline of the West*, he predicted a reaction against the Republic and democracy in his own country. And for Western society as a whole, he could see no alternative to the systematic fostering of an élite of professional politicians on whom the dreadful responsibility of government

[5] Parsons: *Structure of Social Action*, pp. 685–6; "Science as a Vocation," *From Max Weber*, p. 155; "Politics as a Vocation," Ibid., p. 128.

would devolve. From their ranks there would from time to time arise a charismatic party leader who would govern with dictatorial powers. Within this prospect, Weber found no radical contradiction: democracy and charismatic authority did not figure among his irreconcilables. Weber's hankering after personal leadership —along with his ineradicable nationalism—is enough to make us question the whole basis of his political thinking.

In politics, Weber's guidance was frequently dangerous. But as a diagnostician of contemporary society he was without a peer. His delineation of his own time was "unique in its sober realism and its intellectually sophisticated allowance for the immense complexity of the problems, for its ability to draw clear and definite conclusions from such complex materials and yet not fall into dogmatic over-simplification." [6] Weber's mind was never closed. He offered to his contemporaries an "open system of possibilities" in which men were free to create their meanings for themselves.[7]

Thus he has come to be respected in the most diverse intellectual and ideological camps. His standing among social scientists scarcely needs to be argued. The historians hold him in equally high regard. Among democrats he ranks as a friend and mentor of an extreme and salutary tough-mindedness. The neo-Marxists honor him as the man who refused to hate or to outlaw his revolutionary adversaries, who consented to discuss his differences with them frankly and face to face. From his teaching, one of them has written, there took its departure a "rigorous and consequential" Marxism, particularly associated with the writings of his young friend Georg Lukaćs.[8] In similar vein another of We-

[6] Parsons: Introduction to *Theory of Social and Economic Organization*, pp. 74, 84–5.

[7] Löwith, "*Weber und Marx*," p. 212; Weber: " 'Objectivity' in Social Science," *Methodology*, p. 57.

[8] Maurice Merleau-Ponty, *Les Aventures de la dialectique* (Paris, 1955), pp. 38, 42.

ber's younger admirers, the philosopher Karl Jaspers,
has viewed him as a proto-existentialist. In the very way
Weber lived his life, Jaspers contends, the possibilities
of human existence stand revealed. "Through this
man," we can penetrate "to the origin of what is hu-
manly possible," we can "catch sight of what a human
being actually is." [9]

For himself, Weber chose the values of the Enlightenment. Without illusion, with the same sort of desperation with which he made his other choices, he took
his stand with "the best of the eighteenth-century principles of mental integrity and social equity." "The rosy
blush of . . . the Enlightenment," he had written,
"seems . . . to be irretrievably fading," but still he
stuck with it. Not only did Weber possess "an extraordinary ethical sensitivity": he was also one of the last
great exponents of traditional humanist culture. "An
impassioned defender of justice, . . . he proved to be
courageous in his fight against obscurity of thought,
prejudice of judgment, and injustice of action. Ultimately it was the moral dignity of reason which, re-
gardless of historical destiny, constituted his faith." [1]

In this, as in so much else, Weber summed up the
work of his contemporaries. Like them, he had declared
for the Enlightenment *malgré tout*. In common with
Freud, he had proclaimed the supreme virtue of reason
even as he had explicitly recognized the irrational origin of human conduct. In company with Sorel and
Croce—but going far beyond them—he had defined
with a new rigor the epistemological basis of historical
and social investigation: he had established permanently valid criteria for arriving at an understanding of
the human world. Finally, like Mosca and Pareto, he

[9] *Max Weber: Politiker, Forscher, Philosoph* (Bremen, 1946),
p. 56.
[1] *Protestant Ethic*, p. 182; Arnold Bergstraesser: "Wilhelm
Dilthey and Max Weber: An Empirical Approach to Historical
Synthesis," *Ethics*, LVII (January 1947), 109–10.

had given due recognition to the role of élites in history and to the overriding influence of force and unethical behavior in the settlement of human affairs. But he had penetrated more deeply than Pareto into the nature of political action. He had seen that more than force and fraud were involved: politics, he realized, consisted of something beyond mere jungle warfare among embattled power groups; ultimately it was a contest of ethical values.[2]

Alone of his contemporaries, Weber was able to bridge the chasm between positivism and idealism. In the taut formulas of his methodology, he united the residual positivism of Freud and Pareto and Durkheim with what he had found valid in the tradition of Dilthey and Croce. In so doing, he, like them, abandoned to the realm of the irrational—to the unconscious—a vast field that could never be more than partially comprehensible. But in return he had won for social thought a complete autonomy *within* the field in which it had chosen to operate. Self-limitation, he realized, was the prior condition to intellectual liberation: the recognition of the irrational and the insistence on rigorous scientific procedures were only superficially in contrast. As against the dogmatism of the positivist and Marxian traditions, as against the invertebrate "intuitionism" of the idealists, Weber had anchored social thought in a "fictional" theory that asked only to be judged by its results.

---

[2] Rossi: *Storicismo tedesco*, p. 380.

The European Imagination
and the First World War

In the present chapter and the one following, the discussion will shift to a slightly different plane. We shall still be on the "higher" rather than the "lower" level of intellectual history. But we shall be dealing with figures who were closer to the popular world of discourse than were the giants of the generation of the 1890's—slightly younger men in nearly every case, essayists or imaginative writers whose rhythms of thought accorded better with the temper of the general educated public than did the austere lucubrations of the philosophers and social scientists whom we have been considering up to now. We shall be tracing one of the fashions in which the diffusion of the older men's ideas started. The less rigorous writers of a half generation younger than the great intellectual innovators—who, however, still thought of themselves as direct participants in the decisive experience of their elders—served as an initial line of transmission to the true popularizers of the generation following.

Meantime these younger writers were themselves the senior members of the new age group that was coming to maturity in the early twentieth century. In this capacity, they acted as connecting links with a generation that in many respects was in radical contrast with the generation that has up to now occupied our attention. Born in the 1870's, men like Péguy and Hesse, Proust and Mann, could mediate between their elders who had been born in the late 1850's or the 1860's and their immediate juniors, born in the 1880's, who were just reaching manhood in the first decade of the twentieth century. This new generation has yet to be described. It falls outside the sphere of our study, consisting as it does of those whose major period of productivity came after the First World War and, in a number of cases, still continues today. But we need to outline its salient characteristics if we are to understand how it happened that by the outbreak of the war so many of the generation of the 1890's felt themselves to be losing touch with their own spiritual descendants.

1. *The Generation of 1905*

In the retrospect of the war itself, the year 1905 most clearly offered the watershed. It marked the first time for a quarter-century that all Europe seemed astir. The revolution in Russia had come as the first major social disturbance since the Paris Commune of 1871—and for a moment the Socialist parties of France and Germany, Austria and Italy, had faced the embarrassing prospect that they might be obliged to give reality to the Marxist professions that had gradually been transformed into little more than a litany for the faithful. The revolutionary danger soon passed. But the effects of the other decisive event of the year—the First Moroccan Crisis—were not to be eradicated so quickly. From 1905 on, one diplomatic crisis followed on another in regular succession. The shock of Tangiers—as

Péguy put it—"within the space of . . . two hours" introduced a new epoch in his own life, as it did in the history of his country and of the world.[1] For the next decade the youth of Europe lived and breathed in an atmosphere of impending war.

It was this prospect of war service which most sharply marked off the new generation from those who had reached intellectual maturity in the 1890's. By 1905, men like Freud and Weber, Durkheim and Bergson, Mosca and Croce, were already getting too old for front-line duty. Of them, Weber alone put on a uniform during the war, and even he was not permitted to engage in actual combat. The war, when it came, was not *their* war: it was their sons' war. For them the decisive experience had been the intellectual renewal of the 1890's—or perhaps, in the case of the French, the defense of Captain Dreyfus. For the generation of their sons the great event was obviously the war itself. Here we find a dramatic instance of the contrasting experiences that serve to demarcate one age group from another in intellectual history.

Living as it did in a state of nearly constant war alert, the new generation was more impatient than that of its fathers. It respected its elders: in this it differed from the conventional image of a younger generation. But it was looking for something more arresting and dogmatic than its seniors had provided. It admired the discoveries they had made—but it understood these discoveries in cruder fashion. Where the writers of the 1890's had restricted themselves to a questioning of the potentialities of reason, the young men of 1905 became frank irrationalists or even anti-rationalists. This crucial distinction, which so often remains blurred in the history of ideas in our century, was largely a matter of contrasting age groups. The younger men were no longer satisfied with the urbane detachment of their

[1] *Notre Patrie* (originally published in the *Cahiers de la Quinzaine*, October 22, 1905) (Paris, 1915), p. 120.

elders. Everywhere they were in search of an ideal and a faith.

Thus in Germany they began to apply the teachings of Nietzsche in the sense of direct action, and thought of themselves as that "first generation of fighters and dragon-slayers" whom he had called on to establish the "Reich of Youth." One of Nietzsche's self-styled disciples—Stefan George—became their poet: from George they learned to regard themselves as a new spiritual aristocracy, with a lofty if ill-defined mission. The newly formed youth groups gave them an organizational outlet and an intoxicating sense of physical and spiritual liberation. Ten months before the outbreak of the war, in October 1913, representatives of the Free German Youth assembled on the Hohen Meissner hill in central Germany and drew up a melodramatic pledge to "take united action . . . under any and all circumstances . . . for the sake of . . . inner freedom." It was young people of this sort that Weber encountered four years later, when, at a gathering at Burg Lauenstein in Thuringia, he declined to serve as the prophet for whom they longed.[2]

In Italy the years between the turn of the century and the First World War brought into prominence new writers, new reviews, and new political organizations. The reaction from positivism that in Croce's case had expressed itself in rational and measured form, with the younger generation became a kind of spiritual explosion. Nationalism in politics, dynamism and "Futurism" in literature, above all the example—both artistic and personal—of the flamboyant word-magician Gabriele D'Annunzio, marked the changed temper of Italian youth. It was not until the review *La Voce* was founded in Florence in 1908, that some of the new writers were able to collaborate with their elders in

[2] Klemens von Klemperer: *Germany's New Conservatism: Its History and Dilemma in the Twentieth Century* (Princeton, N.J., 1957), pp. 43–6; Marianne Weber: *Max Weber: Ein Lebensbild,* new edition (Heidelberg, 1950), pp. 642–7.

reconciling a moderate type of nationalism with the older liberal tradition.

From his scholarly eminence, Croce watched the growing effervescence with a sympathy tinged with fatherly reproach—much as the elderly Goethe was alternately flattered and embarrassed at the honor paid him by the German Romanticists. This excited stirring, he implied, would be all to the good, if it were properly controlled and moderated. For D'Annunzio, however, he had only words of reproof. It was quite wrong, he insisted, to couple their names in any way: "D'Annunzianism in the proper sense" belonged to the generation that had "grown up since 1890"; he himself and the poet of youth were "spiritually of two different races."

> Though here and there D'Annunzio's art won my admiration, I never felt even a fleeting and sentimental agreement with the ethics which he suggested or preached outright. . . . I cannot remember that I ever for a single moment lost my hold on the distinction between sensuous refinement and spiritual fineness, erotic flights and moral elevation, sham heroism and stern duty.[3]

It was in France, however, that the cleavage between generations was most self-consciously delineated, and it is from here that we shall chiefly draw the literary evidences of a changed temper. In France after the turn of the century, as in Germany a decade earlier, the young people began to declare themselves Nietzscheans. André Gide's *The Immoralist*, published in 1902, is an early example. Subsequently, still younger writers like Alain-Fournier were to recognize the influence, either explicit or unconscious, of Nietzsche on their own thought.[4] But in France the Nietzscheans were

[3] "*Contributo alla critica di me stesso*" (1918) (reprinted as an appendix to *Etica e politica* [Bari, 1931]), translated by R. G. Collingwood as *An Autobiography* (Oxford, 1927), pp. 86–7.
[4] Geneviève Bianquis: *Nietzsche en France* (Paris, 1929), pp. 62–7. Compare the more deprecating statements about Nietzsche

only a minority. It was Bergson, rather, who ranked as the tutelary deity of the new generation. After 1905 the educated youth of France became militantly "Bergsonian."

The young people seized hold of Bergson with avidity and interpreted him according to their own tastes. They read into his teaching the notion of direct-action politics—usually of the Right—which was distinctly in contrast with his own convictions, and of dogmatic religion, on which his personal position still remained obscure. As so often has happened in the history of ideas, the originator of the doctrine lost control of his own creation: his disciples escaped from his tutelary guidance. For the half-decade before the First World War, "Bergsonism" was living a life of its own, almost independent of its founder.

It was a curious phenomenon, this new generation in which the sons were more conservative than the fathers. The latter had done battle for the innocence of Dreyfus and fought the power of the "reactionaries" and the clergy. Their children were as likely as not to embrace the neo-royalism of Charles Maurras and the *Action Française*, or the milder version of conservative nationalism preached by the novelist Maurice Barrès. At the Ecole Normale Supérieure the influence of Lucien Herr, the librarian, and of Jean Jaurès, the great Socialist alumnus, began to wane: Léon Blum—who three decades later was to be prime minister of France, but who at this period still ranked only as a brilliant lawyer and a rather precious *littérateur*—was one of the last of their great converts. And, to the more critical of the younger minds, Blum seemed rather superficial: he still took Jaurès's rolling periods seriously.[5]

Another reason for the declining influence of Socialism—and of Left politics in general—among the edu-

---

in the entry for November 4, 1927, in Gide's *Journal 1889–1939* (Paris, 1948), translated and edited by Justin O'Brien as *The Journals of André Gide* (New York, 1947–9), II, 419–20.

[5] Entry for April 27, 1906, Ibid., I, 181.

cated youth of France, had been the exploitation of
the Dreyfusard victory. Beginning in 1901, the triumphant Radicals had inaugurated a policy of ideological revenge. Freemasons were encouraged to spy on
Army officers of clerical inclinations, and there began
the systematic suppression of religious orders and teaching establishments that culminated in 1905 in the separation of Church and state. As the monks and nuns
emigrated abroad, as weeping children were forced out
of schoolrooms by armed soldiery, "the great pity of
the churches of France" (to use Barrès's phrase) began
to disturb the consciences even of those who had hitherto been neutral in religious matters. And to some of
these, the support that Jaurès was giving to the anti-
clerical campaign seemed like a kind of apostasy. Taking full advantage of his privileged status as an intellectual in politics, Jaurès threw "an oratorical and
poetic veil over the dirty business" by giving it an
"appearance of lofty philosophical reason that to the
naïve" made it "appear sublime." Others, however, like
Péguy or even Proust, could not stomach the fact that
"the same people who had turned the country upside
down in order that it should not be said that in France
a man had suffered on account of his race and his religion," were now "expelling the teaching orders and declaring war on everything religious." [6] As the Jewish
journalist Bernard Lazare put it, the fact that the cleri-
cals had plagued people like himself for years was no
reason to turn around and do the same to them. [7]

In 1900, in intellectual circles, it had been bad form
to be a practicing Catholic. By 1910, while the majority
still consisted of unbelievers—philosophical positivists
for the most part—a growing minority of the sensitive
and discriminating spirits were returning to the faith in
which they had been baptized. A few great conversions

[6] Jérôme and Jean Tharaud: *Notre Cher Péguy* (Paris, 1926),
I, 221, 235–6.
[7] Charles Péguy: *Notre Jeunesse* (originally published in the
Cahiers de la Quinzaine, July 17, 1910) (Paris, 1933), p. 101.

had served as examples—the poet Paul Claudel from the elders, the philosopher Jacques Maritain in the younger generation. It was the latter who was to appeal in vain with the anti-clerical wife of Péguy to ease her husband's torments of conscience by letting her children be baptized.

In 1905 only three or four students at Normale openly professed their religious faith. By 1912 there were perhaps forty—a third of the student body. The great institution that had so long ranked as a "citadel of bantering agnosticism" was gradually being penetrated by the new spirit.[8] And the same thing was going on in other educational centers and other intellectual circles. This changed attitude toward things religious has been admirably documented by André Gide's younger friend and literary associate, Roger Martin du Gard. In his novel *Jean Barois*, published in 1913, Martin du Gard traced the spiritual pilgrimage of his own generation. With an acute sense for the nuances of religious scruple, he depicted the slow transformation of a child's tender, naïve piety into a "Modernist" interpretation of dogma in a symbolic sense. But in the case of the fictitious Jean Barois, as with so many of his actual contemporaries, Catholic "Modernism" could be only an uneasy compromise: the Pope himself was to condemn it. Beyond it lay an aggressive irreligion of a materialist and positivist type, and beyond that in turn a final reconciliation with the Church. In this intellectual progression, Martin du Gard's protagonist seemed typical of the new century. But for religiously minded readers the book had a disconcerting backtwist: Jean Barois's return to Catholicism was denied the character of conscious and responsible choice—it was the despairing product of sickness, personal misery, and fear of death.

Thus Jean Barois is still a transition figure, hovering

[8] Jacques Chastenet: *Une Epoque pathétique: la France de M. Fallières* (Paris, 1949), p. 218.

in unhappy self-division between the skepticism of the older liberal faiths and the dogmatisms of the future. When as a middle-aged man he is faced with two university students come to enlighten him on the new tendencies among French youth, he finds that they are speaking an unfamiliar and rather frightening language. He is repelled by their denigration of science and their cult of force. To him they represent a mere "reaction": in their own eyes they are the bearers of spiritual renewal.

With this contrast, we touch the central ambiguity in the generation of 1905. In France—and the same was true in Germany—during the years just before the outbreak of the war there reigned among the youth a spirit that combined respect for authority with the cult of spontaneous creation. Depending on where they have chosen to lay their emphasis, historians of the epoch have judged it very differently. On the one hand, they have found in it a threatening proto-fascist atmosphere, on the other hand a renaissance of culture and of living brutally cut off at its start. This was the generation of French and Germans of whom the best were to perish in battle—or so, at least, their contemporaries saw it. And the tragic irony of the matter was that they greeted the outbreak of the slaughter with enthusiasm. The more bellicose felt at last within their grasp the life of action for which they had longed. The more reflective welcomed it as a deliverance from unfruitful anticipation: "Better that war should come," they repeated, "than to go on with this perpetual waiting." [9]

---

[9] Pierre Andreu: *Notre Maître, M. Sorel* (Paris, 1953), p. 89, quoting Drieu La Rochelle; Chastenet: *La France de M. Faillières*, pp. 11–12, 353.

ii. *Péguy and Alain-Fournier*

"I have fought all my life on the frontiers," [1] Péguy once wrote, and he meant it in at least two senses. In his blundering, obtuse search for intellectual honesty, in his impatience with the rhetorically facile and the ready-made, he did in fact try to dwell on the frontiers of thought. And from 1905 on, in his insistence on the menace that lay over France, he felt that he was engaged in a perpetual combat to protect his country's borders. It was fitting that he should die at the head of his men in a stubborn skirmish just short of Paris only a month after the declaration of war.

We have encountered Péguy repeatedly in the earlier chapters of this study. He has figured more particularly as a disciple of Bergson and as a friend and intellectual companion to Sorel. Bergson he had first met during his student days at the Ecole Normale Supérieure; the "marvellous teaching" of the extraordinary young lecturer had taken Péguy "by storm."

> He listened in silence, took no part in the discussions, did no written work. Such was the way of this "ardent, gloomy, stupid young man." Bergson took no notice, having been told this was a special case, and he might never have heard the sound of Péguy's voice, had he not stopped him one day in the School corridor: "I know you have put aside your personal work to give us your whole time. You should not do this. You have a book to write, and that should come before everything else," he said, and then passed on. [2]

[1] *Note conjointe* (Péguy's last work, comprising *"Note sur M. Bergson et la philosophie bergsonienne"* and *"Note conjointe sur M. Descartes et la philosophie cartésienne,"* the former originally published in the *Cahiers de la Quinzaine*, April 26, 1914, the latter left unfinished at his death) (Paris, 1935), p. 276.

[2] Daniel Halévy: *Péguy and* Les Cahiers de la Quinzaine (translation by Ruth Bethell of the revised version, published in

Subsequently, after Bergson had been appointed to the
Collège de France, Péguy assiduously attended his lectures. Wrapped in his blue cape, he would sit high up
in the far bank of seats, silently attentive to the message.

Bergson lectured on Friday afternoons. At a quarter
to five Sorel would drop by at the office of the *Cahiers
de la Quinzaine* to pick up Péguy and whatever friends
of his were planning to attend. On Thursday afternoons also *"le père Sorel,"* as the much younger Péguy
affectionately called him, would visit the latter's curious
publishing establishment. Thursday was the time when
the editor was "at home" to friends, critics, and subscribers. In the tiny office the sole chair was reserved
for Sorel; here the elderly polemicist, robust and white-
bearded, would expatiate to the young men from his
vast store of miscellaneous learning and prejudice.[3]

Sorel and Péguy had in common their genuine popular sympathies, their unbending moralism, their impatience with intellectual rhetoric and cant, their
hatred of their country's political and academic élite.
As polemicists, their minds worked in harmony. But in
the range and style of their thought, they diverged
markedly. Sorel, we may recall, was a technician by
training: his mind ran to the abstract; his style was
condensed; he read enormously. Péguy scarcely had
time to read at all; his own education had been literary
and philosophical; and his writing was infinitely prolix.
Sorel in his eccentric fashion touched on the world of
social science: Péguy was exclusively a literary figure.
He was a poet as well as an essayist—indeed, it was as
the author of a long poem on Joan of Arc that in 1909
he first became known to the general reading public.

Thus Péguy offers a link between literature and social thought. Similarly his career suggests an intermedi-

---

France in 1940, of Halévy's *Charles Péguy et les Cahiers de la
Quinzaine*) (London, 1946), p. 29.
    [3] Ibid., pp. 62–5.

ate plane somewhere between the abstract reflections of his elders and the intense political allegiances characteristic of the generation of 1905. Péguy's own ideological position is so special that it fits into none of the conventional categories of French politics. He shared with Maurras and Barrès the role of a nationalist prophet—yet he insisted on his republicanism and his socialist aspirations. He agreed with Alain in championing the rights of the common citizen against the bureaucracy—yet he differed totally with Alain in his judgment of Jaurès, the Radical party, and the anticlerical legislation of the period 1901–5. Durkheim he hated as one of the supreme pontiffs of the "intellectual party" that from its fortress of the Sorbonne ruled the cultural life of France [4]—yet in the tumults of the Dreyfus case he had shouted "rally" and set off with his heavy stick to defend the sociologist's classes from the attacks of nationalist students. Péguy was perpetually cutting across one or another of the cleavages that divided French life into neat compartments. His changes, like Sorel's, bewildered his friends and admirers. Yet in some sense that he alone fully understood, he remained true to an intensely personal concept of what his life and work meant.

To his contemporaries, even to those who disliked what he stood for, Péguy seemed a totally "pure" character—a symbol and leader, only slightly older than they, of the generation that was to be tried by fire in the terrible years after 1914.

In 1894 when, at the age of twenty-one, Péguy arrived at Normale, he was already a very special figure. He was a true son of the people, he was a bit older than his classmates, and he had given advance warning that he would not submit to the sort of hazing that was

---

[4] See particularly the four essays, originally published in the *Cahiers de la Quinzaine*, November 4, December 2, 1906, and February 3, October 6, 1907, and subsequently collected under the title *Situations* (Paris, 1940).

customary at the school. The fact that he had attained
to these rarefied educational heights at all was a tribute both to his own perseverance and to the perspicac-
ity of the teachers who had singled him out for en-
couragement. And it offered the isolated example which
proved that the democratic ideal in French education
was something more than a polite fiction.

Writing five years after Péguy's death and only three
years before his own, Georges Sorel retrospectively
questioned whether his former friend's career as a
normalien had actually been to his advantage. For it
had

> placed him in a milieu for which he felt no sym-
> pathy. Since he did not succeed in bowing to the
> demands that middle-class conventions impose on
> the sons of the so-called ruling classes, he suffered
> all his life from being treated as a rebel by people
> who were complete strangers to his popular in-
> stincts. Moreover, academic rhetoric weighed heav-
> ily on his style, causing him to consider as an
> enrichment of thought, a superabundance of
> epithets, a proliferation of parallel forms, and a
> refinement of unexpected figures of speech, which
> surprise the reader without teaching him very
> much.[5]

At Normale, Péguy, like Durkheim—but for rather
different reasons—was a misfit and an exotic. Among
this band of superlatively articulate young men from
the cultivated classes, Péguy, the son of a widowed
chair-mender from Orléans, was too slow, too somber,
too massively serious about all his concerns. His fellow
students could not help but respect him—a few years
later they and their juniors followed without question
when he assumed command in the street battles of the
Dreyfus era—but they found him a difficult man to
live with. Péguy must have known he was out of place.

[5] "Charles Péguy," *La Ronda*, I (April 1919), 58–9.

In 1898 he took leave of the school. He married, he failed his examinations for the *agrégation*, and then, with the prospects of regular academic advancement cut off, he proceeded to make his own way as an independent journalist in the French intellectual world.

For a brief period he served as the editor of a regular Socialist review. But he soon quarreled with Jaurès, Herr, Blum, and the other party intellectuals, and in 1900 he founded his own unique publication. The *Cahiers de la Quinzaine*—the fortnightly notebooks, as the title may roughly be translated—was not really a periodical at all. Each *cahier* consisted of a separate book or long essay, a large number of which Péguy wrote himself. In a very special sense it was his personal publication: as an artisan from childhood, he devoted his minute attention to every phase of its production; each *cahier*, he insisted, must be perfect, each tiny printer's error tracked down.

The *Cahiers de la Quinzaine* had less than a thousand subscribers, it struggled along perpetually on the verge of financial collapse, but for the first decade of the century it ranked as one of the most original and stimulating publications in the whole of Europe. Péguy brought to it a provincial freshness and an uncompromising stubbornness in argument. And as friends and contributors he gathered around him an unconventional élite of the younger Dreyfusards—plus, of course, the irrepressible Sorel.

Toward the end of the decade, however, the *Cahiers* were shaken by a series of explosions. In 1908, Péguy announced his conversion to Catholicism—a direct slap at the majority of his subscribers, militant freethinkers such as he had once been himself. Two years later, in *Notre Jeunesse*, he lashed out at the exploitation of the Dreyfusard victory—thereby antagonizing another influential group of supporters. Finally, in 1912, there came his break with Sorel. The circumstances of this rupture seem almost too stupid to be true. Julien Benda, one of the numerous intellectual Jews affiliated with the

Cahiers circle, had published a novel entitled *L'Ordination*. Sorel—prude that he was--had condemned it as
pornographic. Hence, when the novel missed receiving
the Prix Goncourt, Péguy blamed the failure on Sorel's
machinations, and asked the latter to visit the *Cahiers*
no more. Sorel stayed away: the two ceased seeing each
other altogether.[6]

Doubtless the split had deeper reasons. Péguy and
Sorel were both cutting across the usual French cleavages, but for a number of years they had been cutting
in opposite directions. At the start they had both been
republican, socialist, and freethinking. But now Sorel
was coquetting with royalism, and Péguy had returned
to the Church. Each had advanced toward the enemy
on the right, but in a different and contradictory fashion. Sorel, we hear, simply did not take Péguy's conversion seriously. And the latter was convinced that
Sorel was doing all in his power to undermine the situation of the *Cahiers*.

During the last two years of his life, Péguy lived in
pitiable poverty and isolation. The *Cahiers* were quite
obviously running dry. And he himself had quarreled
with nearly all his friends. Benda was almost the only
one who remained, and with him, as we shall see, Péguy
had scarcely anything in common.[7] He had become
suspect to the Left. But the Catholics and the Right
were not ready to welcome him: with his marriage still
unblessed by the Church and his children still unbap-
tized, he could not be in formal communion with his
faith. And when in early June 1914, Bergson's books—
despite Péguy's powerfully reasoned arguments—were
put on the Index, the condemnation of his own work
seemed only a matter of time. Two months later Péguy
had every reason to welcome the outbreak of war.

[6] See the accounts in Andreu: *Sorel*, pp. 272–86; Halévy:
Péguy and Les Cahiers, pp. 171–2; Tharaud: *Notre Cher Péguy*,
II, 137–43.
[7] See Chapter 10. But also note Péguy's characterization of
his own relationship to Benda in *Note conjointe*, pp. 62–9.

He had always enjoyed military service, and he departed for the front with joy in his heart. And when he fell with a bullet through his head on the eve of the Battle of the Marne, men recalled the lines he had published nine months earlier:

Heureux ceux qui sont morts dans les grandes batailles Couchés dessus le sol à la face de Dieu.[8]

Péguy wrote of his own literary style: "We shall be obliged to proceed by different approaches and by successive excavations . . . by soundings that we shall push as far as we can, by partial advances, by tunneling, and by all the sapper's arts." Or—changing the metaphor—"even if we do not make interpolations, if we go straight on, without interruption, in the direction and to the extent that . . . reality itself is straight and uninterrupted, [even then] we do not know, we cannot know, whether we shall reach our goal, whether we shall ever arrive anywhere." [9] For Gide, Péguy's writing was a kind of "intellectual stuttering"—a stammer in the thought.[1] This was its weakness, and this was at the same time its strength. When Péguy wrote, he never altered a word: it all came out with the same massive inevitability that was characteristic of the way he lived his life.

Péguy's style of thought represented an effort to apply the Bergsonian metaphysics—an effort to embrace the contours of life itself. Hence there is in it no straight logical sequence. It modulates, rather, from one statement to the next. It proceeds by slight cumulative changes in each succeeding sentence until a new statement is finally reached. Thus the literary mannerisms that annoy Péguy's readers—the repetitions, the endless employment of synonyms (which are seldom, in fact, totally synonymous)—are actually essential to his

---

[8] "Blessed are those who have died in great battles,
  Lying upon the ground in the sight of God."
[9] *Situations*, pp. 8, 105.
[1] Entry for May 7, 1912, *Journals of André Gide*, I, 329.

method. They leave with us an impression of density, of crablike crawling toward a conclusion whose con-tours have at length been fully delineated. At its best, this method may eventually attain to greater clarity than the more conventional approach by logical pro-gression. In its less successful applications, however, as Sorel saw, it turns into mere rhetoric—and this was what Péguy was striving at all costs to avoid.

Péguy scorned mere literary style. In this regard, he was the most un-French of writers. And in this respect also, he was more truly Bergsonian than the master himself, whose prose was usually impeccable. In fact, Péguy's work suggested the technical limitations of the whole Bergsonian approach: language—and more par-ticularly the French language—was simply not built for it.

Péguy had learned at Normale to be Bergson's disci-ple. But before that he had been the son of peasants, and a peasant he remained in the slowness of his thought and the slowness of his expression—which was, perhaps, all the surer for that. Beneath the literary cul-ture with which his formal education had provided him, this was Péguy's solid core. In the *Cahiers*, he said, he would refuse to print anything that was not a product of personal experience—"that we have not gone through ourselves." He demanded total integrity: such was his characteristic contribution to French intellec-tual life.

Considered in this light, the divergent political and social doctrines he espoused have their own stubborn unity. Péguy always thought of himself as a socialist—but a socialist of a quite different breed from the party politicians who tried to monopolize the title. These, Péguy argued, were mere bourgeois demagogues who had no real understanding for what the common people actually thought and felt. His own vision, like Sorel's, was of a *cité* of the future, which would restore the no-tion of pride in honest labor and production. Far from wanting to add the new disorder of social unrest to the old disorder of capitalism, what Péguy was seeking was "to inaugurate, to restore an order, a new, old order; new, antique; in no way modern; an order of hard work, an order of labor, a workingman's order. . . ." [2]

Was he a democrat? Certainly he had no faith in the mere counting of votes and manipulation of majorities. But in a sense in which Sorel could never be numbered among democrats, Péguy was one of them. He had none of Sorel's destructive negativism. Indeed, he was almost childlike in his acceptance of the popular French *mystique* of the Republic and the Revolution. His notion of the good government was apparently that of a broadly based aristocracy of nature founded on hard work and personal worth. And when he had declared himself a Catholic, he brought to his religious faith a similar conviction of the inherent virtue of popular values and the popular understanding of Catholicism. *Charity*, he contended, should be restored to the center of Christian doctrine: the current identification of the Church with the interests of the upper classes was a terrible aberration from the teachings of Christ.

In the France of 1910 Péguy's combination of militant republicanism and Catholicism was something of an ideological novelty. But to Péguy himself, there was no radical contradiction in his double allegiance. Each represented a *mystique*: together they offered the two great systems of belief that had made the French people a unique achievement of history. To Péguy a *mystique* meant what was noble and fresh and bright in a social or religious conviction: a *politique* represented its degeneration into what was petty and self-seeking. "Everything begins as a *mystique*," he declared, "and ends as a *politique*." He was writing specifically of the Dreyfus case. But he was also thinking in more general terms of the whole nature of moral

---

[2] *Notre Jeunesse*, pp. 144–5; see also Félicien Challaye: *Péguy socialiste* (Paris, 1954), Chapter 3.

forces in history and society. Two *mystiques*, he wrote, are much less inimical to each other than are the two *politiques* to which they correspond. Indeed, one might go so far as to say that one *mystique* has more in common with the *mystique* opposed to it than it has with the *politique* that is called by its own name. Thus Péguy saw no contradiction in predicting that "in the same . . . profound movement" the two great *mystiques* of republicanism and Christianity would revive together.[3] Together they would lift France to new heights of fraternal endeavor.

And so after his death in battle Péguy became a symbol of the unity of the French people, which a century and a quarter of political and religious strife had so grievously divided. Like Joan of Arc, whose praises he had sung, Péguy was elevated to the position of a national institution. In the period between the wars he ranked as a minor poet and a major prophet. It was the Second World War, however, that completed his apotheosis. In the occupation and resistance of 1940 to 1944, Péguy spoke with the voice of a martyred people. From extreme Right to extreme Left, in all social classes and all ideological camps, he was quoted again and again as the writer who had shown the French nation the way back to its own soul.

For the French, Péguy obviously has a personal significance in which no foreigner can entirely share. By the same token the French view of him tends to be uncritical: nearly all the Péguy literature is inspired by reverent affection. We who stand a little outside his immediate orbit may try to reach a judgment that is less emotionally colored.

Péguy obviously left behind him no major work of speculative prose. He thought in fragments—in sudden juxtapositions of the unexpected. This was his great strength—indeed, from an intellectual standpoint al-

[3] *Notre Jeunesse*, pp. 17, 27, 50.

most his only strength. Yet we cannot dismiss him as simply a minor essayist: there is something too compelling about him for that. At the same time—just as with his own groping fashion of writing—his significance is difficult to pin down. His thought eludes us. Perhaps the best we can say is that Péguy has a talent for putting familiar things in a way that is so different from the ordinary that their original reality and freshness are restored to them.

Let me give a final example. In a period of almost universal nationalist agitation, in a period when nearly everyone thought he knew what a nation or a people was, Péguy wrote of peoples in a fashion that could not fail to jar and to give pause. For what he said disrupted the clichés both of the nationalists and of the internationally minded humanitarians. Take what he wrote of the Jews, more particularly in his unforgettable portrait of Bernard Lazare, the journalist who almost singlehanded had reopened the Dreyfus case. This picture of a profoundly wounded people, of a "chosen race of anxiety," is suffused with affection. It offers a direct challenge to the cultivated hatred of the anti-Semites. But at the same time it is vaguely troubling. For it has none of the assimilationist sentimentality, the glossing over of distinctions characteristic of "tolerant" Gentiles. On the contrary Péguy pushes his analysis of the dissimilarities between Jew and Christian to the point of intolerable paradox. He dwells on every sign, external or spiritual, of a profound difference in *mystique*. "The Jew," he declares in a passage that has become famous, "is a man who has always read," the Protestant has read for three hundred years, the Catholic for only two generations.[4]

Similarly with his own people. Péguy knew the French people, "poor and Catholic," with a direct experience in which few of his literary countrymen have been able to share. In *Notre Patrie* he caught a vision

[4] Ibid., pp. 72 ff; *Note conjointe*, p. 82.

of what the French actually were like in their moments of naïve enthusiasm. They were tired of Socialist speech-making, bored with the adult-education courses that the Dreyfusards had offered them. What they appreciated was a good show—military music, horses, and marching men. They did not really believe the anti-militarist speeches that they applauded. And this "duplicity" infuriated Péguy. One must be honest about it, he argued, "one must be for or against war," not merely in rhetoric, but with all one's soul. He himself had chosen for war. And, long before most intellectuals had swung around to the same conclusion, he had correctly gauged the temper of his own people. They too had decided for war—as had the Germans also. August 1914 was to show how right Péguy had been.

The act of Péguy's that has taken on the greatest symbolic significance was the pilgrimage he made on foot from Paris to Chartres in June of 1912. According to one account, the young Alain-Fournier accompanied him on a second expedition he made six months or a year later. Another version has it that the latter twice planned to go with Péguy to Chartres and both times was prevented by a last-minute change of plans.[5] In any event, the two were friends, and to the French of their own and succeeding generations they have seemed to represent the same kind of aspirations. Alain-Fournier was thirteen years younger than Péguy; he was gentler —indeed not combative in the slightest; he was exclusively a literary figure and quite uninterested in politics. But he shared with Péguy that striving for spiritual purity which had so deep an appeal for the generation of 1905. And, like Péguy, he perished in battle during the first weeks of the war—simply swallowed up in the

[5] Compare the accounts in Halévy: *Péguy and* Les Cahiers, pp. 169–70, and Robert Gibson: *The Quest of Alain-Fournier* (New Haven, Conn., 1954), pp. 239–40, 286.

inferno of combat, without sight or trace, two weeks after the death of his older friend.

He left behind him the record of an existence that was pathetic in its brevity and its lack of fulfillment. His childhood had been too happy: the son of a village schoolmaster in the center of France near Bourges, he had been surrounded by tenderness, by the reassurance of ancient custom, by the poetic promptings of nature. When he was just turning twelve he had been sent to a Paris *lycée*. Subsequently he studied in Brittany, in England, and again in Paris. He suffered desperately from the brutalities and humiliations of military service. Eventually in shy, tentative fashion he began to write and to win the approval of Gide and other leaders of the literary *avant-garde* in the capital. By the time the war broke out, he had made a small literary reputation of his own. It was all to no avail. Nothing could console him for the loss of the innocence and emotional warmth of childhood. And nothing could make up for the fact that the beautiful girl he had seen a handful of times and whom he had worshiped from a distance had become the wife of another man. For Alain-Fournier also, the war came as a deliverance.

Yet out of the sad fragments of his life, out of the memories of childhood and the disappointments of maturity, he had succeeded in fashioning one great novel. To the generation of 1905, *Le Grand Meaulnes* is the most touching of memorials. It evokes the freshness of a world newly seen, of sensations and emotions to which the full purity of original recognition has been restored. Like the work of Péguy, it is a most un-French affair: there is scarcely an erotic note in it. It lifts us completely out of the nineteenth century—out of its "realistic" world of bourgeois manners and the obsession of adultery. Alain-Fournier's novel leaves all this far behind: it is, rather, the story of a search—a search for innocence and for something more that cannot be explained but can only be divined in our moments of

most intense consciousness. "I am searching," Alain-
Fournier wrote,

> for something still more mysterious. It is the path
> told of in books, the ancient obstructed path, the
> path to which the weary prince could find no en-
> trance. It is found at last at the most forlorn hour
> of the morning, when you have long since for-
> gotten that eleven or twelve is about to strike. . . .
> And suddenly, as one thrusts aside bushes and
> brier, . . . it appears in sight as a long shadowy
> avenue, with at its end a small round patch of
> light.

The secret could be glimpsed but never fully known.
"Our adventure," Meaulnes writes, "is at an end. Winter, this year, is as dead as the grave. Perhaps when we
die, perhaps death alone will give us the key, the sequel
and the end of this adventure that has failed." [6]

III. *The Novelist and the Bourgeois World:*
Gide and Mann

Le Grand Meaulnes was originally published in the
Nouvelle Revue Française from July to November
1913. This fact suggests the spiritual link between the
world of Charles Péguy and the world of André Gide.
For in the realm of pure literature, the *Nouvelle Revue
Française* had something of the same character of self-
conscious integrity and impatience with the "ready-
made" which the *Cahiers de la Quinzaine* stood for in
the realm of writing that was politically engaged.
Founded in 1908, eight years after the *Cahiers*, the
Nouvelle Revue Française was also a product of the stir-
rings of the new century. It aimed at a "classicism" of
thought and expression—"a vindication of the conscious mind" through the exercise of "a rigorous critical

[6] Translation by Françoise Delisle as *The Wanderer* (Boston
and New York, 1928), pp. 156, 176. I have altered the wording
slightly.

vigilance." At the same time it encouraged literary experimentation. These two apparently contradictory goals were not in fact incompatible: in both respects, the review was trying to combat commercialism and cheap sophistication. Within the space of a very few years, the combination proved extraordinarily influential. By 1914 the review had three times the subscription list of Péguy's *Cahiers*. And the publishing house that had been added to it in 1911 was becoming the most select in France; it offered the imprint which the aspiring young author above all desired to have on his work.[7] After the war this position of prestige became overpowering: the *Nouvelle Revue Française* and the affiliated publishing house of Gallimard achieved a near monopoly of first-rate literary talent.

Among the group of six younger writers who had founded the review, André Gide was the most gifted and the nearest to being the guiding spirit. With Gide, we come to a new phenomenon in literary history. Earlier there had always existed the writer as artisan, the literary man who exercised his craft as naturally and un-selfconsciously as any other individual of talent dependent on a public for his livelihood. Up to the late eighteenth century, in fact, this was virtually the sole image of the artist that society knew. Then the Romantic movement had created the notion of the artist as rebel, defiant of convention and alienated from his society. In one form or another, this image had predominated in the public mind throughout the nineteenth century. The Satanic destroyer, the child of scorn, the outcast of special tastes and cultivated depravity—all these had become stock figures in the post-Romantic era.

Gide was something rather different. He was an immensely serious artist, ultra-scrupulous and uncompromising in his literary standards. At the same time he fell

[7] Albert J. Guerard: *André Gide* (Cambridge, Mass., 1951), p. 199; Léon Pierre-Quint, *André Gide: l'homme-sa vie-son œuvre-entretiens avec Gide et ses contemporains* (Paris, 1952), pp. 41–5.

into neither one of the usual categories of rebel or
conformist. He was a product of the cultivated upper
middle class and deeply rooted in its value-system and
way of life. And for the first half of his life he made a
conscientious effort to live—at least externally—in accord with what it expected of him. Eventually the attempt proved impossible: the gap was too wide to be
bridged. Yet Gide did not set himself up in one of the
conventional nineteenth-century poses of alienation.
He worked out his own adjustment to a situation of almost unprecedented difficulty. In the process he created
a twentieth-century image of the novelist nostalgic for
the previous century's world of secure middle-class
values yet forced against his will into opposing those
values and declaring new ones. Thus Gide early realized that his personal existence was taking on a symbolic character—that men younger than he were looking to him for clues as to how the life of literary
creation should be led.

"I have a horror of falsehood," Gide once said to
Jacques Maritain. "That is perhaps just where my Protestantism lurks." [8] Gide's Protestant origin exacerbated
the familiar sense of disparity between the artist and
his milieu, and by the very fact of ancestral difference
from his fellow citizens heightened his consciousness
of the more disturbing differences he felt within himself. The French Protestant community has historically
been distinguished by its pride and the sense of special
status it has derived from its position as a minority
disproportionately influential in business, in public life,
and, above all, in intellectual pursuits. In his consciousness of being a member of a minority—selected out by
God or fate for special purposes and special tempta-
tions—Gide was and always remained a true French
Protestant. And he was in the Calvinist tradition also
in his cult of the perpetual "examination of conscience"
—the ruthless, unremitting search for the unsuspected

[8] Entry for December 21, 1923, *Journals of André Gide*, II,
339.

lapse from grace. Gide's quest for total sincerity—like Weber's—was a secularized variant of the Protestant ethic. The truth had to be found and publicly declared, whoever might be caught up in its wake of suffering.

But how was one to know what the truth was? How was one to distinguish real sincerity from the plausible rationalizations that usually passed by that name? Long before he had read a line of Freud, Gide was tormented by this question. Without suspecting it, he had stumbled on the central problem posed by psychoanalytic theory. Through the characters in his novels, he had learned to test the traps with which the unconscious lay in wait for the unsuspecting—sexual desire lurking under shared religious devotion, murderous impulses behind the charming smiles of adolescent boys. Through his *Journals* he had simultaneously tried to peer down into his own depths—and what he found there would have given pause even to a man who was not, like Gide, a devoted husband, a respectable citizen, and a proud offspring of the Protestant upper bourgeoisie. He had found that he was a very special person indeed, and one of a breed for which middle-class society had reserved its most pitiless contempt.

Gide had first discovered his homosexual inclinations in North Africa in the mid-1890's, when, as an inexperienced young man in his twenties, he had followed the sly promptings of Oscar Wilde. But it was a long way from here to a full recognition of what made him different from others—and farther still to a reconciliation with his own nature. Beyond that—and apparently impossible to attain—lay a frank public avowal of his forbidden desires. Yet in the next three decades Gide was to cover all these stages. One way of reading the quarter-century sequence of his most important work— from *The Immoralist* of 1902 to *The Counterfeiters* and the full version of his autobiography in 1926—is as a progressive revelation of his own ambiguous nature. The literary record is full of half-admissions, sudden reticences, and strategic flights for cover. But as the years advance the declarations become ever more explicit and unmistakable: only the religiously obtuse, like Paul Claudel, could fail to divine what Gide was about.[9]

Above all, it was respect for his wife that held him back from making a full confession. But sooner or later, he knew, the whole truth would have to come out. "Even at the risk of mockery and attacks . . . , he intended to give back their self-esteem to men whom . . . public opinion generally treats as reprobates. He considered that to be his mission. . . ."[1] He knew its dangers. He was familiar with the radically different attitude of Proust, who could never think of his own inclinations as anything other than "infernal," who transposed in his novel the names of the male objects of love into those of women, and who once advised Gide personally: "You can tell anything . . . ; but on condition that you never say: *I*."[2] Yet still Gide was irresistibly impelled to confess all. What Proust and Wilde had tried to deny, he himself would publicly avow: as opposed to the "false martyrdom" of Oscar Wilde, he would face the attack openly and unafraid.

It was not until he was in his mid-fifties that Gide made his full confession. And when it came, it did not arouse the storm of indignation that might have been expected. The years had done their work. There were many people, particularly among the religious, who reacted with horror. But by the mid-1920's the more inquiring and intellectually sensitive had learned— from the behavior of post-war youth, from the half-admissions of other artists, above all, from Freud—to

---

[9] See Robert Mallet, editor: *Paul Claudel et André Gide, Correspondance, 1899–1926* (Paris, 1949).

[1] Jean Schlumberger: *Madeleine et André Gide* (Paris, 1956), pp. 170–1, 176–7.

[2] Entry for May 14, 1921, *Journals of André Gide*, II, 265. See also the entries for the following Wednesday and December 2 of the same year.

accept the notion of the bisexuality of human beings
and the inescapable fact that a significant portion of
each sex felt a compulsion to play the role of its opposite.[3]

Yet one should not minimize the courage of Gide's
act. For the first time, probably, since classical antiq-
ity, a public figure in the Western world had openly
admitted his "forbidden" desires. And thereby he had
made a contribution of no small importance to the
elaboration of a twentieth-century ethic of tolerance
and permissiveness. What Freud had abstractly enunciated in chaste medical language, Gide brought into
explicit discussion before a large literary public. And
as Freud's work had helped to create a more understanding attitude toward extramarital sexual relations,
so Gide's confession was the most important single
document in the contemporary struggle of homosexuals
for humane treatment. In both cases, a statement originally made on the "higher" plane of thought and literature, within a generation had begun to reshape attitudes on the level of semi-popular culture.

The admission of homosexuality was only the more
sensational aspect of Gide's effort to define a contemporary ethic. It was the most tormenting manifestation
of the wider problem of how a man who felt within
himself the warfare of contradictory imperatives could
still manage to bring them into harmony and to become a respectable and self-respecting human being.
The problem was to discover an ethic broad enough to
embrace ways of behavior which society condemned—
and in the process to reconcile things that were customarily treated as radical opposites. Gide, we may repeat, remained a Protestant at heart: he thirsted after
morality and a clear conscience. At the same time he
was more than ordinarily stirred by the impressions of
the senses—and to deny these he felt to be in itself a
kind of immorality, an impiety against nature. Hence,

[3] Pierre-Quint: *Gide,* pp. 26–7, 64–8.

unlike Weber, he did not undertake to settle the problem of ambiguity by proposing rival ethics of polar opposites. He chose to live in the midst of ambiguity—
to entertain simultaneously his own contradictions. He
tried to lead a life that would be moral despite and
even because of its apparent immorality. And in the
process he suggested a definition of human nature as
broad and as troubling as any that the Western world
had known. He sought to prove that one could be an
"immoralist" and yet live with dignity and responsibility and human sympathy.

The discussion of Gide's ethic has taken us far afield
from the central concerns of the present volume. Yet
in a roundabout fashion it may have suggested where
the imaginative writers of the decade prior to the First
World War were beginning to occupy themselves with
themes similar to those that troubled the social theorists. We have seen that Gide shared with Weber an
almost obsessive concern for the ambiguities of human
conduct. The sense of living under high tension—of
striving to hold together the contradictions that were
tearing them asunder—was common to both men. And
along with it there went a conviction that they were
living in historical circumstances in which all fixed
norms were lacking: the old ethic had collapsed—and
it was far from clear where the new one was to be
found.

This sense of a collapse of accepted standards we
have already encountered in tracing the struggles of
Troeltsch and Meinecke with their characteristic Teutonic dilemmas. It has reappeared in Pareto's acid skepticism, in Weber's bleak vision of the future, in the persuasive dissolvent of Freud's psychoanalytic theory. In
the case of these writers, however, a certain ruggedness
of character and an unbending sense of duty kept them
faithful to a few rough-and-ready principles that they
chose to treat as imperatives. One and all they rejected
the title of relativists.

With the imaginative writers it was quite otherwise. In imaginative literature the relativist possibilities that the social theorists had struggled to hold in check were blithely give free rein. In the early twentieth-century novel and drama, relativism became almost a cliché. A recognition of incoherence in ethics and philosophy soon gained acceptance as the contemporary norm. In this sense, the novelists and dramatists completed what the social theorists had either combated or left unsaid. With the innocence of the irresponsible, the imaginative writers quite simply accepted the ultimate conclusions before which the philosophers and sociologists had recoiled.

Thus we find in the early work of Gide and Mann, and in the mature writings of Hesse and Pirandello, an unshocked recognition of the "immoral" as a source of vitality and creation. And where an ethical position is suggested, it is not in terms of a religiously (or even pragmatically) based imperative but as a conscious "construct" of human volition. This sense of the individual consciousness creating its own world suggests another link between social thought and literature: "consciousness," "construction"—the fabrication of a personal world in which the individual self can find existence bearable—these are the key terms that social theory and imaginative literature hold in common.

By the same token the notion of reality in early twentieth-century literature becomes problematical in the extreme. This writing is suffused with the sense of things not being what they appear to be, of contradictory versions of the same reality, of a deeper truth that cannot be explained but can only be glimpsed in moments of heightened awareness. The last of these we have already encountered in the youthful novel of Alain-Fournier. Similarly a feeling for psychological surprise, for the ambiguity of roles, distinguishes the early work of Mann and Gide. It recurs at the end of Proust's *Remembrance of Things Past*, when all stable relationships of character and situation are suddenly revealed as transmuted beyond recognition. It is implicit in the brutal unmasking of character that is at the center of Pirandello's dramas. Indeed, it is in Pirandello that we find the most uncompromising assertion of the dubious nature of psychological reality: Proust and Hesse, Gide and Mann, eventually reveal to us their own notion of the truth; Pirandello is content to leave us suspended in eternal doubt.

Finally, the techniques of "seeing through," of probing in depth, that have occupied us in analyzing the work of Bergson, of Freud, and of Jung most obviously find their reflection in imaginative literature. And by the same process the notion of the unconscious as the storehouse of imperishable memory recurs again and again in the early twentieth-century novel. An obsession with *duration*—with the quality of time-as-experience—is forever returning. A sense of time as it is actually lived, of the work of the unconscious in lengthening and foreshortening it, of its twists and deceptions, gives its special flavor to Alain-Fournier's *Le Grand Meaulnes*, to Mann's *The Magic Mountain*, and, most characteristically, to Proust's *Remembrance of Things Past*. It is for this, more than for any other single quality, that the last of these has come to rank, by common consent, as *the* novel of the early twentieth century.

These concerns that were common to social thought and imaginative literature will first emerge in clear outline when we come to consider the altered circumstances of the immediate post-war years. Meantime it may suffice to observe that in the case of Thomas Mann, the other among our roster of novelists who, alongside Gide, had already achieved a substantial pre-war reputation, the specifically "twentieth-century" qualities of technique and imagination were as yet discernible in only fragmentary form. Their explicit unfolding was to be the product of the post-war era.

Mann's dialectical novel *The Magic Mountain* will figure in the last chapter of the study. For the present we may simply note the parallel between Mann's and Gide's early life and writing. For both of them the problem of ethical relativism was unavoidable: it could not fail to emerge from the clash between the external demands of bourgeois society and the inner necessities of artistic creation. Like Gide, Mann was the offspring of a prosperous upper middle-class family—an urban patrician in whom a cool northern dignity was second nature. And as with Gide, one part of him remained all his life within the formal bounds of inherited respectability. Less emphatically than Gide, but still unmistakably, Mann had also touched on the homosexual note. His short story "Death in Venice" had created a sensation when it appeared in 1911: its sensitive, half-ironic depiction of the fatal passion of an elderly writer for a beautiful boy had awakened admiration among those who followed Stefan George's teaching of an aristocratic ethic based on male companionship.[4] But this was not at all what Mann himself had had in mind. In actuality, he had very little in common with George's ethic of special license and fastidious disdain for the majority of mankind. Nor was he, like Gide, personally committed to an unconventional morality derived from the example of classical Greece. He was, rather, unattached to any conscious ethical position: he was simply trying to conduct his life as an independent artist, working his way free from the attachments of class and prejudice and into a full mastery of his craft.

Far more than "Death in Venice," "Tonio Kröger," published eight years earlier, gives a faithful reflection of the aspirations and disappointments of the young Thomas Mann. It is a story both of liberation from the associations of the author's youth and of a lingering regret for an unproblematical world of well-scrubbed order. It is, in the protagonist's words, the story of "a *bourgeois* who strayed off into art, a bohemian who

[4] Arnold Bauer: *Thomas Mann und die Krise der bürgerlichen Kultur* (Berlin, 1946), pp. 42, 48–9.

feels nostalgic yearnings for respectability, an artist with a bad conscience."

I stand between two worlds. I am at home in neither, and I suffer in consequence. . . .

I admire those proud, cold beings who adventure upon the paths of great and daemonic beauty and despise "mankind"; but I do not envy them. For if anything is capable of making a poet of a literary man, it is my *bourgeois* love of the human, the living and usual. It is the source of all warmth, goodness, and humour. . . .[5]

Like the Gide of the pre-war years, Thomas Mann had not yet learned to bring his contradictions into harmony. A satisfactory reconciliation of opposites would come only in the mid-1920's.

iv. *The Moral Legacy of the War: Spengler and the "Elders"*

As we have traced the careers of the leading members of the generation of the 1890's, we have necessarily at one point or other dealt with their attitude toward the First World War. The war had in no sense been of their making: none of them had as yet held a position of public responsibility, and those who were politically motivated, like Weber, had been obliged to restrict themselves to impassioned warnings of approaching disaster. Nor were they able to fight the war when it came. They were simply spectators—there was no other recourse.

Yet the way in which they understood their role as spectators varied radically. At one extreme were Frenchmen like Bergson and Durkheim—unquestioningly patriotic, indefatigable in their country's service, totally convinced of the justice of their cause. At the other

[5] Translation by H. T. Lowe-Porter in Thomas Mann: *Stories of Three Decades* (New York, 1936), p. 132.

extreme we find the original trio of the critics of Marx —Croce, Pareto, and Sorel—who felt it incumbent on themselves to remain *au dessus de la mêlée* and to adopt an attitude of skepticism toward the aims of both contenders. Croce, as we have seen, at least conformed with what was expected of him as an Italian senator. But Pareto and Sorel were unrestrained in their sarcasms. They found no virtue on either side: they could see nothing more than rival interest groups among the European ruling classes locked together in suicidal slaughter. Sorel in particular was profoundly disillusioned to find that his philosophical master Bergson had joined the chorus of the intellectuals-in-arms.[6]

Of the attitudes in between these extremes, Freud's was closer to detachment than to militancy. He took a decent interest in the Austrian military effort, and he suffered the usual anxieties for the safety of his sons in uniform. But above all else he was impressed with the way in which the war experience had torn off the veneer of civilization and blurred the customary distinction between truth and lies. He was shocked by "the narrow-mindedness shown by the best intellects, their obduracy, their inaccessibility to the most forcible arguments, their uncritical credulity for the most disputable assertions."[7] In the behavior of Europeans at war, Freud found dreadful confirmation of what he had all along been saying about the nature of man.

The three Germans whose names we have so often linked—Troeltsch, Meinecke, and Weber—also strove to maintain their intellectual balance, but they went farther than Freud in the direction of patriotic acquiescence. Despite his fears and his reservations about his country's war leadership, Weber could not help feeling that the conflict was "great and wonder-

[6] Pierre Andreu: *"Bergson et Sorel," Les Etudes bergsoniennes,* III (Paris, 1952), pp. 61–4.

[7] "Thoughts for the Times on War and Death" (first published in *Imago,* V [1915]), authorized translation under the supervision of Joan Riviere, *Collected Papers,* IV (London, 1925), p. 302.

ful" in the devotion it called forth. Troeltsch and
Meinecke, at least in the early years of the war, were
equally caught up in the popular mood of quasi-religious
inspiration. And they agreed wholeheartedly with
Weber's formulation that the Germans bore a "responsibility to history" to keep European civilization
from an exclusive domination by Russian, Latin, and
Anglo-Saxon values.[8]

It is curious to find that even at these rarefied levels
of thought, the attitudes of the intellectuals so closely
parallel those of the populations at large. It seems no
accident that the French are the least questioning, the
Germans are tragically torn between patriotic enthusiasm and half-guilty forebodings, and the two Italians
and an Austrian are almost alone in remaining detached from the struggle. Yet it was this last attitude
that in the retrospect of the 1920's was to seem most
characteristic and most worthy of an intellectual. For
the generation of the 1890's—in the sense of intellectual growth and achievement—the war marked a hiatus
and little else.

When in the winter of 1918–19 the writers and
thinkers of Europe picked up the threads of their interrupted labors and returned to their customary pursuits, they found that the war years had worked significant changes in the intellectual communities with
which they were familiar. The disruption of the ex-
ternals of life through revolutionary violence and economic suffering had barely begun. But in less obvious
ways the tone and atmosphere of intellectual exchange
had altered. For one thing, the end of the fighting
revealed new ideas and new talents that had almost
imperceptibly been maturing during the war years. And
in more concrete terms, a number of works that had
been held up by wartime publication difficulties now all
at once began to appear in the bookstores. The effect

[8] Marianne Weber: *Max Weber*, pp. 571, 626.

was that of a dammed-up stream of thought and creation suddenly released on a public athirst for something more substantial than bulletins from the front.

Thus Vienna, which before the war had seemed like rather a back water, became a major center of philosophical innovation.[9] And in Italy a host of new talents appeared—notably the neo-liberal Piero Gobetti and the Marxist Antonio Gramsci, who were to be cut off by the Fascist repression before they had given the full measure of their capacities. In France the *avant-garde* suddenly became the main guard. The young Surrealists had fastened on André Gide as the herald of the post-war temper. His first really influential work, *Les Caves du Vatican*, which had been published just as the conflict was breaking out, offered a Surrealist model ready to hand. Gide himself had been careful not to give his book any excessive dignity: by calling it a *sotie* or farce rather than a novel, he had emphasized its playful character. And it was with the same sort of humorous, only half-approving curiosity that he followed the extravagant antics of the young. Yet he was rather more pleased than not to be treated as an older playmate by these frolicsome artists and men of letters. It gave him a delicious sense of rejuvenation. "Each new generation," he wrote in his *Journals*, "arrives bearing a message that it must deliver; our role is to help that delivery."[1]

In Germany above all the post-war intellectual scene was almost unrecognizably different from what had come before. Prior to 1914, except in the more raffish atmosphere of Munich, those who were self-consciously refined and distinguished—the sober, dignified writers and professors from the cultivated classes—had maintained an almost unchallenged pre-eminence. With the

[9] See Chapter 10.
[1] Guerard: *Gide*, pp. 227, 232; Pierre-Quint: *Gide*, pp. 58–9, 356; entry for December 26, 1921, *Journals of André Gide*, II, 282. In the English translation *Les Caves du Vatican* is entitled *Lafcadio's Adventures*.

war's end came a general collapse of standards. New fashions in art and literature such as expressionism and "decadence" gripped the attention of the public. And Berlin, which had once had a reputation for formality and stuffiness, replaced Paris as the capital of the more special forms of vice.

Meantime unknown scholars such as Spengler and Keyserling found eager buyers for their suspect wares. These "half-educated" dilettantes—to use the characteristically German term of reproach—offered fervid, sweeping interpretations of the course of world history which made the conventional products of scholarship seem thin fare indeed. A bewildered German public seized on Spengler's self-confident pronouncements to explain the misfortunes that had unaccountably fallen on their country. These readers most frequently came from the political Right. But the mood on the Left was not significantly different. What struck observers about the Germany of the immediate post-war era was the fever of experiment in all political camps. At its best it betokened a promising vitality. But in its more sinister aspects it suggested an intellectual nihilism that a decade later was to become the predominant mood among the youth of the country.

In this volcanic atmosphere, the social thinkers who a generation earlier had ranked as innovators felt themselves in danger of being totally engulfed. Despite their political inexperience, they sought for ways to stem the flood. We have seen how men like Weber and Troeltsch and Meinecke had come to accept the revolution of November 1918 as a dire necessity. A week after the revolution the Democratic party was organized by those elements in German public life who wanted to combine political democracy with the retention of middle-class values. From the start it had a strong intellectual tinge: this was its pride and its weakness. Meinecke and Troeltsch aided in its foundation, Weber briefly supported it, and the philosopher-statesman Walther Rathenau soon became its most prominent public figure. But the party lacked both cohesion and political capacity. Its stand wavered on the issues of burning public concern. It could never decisively make up its mind between free enterprise and a planned economy, nor between nationalist truculence and compliance with the demands of the Allies. Moreover, with the death of Friedrich Naumann in 1919 and the murder of Rathenau three years later, it lost its most forceful political leaders. In the end, the Democratic party proved incapable of survival. By the late 1920's it was in full dissolution.

"We were . . . the conservative reformers," Meinecke lamented, "whose hour struck too late." [2] Those who before the war had thought of themselves as younger liberals in public and faculty discussion were now labeled the "elders" of the Republic. It was their unpromising task to try to chart a middle course in a political situation in which only extremism or apathy responded to the public temper. The younger generation of conservatives would have none of it. Impatient, imperative, anti-intellectualist, schooled in direct action by the war experience—and drunk with the rhetoric of Nietzsche and Stefan George—this new generation detested people who still cherished reasonable and humane values and who were willing to settle for the "mediocrity and philistinism" of the Weimar regime. The great liberals of their fathers' day now seemed like hopelessly antiquated relics of the nineteenth century. As one of Rathenau's assassins put it, his victim, despite the criticism he had directed against the powers of the past,

> is a man belonging to that very time and he is devoted to these powers. He is their last and ripest fruit, and he combines in himself whatever values and ideas, ethos and pathos, dignity and faith it contained. . . . I could not tolerate it if greatness

[2] *Strassburg/Freiburg/Berlin 1901–1919: Erinnerungen* (Stuttgart, 1949), p. 169.

grew once more out of this crumbling and despised
time. . . . I could not tolerate it if this man gave
to the people once more a new faith, if he once
more swayed it in favor of a will and form which
are the will and form of an age which died in the
war, which is dead, three times dead. . . .[3]

Indeed all these "elders" except Meinecke died in
the four years from 1919 to 1923. Yet before vanishing
altogether, they left behind them one great literary
monument. In Germany's bitter years of national discouragement and civil conflict, Ernst Troeltsch had at
last found his authentic voice. The monthly articles he
contributed to the review *Der Kunstwart* under the
signature *"Spektator"* rank as the most judicious and at
the same time the most moving commentary on the
new Republic's struggle for existence. Where in his
theological and historical writings Troeltsch had been
dense, wordy, and confused, in this new journalistic
and polemical vein he went directly to the point. In
their "clarity and frankness of tone," their "analytical
sharpness," and their air of mature consideration, the
"Spectator Letters" belong in that rare category of occasional pieces that have won immortality.[4]

Their underlying theme was the inescapable necessity for the German middle classes to accept the parliamentary Republic—despite everything, despite its
mediocrity, its imitative character, and the "petty self-
seeking" on the part of its rulers. The "frightful dem-
agoguery and provocation" from the Right, Troeltsch
contended, made the task of a responsible German
government almost impossible. And he pleaded with
the noisy opposition to desist. Only if the leading citizens of the country should acquiesce in democracy and
the Republic, not merely "formally" but "with inner

[3] Klemperer: *Germany's New Conservatism*, pp. 115–16,
quoting Ernst von Salomon.
[4] Eric C. Kollman: *"Eine Diagnose der Weimarer Republik:
Ernst Troeltschs politische Anschauungen,"* *Historische Zeitschrift*, CLXXXII (October 1956), 302.

warmth," only then, Troeltsch argued, would it be possible to build for the future. Only when one had affirmed his belief in these institutions "honorably and without reserve," could one begin to think of providing German democracy with an aristocratic and conservative "counterpoise." [5] And then alone would it be possible to salvage and restore those broader values of humanism and rationality that Troeltsch, in common with the other "elders," had most at heart. The "Spectator Letters" terminated only four months before their author's own end. Dying in a state of mortal anxiety, Troeltsch had left behind him a vibrant plea *in extremis* to save the ethical heritage of Europe before it was too late.

Among the younger German conservatives who had scorned and defied the "elders" was the speculative historian Oswald Spengler, whose *Decline of the West* had first been published in the summer of 1918 just before the war's end. Like Troeltsch, Spengler talked of saving what one could of the traditional culture of Europe. But he understood this salvage operation in quite a different sense. Indeed, as we have seen, it was partly as an answer to Spengler that Troeltsch published his own unfinished work on the problems of historical thinking.

The Decline of the West marked the full formulation of a cyclical theory of historical change and a comparative approach to the study of culture which had gradually been establishing themselves among the implicit presuppositions of early twentieth-century social thought. The notion of cycles had underlain Sorel's respect for the values of a simpler age and his skepticism about the "illusions of progress." It had figured more explicitly in Pareto's hypothesis of an alternation between periods in which "persistence of aggregates"

[5] *Spektator-Briefe: Aufsätze über die deutsche Revolution und die Weltpolitik 1918–22*, edited by H. Baron (Tübingen, 1924), pp. 52, 144, 299–300.

was dominant and those in which the "instinct for combinations" held sway. Even Weber had presented the rudiments of a cyclical theory: he had maintained the older unilinear viewpoint only with respect to the rationalization of life in the Western world; elsewhere his doubts about cultural or moral progress and the very statement of the problem in his comparative studies of religion had suggested a view of society in which the primacy of Western history was no longer taken for granted and in which the values of alien civilizations were considered worthy of equal consideration. Indeed by 1914, such a view had become very nearly standard among the more advanced social thinkers: even a man like Durkheim, who in other respects had remained within an earlier tradition, in his capacity as a student of comparative religion quite explicitly espoused a kind of cultural relativism.

The logic of these tendencies Spengler pushed to its extreme limits. The notion of cycles in history and of comparability among the life courses of civilizations— which in the writings of his older contemporaries had remained no more than a working assumption—Spengler made explicit and cast in a harshly dogmatic form. And in the process he dragged out into broad daylight the relativist potentialities that had been lurking in the background of German historical thinking ever since Dilthey first undertook his critique of historical reason.[6] Dilthey and Weber had been acutely conscious of the impossibility of finding within the data of history itself any grounding for final truth or moral value. They had realized that ultimately the historian or social scientist was driven back on an affirmation of his own value-system. In this sense they had been relativists. At the

---

6 I find myself unable to agree with Pietro Rossi's assertion that Spengler "derived the general statement of the problem in his own work" from Dilthey despite the fact that he "never made an explicit reference to Dilthey": *Lo storicismo tedesco contemporaneo* (Turin, 1956), p. 390. I fail to see any influence whatever of Dilthey on Spengler.

same time they had not renounced the attempt to achieve at least a partial "objectivity" and, with it, a sympathetic understanding of alien values. Spengler denied that either was possible. He held that the value-system of one society was a closed book to a member of another culture, and that the best a historian could do was to defend his own ethos with strident self-confidence against all comers. Thus he eliminated the distinction—which was central to the thought not only of Dilthey and Weber but of Croce and Meinecke also—between passion as the origin of historical inquiry and its sublimation into a judgment that might properly lay claim to wider validity.

In practice, however, Spengler did not remain true to the logic of his own position. The very fact that his book dealt with the comparative morphology of civilization suggested his conviction that he himself at least had penetrated to some understanding of alien cultures. Spengler's work was full of contradictions of this sort. In its dogmatic tone, in its determinist assumptions, in its thoroughly unsophisticated application of natural science terminology to the course of human history, *The Decline of the West* represented a relapse into a naïve positivism. At the same time, in its imaginative range, in its breath-taking juxtapositions of examples drawn from the most varied aspects of human culture, it surpassed the boldest flights of idealist thinking. As a work of literature, it was an extraordinary achievement. As history, it quite properly raised doubts on all sides.

In terms of philosophy or social-science method, Spengler's work was a pretty crude performance. Yet it caught the attention of the post-war reading public and throughout the year 1919 maintained an unprecedented rate of sales for a work of such length and difficulty. The explanation is not hard to find. *The Decline of the West* formulated without qualification and with an attractive parade of "scientific" language a view of Western society which Spengler's older contemporaries, like Sorel and Pareto and Weber, had merely sketched out or had left imbedded within their formal methodology. According to this view, the era of "individualism, humanitarianism, intellectual freedom, skepticism" was nearing its end; the new era that was dawning would be characterized by "restrictions on individual freedom . . . , a revival of faith . . . and an increase in the use of force." [7] In the post-war circumstances of national defeat and humiliation, the German reading public could find in Spengler's work a tidy explanation of the calamities that had overwhelmed them—and that were about to befall their neighbors.

It is in this fashion that people have been reading Spengler ever since. It is as a peculiarly telling combination of diagnosis and symptom of a cultural crisis that *The Decline of the West* has maintained its perennial appeal. As diagnosis, Spengler's work showed rare gifts of insight and an almost unmatched talent for finding the striking combination and the dramatic metaphor that would bring the reader up short. As symptom, it expressed with imaginative power and an evocative melancholy a mood that has now been with us for four decades. It is the first of a series of novel and unclassifiable writings that have seemed to mark the end of a cultural epoch.[8]

v. *The Literary Sensations of the Post-War Years: Hesse, Proust, Pirandello*

The success of Spengler's *Decline of the West* was to a very large extent due to the historical circumstances under which it was published. It had been conceived before the outbreak of the war, it had been completed by 1917, and wartime delays alone had postponed its

---

[7] Talcott Parsons: *The Structure of Social Action*, second edition (Glencoe, Ill., 1949), p. 179.

[8] For a fuller statement of this line of thought, see my *Oswald Spengler: A Critical Estimate* (New York, 1952).

publication for another year. Yet it is open to doubt
whether if the book had appeared earlier it would have
found the same reception: it took the war experience
to convince the public of the relevance of what Spengler had to say.

The author of *The Decline of the West* was an unknown in 1918—a former *Gymnasium* teacher in his
late thirties living as a private scholar in Munich. His
sudden fame came as a surprise to everyone. It was
otherwise, however, with three imaginative writers who
also made sensational post-war successes. They were
older men in their forties and fifties, who had begun
their literary labors in the 1890's and who had become
established authors by the outbreak of the war. Yet
none of them had as yet found a wide reading public.
In the sense of universal critical recognition and general
acclaim their success was a post-war phenomenon.

The reception accorded Hermann Hesse's *Demian*
on its appearance in 1919, the excitement occasioned
by the publication of the second volume of Marcel
Proust's *Remembrance of Things Past* in the same year,
and the enthusiastic public response to Luigi Pirandello's great dramas of 1921—these literary sensations
may perhaps give us a clue to the temper of the post-
war reading public. Why did it fasten on these works
in particular? What was there in them which called
forth an especially eager response?

Initially we may note that all these authors were "difficult." It was doubtless this which had denied them
widespread popularity in the earlier part of their creative lives. They were all psychologically oriented, and
they all expressed a viewpoint on life that was commonly considered "disabused," "pessimistic," or even
"cynical." They wrote without illusion—and out of a
kind of inner desperation. They were explorers of the
unconscious: a recurrent theme in their work was the
discrepancy between the apparent reality of common
sense and the inner reality—or realities—of tormented
human beings.

No one of them had any direct relation to Freud. Of the literary men, it was Mann and Gide, rather, who were the self-conscious bearers of the Freudian doctrine. Both had originally worked out their attitude toward human conduct without benefit of psychoanalytic theory. But when they learned of Freud's work, they accepted it without reserve. In the 1930's Thomas Mann became a frequent guest in the Freud household and a particular favorite of the great man's self-effacing wife. And when in the same period Mann turned to new subjects drawn from mythology, he found precious suggestions for his own work in the much controverted *Totem and Taboo*.[9] Characteristically, Gide was more wary. "Freud. Freudianism . . . ," he noted in 1922. "For the last ten years, or fifteen, I have been indulging in it without knowing it." Or, as he wrote with impatience two years later: "Ah, how embarrassing Freud is! And how easily it seems to me we should have discovered his America without him! It seems to me that the thing I should be most grateful to him for is having accustomed readers to hearing certain subjects treated without having to protest or blush. . . . But how many absurd things in that imbecile of genius!" [1]

In contrast to these two, Hesse and Proust and Pirandello never came within Freud's orbit. Hesse, as we shall note in a moment, fell strongly under the influence of Jung—indeed, he is the most "psychoanalytic" of the major creative writers of the post-war era. The other two, so far as I have been able to tell, were thoroughly innocent of psychoanalytic theory. Yet the reception of their writings in the period from 1919 to

[9] Ernest Jones: *The Life and Work of Sigmund Freud*, II: *Years of Maturity 1901–1919* (New York, 1955), p. 387, III: *The Last Phase 1919–1939* (New York, 1957), pp. 170, 199, 205, 347, 462–4; Thomas Mann: *Freud und die Zukunft* (Vienna, 1936), translated by H. T. Lowe-Porter as "Freud and the Future," *Essays of Three Decades* (New York, 1947), p. 422.

[1] Entries for February 4, 1922, and June 19, 1924, *Journals of André Gide*, II, 298, 351.

1921 is of a piece with the acceptance of Freud's own work in those same years. The change in public attitudes—the readiness to try to understand ideas that earlier had been considered incomprehensible, perverse, or depressing—had similar repercussions in the field of imaginative literature and in the field of social theory.

Hermann Hesse was living in self-imposed exile in Switzerland when his *Demian* was published, initially in anonymous form. During the war he had shared with the French novelist Romain Rolland an attitude of pacifist detachment that had infuriated the patriotic. And the same war period had marked the crisis of his own alienation—from his native country, from his family associations, from the whole society that had produced him.

Hesse's origins had already been mixed—Baltic German on his father's side, Swabian and French Swiss on his mother's. He had grown up in a small Württemberg town in the atmosphere of patriarchal family relationships and reassuring tidiness that so often has cradled German men of genius: we are reminded of the similar traditionalist associations in the childhood of Mann and Meinecke. But in Hesse's case, the exotic note—which with Mann was restricted to the inheritance from his Brazilian mother—was characteristic of both sides of the family. Thus, although both Hesse's maternal grandfather and his father were pastors and scholars—again a familiar feature of the biographies of German intellectuals—they were clergymen of a most unusual type: they had served as missionaries in India and brought back with them from their travels a sympathetic understanding for Hindu religion and Sanskrit scholarship.

It was in the family tradition, then, when the young Hesse broke away from his wife and the ordered existence he had tried to devise for himself and went off to India on a voyage of spiritual discovery. And it was also not surprising that after his return from India and his permanent settlement in Switzerland he should have come into contact with Jung. It is unquestionable that Jung's example helped Hesse to self-understanding.[2] This process of unfolding self-awareness was to continue for the next quarter-century: *Demian* marked its first decisive stage.

Thomas Mann has recalled "the electrifying influence exercised . . . by *Demian* . . . on a whole generation just after the First World War. . . . With uncanny accuracy this poetic work struck the nerve of the times and called forth grateful rapture from a whole youthful generation who believed that an interpreter of their innermost life had risen from their own midst —whereas it was a man already forty-two years old who gave them what they sought."[3] Hesse seems to have been aware of the representative character of his novel: it was the only one of his books whose authorship he strove to conceal, and in its intentional ambiguity, the subtitle, "The Story of a Youth," suggested that it could properly be applied to an entire generation.

Two aspects of *Demian* in particular could appeal to young people who had just emerged from the torment of the war. In the first place, the novel was the record of a struggle toward ethical integrity, toward a life that would be in harmony with individual nature. Its first lines stated the theme: "I wanted only to try to live in obedience to the promptings which came from my true self. Why was that so very difficult?" Or, as the author's spokesman put it when he began to be conscious of what he was about: "A man has absolutely no other duty than this: to seek himself, to grope his own way forward, no matter whither it leads."[4] To a generation that felt it had been fed from childhood on nothing

² Edmund Gnefkow: *Hermann Hesse: Biographie* 1952 (Freiburg i. Br., 1952), pp. 15–18, 27–9, 56–7.
³ Foreword to the English translation of *Demian* (New York, 1948), p. x.
⁴ Ibid., pp. 1, 158.

but lies, this simple ethical pronouncement came as a revelation. In Germany, in particular, the young people were sick to suffocation of the hollow pieties of middle-class society—to which there had been added the further indignity of systematic distortion of the truth about the war itself.

This vast impatience with the "respectable" beliefs of the older generation was what had prompted the young political conservatives to refuse the lead of the "elders" of the Republic. But their refusal had been of a brutal, authoritarian type: they had preached the necessity of discipline and the love of combat for its own sake. *Their* novelist was the Free Corps fighter Ernst Jünger. What distinguished *Demian* from the more familiar form of post-war protest—and this was the second source of its peculiar appeal—was its emphasis on individual and humanitarian values. These were old beliefs—values which the young people felt had been dreadfully twisted and perverted to serve a wretched form of society. The present task, *Demian* implied, was not to overthrow them. It was rather to bring them back to their original meaning. "The history of everyone," Hesse wrote, "is important, eternal, divine. For that reason every man, so long as he lives at all and carries out the will of nature, is wonderful and worthy of every attention. In everyone has the spirit taken shape, in everyone creation suffers, in everyone is a redeemer crucified." [5]

Thus the mysterious Max Demian, although he was a Nietzschean "immoralist" and wore the mark of Cain on his brow, was the opposite of an apostle of force or direct action. Despite the laconic frankness of his utterance, he was a humanitarian—and a better one for his very lack of sentimentality. The old world of European society, Demian affirmed, was worthy only of destruction—or rather it was on the verge of destroying itself through its own moral rottenness:

[5] Ibid., p. 2.

> The break-up of an old world is drawing near. . . .
> The world is about to renew itself. It smacks of
> death. Nothing new comes without death.

And then, when the war had indeed come:

> However strongly the world's attention appeared
> to be focused on war and heroic deeds, on honor
> and other old ideals, however distantly and un-
> naturally sang the voices of humanity—all this was
> merely the surface. . . . Deep down, below the
> surface of human affairs, something was in process
> of forming. Something which might be a new or-
> der of humanity.[6]

The author of *Demian* knew the weaknesses in his
own soul—which were also the weaknesses of the German spirit as he had experienced it: infatuation with
death, fantasies of suicide, a sickly social mysticism. In
the general relaxation of moral and intellectual standards that followed the war, countless Germans were
reveling in the indulgence of these spiritual vices.
Hesse took the opposite course: he struggled to free
himself from his private "demons" through a scrupu-
lous examination of conscience. He knew that the price
of his success was alienation from his country and from
middle-class society. But he also knew that the forfeit
was well worth paying if spiritual independence and a
renewal of human fellowship were the result. In this
process of re-evaluation Hesse became one of the first
conscious "Europeans" among twentieth-century writers: his example was to serve as an inspiration to other
Germans who were driven on the road of exile in the
years after 1933.

The first volume of Marcel Proust's *Remembrance of
Things Past—Swann's Way*—had been published a year
before the outbreak of the war. It had caused very little
stir. Gide had turned it down for the *Nouvelle Revue*

[6] Ibid., pp. 194, 203.

Française—a mistake he later regretted with "sorrow and remorse"—and it appeared under the imprint of a less distinguished publishing house. Initially, it had done little to change Proust's reputation as a frivolous social climber and a rather precious designer of occasional pieces. The critics only gradually began to take a more favorable view. Then the war came; further publication was delayed; and during the years of conflict the work swelled enormously until its carefully articulated scaffolding threatened to crack under the strain. In 1919 publication was resumed.

This time the effect was totally different. The second volume of the series,[7] which in the meantime had "migrated" to the *Nouvelle Revue Française,* received the Prix Goncourt amid general public acclaim. The succeeding volumes simply added to an established reputation. Proust was nearly fifty: a hopeless invalid, he had only three more years to live. He died in November 1922, working up to the end on the revision of the concluding volumes of his masterpiece.

Proust's vast novel is so familiar to contemporary readers that we scarcely need elaborate on its major themes. In its psychological structure, it skillfully linked the classic French tradition of meticulous and logically ordered analysis of motive with the newer emphasis on the unconscious associated with the name of Bergson. Proust wrote for a literary audience that was in no sense Freudian. But he found readers who had been prepared by Bergson to grant that the deeper reality of human behavior lay in the invisible work of the unconscious rather than in the sphere of reasoned choice. And he wrote for people whose notions of time and memory had been radically altered by Bergson's revolutionary writings of a generation earlier.

Is it right, then, to call Proust a "Bergsonian" novelist? I think this is true only to a limited extent. Bergson

---

[7] A *l'Ombre des jeunes filles en fleurs* (translated as *Within a Budding Grove*).

himself in his old age seems to have accepted the notion of *Remembrance of Things Past* as a work inspired
by his own precepts: in an essay published in 1934 he
glancingly suggested that before his time no novelist
had succeeded in placing himself "in the flux of the
inner life"—"it was only in places, under the pressure
of necessity," that somebody had done it; "no one had
as yet thought of methodically setting out '*à la recherche du temps perdu*.' " [8] And it is undeniable that
Proust's work rendered the sense of prolongation of the
past into the present that Bergson had sought to convey through the term "duration." In Proust as in Bergson, "the recollection of single, unique, unrepeatable
experiences . . . was assigned a special function in the
quest for the recovery of time and the self," and thus
recollection became "an activity, an operation—not the
passive reproduction of habitual memory responses." [9]
But in Proust's work—particularly in its post-war version—the operation resulted in something more sche-
matized and intellectualized than what Bergson had
envisaged.

Proust had attended Bergson's lectures in the early
1900's. Indeed, through his marriage the philosopher
had become Proust's cousin. Aside from a few acts of
kindness on the part of the older man, however, there
appears to have been little personal relationship between the two. Proust himself, while he admired Bergson and did not reject the adjective "Bergsonian" as
applied to his own work, felt that it gave only an inaccurate idea of what he was doing. Bergson's theories
may have helped him toward a definition of the kind of
novel he wanted to write—but they could scarcely have
told him how to write it. The experience of self, time,
and duration that Bergson had evoked with such caress-
ingly persuasive eloquence was by definition a personal

[8] "Introduction," *La Pensée et le mouvant: Essais et conférences* (Paris, 1934), p. 20.
[9] Hans Meyerhoff: *Time in Literature* (Berkeley and Los
Angeles, 1955), pp. 47–8.

one: an individual either had it or had it not. It bore the character of mystic contemplation and was essentially unteachable. It is perhaps for this reason that Bergson's disciples usually proved so unproductive.

Moreover the philosopher himself did not entirely approve of what Proust had written. He found that it failed to "exalt and brace the spirit" as a true work of art should.[1] In this judgment Bergson was quite wrong. Like so many subsequent readers, he could see only what was bizarre and depressing in Proust's delineation of character. But this was not at all the novelist's intention. He had dwelt on what was repulsive in human behavior simply to display its moral emptiness. In his own life, he had succeeded in his tenacious climb into aristocratic society—but when he had safely arrived there, it left him with a feeling of disgust. These people, Proust realized, were heartless. He had found in them nothing of the warm affection that had shielded his childhood. With the death of his mother in 1905, Proust had given up his worldly existence and retired to his cork-lined bedroom to devote himself to his writing and to the all-absorbing task of recapturing the meaning of his apparently trivial existence. Like Alain-Fournier, he never recovered from the moral shock of expulsion from the world of childhood.

Freud and Bergson had voiced a similar nostalgia. They had expressed a mood that is repeated again and again in the literature of the immediate post-war years. To live without illusion meant to live with sadness. But at the same time it meant that kindness and human feeling were elevated to a position beyond compare as alone giving value to existence. These writers had none of the scorn for their fellow men that has distinguished so many subsequent adventurers into the labyrinth of

[1] André Maurois: *A la Recherche de Marcel Proust* (Paris, 1949), translated by Gerard Hopkins as *The Quest for Proust* (London, 1950), pp. 64, 278. See also Floris Delattre: *"Bergson et Proust," Les Etudes bergsoniennes*, I (Paris, 1948), pp. 39, 61–2, 112–14, 123, 126.

the emotions. For all the disappointments that reality had brought them, they longed for an ideal humanity.

Like Bergson, Proust had no true successors. Those who were to continue the psychological tradition in the French novel—men like Malraux and Mauriac and Montherlant—were to take less gentle a view of humanity. *Remembrance of Things Past*, as its title implies, helped to close rather than to open an intellectual epoch.

In five weeks of the year 1921 Luigi Pirandello wrote two of his greatest plays—*Six Characters in Search of an Author* and *Henry IV*. The following year there came his tragedy *Naked*,[2] another masterpiece. Each of these plays was a resounding success. A new dramatic genre and a new aesthetic attitude seemed to have been born: a wave of "Pirandellismo" swept Italy and the Western world.

To Pirandello, as to Proust, fame was hard won and came late in life. He was fifty-four years old in his year of triumph: he had been publishing verse since 1889, novels since 1901, short stories since 1894, and plays since 1898. A Sicilian and a man of comfortable middle-class means, like Mosca, Pirandello had studied at a German university and was strongly influenced by German poetry. He had had his share of woes: his wife was paranoiac, and the family fortune had been lost in a series of disasters. For the quarter-century up to 1921 Pirandello was dependent for his living on the modest salary of a normal-school teacher.

Before the war Pirandello had been chiefly known as a writer of short stories. Indeed he had originally cast in this form a number of the plots that were later to win popularity as plays. But in their earlier guise these bleak, excessively analytical tales of psychological suffering had repelled the public. Even Croce had been no

[2] *Vestire gli ignudi.*

exception. It is curious to discover that Italy's two most distinguished writers of the twentieth century could not abide each other.

The quarrel had started with the "acrimonious observations" that Pirandello had directed at Croce's *Aesthetics*. The latter had replied with a hostile review in *La Critica* for 1909 of Pirandello's essay *L'Umorismo*. For Croce, humor was simply not a "special category of art." Moreover, as he wrote nearly three decades later, Pirandello's idea of drama was "founded on an incapacity to . . . reason logically." This sort of criticism the dramatist in turn called "the most imbecilic" of all the travesties of his work which were in circulation. No meeting of minds was possible. "The two men were extremely different, not only as thinkers, but as individuals: Croce aristocratic to the depths, urbane and full of jests, rich, world-famous; Pirandello of an honorable middle-class family, acutely sensitive, a bit peevish, always closed in on himself, convinced of the injustice of life and of other people towards himself."

For Croce, "logic and concepts were . . . indispensable instruments. . . . For Pirandello they were the sworn enemies of his art." [3] It is their very lack of apparent logic that gives Pirandello's plays their uniquely disturbing quality. For they present on the stage the private worlds of the individual *dramatis personæ*. Each has his own internal logic: each thinks he understands what his own experience means. (Yet even these individual interpretations display inner contradictions or vary from day to day.) Thus the conflicting notions of reality never meet: Pirandello leaves his characters suspended in limbo eternally arguing with compulsive loquacity their incompatible versions of the facts. As the curtain falls on *It Is So! (If You Think So)*,[4] we

[3] Domenico Vittorini: *"Benedetto Croce e Luigi Pirandello,"* in Francesco Flora, editor, *Benedetto Croce* (Milan, 1953), pp. 559, 561, 564-5.
[4] *Così è (se vi pare)*.

still do not know the truth about the veiled woman who appears in a moment of almost unbearable intensity at the end of the last act. Is she the daughter of Signora Frola, as the latter claims? Is she the second wife of Signor Ponza, as this other character maintains with equal conviction? She can never reveal the truth: for to do so would be to destroy the notion of reality that alone renders bearable the existence of a person she loves.

Pirandello's plays are full of characters of this sort. They flee from intolerable difficulties into the security of illusion. And in the process they construct the private universe that enables them to continue to live. This construction it is the dramatist's own role to tear down: he forces the characters to see themselves in their true image. Thus the concluding scenes of Pirandello's plays are full of cries of anguish, of despairing protests against this cruel violation of emotional sanctuaries. The "madman" who masquerades as the emperor Henry IV protests that "it's a terrible thing if you don't hold on to that which seems true to you today." [5] In this sense—in the stubborn denial of logic and the passionate conviction of individual truth—the insane are the lucky ones. Similarly, the protagonist of *Naked*, when all her pretenses, all her borrowed dignity, have been stripped away, pleads only to be left to die alone and in silence, free at last from the scorn of the respectable.

Pirandello's characters long for social virtue—but they find themselves tricked into situations where they can act only in a disreputable fashion. They are bewildered middle-class people, struggling against hopeless odds to maintain some semblance of ordered existence. It is the unconscious that has tricked them— that has proved the artificiality of the moral codes and the notions of reality which they have attempted to im-

[5] Translation by Edward Storer in *Naked Masks: Five Plays by Luigi Pirandello*, edited by Eric Bentley, Everyman paperback edition (New York, 1957), p. 193.

pose on the fluidity of life itself.[6] Pirandello's plays are the tragedies of people who have lost their way in one universe of discourse and have not been able to find the path into another.

In Pirandello, the spiritual disarray of the immediate post-war epoch is delineated in its bleakest form. Yet the attitude of the author himself is not without pity: there is simply no trace of sentimentality in it. Nor is there a trace of political ideology, national allegiance, or any other conscious social doctrine. The great plays of the early 1920's have reached an unprecedented extreme of abstraction: social cohesion, the familiar world of sense experience, even the individual self—all these have been dissolved. The lack of human communication has become almost total. All that is left is an infinitely poignant awareness of *la condition humaine*— and with it a disappointed longing for a better humanity.

[6] Lander MacClintock: *The Age of Pirandello* (Bloomington, Ind., 1951), pp. 177, 183–4.

The Decade of the 1920's.
The Intellectuals at the
Point of Cleavage

NINETEEN-TWENTY to nineteen twenty-three were years of apotheosis. Within a period of thirty-eight months Sorel and Pareto had died in the fullness of their years, and Weber and Troeltsch had been carried off when still in their fifties. The generation of the 1890's had already begun to thin out: Péguy had been killed in battle in the first weeks of the war, and Durkheim had died exhausted by work and worry as the conflict was drawing to a close.

Yet the greater part of this generation of intellectuals were extremely long-lived; most of them lived on into the 1930's and 1940's and some even into the second half of the century. Their work had straddled the war years, and in the case of a few of them, like Pareto, the world struggle that virtually paralyzed normal intellectual activity had not been permitted to trouble the orderly course of their literary production. Why, then, do we consider the decade of the 1920's as marking a kind of cæsura, a period of summing-up, as the 1890's had been a period of innovation?

Initially, because in case after case we note a flagging or diversion of energy. Or, to put it more precisely, we notice that a period of intellectual triumph in the immediate post-war years is succeeded by a pause in creativity. For the sense of apotheosis did not descend on those alone who were to be carried off by death—on those, like Pareto, to whom a belated recognition came just in time to bring a feeling of fulfillment to their last years. Others, like Freud and the imaginative writers of psychological bent, found that they had suddenly become famous—in the new post-war atmosphere, writings that before 1914 had seemed difficult and esoteric now expressed the dominant mood of the more literate and self-conscious element among Western and Central Europeans.

There were some who completed their major work in the early 1920's and found that they had nothing further to say. Gaetano Mosca was one of these: after the publication of the second volume of his *Elementi* in 1923, he was content to assume the congenial role of mentor and elder statesman which he maintained for nearly two more decades. The case of Croce was somewhat different: as we have seen, in the post-war era Croce kept up a continuous, untroubled literary flow, but he steered it into different channels—public service, polemic, literary reviews, excursions and elaborations, and straight historical exposition. The same sort of reorientation is apparent in the work of a number of major imaginative writers. In the case of André Gide, for example, the decade from the mid-twenties to the mid-thirties marked a sharp psychological break. With the publication of his full confession and the completion of his largest work, *The Counterfeiters*, in 1925, Gide went off on a journey to the Congo and the Chad which profoundly altered his intellectual concerns. And similarly Pirandello, although he continued to deliver a spate of plays right up to his death in 1936, never again attained the level of 1921, his *annus mirabilis*.

We can observe a corresponding turning-point in the life of Freud. With the publication of *The Ego and the Id* in 1923, the corpus of his basic writings was completed: from this point on Freud was simply to modify details in a fully constructed theory that was more and more winning general recognition. And in 1923 he also underwent the radical surgery that gave him sixteen more years of life but at the same time reduced his working powers and made pain his daily companion. The late twenties and thirties saw Freud turning toward speculation on society and religion: such books as *The Future of an Illusion, Civilization and Its Discontents*, and *Moses and Monotheism* suggest the later Freud, metamorphosed from a physician into a seer and sage.

In all these cases, a pause, a change, or a cessation in creative energy did not occasion a waning of public attention. On the contrary, nearly all the survivors of the generation of the 1890's ranked as intellectual leaders as long as they lived. What loss of influence they experienced did not manifest itself openly: it appeared in their being honored more with respect than with understanding and in a certain impatient surprise that these old men could prove so hardy: by the end of the Second World War, Thomas Mann was nearly without esteem in his own country, and the younger Italian intellectuals were displaying a growing restiveness under the half-century-long domination that Croce had imposed upon them.

The great exception was Henri Bergson. He alone experienced the supreme calamity of outliving his glory. To him, as to the others, the post-war years had brought their harvest of honors. He had seemed the obvious choice for president of the commission for intellectual co-operation set up under the auspices of the League of Nations, and in 1927 he had received the

Nobel Prize. But meantime illness had struck him even more severely than Freud, and during nearly the whole decade of the 1920's his writing could progress only with pitiable slowness. When his last book, *Two Sources of Morality and Religion,* finally appeared in 1932, it came as a disappointment and an anticlimax. Bergson's incomparable style had weakened, and his reasoning—never too rigorous—had become still looser. Above all, in a philosophical sense, he had fallen into irrelevance.

A drastic shift in philosophical interests had caught Bergson unaware. While he alone directly suffered from it, the philosophies of Croce and James were also threatened, and the more speculative sociologists like Weber could consider themselves similarly rebuked. This is the first of two signs of the altered intellectual prospect to which we must now turn our attention.

1. *The New Philosophical Interests*

In the preceding chapters, we have had occasion more than once to note the appearance of younger men whose work challenged the presuppositions on which the major social doctrines of the early twentieth century had been based. In Germany in particular, such intellectual phenomena as Karl Barth's religious neo-orthodoxy and Georg Lukács's neo-Marxism have suggested an abandonment of cultural permissiveness and skepticism and a return to more militant formulations of belief. This intellectual revulsion may be viewed as another manifestation of that rejection of the "elders'" lead that we have already observed in the sphere of post-war politics. By the early 1920's, in abstract thought as in ideology, the example of men like Weber and Troeltsch had begun to appear old-fashioned. The generation of students that reached the universities immediately subsequent to their deaths found a different kind of intellectual excitement in Lukács's *Ge-*

schichte und Klassenbewusstsein, published in 1923, and in Max Scheler's *Die Wissensformen und die Gesellschaft,* which three years later outlined the elements of a new discipline called the "sociology of knowledge."

The two philosophers, however, in whom the younger generation could find the most powerful stimulus, were Husserl and Heidegger. The related doctrines of phenomenology and existentialism associated with their names departed notably from the tradition of European philosophy of which Croce and Bergson had been the most prominent pre-war representatives. Phenomenology devoted a painstaking attention to the minute details of human experience. Existentialism, in its lineal descent from Kierkegaard, shared the Danish theologian's hostility to the tradition of the Enlightenment. If Husserl's work pointed toward a meticulous analysis of ideas that would make the work of Croce or Bergson appear amateurish and slipshod, Heidegger's tragic view of existence broke sharply with the serene and optimistic attitude that still linked the leading French and Italian philosophic schools with the thought of the eighteenth century.

Yet, more broadly considered, the growing influence of existentialism that was to reach its height at the end of the Second World War betokened more a shift of emphasis than a redefinition of the presuppositions of philosophic investigation. Existentialism continued to range over the traditional pastures of metaphysics, ethics, and social philosophy, and its practitioners were not afraid to make statements for which strictly scientific evidence was lacking. Both Husserl and Heidegger echoed Bergson's faith in intuition. And in common not only with Bergson, but, in certain respects, with Croce also, existentialism was obsessed with the problems of historicity and the "experiential qualities of time." "All existentialist thinkers assign to the category of time a central place in their metaphysical systems. . . . The point of departure is . . . temporality, or historicity . . . ; the point of arrival is usually an attempt . . . to . . . 'transcend' this temporally situated mode of man's existence." [1]

Moreover, in the 1920's the influence of existentialism was still largely confined to Germany. It was pragmatism, rather, that had suggested some of the new concerns that were to be characteristic of the period from about 1920 to the present. Pragmatism, as William James had asserted, was "a mediating movement in philosophy": it aspired to "a total, metaphysical, systematic view of reality without losing sight of scientific and logical detail or of human problems"; it stood "between the more traditional view of philosophy as world-view and the more recent analytic tendencies." [2] These analytic tendencies broke still more radically than had phenomenology or existentialism with the pre-war formulation of philosophical problems.

Just as it was a non-Continental, William James, who had acted as the revivifying force in European thought in the decade and a half preceding the outbreak of the First World War, so it was an Englishman, Bertrand Russell, who became the progenitor of analytic philosophy on the European Continent in the post-war years. The publication of Whitehead and Russell's *Principia Mathematica* in the years 1910 to 1913 can conventionally be taken as the starting-point of the effort to fuse the methods of philosophy and mathematics and by so doing to bring greater rigor into the conceptual framework of both of them. Three decades later Lord Russell described the philosophy of logical analysis in its broadest terms as one having "the quality of science. . . . It has the advantage, as compared with the philosophies of the system-builders, of

---

[1] Hans Meyerhoff: *Time in Literature* (Berkeley and Los Angeles, 1955), pp. 138–9.
[2] Morton White: *The Age of Analysis* (New York, 1955), p. 19. See also White's *Toward Reunion in Philosophy* (Cambridge, Mass., 1956) and Charles W. Morris: *Logical Positivism, Pragmatism, and Scientific Empiricism* (Paris, 1937).

being able to tackle its problems one at a time, instead
of having to invent at one stroke a block theory of the
whole universe."

From the standpoint of intellectual clarity, all this
was doubtless a gain. But the shift to the mathematical-
logical method also implied an enormous sacrifice:

> There remains, however, a vast field, tradition-
> ally included in philosophy, where scientific
> methods are inadequate. This field includes ulti-
> mate questions of value; science alone, for ex-
> ample, cannot prove that it is bad to enjoy the
> infliction of cruelty. Whatever can be known, can
> be known by means of science; but things which
> are legitimately matters of feeling lie outside its
> province.[3]

It was in Vienna that Russell found his most coherent band of disciples. In 1923—a date which we have
encountered again and again in the past few pages—a
group of younger men mostly drawn from the natural
sciences organized the "Vienna Circle." Besides Russell, its tutelary spirit was the mathematical logician
Gottlob Frege, and its most articulate spokesman was
the thirty-two-year-old Rudolf Carnap. Highly conscious of themselves as a cohesive, militant philosophic
school, the members of the Vienna Circle initially
referred to their doctrine as "logical positivism."
Although they later changed this label to "logical
empiricism," as less associated with outmoded nineteenth-century teachings, it was the word "positivism"
—perhaps for the very reason that it was more contro-
versial—that stuck in the public consciousness.

Similarly the pronouncement that occasioned the
greatest stir abroad was not an official emanation of the
Circle. Ludwig Wittgenstein was more eccentric, extreme, and undisciplined than the charter founders of

[3] Bertrand Russell: *A History of Western Philosophy* (New
York, 1945), p. 834.

logical positivism, and his interests were primarily linguistic rather than mathematical. Yet his *Tractatus Logico-Philosophicus*, first published in Vienna in 1921, was to give most people their notion of what logical positivism was after, and was to become the most influential philosophical work of the post-war years.

Wittgenstein's book was cast in a consciously provocative form. Less than a hundred pages in length, it tossed at the reader—to be accepted *en bloc* or not at all—a series of terse, hermetic "propositions," most of them presented as self-evident and all billed as "of equal value." Starting from the proposition that "what can be said at all can be said clearly," Wittgenstein proceeded to prove that there was indeed very little that could be said—and that this little could all be expressed very briefly either in logical symbols or, preferably, in the language of ordinary speech. "Most propositions and questions," he asserted, "that have been written about philosophical matters, are not false, but senseless. . . . And so it is not to be wondered at that the deepest problems are really *no* problems. . . . Hence also there can be no ethical propositions." And he concluded that both mysticism and skepticism—which was "*not* irrefutable, but palpably senseless"—could find no place in a scientifically conducted philosophical investigation.[4]

By this path Wittgenstein brought himself to the final assertion that the "right method of philosophy" would be simply to state "the propositions of natural science, *i.e.* something that has nothing to do with philosophy: and then always, when someone else wished to say something metaphysical," to demonstrate to him the error of his ways. Eventually, even Wittgenstein's own propositions would prove to be unessential:

[4] Ludwig Wittgenstein: *Logisch-Philosophische Abhandlung* (Vienna, 1921), translated with parallel German text as *Tractatus Logico-Philosophicus* (London, 1922), pp. 27, 63, 183, 187.

he who understands me finally recognizes them as
senseless, when he has climbed out through them,
on them, over them. (He must so to speak throw
away the ladder, after he has climbed up on it.)
      He must surmount these propositions; then he
sees the world rightly.
      Whereof one cannot speak, thereof one must be
silent.[5]

There was a certain irony in the fact that Wittgenstein and the young philosopher-scientists of the
Vienna Circle should have been taking up again—under
the banner of intellectual liberation—positions that
had apparently been definitively abandoned thirty
years earlier. At first glance it might appear that European philosophy since the 1890's had come full circle. The generation of the sons was refurbishing the
doctrines of their grandfathers against whose iron domination the generation of their fathers had battled so
hard for independence.
      It is true that in this case, as so often in the history
of philosophy, the passage from one generation to another had a good deal to do with making the word
"positivism" and the linkage of science with philosophy
once again acceptable. Yet the new positivism was far
from being a mere revival of its nineteenth-century
predecessor. Its aims were more modest and its definition of science more sophisticated. The neo-positivists
no longer believed it possible to establish an unquestioned series of cause-and-effect relationships over the
entire field of human activity. Wittgenstein had in fact
cast doubt on the whole idea by asserting that "belief
in the causal nexus" was a "superstition" and that it
was an "illusion" that "the so-called laws of nature"
were "the explanations of natural phenomena." The
sole necessity in nature was a *logical* necessity." [6]
Hence it was only by abandoning vast portions of the

      [5] Ibid., pp. 187, 189.   [6] Ibid., pp. 109, 181.

field that Comte and Spencer and Taine and the others had originally staked out for scientific cultivation that the neo-positivists of the twentieth century were able to rehabilitate the scientific method in philosophy. Leaving aside as questions of value or metaphysics nearly all the topics that had traditionally seemed most important to philosophers, they were to restrict themselves to those problems alone that could be formulated without ambiguity in logical or symbolic language.

In this context, the old positivist anti-positivist controversy could be considered as superseded. The battles of the 1890's could be dismissed as rather fusty affairs in which the contestants themselves had never really known what they were talking about. Russell, Frege, and their descendants had now at last made matters clear.

Yet there was a final aspect to the change that was not so readily apparent. Just as poetry and painting and music in the twentieth century had become more esoteric and "difficult," less accessible to the man of ordinary cultivation and perception, so now philosophy was taking the same course. A person of a reasonable level of education could read Bergson or Croce with ease and pleasure, as literature and moral teaching. He could not do the same with Wittgenstein. The door to philosophical knowledge had apparently been slammed in his face, and for another two decades Europe was to be without a philosophy that could speak to the ordinary citizen about problems close to his most pressing concerns.

11. *The Social Question*

When such a philosophy did at length appear, it was to carry the words "engagement" and "commitment" as moral imperatives. The post-1945 vogue of French existentialism grew directly out of a situation in which

a concern with social problems appeared an inescapable
necessity.

This is the second aspect of the altered intellectual
prospect to which we earlier referred. During the
greater part of the 1920's it might still be possible to
live and to philosophize as though the times were in
some sense "normal." Yet already the range—both
geographical and psychological—through which the
mind might comfortably wander had sensibly narrowed. The war had revealed the fragility of civilized
values among the populations of Western and Central
Europe. The advent of Bolshevism had cut off Russia
from the community of liberal intellectuals. And the
triumph of Italian Fascism had shaken up consciences
at least as deeply by bringing a major Western country,
for the first time in a half-century, under a government
strenuously hostile to free speculation. It was no accident that Croce and Mosca as intellectual opponents
of the new regime found themselves in the mid-twenties uncertain what course to follow. And it was also
not accidental that Croce—and subsequently Meinecke
in Germany—eventually came around to a militancy in
defense of free institutions which was in radical contrast with their earlier insistence on the historian's
aloofness from political controversy.

Under the comparatively mild tyranny of Mussolini,
an attitude of uncertainty or of intellectual detachment
was still possible. But as the decade closed, the coming
of the great depression and the National Socialist
menace seemed to render all such compromise positions
intolerable. By the 1930's an increasing number of
European intellectuals were concluding that an attitude
of political commitment was the only possible choice.
A few—a very few—opted for fascism. Of the truly
great, Heidegger and Jung alone entered into com-
promising associations with the Nazi regime.[7] The ma-

[7] On Jung, see the detailed evidence presented in Edward
Glover: *Freud or Jung?* Meridian edition (New York, 1956), pp.
147–52.

jority of Europe's intellectual leaders, whether in exile, the self-conscious urgency of Popular Fronts, or the muted suffering of "inner emigration," chose the course of resistance to what the fascist leaders had proclaimed as the predestined future.

With his customary sensitivity to new currents, André Gide had been caught up by the imperative of political and moral engagement rather earlier than the rest. The trip to French Equatorial Africa which he had originally embarked on as a recreation from literary activity had led to a revelation of abuses and a mounting indignation that were eventually to take him into the Communist camp. But he was also quicker than the others to appreciate the dangers that the intellectual encountered in subordinating himself to an organized political movement. It was not only that a visit to the Soviet Union, ten years following his journey to the Congo, disclosed to him the brutal truth about Communism in practice. There came also a realization that his concern with the social question had "poisoned" his life and damaged his creative activity. As a loyal party supporter, he discovered, the intellectual had the choice between silence and "going astray": neither was compatible with the traditional definition of his function.[8]

Inevitably it was in Germany, where the political pressures were most intense and the tradition of the intellectual's disassociation from practical concerns most clearly established, that the new impulse toward commitment produced the greatest inner conflict. Here the writer or philosopher had nearly always been hostile to popular judgments and practical criteria of value. It had been to escape the pressures of organized opinion that Nietzsche, and after him Hermann Hesse, had

[8] Letter of May 16, 1947, published as appendix to Albert J. Guerard, *André Gide* (Cambridge, Mass., 1951), p. 241; entry for December 29, 1932, in *Journal 1889–1939* (Paris, 1948), translated and edited by Justin O'Brien as *The Journals of André Gide* (New York, 1947–9), III, 252.

fled to Switzerland, and it was in the form of escape—whether as exile or as inner withdrawal—that the German intellectual's reaction to Nazism most commonly expressed itself. In the choice between propaganda and silence, by far the larger number decided for the latter. Thomas Mann was almost alone in successfully combining political propaganda with a maintenance of his earlier level of artistic production.

In any case, the very fact that the choice had presented itself in these terms betokened a drastic change for the survivors of the generation of the 1890's. It suggested that they had perhaps outlived their era, and that the years following 1933 would be an age of iron for which their intellectual preparation had ill equipped them. Economic ruin, political upheaval, exile, the threat of war—all these were profoundly altering the character of their existence. In the new Europe of political terror and impending war, what place was there for the *freischwebende Intelligenz?* It might well be that the freely speculating intellectual had become no more than a useless relic of the eighteenth and nineteenth centuries.

III. *The Role of the Intellectuals: Mann, Benda, Mannheim*

By the mid-twenties, the two separate and contradictory tendencies that we have been tracing had begun—paradoxically enough—to reinforce each other in necessitating a redefinition of the intellectual's role. For both of them implied an impatience with the traditional conception of what the European philosopher or moralist should do. From neither of these standpoints was it possible any longer to maintain that a major writer should concern himself with the whole range of human problems—that he should survey with

Olympian calm the social doings of his fellow men and, after a suitable parade of literary and historical learning, and a minimum of reflection on his presuppositions, come to certain rather majestic conclusions about what constituted the true, the beautiful, and the good. This was what the European intellectuals had been doing ever since the species first came into existence, and it was what they had continued to do in the first two decades of the twentieth century. In this sense, philosophers and sociologists such as Croce and Bergson and Weber—even Freud in his more speculative writings— had been in direct descent from Aquinas or Montaigne. And a deviant like Sorel—however much he had railed at the intellectualist tradition—had always remained a moralist at heart. Up to about 1920 no sharp division between literature and social science had been drawn, and the intellectual still felt himself as free as Goethe to roam at will throughout the varied domains of human activity.

To the new school of logical positivism, however, such dilettantism was totally unacceptable. And to the advocates of social "commitment" it appeared, for quite different reasons, equally suspect. To the latter, the intellectual's traditional claim to a special status and to the right of suspended judgment seemed an intolerable frivolity in an era of agonizing choices in which each self-conscious individual, without exception, was in duty bound to stand up and be counted. By the mid-twenties, then, there had begun to loom up a vastly altered intellectual prospect in which the old confident generalizing would find no place: the meticulous scientists of words and symbols and the "terrible simplifiers" of Jacob Burckhardt's nineteenth-century nightmare, in their mutually incompatible endeavors, would have the field all to themselves.

Under these circumstances, it is not surprising that in the years 1924 to 1929—the six deceptive years of post-war Europe's apparent stabilization and prosperity

—three major works, totally unrelated in character and totally independent of each other, should have sought to redefine in contemporary terms the function and calling of the European *literati*.

The first word came from a novelist. For Thomas Mann the war years had been a period of trial and tragic ambivalence. He had interrupted work on what was to be the second of his major novels, *The Magic Mountain*, and he had felt incapable of sustained creative effort. The one substantial product of this period, the *Betrachtungen eines Unpolitischen* (Reflections of an Unpolitical Man), ranks, by general consent, as the least fortunate of his whole literary output. In writing it, he had felt obligated to assume a propagandist role. He had believed it incumbent on him to make his personal contribution to his nation's war effort by defending the German "cultural" values of hierarchy and inner experience against the merely "civilized" democracy and literary-minded humanitarianism of the West. Yet his own hesitations had penetrated the propagandist surface of his work: in passage after passage, he had been obliged to recognize the extent to which he himself was a *Zivilisationsliterat*—a "civilized" intellectual.

Hence when *The Magic Mountain* finally appeared, six years after the war's end, both its scope and its intellectual emphasis had vastly altered. It had grown from a brief, half-jocular companion piece to "Death in Venice" into an immense *summa* of Mann's recurring interests—the aesthetic, erotic, and destructive function of disease and death, the ambiguous relation of the artist to bourgeois society, the incompatibility between German national values and European democracy, and the dubious ideal of a wider humanity. By the 1920's Mann was ready to grant a respectful and even a sympathetic hearing to the "civilized" values that he had attacked so bitterly in his wartime reflections. In this respect *The Magic Mountain* marked the transition between the early Mann in his self-con-

sciously alienated and unpolitical guise and the later
Mann of humanist affirmation.

Thus the book that eventually became the most influential German novel of the inter-war years was a
great deal more than a work of imaginative literature.
It had a public, political aspect that Mann's contemporaries were quick to recognize. Already in 1922, he
had begun to take a more affirmative stand toward his
nation's new "Western" institutions in his influential
address entitled "The German Republic." Two years
later the generally favorable reception of *The Magic
Mountain* suggested that the German reading public
had found a new and more subtle literary-cosmological
breviary to balance Spengler's "narcotic" *Decline of
the West*. In fact the publication of his great post-war
work established the still hesitant Mann—quite to his
own surprise—as a kind of novelist-laureate of the Weimar Republic.

The "public" aspect of *The Magic Mountain* was
already apparent in its structure and presentation. Its
very locale—a tuberculosis sanitarium high up in the
Swiss Alps—gave it a quality of stylization and abstraction, of an artistically imposed isolation from the concerns and relationships of everyday living. "The *milieu*
of the sanitarium, which removes its inmates both in
time and space from their customary associations, has
the advantage of an epic possibility scarcely attainable
in other communities—the life of the spirit confronting
death." It is a *milieu* in which even an "average" individual, freed from the bonds of practical endeavor,
can learn to meditate on ultimate values—a *milieu* in
which disease itself becomes the teacher who warns
never to take for granted the categories that are simply
assumed in the "flatland" down below.[9]

Hence as a novel of education—the form in which it
most obviously offered itself to the reading public—
The Magic Mountain conveyed a rarefied atmosphere,

[9] Arnold Bauer: *Thomas Mann und die Krise der bürgerlichen
Kultur* (Berlin, 1946), pp. 66–9, 71.

a sense of compression in space and dissolution in time, that were lacking in its picaresque prototype *Wilhelm Meister*. It traced a search for enlightenment through the dialectical method dear to four generations of German thinkers: two self-appointed preceptors were to struggle for the soul of a quite ordinary scion of the upper middle class sent them by accident from the world of practical activity.

Thomas Mann himself has put on record the simplicity of his original conception: "a kind of pedagogical story, in which a young man, cast adrift in a morally dangerous abode, was placed between two equally droll educators, between an Italian *littérateur*, humanist, rhetorician, and disciple of progress, and a somewhat disreputable mystic, reactionary, and advocate of unreason." [1] But in the more than decade-long process of composition, *The Magic Mountain* had changed from a *scherzo* into a novel of a high, if frequently ironical, seriousness. The Italian humanist Settembrini had become far more than the "windbag" or "organ-grinder" that the young protagonist called him in moments of irritation: he was transmuted into a pathetic and even dignified figure, who, for all his superficiality and obtuseness of thought, stood for the abiding values of reason, justice, and love of humanity inherited from the Enlightenment. And his antagonist Leo Naphta— combining in his own person the appropriate illogicality of Jewish origin and Jesuit training—had grown through the years from a "disreputable" eccentric into a towering personification of the forces of terroristic orthodoxy unleashed by the war and its aftermath, pointing with uncanny insight to the still more disciplined and pitiless terror of the decade to come. Even the protagonist, the young engineer from Hamburg, Hans Castorp, although still deceptively labeled as "simple," had become an apt pupil qualified to judge in his own right: at the end of the book he had as-

[1] Cited in *ibid.*, p. 70.

sumed the dominant role, as he sat by Settembrini's bedside, listening to the latter's explanations of the crisis of July 1914 with the tolerant, affectionate respect that one grants to an old teacher to whom one owes much but from whom one can learn nothing further.

In the vast dialectical battles on the *Zauberberg*, it was Naphta who seemed—particularly to Mann's readers of the 1930's and 1940's—to have made the more convincing case. He spoke with the voice of militant irrationalism, and in his triumphant affirmations of the virtues of illogicality, disease, and terror he appeared to epitomize what Jung had called the shadow side of twentieth-century psychology. Yet it was Settembrini who had the last word. After his antagonist's non-logic had reached its inescapable conclusion in the taking of his own life, the Italian humanist had had the pedagogical field all to himself. Failing in strength but buoyant to the end, Settembrini gave the last encouraging counsels that sped Hans Castorp on his way back to the flatland to serve his country in war. "One can only suppose that in allowing the Jesuit to kill himself and Settembrini to live on, Thomas Mann is acknowledging the right to survival of his old enemy, the 'Zivilisationsliterat.' " [2]

The same impression is confirmed in the central passage of the whole book—the sentence that marks the culmination of Castorp's education, and the only sentence in the corpus of Mann's writings printed entirely in italics: *"For the sake of goodness and love, man shall let death have no sovereignty over his thoughts."* [3] The values of the Enlightenment, the ethical abstractions that had provided the great European moralists with their *raison d'être*—the values to which Croce and Mosca, Freud and Weber, Durkheim and Bergson had remained faithful—are here endorsed without doubt or qualification.

[2] J. M. Lindsay: *Thomas Mann* (Oxford, 1954), p. 49.
[3] *Der Zauberberg* (Berlin, 1924), translated by H. T. Lowe-Porter as *The Magic Mountain* (New York, 1927), p. 626.

Yet a final ambiguity remains. Castorp proves unable
to hold firm to the vision of truth to which he had attained in a moment of exaltation; the reconciliation
of humanism with its necessary foundation of cruelty
reveals itself as a synthesis too tenuous to last. Toward
the end of the book we find him making a confession—
a highly damaging confession from the standpoint of
"enlightened" values: "In defiance of Herr Settembrini, I declared myself for the principle of unreason,
the *spirituel* principle of disease, under whose aegis I
had already, in reality, stood for a long time back." [4]
And the individual to whom the confession is made,
Mynheer Peeperkorn, suggests a still more damaging
association. For it is quite apparent that Peeperkorn
stands for the elemental power of human personality
divorced from logic, charity, or the golden mean—for
pure *charisma*, unalloyed by intellect or morality. It is
true that this third preceptor, like Naphta, conven-
iently removes himself as a pedagogical influence by
taking his own life. And it is equally true that Castorp
is eventually "saved" by his enforced return to the flatland. Yet one cannot help wondering how the author
could have resolved his educational dilemma except by
the *deus ex machina* of the outbreak of war.

Thus the riddle of Peeperkorn is left in suspense. We
are told that in his commanding presence the dialectics
of Settembrini and Naphta seemed reduced to mere
irrelevancies. "No spark leaped nimbly from pole to
pole, no flash of lightning, no current. The intellect
which should in its own opinion have neutralized the
presence was neutralized by it." [5] The two self constituted educators found their brilliant reasoning collapse before this majestic, essentially stupid personality for whom words were simply compelling sounds that
carried no defined meaning.

And so Thomas Mann had revealed something beyond Naphta, beyond the merely intellectual propaga-

[4] Ibid., p. 769.   [5] Ibid., p. 743.

tion of terror. It was a theme to which he was to return in more specific form in his short story *Mario and the Magician*, published in 1930. A transparent allegory of Italian Fascism, *Mario* took up again in terms of sharp warning the dangers of "magic" and personal magnetism. The implication was that the Naphtas of this world, for all the inhumanity of their doctrines, had at least remained within the bounds of conversation and intellectual exchange. The thread of the Enlightenment had been stretched to its farthest limits but not yet entirely broken. With Mynheer Peeperkorn and the magician Cipolla a new species of humanity had appeared. Between them and the European *literati* no sort of understanding was possible.

In the dialectical conflict between Naphta and Settembrini, Thomas Mann had left the issue unresolved. Three years later—in 1927—a French philosopher of the same generation aligned himself unequivocally with the tradition of the Enlightenment. In Julien Benda's *The Betrayal of the Intellectuals* the contestants were not quite identical with those who had battled on the *Zauberberg*: in shifting from a Germanic to a French setting, the argument had lost much of its subtlety. But by the very fact of simplifying the issues, Benda was able to make his polemic cut more sharply. For it was not his intention to give credit to the intellectual innovators of his time or to recognize the nuances that separated one writer from another; he was not interested in the enhancement of understanding that had come from the thirty-year critique of the Enlightenment. He simply wanted to sound an alarm.

For this he was ideally qualified. A Jew by family tradition if not by formal practice, Benda had been born in Paris in 1867: like his co-religionists Bergson and Blum—the former eight years older, the latter five years younger—he remained all his life a Parisian to the marrow. His parents, he felt, had left their temperamental divergences imprinted on his character: in his later years he described himself as the "product of a Jew of the ancient Orient, in love with eternity and scornful of contingence, joined to a petulant Parisian Jewess . . . with the itch for writing." [6] At the same time, their unquestioning love, the atmosphere of warm family affection in which he had grown up, had given him a sense of inner security that never deserted him.

His had been a childhood without problems or painful psychological cleavages. The abstract republicanism of his upbringing—so characteristic of French Jewish families in the last decades of the nineteenth century—was simply confirmed by his schooling; in Benda's case, as opposed to the classic conflict that faced young Frenchmen of Catholic background, there was no opposition between what was taught in the state school and the values that had been inculcated at home. Similarly the austere intellectualism of the *lycée* found in the adolescent Benda a mind already prepared for enthusiastic acceptance. Mathematics was his joy; a rhetoric based on Latin models seemed to respond to the demands of his inmost being and gave him a bare, muscular style that was to serve him well in controversy; but the academic philosophy of his day repelled him by its discursiveness. When still a child he had found the philosopher who was to remain his model for life—need one name him?—Spinoza.

In the very gaps in his education an older Benda looking back on the conflicts of his middle years was to discern further explanations for the tight coherence of his convictions. His family had had small esteem for non-logical values based on history and religion; energy, physical courage had been little honored; his ancestors "had never held functions of command." [7] One could find no sharper contrast with the ideals that inspired those who were to be the targets of his future attack—the monarchists, the authoritarians, the apostles of na-

<hr />

[6] *La Jeunesse d'un clerc* (Paris, 1936), p. 36.
[7] Ibid., p. 53.

tional dynamism. These might be the socially fashionable doctrines of his mature years—but to the allures
of society and intellectual fashion Benda was singularly
unsusceptible. Unlike Bergson or Blum, he came from
relatively modest circumstances and had not attended
one of the famous *lycées* where young Parisians of
promise and prominence struck up intellectual alliances
and came to think of themselves as the leaders of their
generation. For himself Benda had no sense of his
generation and was quite content to stand apart. The
"mandarin" aspects of the French intellectual's existence satisfied him entirely: as in childhood, he continued "to think . . . that the great human examples
are those who can find joy . . . in remaining quietly
in a room with pen and paper." [8] He enjoyed a personal
independence as complete as the modern world can
offer—a comfortable private income, no job, no wife,
no child. And as a man just turning thirty he had experienced the one decisive event that would dictate for
the rest of his life his notions of political right and
wrong—again the reference is obvious—the Dreyfus
case.

Like Bergson and Durkheim, Sorel and Péguy, Benda
had fought in the ranks of the Dreyfusards. And he had
been one of the numerous Jewish supporters of and
contributors to the *Cahiers de la Quinzaine*. Indeed,
as we have seen, it had been a disagreement over Benda's novel *L'Ordination* that had precipitated the rupture between Sorel and Péguy in 1912.

The events of 1917 and 1922 had given him occasion
to think through once again his essential convictions
about human rationality. It is against this background
of the triumph of Lenin and Mussolini that his *Betrayal of the Intellectuals* needs to be viewed. Such a
book could not have been written before the mid-
twenties. And by that time circumstances so manifestly
called for it that it evoked an immediate response. In

[8] Ibid., p. 73.

brief, Benda's compact, combative little book warned of the retreat from civilized values that had already occurred—and in particular ascribed to the European intellectuals a major responsibility for it.

From the early Middle Ages, Benda maintained, the "clerks" or intellectuals had constituted a class apart, dedicated not to earthly but to transcendent concerns. Their great "treason" of contemporary times had arisen from their *"desire to abase the values of knowledge before the values of action.* . . . About 1890 the men of letters, especially in France and Italy, realized with astonishing astuteness that the doctrines of arbitrary authority, discipline, tradition, contempt for the spirit of liberty, assertion of the morality of war and slavery, were haughty and rigid poses infinitely more likely to strike the imagination of simple souls than the sentimentalities of Liberalism and Humanitarianism." [9] Hence instead of resisting the popular drive toward an intensification of racial, class, and national passions, they had abetted it. Far from constituting themselves as an opposition to the new irrationalism, they had become its spokesmen.

The nineteenth-century Germans had been their original teachers, and Nietzsche had been their precursor. Philosophically they had managed to combine a neo-romantic reliance on "artistic sensibility" with a positivist insistence that "they consider only the facts." But this inconsistency had not troubled them: they prided themselves on their pragmatism. What united them, rather, was a metaphysics without precedent in history which preached "adoration for the contingent, and scorn for the eternal." [1]

By this route, then, Benda was led to include in a sweeping indictment not only such minor and essen-

---

[9] *La Trahison des clercs* (Paris, 1927), translated as *The Betrayal of the Intellectuals*, Beacon paperback edition (Boston, 1955), pp. 119, 135. See also Robert J. Niess: *Julien Benda* (Ann Arbor, Mich., 1956), Chapter 7.

[1] *Betrayal of the Intellectuals*, pp. 78, 94, 137.

tially propagandist figures as D'Annunzio, Barrès, Maurras, and Kipling, and a middle-rank moralist like Péguy, but also such major intellectual creators as Sorel and Bergson. The former Benda condemned for his doctrines of violence and his "glorifications of the *homo faber*," the latter for his "exhortations to consider everything only as it exists *in time*, that is as it constitutes a succession of particular states, a 'becoming,' a 'history,' and never as it presents a state of permanence beyond time." In the case of Bergson, Benda could attack only the implications of the new metaphysics; it was obvious that the philosopher of the *élan vital*, unlike Péguy and Sorel, did not personally advocate a warrior ethic. Similarly with Durkheim, Benda could do no more than parenthetically offer reproaches for a neglect of the "notion of good in the heart of eternal and disinterested man." And when he came to William James, Benda confined himself to noting the American philosopher's attitude of approval toward the Spanish-American war and characterizing the "preaching of *Pragmatism*" in its various forms as the "cult of the strong state and the moral methods which ensure it." [2]

As the foregoing enumeration reveals, *The Betrayal of the Intellectuals* drew most of its examples from contemporary France. Here indeed the lines of intellectual cleavage were almost as sharp as Benda had defined them, and in rough terms corresponded to the political division between authoritarians and republicans. Outside France, however, the situation was quite different. One wonders what Benda would have made of a thinker like Pareto—a prime "traitor," if one considered only the surface of his doctrine, yet rooted in the tradition of the Enlightenment. For the subtleties and the ambiguities of German and Italian thought, Benda manifested little concern. His book—despite its constant insistence on eternal values—betrayed a pro-

[2] Ibid., pp. 39, 74, 79, 98–9, 101.

foundly parochial outlook. It was Parisian-French—
classical, formally logical, intellectualist. The mark of
the First World War was unmistakably upon it: Benda
never thought of apologizing for his distaste and fear
of things German. Yet his work had the characteristic
strength of the parochial in its simplicity and robust
certainty.

At a deeper level of criticism one may suggest that
Benda's failure to make his presuppositions explicit
gave him an unfair polemical advantage. Essentially
what he was doing was taking his stand with the major
tradition of Western philosophy from Socrates to
Kant. Outside this path, he implied, no firm footing
was possible: all around lay the quicksands of relativism and pragmatism. The nobility of such an attitude is unchallengeable. It appears with particular
force toward the close of Benda's book, where he warns
of the fragility of civilized values as the West has
known them. "If humanity loses this jewel, there is
not much chance of finding it again. . . . People forget that Hellenic rationalism only really enlightened
the world during seven hundred years, that it was then
hidden . . . for twelve centuries, and has begun to
shine again for barely four centuries." [3]

At the same time, this synopsis of two millennia of
intellectual history is staggeringly oversimplified. If
Benda had stated his presuppositions more explicitly, it
would have been apparent how heavily he was stacking
the cards against his adversaries. He was suggesting that
salvation—indeed the most elementary intellectual honesty—lay only within the Western rational tradition *as
narrowly defined by him.* For the moral dilemmas that
practicing intellectuals daily confront in contemporary
life, he showed scant sympathy. His ethical rigor and
absolutism reflected the serenity of his own career, and
the fact that the one great crisis of his life—the Dreyfus
case—had been blessedly simple. The Dreyfus case has

[3] Ibid., pp. 156, 158–9.

not repeated itself: its successors in more recent times have been far more ambiguous. And the precept that Benda offered in such emergencies—that the Athenian state was behaving correctly *as state* in presenting Socrates the hemlock, while Socrates *as intellectual* was also correct in making no attempt to escape it—was perhaps sufficient for a man without a family, but for the run of intellectuals offered no adequate guide.[4] (In circumstances similar to Socrates', Galileo had chosen the opposite course.) Had they followed to the letter the advice Benda offered, few European intellectuals would have survived the two decades subsequent to the publication of his book.

Similarly with regard to his more abstract categories. Benda never gave his intellectual adversaries credit for keeping faith with the spirit of the Enlightenment even as they tried to broaden its methods. In the first place, he allowed them no sufficient opportunity to state their case. The greatest of them—Croce, Freud, Weber—are absent from his pages. "This is the weakest point in M. Benda's argument; he compares the minor clerks of our time with the major clerks of other ages." [5] And those of the great who do appear in his book, like Nietzsche and Bergson, figure in travestied form. Benda, as he frankly admits, is concerned only with the *tendency* of a man's thought ("though I know perfectly well that in reality this teaching is something far more complex"): "Nietzsche as a humanitarian . . . had no influence at all, and my subject is the influence which the 'clerks' have had in the world, and not what they were in themselves. . . . Need I say that Nietzsche, who seems to me a bad 'clerk' from the nature of his teaching, seems to me one of the finest from his entire devotion to the passions of the spirit alone?" [6]

But what sort of logic is this? Benda repeatedly asserts his radical opposition to any *practical* criterion.

[4] Ibid., p. 171.
[5] Ibid., Introduction by Herbert Read, p. xxii.
[6] Ibid., pp. 34, 130n, 179.

Yet in judging Nietzsche and his like he seems to have fallen into the grossest sort of pragmatism. Was it Bergson's fault that his doctrines gained popularity and were perverted to obscurantist and nationalist ends? The princes of the mind are not always without honor in their own time. If Benda can treat so unjustly two such lofty-spirited intellectuals as Nietzsche and Bergson, is it not possible that there is a deep flaw in his whole argument?

The basic trouble with Benda was that his intellectual range was too narrow. He wore his Cartesian categories and his traditional metaphysics like blinders, and they denied him any sympathetic understanding of the creative achievements of his contemporaries. To him the intuitive approach was anathema without qualification. True to the strict observance of the Enlightenment, he could not imagine how the uses of intuition could possibly be reconciled with it. He saw all too clearly the dangers of intuitive thinking in its destructive, hateful, and irrational guise. He was blind to its potentialities for disinterested investigation and creation. As a moral remonstrance and a call to a long-overdue examination of conscience, *The Betrayal of the Intellectuals* was a major monument of twentieth-century thought. As a summary of past achievement and a guide to the role of intellectuals when the second quarter of the century opened, it was glaringly insufficient.

The last of the three works of intellectual summation that we have singled out as directional signposts for the middle and late 1920's—Karl Mannheim's *Ideology and Utopia*—was less obviously a defense of the Enlightenment than its two predecessors. In fact what it owed to the rationalist tradition was so well concealed under German sociological paraphernalia as frequently to pass unnoticed. Yet the author's intent should have been unmistakable. His book aimed at "inquiring into the prospects of rationality and common understanding" in an era that apparently "put a premium upon irrationality and from which the possibilities of mutual understanding" had all but disappeared.[7] And when he came to write of the Enlightenment itself he stressed its "fresh and youthful quality," its "suggestive and stimulating atmosphere," whose "central elements . . . were open to the clear light of day" and which "appealed to the free will" by keeping alive "the feeling of being indeterminate and unconditioned. . . . Its abstractness, which was only gradually uncovered by the criticism of the right and left, was never felt by the original exponents of the idea."[8]

Moreover, like Benda, Mannheim was trying to rescue the tradition of abstract, categorized thinking from the shoals of pragmatist method. But he was not proposing to follow his French predecessor in throwing overboard the whole Jamesian and Bergsonian baggage. Rather he was attempting to integrate their notions—and the work of Freud as well—into a grand synthesis that would at last make possible civilized communication among the various competing philosophical and ideological schools. A synthesis it would be—but of a loose and permissive variety. To distinguish his approach from the relativism that he wished to transcend, Mannheim called it "relationism." Viewed from this angle, knowledge would be "by no means an illusory experience"—as it presumably was when viewed relativistically. On the contrary, "all of the elements of meaning in a given situation" would "have reference to one another and derive their significance from this reciprocal interrelationship." The approach would be "dynamic": the observer of society would try to keep all sorts of shifting relationships in uneasy balance. And it would actually be of advantage—in making his

---

[7] Preface by Louis Wirth to *Ideology and Utopia* (expansion and translation of *Ideologie und Utopie* [Bonn, 1929]) (London and New York, 1936), p. xxv.

[8] Ibid., pp. 205–6.

thought "flexible and dialectical, rather than rigid and dogmatic"—if he were not to try for an unattainable detachment and were rather to "incorporate into his vision each contradictory and conflicting current." [9]

It was perhaps this frank entertainment of contradictions that gave *Ideology and Utopia* its very special appeal. "Rarely has a sociological study succeeded in arresting the attention of so wide a public. Not only sociologists but economists, historians, philosophers, and theologians, too, participated in the discussion." There was something in it for everybody. Its basic categories of social analysis had been derived from Weber— but to them there had been added Scheler's notion of the collective origin of abstract ideas. And in the process Weber's procedure had been still further relativized. In Weber's work, values alone bore a purely subjective character; scientific knowledge retained a quality of "objectivity." With Mannheim, the order had been reversed. The values themselves possessed a kind of objective stability—it was the criteria of "objective" knowledge that fluctuated.[1] Thus however much Mannheim might protest that his own point of view was not relativistic, it was difficult to detect where the difference lay. As in Weber—but still more clearly than in Weber's case—*Ideology and Utopia* made it apparent that the student of society could never find rest in his quest for certainty.

Or perhaps there was one resting-place that the author himself never specifically mentioned. Like so many German thinkers of the 1920's, Mannheim owed a heavy debt to Marx. A Social Democrat in political sympathy, he was obsessed with Marxist memories. Not that he was dogmatic about them—on the contrary, he repeatedly emphasized the variety of determinants besides class position that went into forming the *Weltan-*

[9] Ibid., pp. 76, 88n.
[1] Hans Speier: "Karl Mannheim's *Ideology and Utopia*," *Social Order and the Risks of War: Papers in Political Sociology* (New York, 1952), pp. 190, 192.

schauungen of individuals and groups.[2] Yet the social conditioning of human thought remained uppermost in his mind; he had little understanding for the groping toward universals which still characterized thinkers like Freud and Weber and which Benda had just defended with such confident belligerence. A conviction of the ultimate autonomy of man's higher mental processes revealed itself only fitfully in his work—as, for instance, when he wrote of the Enlightenment. Mannheim's effort to absorb into the Marxist tradition the more significant innovations of his contemporaries was only partially successful: in the final amalgam too much of Marx remained.

In retrospect, one can see in the circumstances under which he had written his book the elements of high historical drama. Germany in the late 1920's—deceptively prosperous, deceptively orderly—offered the fitting stage for a last effort to present a progress report on what European social thought had accomplished in the past half-century. Never in European history had there been a population better educated and culturally more aware. Never had the conflict of ideologies been more intense. Weimar Germany offered nearly ideal laboratory conditions for observing a situation in which all values had been called into question and the living "roots from which human thought had hitherto derived its nourishment were exposed." On the edge of a precipice, the more perceptive of the German intellectuals had attained to an intensity of consciousness that recalled the reputed clairvoyance of the dying.

Mannheim himself was aware of the drama of his position. The historical opportunity, he wrote, demanded to be grasped before it was too late:

> At this point in history when all things which concern man and the structure and elements of

---

[2] Robert K. Merton: "The Sociology of Knowledge," in Georges Gurvitch and Wilbert E. Moore, editors: *Twentieth Century Sociology* (New York, 1945), pp. 377, 383.

history itself are suddenly revealed to us in a new
light, it behooves us in our scientific thinking to become masters of the situation, for it is not incon-
ceivable that sooner than we suspect, as has often
been the case before in history, this vision may disappear, the opportunity may be lost, and the world
will once again present a static, uniform, and in-
flexible countenance.[3]

Hence his book pursued a number of only loosely
related goals. The very pluralism of Mannheim's thinking and the form of three virtually free-standing essays
in which *Ideology and Utopia* was cast, contributed to
its multi-purpose character. Ostensibly—as its title implied—it was a discussion of the conflict of ideologies,
or rather, to use Mannheim's own terminology, the interaction among the attitudes of "ruling groups" that
were "intensively interest-bound" (*i.e.*, ideologies in
the narrower sense) and the viewpoints of "oppressed
groups . . . intellectually . . . strongly interested in
the destruction and transformation of a given condition
of society" (which Mannheim chose to call utopias).
The author's method consisted of pushing to its logical
conclusion the technique of "radical unmasking" that
had originally been a Marxian discovery.[4] If, Mannheim implied, this stripping away of one's adversaries'
illusions—and with them one's own—could only be
carried out with sufficient rigor, mutual understanding
and even, perhaps, reconciliation would be the paradoxical result.

Logically, then, Mannheim did not need to hide his
own sympathies. Within the terms of the method that
he had devised, it was sufficient if he clarified the basis
of his preferences and tried to relate them "dynami-
cally" to the prejudices of others. To the careful reader
it was readily apparent that the author of *Ideology and
Utopia* preferred the vitality of the latter type of world-

[3] *Ideology and Utopia,* pp. 38, 76.
[4] Ibid., pp. 36, 37.

view to the static repose of the former. His heart went out to the utopias—with the significant exception of "the sombre depths of Chiliastic agitation," whose twentieth-century incarnation was the syndicalist vision that had inspired Sorel. Mannheim's own utopian sympathies were more practical, earth-bound, and optimistic: they lay somewhere between Marx and the Enlightenment. And his fidelity to this type of thinking frequently blinded him to the tenacity of ideologies hostile to it. Fascist movements—to cite the most important case—he underestimated as "transitory formations" emerging during periods when individuals had "lost or forgotten their class orientations." [5]

But we should be very wrong to dismiss Mannheim's utopian attachments as mere sentimentality. His book might offer a maddening alternation between perception and windy verbiage. At its best, however, it shot perspectives into the future which can still bring the reader up short. His concluding vision of a world without utopia is chilling in its contemporary relevance. It is impossible to read today his strictures on the "barrenness" of a society "absorbed by its interest in concrete and isolated details" and a sociology "split up into a series of discrete technical problems of social readjustment" without applying them to the present situation in the United States. For his own generation, Mannheim implied, so "prosaic" an attitude was impossible. "It would require either a callousness which our generation could probably no longer acquire or the unsuspecting naïveté of a generation newly born into the world to be able to live in absolute congruence with the realities of that world, utterly without any transcendent element." [6]

And so by the close of his book Mannheim had been led to a prophetic position almost Spenglerian in its bleakness:

[5] Ibid., pp. 127, 205–6.
[6] Ibid., pp. 225, 228, 230.

The complete disappearance of the Utopian element . . . would mean that . . . human development would take on a totally new character. . . . We would be faced then with the greatest paradox imaginable, namely, that man, who has achieved the highest degree of rational mastery of existence, left without any ideals, becomes a mere creature of impulses. Thus . . . just at the highest stage of awareness, when history is ceasing to be blind fate, and is becoming more and more man's own creation, with the relinquishment of utopias, man would lose his will to shape history and therewith his ability to understand it.[7]

"And therewith his ability to understand it"—like Dilthey, like Croce, Mannheim believed that the understanding of history could arise only from acting in it. To him, as to his great predecessors of the generation of the 1890's, thought was not a detached and static affair: it was intimately involved in the processes of living. In this view, the intellectual was no mere observer. He represented the conscience of his society—perched perilously between the danger of betraying his trust through failure to give a clear lead, and the opposite "treason" of lending his pen to the purposes of propaganda. Benda—under French conditions—had been more conscious of the latter danger. Mannheim—from a German perspective—saw the greater peril in detachment and apathy. When, four years after the publication of his book, the catastrophe came, the behavior of most German intellectuals proved him right.

Hence when he strove to bind together in tense reconciliation the divergent philosophies and ideologies of his time—to integrate into the rationalist tradition certain of the "irrationalist" tendencies that Benda had refused to countenance—he was as concerned as Benda had been with the role of the intellectual in contem-

[7] Ibid., p. 236.

porary society. And—as we have just noticed—he defined this role in similar terms. Like Benda, he traced the sense of special function that still characterized the European intellectuals to their position in the Middle Ages as privileged "clerks." But he differed from his predecessor in stressing the ambiguity as well as the "unexampled intellectual richness" that had resulted from the "disruption of the . . . monopoly of the church." This was a problem that went at least as far back as the sixteenth century. Since the First World War, however, it had grown inordinately acute. The intellectual's relation to the society in which he lived had become dubious in the extreme. For his own part, Mannheim could see only four possible choices—affiliation "with the radical wing of the socialist-communist proletariat"; skepticism "in the name of intellectual integrity" (as in the case of Max Weber and Pareto); seeking "refuge in the past" through "attempts to revive religious feeling, idealism, symbols, and myths"; and a withdrawal from the world and conscious renunciation of "direct participation in the historical process."[8] It was this last possibility that Mannheim had in mind when he traced the outlines of a future without utopia.

Of these, only the second, he believed, held any creative possibilities. Despite its negative features, it possessed the virtue of "frankness," which was perhaps the best that could be expected in an era when utopian hopes were fading. The great advantage of the intellectuals, Mannheim argued, was that they alone constituted "a relatively classless stratum . . . not too firmly situated in the social order. . . . Participation in a common educational heritage progressively tends to suppress differences of birth, status, profession, and wealth, and to unite the individual educated people on the basis of the education they have received." Hence they alone could become the vehicles of "dynamic in-

[8] Ibid., pp. 11, 233.

tellectual mediation"—a last supreme effort to bring
about public understanding through entering into a
sympathetic internal comprehension of each of the mutually destructive ideologies and utopias that were tearing European society apart. Their intervention offered
the only faint hope of arresting the drift toward catastrophe.[9]

An illusion, of course—and yet Mannheim seems to
have known it was an illusion even as he wrote. In his
many-layered, involuted thinking, the line between intellectual clarity and the partial self-deceptions by
which men live was never fixed. Indeed, in the fluid
social universe that he had delineated, to draw such a
line would appear to be naïveté or nonsense. Similarly
the desperate hope that he had vested in the European
intellectuals had its own elements of ambiguity: the
role he assigned them lay somewhere between the new
ethic of "engagement" and the more traditional conception of the "unattached" (*freischwebend*) thinker
or writer. On balance, it leaned toward the latter. The
final relevance of *Ideology and Utopia* was as a defense
and justification of the *Freischwebender* on the brink
of disappearance.

The generation of the 1890's had begun their work
and completed the major outlines of their thought in
a privileged era. Riding the final wave of the century-
old faith in progress, they had enjoyed the last great
period of peace and security that Europe was to know.
Profiting by the comforts, the facilities that modern
technology offered, they were to witness only in their
later years—when their world-view had already been
formed—the new face of technology in its destructive
guise. They had passed their youth at the climax of the
Enlightenment—and simultaneously had inaugurated
its most probing critique. Indeed, it was their very certainty of "enlightened" values (however much they
might jibe at them) that had enabled them to strip

9 Ibid., pp. 137–8, 168, 231.

away so mercilessly the illusions with which these values had become encrusted. Their own psychological security—their confidence in such unstated assumptions as humane behavior and intellectual integrity—had given them the inner strength to inaugurate an unprecedented examination of conscience. Perched between two eras of dogmatism—the old dogmas of positivism and Marxism behind them, and the new certainties of "commitment" and exact logic in the future—they could afford the luxury of suspended judgment. The philosophies of urbane doubt—skepticism, pragmatism, pluralism—held no terrors for them.

Hence the quality of serenity, of an untroubled entertainment of contradictions, that we have noticed in the writing of a Croce or a Bergson. They led privileged lives of contemplation: never again were intellectuals to be so free from the petty harassments that have exasperated the existence of their fellows in most of the eras of European history—financial need, interference by the public authorities, and the sense of personal danger. They were the last of the great *Freischwebende*. Karl Mannheim, a late arrival in their fraternity, might sum up their role and try to redefine it to conform to the vastly altered situation he saw approaching. But he could not revitalize a way of life that was already disappearing. For the next two decades at least, the "unattached intellectual" was to be everywhere on the defensive.

IV. *A Generation in Retrospect*

From the perspective of the post-Second World War era, the work of the generation of the 1890's can be viewed as a "first attempt" at accommodation to a "new conception of reality." It represented a great deal more than a "return of the older idealism"—although the restatement of certain familiar idealist principles, in vastly altered form, was one aspect of this wider revolution in thought. In their most general significance,

the three decades from about 1890 to the early 1920's
marked the period in which the more imaginative
thinkers came to the conclusion that "the former con-
ceptions of a rational reality" were insufficient, and
that human thought would have to make "concessions"
to a reality that could no longer be conceived as an orderly system. In this process of concession and adapta-
tion, the "activity of human consciousness" for the first
time became of paramount importance. For consciousness seemed to offer the only link between man and
the world of society and history.

"The nature of reality" itself "no longer afforded a
coherent totality": the natural world and with it reality
in the broader sense were now seen as approachable
only through conventional fictions. "But society, which
represented the mediating sphere between man and
this general reality and partook of elements of both,
was still accessible to man." [1] As Vico had declared
two centuries earlier, man was capable of understanding the "civil world" *because he had made it.* By an effort of imaginative *construction,* human thought could
mimic the process of creation, and hence of understanding.

Croce himself even before the turn of the century
had expressed a similar idea with his customary vigor
and felicity:

> We no longer believe . . . , like the Greeks, in
> happiness of life on earth; we no longer believe,
> like the Christians, in happiness in an other-
> worldly life; we no longer believe, like the opti-
> mistic philosophers of the last century, in a happy
> future for the human race. . . . We no longer be-
> lieve in anything of that, and *what we have alone
> retained is the consciousness of ourselves, and the
> need to make that consciousness ever clearer and*

[1] Leonard Krieger: "The Intellectuals and European Society,"
Political Science Quarterly, LXVII (1952), 232-3.

more evident, a need for whose satisfaction we turn to science and to art.[2]

In the years after 1920 the new attitude toward consciousness and society that had originally been developed in Germany and France and Italy began to win an increasing number of adherents in other parts of the Western world. Figures as diverse as Ortega y Gasset in Spain and Collingwood or Malinowski in England suggest the varied forms in which this spreading influence manifested itself. In the United States such pioneering books as Harold Lasswell's *Psychopathology and Politics,* Talcott Parsons's *Structure of Social Action,* and the historical speculations of Carl Becker broke sharply with the older academic tradition. By the outbreak of the Second World War, the psychoanalytic approach to human motivation, an ideal-type method in social study, and a canon of historical research derived from neo-idealist premises, had become the distinguishing marks of the livelier thinkers in a wide variety of fields. In imaginative literature a comparable change had occurred: throughout the Western world the notion of "realistic" treatments based on positivist assumptions had been almost completely discredited.

But this changed attitude, as we noted a moment ago, taxed the intellect inordinately with its complex arrangement of concessions and adaptations. It was a tenuous synthesis that constantly threatened to break down in one direction or another. It had originated in a revolt from positivism—explicit or implied—yet it retained from the positivist faith its trust in the procedures of exact science. It marked a revival of idealist thinking—yet it rejected the idealist belief in the eternal character of spiritual values. It found its clearest expression in pragmatism—yet pragmatism without

[2] Quoted in Mario Corsi: *Le origini del pensiero di Benedetto Croce* (Florence, 1951), pp. 20–1.

qualification robbed it of its subtleties and reduced it to a rough rule of thumb. Most obviously it had questioned the potentialities of human reason—yet "irrationalism" was merely a crude deformation and degeneration of what the generation of the 1890's had proposed.

The question of rationality is the crucial one—the final test of what was viable and what was transitory in the intellectual labors of this generation. In defining their attitude toward reason, the social thinkers of the early twentieth century were obliged to walk the edge of a razor. On the one side lay the past errors of the eighteenth century and of the positivist tradition. On the other side lay the future errors of unreason and emotional thinking. In between there remained only the narrow path of faith in reason despite and even because of the drastic limitations with which psychological and historical discovery had hedged it: however much "intuition," free association, and the other unorthodox techniques of investigation might have broadened the criteria of evidence in social thought, reason alone remained the final control and arbiter.

Even the greatest members of this generation found it impossible to walk the thin line with an invariable sureness of step. Bergson and Sorel eventually succumbed to a kind of social mysticism. Freud began his work with an unsophisticated trust in mechanistic explanations which he never explicitly abandoned. Yet by the end of his life he had crossed over to the extreme opposite of letting his speculative imagination roam virtually free of rational check. Pareto never properly understood that values—however irrational their origin—could be treated as something more than a residual category: he never appreciated the difference between human folly and a coherent value-system. Croce in the early part of his career had understood the elements of this distinction. But as his life advanced he had gradually and almost imperceptibly shifted the meaning of his central historical principle. His doctrine that the rational alone could be the subject of history had begun as the simple and unobjectionable statement that history necessarily dealt with what was capable of rational explanation. As eventually defined, however, it proposed a drastic narrowing of the historian's intellectual sphere—the virtual exclusion from history, as mere incoherence, of the whole realm of non-rational conduct.

Thus by the 1920's and 1930's Croce and Freud were crossing in opposite directions the thin divide on which the contrasting perils of intellectualism and fantasy had momentarily been transcended. Yet paradoxically enough, both of them, in their final guise, figured more as men of letters than as social scientists. For by the time of their deaths the divorce between literature and social science was an accomplished fact. By the mid-century the exact logicians and the men of science had left far behind the Crocean notion of reason and logical method and were shrugging their shoulders at Freud's meta-historical speculations. Between rational method and literary meaning a chasm had opened.

Max Weber had been acutely aware of the danger. In his effort to transcend the positivist-idealist polemic, he had striven for formulations that would keep together the sphere of logic and the sphere of value. In so doing, he alone invariably held to the central understanding of his whole generation. He alone never wavered in his insistence that *both* reason and illogic were essential to the comprehension of the human world. While reality, he implied, was dominated by unreason, it was only through rational treatment that it could be made comprehensible. Yet Weber's intellectual coherence had been acquired at the price of a psychic tension that was almost too much for the human mind to bear. For a brief decade or two he and his generation had striven to keep reason and emotional value in precarious balance: it was not surprising that the two should so soon have parted company.

Bibliographical Note

I DO NOT BELIEVE that this study requires a formal bibliography. The footnotes give sufficient indication of the range of the original works and secondary accounts on which I have drawn.

It is relevant to suggest, however, the types of literature that I have found most useful. From formal histories of the various learned disciplines I have derived little profit. Nearly all of them have proved to be either too impressionistic or too technical for my purposes. A number of biographical studies, on the contrary, I have found indispensable: it is difficult to see how I could have written certain chapters without the aid of Ernest Jones's great work on Freud, of Marianne Weber's sensitive and illuminating account of her husband's career, of the solid studies of Sorel's life and doctrines with which Andreu and Humphrey and Meisel have recently provided us.

In the case of Bergson and Croce, Durkheim and Pareto, I have been thrown more on my own devices. On Bergson one is obliged to take one's choice: virtually all the available literature is either uncritically pious or devastatingly hostile. For Croce a major work of reinterpretation is still lacking—yet the recent studies by such writers as Caponigri, Chabod, Corsi, De Caprariis, and Sprigge suggest the elements of a new evaluation. For Durkheim and Pareto, Parsons's *The Structure of Social Action* is an indispensable guide.

Indeed it is one of three extraordinary works of synthesis on which I have relied most heavily.

The other two are both by Italians—Antoni's *Dallo storicismo alla sociologia* and Rossi's *Lo storicismo tedesco contemporaneo*. Although covering much of the same ground, they contrast sharply in their philosophical approach: the former, by a respected elder scholar, is frankly Crocean; the latter, the work of a brilliant neophyte, leans toward social science in the Weber tradition. That my own viewpoint inclines toward the latter should be apparent from a reading of my sixth and eighth chapters.

I might add that all translations in the text, except where otherwise indicated, are my own. In every case I have referred the reader to the English translations both of original and of secondary works, where such are available. When mentioning titles in the text, I have ordinarily left in the original language only those which have not yet been translated. In a few cases, however, I have refrained from reproducing a translated title that struck me as misleading or inappropriate.

Index

A NOTE ON THE AUTHOR

H. Stuart Hughes was born in 1916 in New York City. He received his A.B. from Amherst College and his A.M. and Ph.D. from Harvard. Before the Second World War he also studied in Europe, at Heidelberg University and the University of Munich, and worked in the Archives Nationales in Paris, where he did research on a John Harvard Traveling Fellowship.

Mr. Hughes taught history at Brown University before he enlisted in the Army as a private in 1941. By 1944 he was Chief of the Research and Analysis Branch of the Office of Strategic Services in the Mediterranean Theater; later he held the same post in Germany. He was relieved from active duty as a lieutenant colonel in 1946.

Since then he has been Chief of the State Department's Division of Research for Europe; Assistant Professor of History at Harvard; Associate Professor and Professor and head of the Department of History at Stanford; and, since 1957, Professor of History at Harvard. He has also been a Visiting Member of the Institute for Advanced Study at Princeton, a Fellow at the Center for Advanced Study in the Behavioral Sciences at Stanford, and the holder of a Guggenheim Fellowship.

Mr. Hughes is the author of three books besides *Consciousness and Society—An Essay for Our Times* (1950); *Oswald Spengler: A Critical Estimate* (1952); and *The United States and Italy* (1953). He also edited *Teachers of History: Essays in Honor of Laurence Bradford Packard* (1954). He lives in Cambridge, Massachusetts, with his wife and two young children.